THE
PARTNERSHIP

THE
PARTNERSHIP

FIVE COLD WARRIORS AND THEIR QUEST TO BAN THE BOMB

PHILIP TAUBMAN

HARPER

An Imprint of HarperCollins*Publishers*
www.harpercollins.com

HarperCollins books may be purchased for educational, business, or sales promotional use. For information, please write: Special Markets Department, HarperCollins Publishers, 10 East 53rd Street, New York, NY 10022.

Title page photographs *(left to right)*: Sam Nunn, Sidney Drell, Henry Kissinger, George Shultz (photographs by Neil Spence), Bill Perry (© 2010 Rod Searcey).

FIRST EDITION

Designed by Renato Stanisic

Library of Congress Cataloging-in-Publication Data

Taubman, Philip.

The partnership : five cold warriors and their quest to ban the bomb / by Philip Taubman.

p. cm.

ISBN 978-0-06-174400-6 (hardback)

1. Nuclear weapons—Government policy—United States—History—20th century. 2. Nuclear disarmament—United States—History. 3. Drell, Sidney D. (Sidney David), 1926– 4. Kissinger, Henry, 1923– 5. Shultz, George Pratt, 1920– 6. Nunn, Sam. 7. Perry, William James, 1927– I. Title.

U264.3.T38 2012

327.1'747092273—dc23

2011028258

---

12 13 14 15 16   OV/RRD   10 9 8 7 6 5 4 3 2 1

FOR LORI MARCH WILLIAMS

CONTENTS

PREFACE

Shortly before noon on a September morning in 1988, the desolate Central Asian steppes heaved toward the sky and a concussive thud shook the air. I braced myself as a shock wave rippled swiftly across the arid landscape. It hit with a jolt, nearly knocking me off my feet.

A nuclear bomb, ten times more powerful than the one that destroyed Hiroshima, had just exploded half a mile belowground at the Soviet test site in Kazakhstan. I was there to cover the test for the *New York Times*, and among the first group of Americans to witness a Soviet nuclear test. As the brown grass and dry soil that had levitated into the air settled back to earth, several dozen Soviet and American officials stood in awed silence, then slowly broke into relieved applause.

I had read John Hersey's riveting account of the atomic bombing of Hiroshima in 1945 and seen harrowing film footage of the burned, shell-shocked victims in that city and Nagasaki. I had rushed with high school classmates in New York to the nearest fallout shelter during air raid drills at the peak of the Cuban Missile Crisis in 1962. But until that September morning at the Semipalatinsk test site, I did not viscerally understand the brute force of a nuclear bomb.

The memory of that day stayed with me, a disturbing reminder of the destructive power that could be unleashed by terrorists, warring states, or even the accidental launch of a nuclear warhead by Russia, India, Pakistan, or the United States.

While, twenty years after the Soviet test, I contemplated retirement from the *Times*, I found myself in conversation one day
with Sidney Drell, a physicist I had first met when I was a student
at Stanford University in the 1960s. As we talked, I learned Drell
was part of an audacious quest to abolish nuclear weapons. The
campaign's marquee leaders were men I knew well from Cold War
headlines, and in some cases, men I had covered as a reporter for
the *Times*: Henry Kissinger and George Shultz, former Republican
secretaries of state; William Perry, a former Democratic defense
secretary; and Sam Nunn, the onetime Democratic chairman of
the Senate Armed Services Committee.

The four statesmen, with a powerful unpublicized assist from
Drell, declared their commitment to eliminate nuclear weapons in
an op-ed in the *Wall Street Journal* in January 2007. The article outlined a road map to abolition with clear, feasible steps that could be
addressed in the short and medium term to reduce nuclear threats.
They called for downgrading the alert status of nuclear weapons
to reduce the danger of accidental or unauthorized launch, trimming the size of nuclear forces, eliminating short-range nuclear
weapons, and improving the security of nuclear arms and stocks of
fissile materials.

The article proposed halting the production of fissile material
for weapons. It also recommended steps to get control of the uranium enrichment process so that nations that need the uranium
for nuclear power plants or research reactors can obtain it from
international organizations instead of building plants that can also
produce weapons-grade highly enriched uranium.

The article stunned the nuclear weapons cognoscenti, a cloistered community of defense analysts, technocrats, and policymakers deeply invested in the proposition that nuclear weapons are the
bedrock of American foreign policy.

Here, like a bolt from the blue, was a bipartisan group of eminent Cold Warriors eager to upend the atomic applecart. The

article couldn't be dismissed as the work of pacifists or antinuclear campaigners. It was the hardheaded vision of men who had played central roles in building, managing, and wielding America's nuclear arsenal during the Cold War.

Fearing that the twentieth-century era of nuclear stalemate was turning into a twenty-first-century era of nuclear terrorism, failed states, and an ever expanding array of nuclear threats, the men proposed setting a new course before the unthinkable could happen—the destruction of New York, Washington, London, Moscow, Tokyo, or another urban center by terrorists armed with a nuclear bomb. If not a nuclear weapon, a radiological bomb—a conventional explosive device packaged with radioactive materials like plutonium that could expose thousands of people to lethal doses of radiation and make a downtown area uninhabitable for months. (The radiation leakage from crippled Japanese reactors after the catastrophic 2011 earthquake and tsunami made the radiological threat all too tangible.)

In 2008, already inclined to turn my attention to book writing, I decided to step back from daily newspapering to tell the story of the five-man partnership and draw attention to the rising nuclear threat. Tracing the genesis of their joint effort took me on an historical journey through the Cold War and to places in the United States and abroad where the men have pitched their vision since 2007. I investigated the threat of nuclear terrorism in the United States, explored nuclear smuggling routes in Europe and the Caucasus, and spent time at some of the national laboratories that are part of America's nuclear weapons complex. This book is the result.

As I spent time with the men in formal and informal settings, I found their partnership more complicated than the unanimity of the *Wall Street Journal* article implied. The advent of the new nuclear age propelled the men to reexamine their assumptions about nuclear weapons, especially after the terror attacks on September

11, 2001. But they reached agreement only after months of hesitation and indecision, and might never have acted were it not for the spadework of Max Kampelman, an unsung Reagan administration arms negotiator, and Steve Andreasen, an unassuming nuclear policy expert. Kampelman and Andreasen rekindled discussion about nuclear disarmament and Shultz, Kissinger, Perry, Nunn, and Drell picked up the idea and ran with it.

To find common ground, the five men had to bury past quarrels, overcome political and ideological differences, and stand fast against a wave of criticism. Along the way they developed a productive, often lighthearted partnership. Even so, significant differences remain to this day, largely hidden from public view. That's not surprising, given the complexity of the issues involved and the difficulty of capturing nuances in an op-ed article and other abbreviated pronouncements. Still, Henry Kissinger's private misgivings about the enterprise, described by a number of people, are striking.

And while the men all publicly subscribe to the high-minded goal of reducing nuclear threats, other factors clearly played a part in building and sustaining their alliance—a desire to burnish reputations, maintain leadership roles, vindicate past policy prescriptions, or just linger in the limelight.

Whatever it is that motivates the men, they often operate with the intensity and energy of men half their golden age. At a time of life when many people might be slowing down, they seem to be speeding up, flying through the night to get to distant destinations, defying jet lag as they campaign for nuclear disarmament around the world. During the past few years, Perry has traveled to Moscow, Beijing, London, Rome, Sydney, Ottawa, Tokyo, Helsinki, New Delhi, Berlin, Vienna, Geneva, Seoul, and Pyongyang, not to mention several trips a month to Washington.

Then, unpredictably, come moments when the fevered pace catches up with them, revealing a poignant frailty: Perry repeatedly nodding off at a conference in Rome, Kissinger slumping forward in his seat at a Berlin meeting, Drell momentarily crumpling to the ground as he exited a San Francisco reception, Shultz leaning on a fellow passenger's arm as he stepped gingerly through the snow on a wintry night at Le Bourget Airport outside Paris.

It was hard at such moments not to wonder why they press on, why they seem so determined to rid the world of nuclear weapons. The answer rests in part on the present danger they perceive, but also on the arc of their Cold War careers.

For each of the five men the call for abolition represents the culmination of a personal journey across the nuclear age. They were young men, Nunn just a boy, when an atomic bomb obliterated Hiroshima. They came of age as new technologies—the hydrogen bomb, intercontinental ballistic missiles, and the miniaturization of nuclear warheads—brought the world to the brink of annihilation. In the prime of their lives, they played pivotal roles in managing America's defenses and perfecting new intelligence-gathering technologies. During those Cold War years, each man found himself dealing with the sobering realities of the nuclear era. Almost imperceptibly, their thinking about the bomb evolved and their doubts about controlling it grew. Then, late in life, they looked at the world they had helped make and realized it was too dangerous, too near a new kind of nuclear conflagration, to hand off unaltered to their grandchildren.

The five men were as surprised as the nuclear weapons fraternity when their initiative attracted worldwide support. In just a few years, their long-shot campaign has gained traction in government offices, corporate boardrooms, evangelical Christian churches, and school and college classrooms. It has induced sitting presidents and foreign ministers to embrace ideas not long ago ridiculed as radical and reckless. Global Zero, a parallel antinuclear campaign launched twenty-three months after the *Wall Street Journal* article, now claims a long list of prominent supporters, including dozens of former presidents, prime ministers, and diplomats. A high-powered international commission on nuclear threats, sponsored by Australia and Japan, issued a report in 2010 calling for the elimination of nuclear weapons, including a detailed action plan to reach that goal.

In awarding the 2009 Nobel Peace Prize to Barack Obama, the Norwegian Nobel Committee, it seemed, was indirectly honoring Shultz, Kissinger, Perry, Nunn, and Drell, whose efforts to eradicate nuclear weapons have powerfully influenced Obama.

I was drawn to the subject partly by my own concerns about the spread of nuclear weapons and technology and the realization that it could well be just a matter of time before a terrorist group like al-Qaeda gets its hands on a nuclear weapon. On September 11, 2001, I listened to radio news reports about smoke rising from the North Tower of the World Trade Center as I finished breakfast at my Manhattan apartment, then stared in disbelief at live televised images of a passenger plane piercing the South Tower and exploding into a hellish fireball. I grabbed my briefcase and raced downtown to the *New York Times* headquarters to help put out the next day's newspaper. As I headed to work, dazed survivors were already streaming north from lower Manhattan. I was fortunate not to be near the World Trade Center, or to lose relatives or friends in the inferno and collapse of the towers, but like all New Yorkers that day, I felt a level of anger and fear I had not known before.

During a three-decade career at the *Times*, I specialized in national security affairs, often from a ringside seat in Washington and Moscow. Nuclear weapons and their central role in the Cold War were an inescapable reality. Like other journalists immersed in foreign policy and defense issues, I became conversant in the recondite realm of nuclear strategy and technology. The technical argot about nuclear weapons—terms like *counterforce* for military targets and *countervalue* for civilian populations—seemed intended to mask the chilling reality that the United States maintained a nuclear arsenal designed to kill 100 million people in the Soviet Union. The Kremlin was prepared to do the same to us. The doctrine of nuclear deterrence was more transparently labeled "massive retaliation" and "mutual assured destruction," the latter of which appropriately went by the shorthand "MAD."

I was present in Reykjavik, Iceland, in October 1986 when President Ronald Reagan and Mikhail Gorbachev, the Soviet leader, momentarily considered the elimination of nuclear weapons. Like other reporters at the summit meeting, I was caught off guard by the unexpected talk of abolishing nuclear weapons and the confusion that surrounded the abrupt end of the Reagan-Gorbachev discussions. Reagan and George Shultz, who participated in the talks as secretary of state, were widely criticized for even entertaining the thought. But as the postsummit fog cleared, a new landscape came into sight. Washington and Moscow were willing, for the first time, to reduce their nuclear arsenals rather than just setting ceilings on them.

When the Cold War ended in 1991 with the disintegration of the Soviet Union, I was hopeful that the pace of nuclear arms reductions would quicken. It did. The grotesquely inflated American and Russian arsenals came down from their Cold War zenith of roughly 70,000 warheads all told. The number is closer to 22,000 today. Thanks to timely legislation crafted by Sam Nunn and Senator Richard Lugar, his Republican colleague, the United States pursued an enlightened program to help Russia secure its nuclear weapons and fissile materials and keep its nuclear scientists from selling their expertise abroad. China, which developed the bomb in 1964, maintained a relatively small arsenal, as did India and Israel. The other nuclear weapons states, Britain and France, were responsible guardians of the bomb.

But the momentum stalled and nuclear threats began to escalate again. Abdul Qadeer Khan, a Pakistani nuclear scientist, helped his countrymen develop the bomb and ran a lucrative global black market in nuclear technologies that spread weapons programs to dictatorial regimes in North Korea, Libya, and Iran—all prepared to pay a premium to crash the nuclear club. In 1998, India ended any ambiguity about its weapons program by conducting an underground test that was easily detected. Pakistan soon answered with tests of its own—the first proof that it had nuclear weapons—igniting a volatile arms race on the subcontinent. North Korea developed a bomb program, and tested a nuclear device in 2006. Iran seems determined to do the same. Despite American and Russian efforts to improve security at nuclear storage facilities around the world, the key ingredient of a crude nuclear bomb—highly enriched uranium—seems vulnerable to theft at dozens of poorly guarded sites in dozens of countries. The operation of nuclear power plants depends on enriched uranium, requiring the constant production of new stocks of fissile material that can relatively easily be brought up to bomb-grade standards. September 11, 2001, made people realize that terrorists intent on inflicting as much damage as possible might strike again someday with a nuclear weapon.

The conversion of Shultz, Kissinger, Perry, Nunn, and Drell from stalwart Cold Warriors to champions of disarmament illuminates the unsettling reality that the nuclear balance of terror has been supplanted by a different but equally disturbing threat—nuclear terrorism and the spread of nuclear weapons technology and materials to dangerously unstable nations.

As Secretary of Defense Robert M. Gates said before leaving office in 2011, "If you were to ask most of the leaders of the last administration or the current administration what might keep them awake at night, it's the prospect of a weapon or nuclear material falling into the hands of Al Qaeda or some other extremists. And it doesn't have to be a weapon. It could be nuclear material with regular explosives and produce a degree of contamination that would be catastrophic." That threat did not end with the killing of Osama bin Laden in 2011.

I admire what the men have done in their joint campaign, and observed them at close range for the past few years. I traveled the world with Shultz when he was secretary of state, reporting on his diplomatic adventures on four continents. He kept his distance from reporters, not always the norm for secretaries of state. But an exception was made for tennis. Before one trip, he quietly told me to bring along my racquet. I did, and we played doubles in Rio and Moscow, the only times in many decades of trying to master the game that I stepped on a tennis court in the company of ball boys, with a doctor standing by at courtside. Though Shultz's mobility was limited by a bum knee, he returned every ball within striking distance, often stroking crosscourt or down-the-line winners.

Drell, Shultz, and Perry welcomed the book project, gave me access to their work, and agreed to multiple interviews. Our common base at Stanford made the logistics convenient. Nunn cooperated fully, too, as did his able colleagues at the Nuclear Threat Initiative, a Washington, D.C.–based nonprofit organization dedicated to reducing nuclear and other unconventional threats. Kissinger, bruised over the years by *New York Times* news coverage and editorial commentary that he considered unfair, was suspicious from the outset, and remained so, I'm sure. He once asked me if I intended to make him "the villain" of my book. But we found time to talk, thanks to an introduction by Shultz, and Kissinger condoned my appearance at several group gatherings and a three-day trip the men made to Berlin and Munich in 2010.

The Cold War history found in these pages is selective. It primarily tracks the careers of the five men, focusing on the roles they played in managing America's nuclear arsenal and deterring the threat of a Soviet nuclear attack. I have attempted to place the men in the broader context of their time, but deliberately do not dwell on other aspects of their government careers, such as George Shultz's role as an economic policymaker during the Nixon administration and Henry Kissinger's extensive nonnuclear diplomatic history. Nor do I deal at length with the broad array of nonnuclear defense issues tackled by Bill Perry during his stints at the Pentagon, Sam Nunn's leadership on conventional military matters, and Sid Drell's work as a theoretical physicist.

Most Americans consider an act of nuclear terrorism a remote threat, if they have thought about it at all. The economic tribulations of recent years, along with other pressing problems close to home, command attention. American men and women are losing their lives fighting a distant war and elusive foe in Afghanistan. The reinvention of Iraq as a secular democracy in the heart of the Middle East remains a costly work in progress. In the wake of the Cold War, nuclear threats are easy for most Americans to overlook. That may have started changing after the radiation scare in Japan. I hope so. Complacency and inattention are an invitation to a disaster the likes of which the United States has never experienced.

Henry Kissinger said it well: "Our age has stolen the fire from the gods. Can we confine it to peaceful purposes before it consumes us?"

PART I

Confronting the Threat

CHAPTER ONE

*I don't think anybody would accuse these four
gentlemen of being dreamers.*
—PRESIDENT BARACK OBAMA

World leaders, including the president of the United States,
were gathering in New York in 2009 for the annual
autumn meeting of the United Nations General Assembly. Vehicles cleared to enter the area around the United Nations complex
were channeled into barricaded lanes to be searched before they
could move on. Security agents manning barriers at the corner of
Second Avenue and Forty-Fourth Street sealed off the sidewalks
around the Millennium UN Plaza Hotel, a half block away.

It was an eerily familiar scene for Henry Kissinger, George
Shultz, Bill Perry, and Sam Nunn as they entered the polished
lobby of the hotel. Each of them had helped shape American history during some of the most tumultuous decades of the Cold
War. In their heyday, they lived in the white light of high-intensity
diplomacy and politics, surrounded by aides and blanketed in
multiple levels of security. Each played a pivotal role in building,
maintaining, and managing America's mammoth arsenal of nuclear weapons.

Now they were back at center stage, animated by an improbable cause—the eradication of nuclear weapons. Though
grayer, and in some cases rounder, than during their years in

Washington, they were instantly recognizable to anyone familiar with postwar American history.

There was Kissinger, age eighty-five, short, rumpled, enveloped by the gravelly German accent that is his calling card, still turning heads and cutting a power swath across the room. As Richard Nixon's national security adviser, secretary of state, and courtier, the precociously brilliant Harvard professor had bedazzled Washington with high-wire diplomacy and won a Nobel Peace Prize but lost his bearings in the jungles of Southeast Asia and the vengeful paranoia of the Nixon White House. He had immigrated to the United States from Germany at age fifteen and rocketed through the academic world, propelled by a richly textured intellect, high ambition, and a disarming, some would say solicitous, charm that endeared him to powerful members of the eastern establishment like Nelson and David Rockefeller. His partnership with Nixon produced strategic breakthroughs like Nixon's 1972 trip to China and foreign policy debacles like the expansion of American military operations in Southeast Asia. After leaving Washington at the end of the Ford administration, he built a profitable and influential business as a consultant to American and foreign clients and circulated easily in the tony precincts of New York and Washington society.

He was joined at the hotel by Shultz, age eighty-eight, his posture still as erect as that of the Marine he had been during the bloody Pacific landings of World War II. Moving more slowly than he once did, the former secretary of state still commanded attention in an elegant suit, bow tie, and colorful handkerchief tucked neatly in his breast pocket. The holder of four cabinet posts under two presidents, he was a supremely confident, self-contained economist and academician who as a newcomer to defense policy helped Ronald Reagan redirect relations with the Soviet Union and imagine a world without nuclear weapons. Shultz didn't need to win his way into the world of Wall Street and the Ivy League—he grew up in it, the son of a well-respected New York expert on the securities markets. Shultz was a prep school and Princeton graduate with a Ph.D. in economics from the Massachusetts Institute of Technology; he seemed equally at home in the academy and in Washington, a man who radiated probity, pragmatism, and Republicanism. So much so that Richard Nixon, angered by Shultz's refusal to sic the Internal Revenue Service on White House critics, once called him a "candyass."

Perry followed, age eighty-two, almost lost in the shadows, his slight frame and quiet demeanor overmatched by the star power of Kissinger and Shultz. A high-tech wizard and mastermind of inventive Cold War weapons systems, including stealth aircraft, he had played a pivotal role as Bill Clinton's defense secretary in dismantling the nuclear arsenals of Ukraine and two other former Soviet republics after the disintegration of the Soviet empire. Born into a blue-collar family in western Pennsylvania, he had parlayed a gift for technological ingenuity and management into a successful defense business and high-powered Washington career. A man of uncommon competence and modesty, he commanded the respect of Democrats and Republicans alike. In 1996, Osama bin Laden addressed a threatening poem to Perry, then secretary of defense, shortly after calling for a jihad, or war, against American troops stationed in Saudi Arabia.

Last came Nunn, at age seventy-two the kid of the group, his round face accented by large, owlish spectacles, looking as if he had just stepped off the Senate floor. A courtly, canny, gregarious Georgia lawyer, he had became a Senate baron in the 1980s, a putative presidential candidate and an oft-mentioned but never appointed prospect for defense secretary or secretary of state. Born in rural Georgia, he had followed the path of Representative Carl Vinson, his great-uncle and political mentor, to become an expert on military affairs and chairman of the Senate Armed Services Committee. Thoughtful, hardworking, and inherently conservative, he had played a vital role in just about every defense issue for twenty-five years, until his retirement from the Senate in 1997. After a brief hiatus, he became cochairman of the Nuclear Threat Initiative (NTI), a well-funded, nonprofit organization dedicated to reducing the threat of weapons of mass destruction. NTI, over time, became the secretariat for the nuclear disarmament campaign launched by Nunn, Shultz, Kissinger, and Perry.

They formed an unlikely quartet. Two Republicans, two Democrats, four men who had made their way to Washington from very different hometowns and backgrounds but shared a yen for power and public service and a common interest in keeping America's defenses strong. Their paths had intersected often over more than five decades, sometimes in collaboration, sometimes in conflict. As presidencies passed, the direct and indirect links between the men grew as they, in effect, handed critical levers of American foreign and defense policy back and forth across administrations.

Each in his way had played a starring role in the Cold War. All held power at a time when American security was based on an overpowering array of nuclear weapons designed to keep the Soviet Union at bay and guarantee that any attack on the United States or its allies would be met with a devastating response.

But with the end of the Cold War, the appearance of failed states, the rise of terrorism, and the spread of nuclear know-how and materials, Kissinger, Shultz, Perry, and Nunn grew wary of the nuclear gospel. They stunned the world on January 4, 2007, by calling for the elimination of nuclear arms, in a brilliantly subversive op-ed article in the *Wall Street Journal*. The language was cautious and precise, the product of days of drafting and painstakingly negotiated revisions, but the message was unmistakable: four eminent Cold Warriors, setting aside ideological and political differences, favored a radical break with postwar defense strategy. It was roughly equivalent to John D. Rockefeller, Andrew Carnegie, J. P. Morgan, and Jay Gould calling for the demise of capitalism, or

Bill Walsh, Joe Montana, Jerry Rice, Peyton Manning, and Tom Brady saying the time had come to rid football of the forward pass.

Their reasoning was sound and, by the stolid standards of defense patois, direct about the rising threat of nuclear terrorism.

"Nuclear weapons today present tremendous dangers, but also an historic opportunity. U.S. leadership will be required to take the world to the next stage—to a solid consensus for reversing reliance on nuclear weapons globally as a vital contribution to preventing their proliferation into potentially dangerous hands, and ultimately ending them as a threat to the world."

The men warned that with North Korea already armed with nuclear weapons and Iran not far behind, "the world is now on the precipice of a new and dangerous nuclear era." They cautioned that terrorists with nuclear weapons, operating outside the bounds of traditional defense theory, would not be deterred from using them by fear of nuclear retaliation.

The article called for specific steps to decrease nuclear dangers in the near term, including reductions in nuclear arms, eliminating short-range nuclear weapons like nuclear-tipped artillery shells, securing stocks of weapons-grade highly enriched uranium and plutonium, and ending the production of fissile materials for weapons.

As the four men greeted diplomats from more than a dozen countries in the Landmark View Conference Room on the twenty-ninth floor of the Millennium Hotel, they were pressing ahead with their quest to rid the world of nuclear weapons.

The idea itself is not new. Almost from the moment the first atom bomb was tested in the New Mexico desert on July 16, 1945, scientists, statesmen, theologians, philosophers, and concerned citizens have questioned the legitimacy of nuclear weapons as instruments of war and politics. Albert Einstein, who alerted President Franklin D. Roosevelt to the potential military uses of the atom in 1939, pressed for nuclear disarmament after the destruction of

Hiroshima and Nagasaki. Many of the Manhattan Project scientists who built the first bombs banded together in 1945 to establish the Federation of Atomic Scientists in hopes of preventing a nuclear arms race. J. Robert Oppenheimer, the physicist who directed the scientific work of the Manhattan Project, opposed development of the hydrogen bomb.

The atmospheric testing of absurdly powerful hydrogen bombs in the 1950s and early '60s—the largest a Soviet monster equivalent to 50 million tons of TNT, more than three thousand times greater than the Hiroshima bomb—spread radioactive fallout around the planet, fueling public opposition to the weapons. Antinuclear groups sprang up around the world. Hollywood abetted the cause with pithy films like *On the Beach* and *Dr. Strangelove or: How I Learned to Stop Worrying and Love the Bomb*. The nuclear freeze campaign, an effort to get the United States and Soviet Union not to build any more weapons, inspired mass demonstrations in the early 1980s, including a rally of some one million people in New York's Central Park in 1982. The next year, the National Conference of Catholic Bishops issued a Pastoral Letter on War and Peace intended, it said, "to provide hope for people in our day and direction toward a world freed of the nuclear threat."

Starting with Harry Truman, every president has talked in one way or another about ridding the world of nuclear weapons. The first major effort to control the weapons came on Truman's watch in early 1946 when Dean Acheson, undersecretary of state, and David Lilienthal, chairman of the Tennessee Valley Authority, produced a report recommending that nuclear weapons be put under international control. The plan died aborning in the United Nations. President Dwight D. Eisenhower was so concerned about nuclear war that he wrote in his diary toward the end of 1953, "As of now the world is racing toward catastrophe."

In an eloquent address to the United Nations General Assembly in 1961, President John F. Kennedy said, "Today, every inhabitant of this planet must contemplate the day when this planet may no longer be habitable. Every man, woman and child lives under a nuclear sword of Damocles, hanging by the slenderest of threads, capable of being cut at any moment by accident or miscalculation or by madness. The weapons of war must be abolished before they abolish us."

Lyndon Johnson signed the Nuclear Non-Proliferation Treaty (NPT) in 1968. It is an enlightened accord that, among other things, committed the United States and other nuclear weapons states to "pursue negotiations in good faith on effective measures relating to cessation of the nuclear arms race at an early date and to nuclear disarmament, and on a Treaty on general and complete disarmament under strict and effective international control." In return, nations that had not already developed nuclear weapons agreed not to do so. After signing the agreement, Johnson said, "This is a very reassuring and hopeful moment in the relations among nations." He described the treaty as "the most important international agreement since the beginning of the nuclear age."

In his 1977 inaugural address, Jimmy Carter called for the "elimination of all nuclear weapons from this Earth." Ronald Reagan prized the idea and momentarily put it on the negotiating table with Mikhail Gorbachev, the Soviet leader.

The NPT treaty remains in effect today, but progress toward disarmament has been fitful. In 1963, John Kennedy predicted that by the 1970s, "15 or 20 or 25" nations would own nuclear weapons. He said, "I regard that as the greatest possible danger and hazard." He was wrong about the number, thanks in part to the treaty. Over the decades, a number of nations that started down the path to developing nuclear weapons gave up their programs or plans to start one, including South Africa, Libya, Brazil, Sweden, Norway, and South Korea.

But as this book went to press, there were still more than 22,000 nuclear warheads in nuclear arsenals around the world, better than 90 percent of them American or Russian. And the roll call of nuclear weapons states has grown since 1968. In addition to the United States, Russia, Britain, France, and China, all of which are party to the Non-Proliferation Treaty, the roster now includes Israel, India, Pakistan, and North Korea, none a signatory to the treaty. Iran appears to be next in line to join the club.

Despite the treaty, the notion of nuclear disarmament never amounted to much more than a rhetorical flourish for most American leaders throughout the Cold War. Reagan was ridiculed for backing the idea. When General Lee Butler, once the commander of American strategic nuclear forces, unexpectedly called for the elimination of nuclear weapons in the mid-1990s, he was summarily excommunicated from the bomb brotherhood. His reputation, friendships, even his livelihood were threatened by his action. The administration of President George W. Bush seemed content to see a 2005 international conference designed to buttress the NPT treaty dissolve in disarray, suggesting the United States had little interest in making a "good faith" effort to work toward nuclear disarmament.

Now, thanks largely to the efforts of Shultz, Kissinger, Perry, and Nunn, the idea is taken seriously. Perry sometimes recalls a phrase from Victor Hugo to capture the shift. "More powerful than the tread of mighty armies is an idea whose time has come." If these sober-minded masters of the nuclear universe fear that a nuclear catastrophe is imminent, if, after a lifetime of living with the bomb, they are urgently calling for the abolition of nuclear weapons, then the rest of us would do well to listen.

President Barack Obama is. "I don't think anybody would accuse these four gentlemen of being dreamers," he said. "They're hard-headed, tough defenders of American interests and American security. But what they have come together to help galvanize is a recognition that we do not want a world of continued nuclear proliferation, and that in order for us to meet the security challenges of the future, America has to take leadership in this area."

Even if the realization of a world free of nuclear weapons remains a daring, distant vision, the goal has gained sufficient propulsion in the past few years to drive forward a number of practical steps to reduce the risk of nuclear attack.

Just hours before the four men gathered at the Millennium Hotel, President Obama, responding in part to their alarm, chaired a meeting of the UN Security Council that unanimously endorsed the goal, as well as several concrete steps to decrease nuclear dangers.

Since the founding of the United Nations in 1945, the Security Council had convened just three times with fifteen heads of state in place as leaders of their delegations. This was the first time the president of the United States had chaired a Security Council meeting. Obama told the council: "This very institution was founded at the dawn of the atomic age, in part because man's capacity to kill had to be contained. And although we averted a nuclear nightmare during the Cold War, we now face proliferation of a scope and complexity that demands new strategies and new approaches. Just one nuclear weapon exploded in a city—be it New York or Moscow; Tokyo or Beijing; London or Paris—could kill hundreds of thousands of people. And it would badly destabilize our security, our economies, and our very way of life.

"The historic resolution we just adopted enshrines our shared commitment to the goal of a world without nuclear weapons. And it brings Security Council agreement on a broad framework for action to reduce nuclear dangers as we work toward that goal."

He pointed to Kissinger, Shultz, Perry, and Nunn, seated at his invitation in the Security Council chamber, as he told the council that the goal of eliminating nuclear weapons could unite disparate peoples in common cause, including Democrats and Republicans in the United States.

"We were just sitting in the corner, looking on with amazement and pleasure," Nunn later said.

Unbeknownst to Obama, one of his Republican predecessors,

George H. W. Bush, had quietly informed Shultz that he, too, favored abolition, even though his son had brushed off the initiative while president. The first President Bush had written to Shultz in early 2007, while George W. Bush was still president. The letter said: "Thank you so much for the information that you sent me regarding a nuclear weapons free world. Inasmuch as George is President of the United States, I determined long ago that I would not publicly take positions that might be seen to be contrary to the positions taken by his Administration. Having said that, I would love to see 'a world free of nuclear weapons;' and the steps you outline seem most reasonable to me."

The dinner gathering at the Millennium Hotel capped the triumphal day for the four men. As the dusk deepened outside and the lights of the Manhattan skyline sparkled through the panoramic windows, Kissinger and Nunn conversed by the bar with Kanat Saudabayev, the foreign minister of Kazakhstan. They were joined by Egypt's foreign minister, Ahmed Aboul Gheit. Kissinger's basso profundo rumbled through the room as he described his tour of duty as a young counterintelligence officer in the U.S. Army in his native Germany not long after World War II ended.

Bill Perry talked quietly in another corner with Rolf Ekéus, chairman of the Stockholm International Peace Research Institute. Seated at one end of the elongated rectangular dinner table, Shultz conferred with several colleagues of Sam Nunn who traveled with him to New York.

The two dozen or so guests took their seats. Ekéus, one of the dinner hosts, welcomed everyone. Then Shultz rose to speak. A few months shy of his eighty-ninth birthday, he spoke softly but with clear conviction.

"I know all four of us were very moved by what happened today," he said. "I think we have seen that we have gotten past the argument of whether we should get rid of nuclear weapons or not, and moved to a different question—how do we get there from here?"

Perry spoke next. Thin but fit, with his words ever so slightly slowed by a mild stroke several years earlier, he recalled speaking to a group of foreign ministers in 2008. "It was in some ways a very interesting meeting, but I also had a very strong impression that I and others who were pushing for limited nuclear weapons were swimming upstream, and the current was very, very powerful against us. Contrast that with today, and today really for the first time I had the impression that it was going with the current. What a difference a year makes."

An idea that not long ago was considered utopian was suddenly a centerpiece of American foreign policy. Fifteen heads of state, including the Russian and Chinese presidents and British prime minister, had embraced the idea that morning. A host of former top American officials, Democrat and Republican, supported the concept.

Still, no one believed it would be easy, or that the goal would be achieved anytime soon. And abolition is not likely to be a pristine state in which nuclear weapons are forever banished. Nuclear weapons can be disassembled, dismantled, and destroyed. They cannot be uninvented. Nor can fissile material be erased from the earth. Any plausible scheme for a nuclear-free world must grapple with that reality. The most cogent proposals couple abolition with the latent ability to reproduce nuclear weapons if the international nonnuclear consensus breaks down. Shultz, Kissinger, Perry, and Nunn are exploring such an approach, known in nuclear circles as reconstitution. It would permit the United States and other nations to maintain the infrastructure, materials, and skilled workforce needed to build new weapons someday.

Even with that backstop, opponents of abolition have warned it is an ill-advised, even dangerously misguided vision that would damage American security and lead to more, not less, international conflict. Entrenched interests in the military services, national laboratories, strategic think tanks, and other bastions of the nuclear weapons priesthood are already mobilizing to block the disarmament movement. James Schlesinger, a former defense secretary, mockingly told a crowd of defense analysts at a symposium in Omaha, Nebraska, in 2010, "The dividing line between vision and hallucination is never very clear." The audience, hosted by the Pentagon's nuclear weapons combat commander, roared with appreciative laughter.

Two prominent Democrats—former defense secretary Harold Brown and former CIA director John Deutch—responded to the Shultz-Kissinger-Perry-Nunn op-ed article with their own *Wall Street Journal* rejoinder. "We agree that the strongest possible measures must be taken to inhibit the acquisition of and roll back the possession of nuclear weapons. However, the goal, even the aspirational goal, of eliminating all nuclear weapons is counterproductive. It will not advance substantive progress on nonproliferation; and it risks compromising the value that nuclear weapons continue to contribute, through deterrence, to U.S. security and international stability."

The new prominence of nuclear disarmament was due largely to the efforts of Shultz, Kissinger, Perry, and Nunn, and the less visible but critical analytical work and passion of Sidney Drell, an accomplished physicist, longtime government consultant on defense issues, colleague of Shultz and Perry at Stanford University, and onetime backstage adviser to Kissinger. Over four decades of advising the government on some of America's most secret and critical defense projects, he worked with seven presidents. In the 1990s alone, his leadership on nuclear weapons issues contributed to important safety enhancements for America's nuclear arsenal, the Clinton administration's endorsement of a nuclear test ban treaty (rejected by the Senate), and establishment of the National Nuclear Security Administration, a federal agency that, among other things, is rounding up vulnerable stocks of fissile material around the world. Drell played a critical role in drafting the *Wall Street Journal* article. "All four of us would say Sid, as much as anybody, is responsible for pushing this along," Shultz said. McGeorge Bundy, President Kennedy's national security adviser, once said of Drell, "He's the best man in the field on the intersection of science, technology and arms control."

There was more to the nuclear disarmament declaration in the *Wall Street Journal* than the dry, analytical prose suggested. It was also an effort by each man to bring a lifetime of engagement with nuclear weapons to a promising, positive culmination, to take a final run at tackling problems that had haunted them for years and eluded resolution while they were in power.

How the five men came to know one another, how they worked together or in opposition on defense issues across a span of six decades, is a quintessentially American story of the nuclear age. Like so many men and women in their generation, the five men were drawn to public service by the ideological and political contest between the United States and the Soviet Union. The Cold War may not have required the flat-out mobilization of national resources as World War II did, but it permeated American life and molded the worlds of science, industry, education, and politics in countless ways. Science and industry adapted and expanded to meet the need for new weapons systems. Defense funding gave universities the motivation and means to turn out more scientists and engineers and Soviet experts. Debates over defense drove and distorted presidential and congressional campaigns.

Shultz, Kissinger, Perry, Nunn, and Drell were very much products of their time. The possibility of a superpower nuclear conflict colored their lives and the fields they entered—science, statecraft, and politics. Their involvement with nuclear issues began at the outskirts of power in the worlds of scholarship, defense research, and local government, then gravitated to the centers of power in Washington. They came to the capital to serve their country, to flex their newfound power, to wage the Cold War, to advance their own fortunes, but more than anything, they came to help the nation prevail in the long struggle with the Soviet Union and to do what they could to prevent a nuclear war. What they saw and did during those years left them convinced that nuclear weapons must never be used again.

The ties between the men unfurled across multiple presidencies as they rotated in and out of Washington. They were, of course, but a small contingent among the thousands of Americans who played leading roles during the Cold War, and they did the bidding of the presidents they served while in executive branch posts. But their contributions were notable, and tell the tale of how the nation struggled to simultaneously manipulate and contain the destructive power that scientists let loose in the New Mexico desert in 1945.

Bill Perry and Sid Drell were the epitome of Cold War citizen-scientists. They helped make the hardware that made the Cold War manageable and, ultimately, winnable. Henry Kissinger and George Shultz, scholars turned diplomats, devised and directed strategies that shaped America's Cold War diplomacy, for better or for worse. Sam Nunn, the politician, became the Senate's leading authority on Cold War military matters.

Not surprisingly, much of what the five men did during the Cold War was aimed at maintaining America's defenses and ensuring that its nuclear weapons were reliable and could be swiftly and accurately delivered to targets across the Soviet Union by missiles or bombers. They were dedicated Cold Warriors. And by that yardstick, their present effort to eliminate nuclear weapons seems all the more improbable. Henry Kissinger, after all, approved the development of multiwarhead clusters that could be loaded atop missiles and aimed at different targets, a fateful step that made the Cold War even more volatile by making land-based missiles vulnerable to attack. He also risked nuclear miscalculation when he and Richard Nixon used American nuclear force exercises in 1969 to unnerve the Kremlin about American intentions in Vietnam and again in 1973 to keep Moscow from intervening in a Mideast war. Bill Perry played a pivotal role in the development of advanced missiles, submarines, and warplanes designed to carry nuclear weapons. Sam Nunn made sure that the Senate funded those and scores of other nuclear weapons programs. Sid Drell applied his expertise to numerous defense projects.

But another, more temperate thread runs through their Cold War careers, one that offers some hint of the destination where they find themselves today. It was most pronounced with George Shultz, who as a newcomer to defense policy in the 1980s joined Ronald Reagan in search of a strategy that would de-emphasize nuclear weapons and ultimately displace them at the heart of American military power. Kissinger as a young scholar at Harvard in the 1950s questioned whether a defense strategy built around the profligate use of nuclear weapons was credible or effective. Later, as national security adviser and secretary of state, he made arms control negotiations a centerpiece of American foreign policy and sought to limit U.S. nuclear war fighting plans.

Perry and Drell helped develop intelligence-gathering technologies that stabilized the Cold War by giving Washington a better reading on the size and firepower of Soviet forces. They both stressed the need for arms control and Perry, as defense secretary, took the lead in getting Ukraine, Kazakhstan, and Belarus to dismantle their nuclear arsenals after the 1991 disintegration of the Soviet Union. And Nunn repeatedly used his influence in the Senate to advance programs that reduced the risk of nuclear war and crafted legislation that provided critical American support to Russia to secure its nuclear weapons and materials after the Soviet Union collapsed.

None of the five men would call their current effort an act of repentance for their leading roles in maintaining the Cold War nuclear balance of terror. Nunn, for one, bristles at the idea. "Some people take great delight in saying, 'Well, these guys have gone through the Cold War, they're the ones who supported nuclear weapons, they're the ones who wanted a very large arsenal to confront the Soviet Union, and now they've seen the light, they've changed their mind after all these years.' I think that is not only simplistic, I think it's grossly misleading."

Nunn is right, in the sense that he and the other men long had doubts about nuclear weapons and tried, in different ways, to diminish the danger of nuclear war.

Yet there is an undeniable patina of atonement inherent in their effort. Having witnessed the birth of the nuclear age in 1945 and devoted the best years of their lives to sustaining America's nuclear might, they seem determined in their twilight years to convince the world that nuclear weapons must be abolished before it is too late to prevent the destruction of New York, Washington, London, or some other urban center.

A friend of Nunn and member of the NTI board said of Nunn's role, "It seemed a little out of character. It's really amazing what happens when people get older. There comes a moment for whatever reason that you have an epiphany."

Perry comes closest to a sense of expiation. "My generation was responsible for building up this fearsome nuclear arsenal," he sometimes tells his Stanford students. "I helped create these deadly weapons, and therefore I believe that I have a special responsibility to dismantle them."

A man who knows the men well, Albert "Bud" Wheelon, the founder of the CIA's Directorate of Science and Technology, put it this way: "I think Samuel Johnson said it best. There's nothing that focuses a man's mind like the certain knowledge that he's going to be hanged in a fortnight. You know, with all the things you've done, time is running out. . . . They bring a unique set of credentials; they've been right most of the time. They've seen it all. They deserve to be listened to. They have a platform; they have a voice that only they have. And the question is, how are they going to use the short time that remains?

"They had a certain amount of equity, and it will be gone when their voice is stilled. So let's shout while we can."

CHAPTER TWO

*In my view, whatever problems we have with Henry's
reluctance in some aspects of this mission, these problems are more
than offset by the value that he brings to the group.*
—BILL PERRY

Stage-managing the disarmament initiative can be a tricky task
when the five men take their show on the road. That was
evident in 2011 when they rolled into London in late spring for
a two-day nuclear policy conference with a star-studded group
of former national leaders from eighteen nations. At the first session in the gilded halls of Lancaster House, an eighteenth-century
palace adjacent to Green Park, Henry Kissinger's seat was unexpectedly vacant as the discussion commenced. He had also been
absent the prior evening when George Shultz, Sam Nunn, and Bill
Perry discussed their ideas with more than a dozen members of
Parliament who had gathered at Portcullis House in Westminster
to meet with the Americans.

Kissinger wasn't deliberately snubbing his partners. He was
promoting his new book about China, which had been published a few weeks earlier. While in London, he attracted a good
deal of attention, including prominent visibility in the *Financial
Times* and the *Sunday Telegraph*, which published extended interviews with Kissinger. Neither included a word about the nuclear
initiative or a mention of Shultz, Perry, or Nunn. On the day

of the first session at Lancaster House, he met with George Osborne, chancellor of the exchequer. Prime Minister David Cameron dropped in on the meeting.

It was not the first time, nor would it be the last, that Kissinger's celebrity overshadowed the other men. The imbalance was
ironic. Of the five men, Kissinger seems to be the least invested
in the nuclear initiative. He was the last to sign the *Wall Street
Journal* article and at times has sounded wobbly about the cause,
telling several friends that he doesn't really subscribe to the goal of
eliminating nuclear weapons. "He doesn't believe it," one friend
said. "He'd love to figure a way to get out of it." James Goodby, a
former American diplomat and arms negotiator who has worked
closely with the men in recent years, said, "He's blown hot and
cold. George Shultz has to keep pulling him back, pulling him
back. But he certainly is a very effective spokesperson. People
listen to him and he has such a reputation in the world that when
he signs on to something, it really makes quite a lot of difference."

The more time one spends with the five men, the more it becomes evident that the united front they present in public masks
disagreements, past and present. For the most part, they have put
bitter Cold War disputes behind them, but tensions occasionally
crack the comity.

Shultz seems to be the most committed to their joint enterprise
and the most impatient to see its goals realized. At ninety, he is also
the oldest, but age is not the reason. The real explanation is his jaundiced view of nuclear weapons as a legitimate instrument of war.
Unlike his partners, he was never fully invested in nuclear weapons,
never totally subscribed to the idea that they were an irreplaceable
component of American defense. "I had never learned to love the
bomb—or the ballistic missile that carried it," he once said.

After he got involved in defense policy in 1982 as secretary
of state, he shed many of the conventional nuclear views he had
and followed Ronald Reagan's lead in questioning the most

fundamental tenets of the nuclear age, even the weapons themselves. In his view, American and Soviet war-fighting blueprints that anticipated the deaths of hundreds of millions of people "were insane, just insane."

For Shultz, the undeclared leader of the quintet, the *Wall Street Journal* article inaugurated a final drive to realize the goal of a world free of nuclear weapons that Reagan and he were ridiculed for entertaining at the 1986 Reykjavik summit. Kissinger calls Shultz the "spiritual father of this enterprise."

Shultz and Reykjavik are inextricably linked. "I think it probably did bother him that something that was so obviously right in his view and in Reagan's view was so roundly criticized and little understood," Goodby said. "The whole experience got seared into his soul, in a way, and it bothered him and he wanted to do something about it and did. . . . It's not just an intellectual thing with him, but a fairly emotional thing."

In Shultz's view, progress toward eliminating nuclear weapons would be a crowning achievement. He can sound positively frisky about the issue. "I'm very optimistic," he told a gathering in Paris one day. "I really think we can get somewhere, that's why I feel as though, with the years I have left, it's the subject I've spent my time working on and worrying about."

For Perry, the effort is the continuation of the work he did during the Clinton administration to dismantle nuclear arsenals left behind in the wreckage of the Soviet empire. "Bill sees his great success in denuclearizing the non-Russian parts of the USSR and thinks of this as another big step worth doing," Harold Brown, the former defense secretary, said.

Perry's role also reflects a desire to leave a legacy less defined by the cutting-edge weapons he helped create during the Cold War than by his devotion in more recent times to eliminating the deadliest weapons of all. Yet Perry, like Kissinger, has at times confounded his fellow abolitionists by publicly questioning whether the elimination of nuclear weapons is a plausible goal. When Perry and Brent Scowcroft, a skeptic about abolition, cochaired a 2009 Council on Foreign Relations study group on nuclear weapons, they raised doubts about the goal in the group's final report. In a joint preface, they said, "It will at a minimum be many years before the goal of zero nuclear weapons can be realized, and thus the United States should set a goal of reaching what some have called a base camp or vantage point. . . . When that goal is reached, it will be possible to reevaluate whether geopolitical conditions permit moving closer to the elimination of nuclear weapons. That decision need not be made now and, indeed, it is not possible now to envision the geopolitical conditions that would permit moving toward the final goal." Perry and James Schlesinger sounded a similar note in a task force report they prepared for Congress.

When asked if he read the Perry-Scowcroft language as a retreat, Shultz said, "That's the way it read to me, too. But when you talk to Bill, he says, no. He thinks that he's brought them a long ways, and Scowcroft has come a long way towards us, but not all the way." Despite the Perry-Scowcroft language, Shultz said he did not doubt Perry's commitment.

Perry was unapologetic about the reports. "I saw my duty on those two commissions was to get the best possible report I could get," he said. Perry and Scowcroft managed to work out compromise language that each of them could live with. That was not the case with Schlesinger. "Jim and I don't have that kind of relationship," Perry said. "And to compound the issue, that commission became very quickly polarized."

Perry nearly resigned in protest from the congressional commission. When he took the draft report back to his hotel to read, he found it was heavily tilted toward Republican views. "I came back the next day and I said, 'This is my last meeting. I've read this report. It's too far from what I'm willing to sign. I'm not willing to simply fight over every word in this thing, so I'm just withdrawing from the commission.' And that was not meant as a gambit or as a ploy. I decided to leave. And so I made my little fifteen-minute speech and started packing my things to go." The other members appealed to him not to quit, and wording acceptable to Perry was ultimately adopted.

For Nunn, the nuclear disarmament initiative is a logical extension of his Senate push to reduce NATO's reliance on battlefield nuclear weapons to repulse a Warsaw Pact invasion of then West Germany and Western Europe and his legislative initiative, with Senator Richard Lugar, to secure Soviet nuclear weapons and materials as the Soviet Union collapsed in the early 1990s. Yet he warmed to it slowly after retiring from the Senate in 1997 and later becoming cochairman of the Nuclear Threat Initiative. Nunn and Ted Turner, the Atlanta billionaire who founded CNN, created NTI in 2001. It was initially funded by Turner and later generously supported by Warren Buffett, the financier and philanthropist.

When NTI was established, Nunn was wary of Turner's desire to commit the organization to the elimination of nuclear weapons, fearing the goal would prove divisive and impede its threat reduction agenda. By the time Shultz and Nunn started talking about a new initiative in 2006, Nunn's views had evolved. He was more receptive to abolition, believing the audacious idea would rally support for interim steps to better manage nuclear arsenals and materials. In the end, as ministers to the antinuclear flock, Nunn and NTI could ill afford to let others trump their leadership. Once he swung around in favor of abolition, Nunn became an unwavering advocate.

"I think he very quickly saw that there was something going on that would perhaps undercut his standing as the preeminent guru in the field, and so he pretty quickly signed on to it, and he is now one of the fairly effective advocates of the whole scheme," Goodby said.

Nunn harbors his own doubts, not about the goal or the steps, but about how quickly the goal can be achieved and how profoundly geopolitics must change to make the abolition of nuclear weapons possible. "I don't see this as saying that we're taking the world as it is now and simply getting rid of nuclear weapons," he said. "I think you have to change the world. And I don't want to make it sound like that's forever, but I think it's what you have to do."

Kissinger shared Nunn's concerns, and along with Nunn, first considered endorsing the principles outlined in the article but not signing on as coauthor. "I confess when it started, I joined because of my respect for my colleagues and I might not have gone all that distance had I done it by myself," Kissinger said.

Harold Brown put it this way: "Henry's always hard to understand. I think Henry periodically feels the need to be a good guy, and that's why he signed on to this."

Most of Kissinger's four accomplices were not eager to talk about his doubts. One of them, asking not to be quoted by name, said, "When Henry's friends say, 'Henry, how could you do anything so outrageous after your history,' I think Henry, at that stage, just sort of mutters."

Perry didn't flinch when asked if he was aware that Kissinger has told friends he disagreed with the group. "He's told me that, too, on occasion," Perry said. "And what I make of it is that he doesn't agree with much of it, and he's constantly harangued by his friends on the right and whose friendship he wants to keep.

"So why did Henry agree to be a part of this?" Perry asked aloud. "For one thing, I think it was important for him to be a part of this group and of this movement, even though he didn't fully agree with it. It certainly put him front and center on a very important issue of the day. And Henry likes to be front and center of big policy issues of the day, and this put him in that position, even though he didn't fully agree with all of the conclusions. So that is a fact. And that's my interpretation of how that happened."

Despite the wavering, Perry still regards Kissinger as an asset. "He's been a very important part of it," he said. "His reputation around the world has been a very important asset to us, particularly in Russia, particularly in China. . . . In my view, whatever problems we have with Henry's reluctance in some aspects of this mission, these problems are more than offset by the value that he brings to the group, particularly in opening doors at very high levels in a few foreign countries."

Kissinger's concerns, coupled with his often extended flyspecking of joint pronouncements before publication, clearly makes the other men impatient at times. Shultz and Perry were visibly relieved in early 2011 when Kissinger finally signed off on a joint op-ed article about nuclear deterrence policy that he had held up for weeks. But the other men would be the first to say that Kissinger's intellectual horsepower has enhanced their work and his international fame has given their campaign a degree of star power the others do not generate. Kissinger's unparalleled access to government leaders abroad has made it possible for the men to meet several times with top Russian and Chinese leaders.

When asked about Kissinger's apparent ambivalence about abolishing nuclear arms, Shultz would not acknowledge any daylight between his views and Kissinger's. "Well, he signed it," Shultz said of the *Wall Street Journal* piece. Referring to a documentary film about nuclear disarmament that features Shultz, Kissinger, Perry, and Nunn, Shultz continued, "And you've seen the *Nuclear Tipping Point*. He made all those statements. There they are. They're on the record." In the film, Kissinger speaks as a firm supporter of the abolition initiative.

Nunn said he understood Kissinger's concerns about moving too quickly toward nuclear disarmament. "First, let's remember that this is a very complex public policy issue that the four of us have distilled down to the 'vision and steps' agenda," he said. "There is bound to be some nuance in talking to any one of the four of us, in particular, given that we have been working together on this now for four years.

"Second, I can't comment on what someone else might have said to someone else privately. But on the question of the public record—much of which I've been a firsthand witness to—Henry has been a consistent, clear, and invaluable advocate of the vision and the steps as a way of framing this broad and diverse nuclear policy agenda for governments and publics."

Kissinger openly acknowledged he was initially wary of signing the op-ed article but said he came around because he thought it might jump-start some constructive new thinking about nuclear weapons.

"Both Sam and I decided to go all the way because we could agree with the specifics," he said. "We might disagree on the feasibility of the zero option, but I agree with Sam, who says it's like going up a mountain. You've heard that phrase. I agree with that. And so it might be that as interim steps evolve, and as a global dialogue develops, that necessities will appear that bring people at least to the point where I started, of pushing the use of nuclear weapons to the fringes. And then once we are there, to go beyond that."

It is hard not to see Kissinger's involvement as motivated at least in part by a desire to burnish his image late in life. "This is an historic initiative, and he likes to be part of history," one friend said. Multiple invitations to meet with President Obama in the Oval Office, along with Shultz, Perry, and Nunn, have been an unexpected dividend.

But to be fair, controlling nuclear weapons has long been a Kissinger cause. He made his first mark on the national scene in the 1950s with a bestselling book, *Nuclear Weapons and Foreign Policy*, which called for limiting a nuclear conflict. While he waffled on a key issue during the Nixon administration—the arming of American and Soviet missiles with multiple warheads—he made nuclear arms control an American priority during his tenure as national security adviser and secretary of state. "Henry Kissinger did more than almost any secretary of state to get strategic nuclear arms control onto the national agenda," said Goodby, who was involved in many of the arms negotiations. The results were major accomplishments: the 1972 Anti-Ballistic Missile Treaty (ABM) and the Strategic Arms Limitation Talks (SALT), which culminated in an interim agreement signed by Nixon and Leonid Brezhnev, the Soviet leader. Kissinger also tried, without great success, to get the Pentagon to limit its nuclear war-fighting plans.

Drell is the conscience of the group, though he, too, is a latecomer to abolition. "You've got to seek these goals in a sensible way," he said. "It's not just an empty vision. . . . And that's why I was late coming around to saying go to zero, because I didn't see any practical way of urging that. You can't say that's a goal, but what do we do today, tomorrow, this year, or next year?"

Drell has wrestled throughout his career with the moral dimensions of nuclear weapons and attendant concepts like nuclear deterrence and first-use policy, the doctrine that a nation is prepared to initiate a nuclear exchange if it believes an enemy nuclear attack is imminent. He churned out dozens of technical papers and philosophical essays about nuclear weapons over the years and led numerous scientific studies about arms control matters.

He befriended Andrei Sakharov, the beleaguered Soviet nuclear physicist and human rights campaigner who bravely disowned the weapons he helped develop and questioned the tyranny of the Kremlin. When the Soviet government forcibly hauled Sakharov from his Moscow apartment in 1980 and put him under house arrest in Gorky (Nizhny Novgorod), Drell rallied support for him in the West and became a dear friend of Sakharov and his wife, Yelena Bonner. Though Drell viewed the elimination of nuclear weapons as an impractical goal during the long standoff with the Soviet Union, and pointedly argued against the goal in a 1989 public debate, he was always an arms controller at heart. In 1983 he cofounded the Center for International Security and Arms

Control, a Stanford organization that brought scientists and social scientists together to discuss defense issues.

It is difficult at times to square that role with Drell's active involvement in dispensing scientific advice to the White House during the Vietnam War. Drell does not see a moral or intellectual conflict in that service and his sincerity is genuine when he says he felt an obligation as a citizen scientist to render his best advice to the nation on esoteric technical matters, many unrelated to Vietnam, even during politically charged times. His fierce dedication to nuclear arms control and his thoughtful approach to nuclear issues belie the Vietnam-era depiction of Drell by some critics as a morally deficient figure.

WITH SEVERAL LARGE egos involved, the collaboration among the five men can be a complicated affair. Kissinger and Nunn are the extroverts, bantering with their colleagues, recounting droll anecdotes, disarming others with sly humor.

"You need your cardiologist on hand when you dine here," Kissinger advised the group one evening in 2010 as they warily examined the menu at Franziskaner, a Bavarian restaurant in Munich. He promptly ordered the "Franziskaner sausage plate," featuring five kinds of sausages, mashed potatoes, sauerkraut, and horseradish. He washed it down with two large glasses of beer.

After an especially flattering introduction at a large dinner in California, Kissinger stepped up to the microphone. "I appreciate the kind remarks," he said. "They leave me in a position in which I found myself once at a cocktail party where a lady came up to me and said, 'I understand you are a fascinating man. Fascinate me.' It was one of the less successful conversations that I've had."

Nunn was often guarded and dreary while serving in the Senate, leading a *New York Times* reporter to ask in a 1987 magazine profile, "Is Sam Nunn too smart, too conservative and too dull to be president?" These days his folksy side is showing. He seems to relish his new role as a champion of nuclear disarmament, even poking fun at himself. One day he recounted how, as a young House aide in 1962, he was instructed to read the Army, Navy, and Air Force procurement manuals, dense tomes packed with mind-numbing bureaucratese. "I read every word of the procurement manuals," he said. "Everybody wants to know why I'm boring. That was the way I started. I was a very colorful guy before that."

He even ventured onto *The Colbert Report* in 2010 to banter with Stephen Colbert. He held his own as Colbert peppered him with antic, barbed questions.

"How about this, would this work?" Colbert asked Nunn. "If any nuclear bomb goes off from a terrorist organization, we just automatically nuke North Korea or Iran—without even investigating—we just say, boom, tag, you're it. And that will encourage those countries to try to keep nuclear weapons out of the hands of terrorists even harder than we do because they know if anything happens, we pull the plug on them. What about that?"

Nunn: "Stephen, I have to confess, I hadn't thought of that answer."

Colbert: "You surprise me, sir. Sam Nunn was always known as being a Democrat you could trust on defense. Head of the Senate Armed Services Committee. Have you gotten soft with your peace-nik friends putting your flowers down the barrels of the guns?"

Nunn: "Well, I would not think that George Shultz or Henry Kissinger or Bill Perry, secretary of defense, secretaries of state, are in that category."

Shultz often maintains an impassive, Buddha-like presence in public, but can be quite puckish when the mood is light. A photo of Shultz dancing with Ginger Rogers occupies a place of honor on his conference room wall at Stanford. It is signed by Rogers, with the inscription, "For the first two minutes, I could swear I was dancing with Fred."

At a 2010 San Francisco holiday party a few nights before his ninetieth birthday, Shultz bounded from his chair to take the microphone from the bandleader after the group played "Georgia on My Mind." The song, he told the dinner guests, reminded him of the time he had presented Eduard Shevardnadze, the Soviet foreign minister, with a revised version of the tune with the lyrics zanily rewritten to refer to Soviet Georgia, Shevardnadze's homeland. Shultz exuberantly sang a few bars of the variation before relinquishing the microphone. A few evenings later, at an extravagant black-tie birthday gala organized by his effervescent wife, Charlotte, Shultz emphatically rejected the idea that the party marked the end of his active life. "I'm still in the game!" he whooped.

The high-spirited conviviality sometimes masks long-simmering disputes among the men. Shultz and Kissinger, once bitterly at odds over how to deal with the Soviet Union, don't dwell on past disagreements. In 1987, just to cite one example of the bad blood, Kissinger and Richard Nixon coauthored a scorching opinion piece in the *Los Angeles Times* attacking Reagan and Shultz for their approach to the Kremlin, especially their discussion with Mikhail Gorbachev about eliminating nuclear weapons. "Soviet strategy since the end of World War II has been to exploit the West's fear of nuclear weapons by calling repeatedly for their abolition," they warned. "Any Western leader who indulges in the Soviets' disingenuous fantasies of a nuclear-free world courts unimaginable perils."

Anatoly Dobrynin, the longtime Soviet ambassador in Washington, recalled in his memoirs that Kissinger told him in 1984 that Reagan and Shultz were fumbling relations with Moscow. "He stressed that the Reagan administration had no coherent program to deal with the Soviet Union because Reagan had never thought about it seriously, and the State Department was characteristically lacking in initiative and courage to suggest new ideas."

These and other slashing attacks seemed to belie Kissinger's comment in 1982 that "if I could choose one American to whom I would entrust the nation's fate, it would be George Shultz."

When reminded that Nixon and Kissinger had hammered Reagan and Shultz, and that Nixon even questioned his suitability to be secretary of state, Shultz said, "They're entitled to their opinions. But it turned out I was right and they were wrong about the biggest issue we faced, namely how to deal with the Cold War."

But the mood quickly lightened as Shultz merrily recounted Kissinger's grudging acknowledgment that Shultz had been right. "He would never say this in public," Shultz said. Then imitating Kissinger's occasionally unintelligible rumble, he gently parodied Kissinger's comment to him: "'Mostly we agreed, but on one big thing we disagreed, and you were right and I was wrong. But if it had turned out that the Soviet Union *wruhwruhwruh*, I would have been right.'

"I said, 'Well, but it turned out you were wrong.'"

Laughing at his memory of the conversation, Shultz added, "Henry and I are pretty good friends. We can josh about that."

Yet a hint of old animosities flares up occasionally, or so it seems. At a dinner in 2010, Shultz warmly introduced Kissinger as the keynote speaker. When Kissinger finished his talk, Shultz, usually a man of exquisite manners, playfully but awkwardly joked about Kissinger's penchant for manipulation. He told the two hundred or so dinner guests that he had just realized the real reason Kissinger favored eliminating nuclear weapons: he could not manipulate them. "Henry loves to manipulate things," Shultz said.

The comment drew a chilly stare from Kissinger, who stepped back to the microphone to offer a tart riposte. "I have to say that when you are in a crisis, you have to move things around in a crisis, that's your job, but manipulating them is not the purpose of being in office. The purpose of being in office is to protect the security of the United States, and to contribute to creating a better world. . . . My problem with nuclear weapons is not that I can't move them around. My problem is that if you move them around, you have consequences that are out of proportion to anything that you might want to achieve. That's the fundamental reason."

Shultz and Nunn have their own history of disagreements. Their present friendship might surprise Washington veterans who recall testy relations between the State Department and Nunn when the Reagan administration argued that the 1972 ABM Treaty permitted development of space-based missile defenses. Nunn led a Senate revolt on the issue, warning that it could lead to a "constitutional crisis." He contended the administration's claim was based on a "complete and total misrepresentation" of the Senate ratification history. Nunn also chastised Shultz and Reagan for discussing the elimination of nuclear weapons with Mikhail Gorbachev in Reykjavik.

Yet while Nunn and Shultz were policy antagonists, they were competing amicably at two of Washington's top golf courses, Congressional and Burning Tree. "He's a much better golfer," Shultz said, not an easy admission for the intensely competitive former secretary. Nunn, who regularly scored in the 70s in those days, called Shultz a "pretty good golfer." He had one quirk, Nunn recalled. Shultz relished extremely complicated betting schemes. They would place dollar bets on who would place closer to the pin. Anyone who hit a tee shot off a tree and still made par would win a dollar. Shultz dubbed the tree shots "woodsies." "George would always say his ball hit two trees," Nunn said. "He'd claim if he made par after that, he got two woodsies." Alex Shultz, one of George's sons, knows the routine well. "It was a complex game," he once told an interviewer. "It always seems like you're winning, and then at the end, you owe him money."

When Nunn's description was recounted to Shultz, he smiled. "You get away with what you can," he said.

Perry, despite his standing as a former defense secretary, is preternaturally modest. So much so that some defense experts questioned whether he had sufficient moxie to be secretary of defense. Senator Robert Byrd, the West Virginia Democrat, quickly deflated the issue at Perry's 1994 confirmation hearing by observing that in his forty years in the Senate, he had never seen humility in a cabinet officer, and that it was time to give it a try.

While Shultz, Kissinger, and Nunn are drawn to center stage, Perry flees from it. "I don't seek publicity," he said. "To me it's not an advantage. When I have my picture taken or I testify or when I go give a news account, I'm doing it because it's my responsibility to do it, not because I want to do it. And so I guess I tend to gravitate away from the center of those things. Whereas Henry—that sort of thing forms naturally around him."

One evening at Universal Studios in Hollywood, as they arrived for the premiere of *Nuclear Tipping Point*, Nunn and Shultz and their wives jauntily stepped across the red carpet as the paparazzi snapped photos. The men clearly relished the Tinseltown treatment. They paused in the klieg lights to field questions from reporters as Jon Voight appeared. Ted Turner warmly welcomed Nunn. Moments later, Shultz and his wife enthusiastically greeted then California governor and longtime Hollywood star Arnold Schwarzenegger. Meanwhile, Perry and his wife, Lee, inconspicuously entered the theater without attracting so much as a glance from the photographers. (Kissinger did not attend the event.)

When President Obama hosted a White House screening of *Nuclear Tipping Point*, Shultz, Kissinger, and Nunn drew most of the attention from several dozen of the government's top national security officials at a reception in a ground-floor hall overlooking the Rose Garden. At an appearance by the four at the American Academy in Berlin, Perry sat so far to the side of the stage that he was outside the reach of the academy backdrop and barely visible to many in the audience. Whenever the four men appear together, Perry's brevity invariably contrasts with the orotund remarks of his more loquacious colleagues. He frequently says more in a few words than they say in many. He never seems to travel with more than a pint-size carry-on suitcase that he drags behind him like an obedient puppy. At the airport in Munich, he uncomplainingly endured an extensive security check, unpacking all his belongings and partly disrobing for a guard who obviously had no idea that the unassuming man standing before him was a former American defense secretary.

But for all his modesty, Perry can be quite assertive and opinionated. When he chairs large gatherings of defense experts, he crisply directs the conversation and does not hesitate to challenge the views of other participants and put his imprint on the discussion. Active-duty generals and admirals travel to California frequently to consult with him. During his stints at the Pentagon, he was regarded as a decisive leader and risk taker who was prepared to bet the bank on the development of untested new technologies like stealth airplanes.

Drell, less prominent than the others, sometimes watches his colleagues with detached amusement. But he expects to be treated with respect. When shown an e-mail message from Nunn to Shultz, Perry, and Kissinger that relegated Drell to the "cc" line along with several staff members at the Nuclear Threat Initiative, Drell grimaced.

Shultz is the paterfamilias of the group, the patient diplomat who keeps everyone on board during rocky periods when one or another of the men seems to be straying. Coaxing, cajoling, sometimes playing to the vanity of his partners, he has kept the consensus alive for more than four years, four joint op-ed articles, and a flurry of public appearances. Though Nunn shares leadership duties with Shultz, and the initiative is mostly funded, staffed, and publicized through NTI, Nunn courteously defers to Shultz on many matters.

While the five men act in concert and hold periodic conference calls to consult about next steps and public appearances, the men tend to pair off in subgroups.

An informal West Coast group is anchored by Shultz and Drell. Shultz relies heavily on Drell for technical knowledge and perspective and the two have clearly formed a close, mutually respectful friendship. Sensing that Drell might feel slighted by the public fanfare surrounding the four more prominent men, Shultz looks for opportunities to spotlight Drell. When the American Academy of Arts and Sciences decided to award the prestigious Rumford Prize to Shultz, Kissinger, Perry, and Nunn in 2008, Shultz made sure that Drell was included.

Perry, whose Stanford office is a short walk from the campus building where Shultz and Drell work, confers with them frequently, but tends to operate in his own orbit. His hectic travel schedule keeps him on the road constantly.

An East Coast group revolves around Nunn and his colleagues at NTI. Nunn and Kissinger seem to think alike on many matters. In agreeing to call for the elimination of nuclear weapons, Kissinger seemed most reassured by Nunn's involvement. He said he frequently consults with Nunn on nuclear weapons issues.

Drell and Kissinger, who have known each other since 1960, maintain a friendship that is at once wary and warm. United by their nuclear initiative, they sometimes kid one another about overcoming their political disagreements. At a meeting in London in 2008, Kissinger pulled Drell aside and told him, "Sid, we've come a long way since the 1960s. It worries me that we now agree on so many things."

What brought Kissinger and Drell together in recent years, and fuses the five men in common cause, is their conviction that the world stands at a nuclear pivot point. If urgent steps are not taken to rein in nuclear weapons and prevent the spread of nuclear technologies and fissile materials, they believe, a catastrophic attack is virtually inevitable.

An enemy of the United States today is more likely to detonate a nuclear weapon in New York, Washington, or some other

American city than was the case at the height of the Cold War. Just short of that, a terror group could set off a powerful conventional bomb packed with plutonium or highly enriched uranium, a device known as a dirty bomb. It would blanket a large area with lethal radioactive debris, sickening thousands of people and making the business district of a city uninhabitable for years.

"We are in a race between cooperation and catastrophe," Sam Nunn sometimes says. At the moment, cooperation is losing. The world today is filled with nuclear dangers—and insufficient efforts to overcome them. The result could be every bit as devastating as the atomic bombing of Hiroshima.

CHAPTER THREE

*Our number one concern is the acquisition of fissile
material by a terror group.*
—AMERICAN INTELLIGENCE OFFICIAL

T he workday was just beginning in Hiroshima on Monday,
August 6, 1945. The sun was bright and warm as commut-
ers made their way to offices by foot or bicycle, children headed
to school, and citizens tended to a number of civil defense projects
around the city. Earlier in the morning, officials had called off
an air raid alert after a weather plane passed uneventfully overhead. After four years of war, people were thankful that their city
had largely escaped the ruinous American bombing raids that had
damaged other Japanese cities.

At approximately 8:15 a.m., a 9,700-pound uranium bomb,
dubbed "Little Boy" by its American makers, exploded roughly
1,900 feet above Hiroshima.

"Those closest to the explosion died instantly, their bodies turned
to black char," an American account recalled. "Nearby birds burst
into flames in mid-air, and dry, combustible materials such as paper
instantly ignited as far away as 6,400 feet from ground zero. The
white light acted as a giant flashbulb, burning the dark patterns of
clothing onto skin and the shadows of bodies onto walls."

Those not incinerated by the blast were terribly burned or
bloodied by flying shards of glass. "Within minutes 9 out of 10

people half a mile or less from ground zero were dead. . . . Nearly every structure within one mile of ground zero was destroyed, and almost every building within three miles was damaged.

"The numerous small fires that erupted simultaneously all around the city soon merged into one large firestorm, creating extremely strong winds that blew towards the center of the fire. The firestorm eventually engulfed 4.4 square miles of the city, killing anyone who had not escaped in the first minutes after the attack."

The United States estimated that 70,000 people died as a result of the initial blast, heat, and radiation effects. By the end of 1945, a government report said, the death toll was probably over 100,000. "The five-year death total may have reached or even exceeded 200,000, as cancer and other long-term effects took hold."

It is understandably hard for Americans to contemplate an attack of that magnitude somewhere in the United States. It would be a day unlike any other in American history. One way to think about it is to recall the terror attacks of September 11, 2001, and imagine an assault that would make that awful day seem like a pinprick. All the loss of life on 9/11, the dislocation, the families that lost loved ones in the towers of the World Trade Center, the hundreds of New York firefighters who perished when the buildings collapsed, the men and women who began a beautiful late-summer day at work in the upper stories of the towers, then jumped out of windows, preferring to die instantly rather than burn to death, the soldiers and civilians who died at the Pentagon, the disintegration of United Airlines Flight 93 when it plunged into a Pennsylvania field—all that horror would be thousands of times worse in a nuclear attack.

A dirty bomb would produce fewer casualties and much less damage to buildings but the aftermath would still be devastating. The spread of highly radioactive particles would probably prove fatal to people near the blast site, could produce debilitating radiation sickness in thousands of others in the immediate vicinity, and could contaminate many square blocks of office buildings, restaurants, and residential quarters. If the bomb were loaded with plutonium, dangerous levels of radiation would persist for years. The mass evacuations, and attendant fears, generated by radiation, the invisible killer, were evident in Japan when the reactors at the Fukushima nuclear plant failed after a massive earthquake and tsunami in 2011.

Unfortunately, the possibility of a nuclear attack is increasing rather than diminishing two decades after the end of the Cold War. President Obama put it well when he addressed nuclear dangers during a 2009 visit to Prague. "Today, the Cold War has disappeared but thousands of those weapons have not," he said. "In a strange turn of history, the threat of global nuclear war has gone down, but the risk of a nuclear attack has gone up."

North Korea has the bomb and Iran is trying to get one. Bomb-making technology is easy to acquire. Fissile material needed for a bomb, especially highly enriched uranium, is plentiful and poorly protected in many places. More of it is produced every day at enrichment plants around the world to fuel civilian nuclear reactors. Despite the Japanese reactor disasters in 2011, the long-term demand for electric power generated from sources other than fossil fuels like oil and coal is sure to lead to the construction of new nuclear power plants in the years ahead. As long as uranium is enriched for power-plant reactors, the risk of diversion and theft will remain high. The danger is likely to increase as new enrichment technologies are perfected, including the use of the concentrated light of laser beams to purify uranium. The process, perfected by two scientists in Australia and adapted by General Electric, could transform the production of bomb-grade fuel from an industrial-scale enterprise to one that a scientifically sophisticated terror group could master. Iranian scientists appear to have already perfected laser enrichment at a laboratory level. Under current circumstances, terrorists stand a decent chance of producing a makeshift nuclear weapon, known in counterterrorism circles as an Improvised Nuclear Device, or IND. If they can't fabricate their own weapon, there is always the possibility that they could smuggle one out of Russia, buy one from North Korea, or obtain one from Pakistan, or from Iran if Tehran takes the final steps necessary to develop nuclear weapons.

The use of a nuclear weapon would profoundly change the United States or any other target nation. The catastrophic consequences of a nuclear attack go far beyond the horrific bloodshed and physical destruction that would cripple a city like New York. As devastating as that damage would be—hundreds of thousands of people killed or maimed, a huge swath of the city reduced to rubble or burned-out neighborhoods—the longer-term impact would be equally unthinkable. The American economy would be paralyzed, the psychology of the country would be altered, and the delicate balance between security and liberty that lies at the heart of American democracy would be wrenched in favor of security.

"When this first bomb, this first terrorist bomb is unleashed," Bill Perry said, "it not only will transform people's thinking, it leads us to a different course of action. It will probably lead us to the wrong set of actions. Because it caught us by surprise, because people will only begin to realize what the truly terrible consequences are going to be, we will overreact in a way that will threaten our civil liberties, threaten our democratic form of government."

The Preventive Defense Project, a Harvard–Stanford partnership, described the likely consequences if a 10-kiloton weapon, about two-thirds the size of the Hiroshima bomb, were detonated in New York, Washington, or San Francisco.

"The downtown area would be obliterated. Just outside the area leveled by the blast, people wounded by flying debris, fires, and intense radiation would stand little chance of survival: emergency workers would not get to them because of the intense radiation, and in any event their injuries (burns and acute radiation exposure) would require sophisticated and intensive medical care to offer any chance of survival; only a fraction of them could hope for such care. Further downwind from the detonation point, a plume of radioactive debris would spread. Its shape and size would depend on wind and rain conditions, but the area over which people who did not shelter themselves or flee within hours would receive lethal doses within a day would range from five to ten square miles: the area of Brooklyn for New York, northwest Washington for Washington, DC, or the upper peninsula for San Francisco."

Like the 9/11 attacks, the impact would ripple across the country, but this time the inhabitants of other cities, fearing they could be next, might flee to safer ground, clogging escape routes. Financial markets would come to a standstill for weeks, not days. And the optimism, resilience, and sense of perpetual reinvention and renewal that have propelled American society throughout its history would be gravely, perhaps irreparably, damaged.

The very thought of it is so disturbing, so outside the realm of our daily lives, that it seems the stuff of Hollywood thrillers and video games. We think, that could never happen. Compared to the tribulations of the day, it's a remote, abstract concept. And even if it is a possibility, the natural reaction is to assume little can be done to stop determined terrorists.

It is, as Perry says, a "low-probability, high-impact event." Unfortunately, that equation can lead to inattention and indifference. As Perry said, "It's the remote contingencies that we have a hard time preparing for either physically or psychologically." Perry thinks of it this way: "Things that haven't happened are not going to happen. People have a hard time grasping, understanding, just how horrible it would be and how much it would change their lives. And maybe it won't happen. I think the more general question is how in your own life do you prepare for an event that would be catastrophic but only has one chance in a hundred of happening? Generally you deal by dismissing it rather than preparing for it."

"We have to get past the mental block that says it's too terrible to think about," W. Craig Fugate, administrator of the Federal Emergency Management Agency, told the *New York Times* in late 2010. "We have to be ready to deal with it."

The *Times'* story about government guidance on how to survive a nuclear attack probably came as a shock to many readers. The subject seemed like a throwback to the 1950s, when civil defense planning was the rage and government officials crisscrossed the nation urging citizens to build fallout shelters in their backyards or apartment house basements. Unfortunately, surviving a nuclear attack is not an outdated or abstract issue. Fugate and his colleagues are worried about a terrorist nuclear attack. The government's recommendation: seek shelter in any stable building, or even a car, after the bomb goes off, rather than fleeing. Japanese authorities initially issued similar instructions to citizens living near the damaged Fukushima reactors. The American guidance grew out of studies showing that the number of casualties could be sharply reduced if people avoided exposure to lethal airborne radiation that would come with a nuclear explosion. Much of the radioactive plume would disperse within twelve to twenty-four hours.

Shultz, Kissinger, Perry, Nunn, and Drell fear that the prospects of a terrorist nuclear strike are increasing as nuclear weapons and the means to make them proliferate. Their concerns are echoed in a torrent of sobering books, papers, websites, and blog postings produced by government officials, scholars, and other nuclear experts warning that it is only a matter of time before terrorists obtain the knowledge and ingredients to make a bomb. Much of the work is consumed by a limited, already well-informed audience and it either doesn't reach most Americans or fails to register with them.

Matthew Bunn at Harvard's Belfer Center for Science and International Affairs, supported by funding from the NTI, has for several years produced a carefully researched annual report about nuclear threats called *Securing the Bomb*. The most recent edition reports some progress over the last decade in reducing nuclear arms and securing the fissile materials needed to make them. But the overall picture remains grim. While American and Russian arsenals have been sharply reduced since the end of the Cold War, and will go down further under the arms reduction treaty negotiated by the Obama administration and Kremlin leadership, that progress offers little comfort.

Bunn rightly cites four factors that, taken together, paint an ominous picture: al-Qaeda is seeking nuclear weapons; a sophisticated terrorist group could make a crude nuclear bomb if it got enough of the needed nuclear materials; there have been more than eighteen documented cases of theft or loss of plutonium or highly enriched uranium; nuclear smuggling is extraordinarily difficult to stop.

The vulnerability of nuclear facilities was evident in a particularly disturbing South African incident. Just after midnight on November 8, 2007, two groups of armed men broke into South Africa's nuclear complex in Pelindaba, not far from Pretoria, the capital. While South Africa was still under apartheid rule in the 1970s and '80s, the government built the secret complex, and with Israeli help, produced a small number of nuclear weapons. The complex remained intact after South Africa voluntarily gave up its weapons program in 1991. It housed half a ton of highly enriched uranium at the time of the break-in.

The raiders, apparently assisted by employees at the complex, breached an electrified security fence, advanced past security cameras, and burst into the complex control room without drawing any response from security guards. The four gunmen quickly overpowered two people in the control room, shooting one in the chest. Meanwhile, two other armed men cut through the fence and opened fire on a guard. By the time security units reached the control room, the men had fled with several cell phones, but no enriched uranium.

South African authorities called the attack a botched burglary attempt unconnected to the stockpile of fissile material. Four years later, the motivations of the gunmen remain publicly unknown. Whatever the aim of the attackers, the incident showed that even an ostensibly well-secured nuclear installation could be successfully invaded.

One of the primary nuclear threats today comes from stateless terror groups like al-Qaeda and their offspring. They would not hesitate to use a nuclear weapon. Since the 1970s, at least three terrorist groups have tried to obtain or produce nuclear weapons. The Baader-Meinhof Gang, the left-wing German group that flourished in the 1970s, attempted unsuccessfully to steal nuclear weapons from an American military base in Western Europe. In the 1990s, Aum Shinrikyo, the Japanese organization that staged a chemical weapon attack on the Tokyo subway system in 1995, tried to buy nuclear weapons from Russia. And al-Qaeda has made no secret of its desire to acquire nuclear arms.

In 1998, Osama bin Laden declared it was a "religious duty" of al-Qaeda members to get nuclear weapons. Crude drawings of nuclear weapons were found in al-Qaeda quarters in Afghanistan after the American military intervention there in late 2001, and there is evidence that bin Laden, the al-Qaeda leader at the time, met with two Pakistani nuclear scientists before the September 11 attacks. American intelligence agencies have repeatedly warned that al-Qaeda is seeking to acquire nuclear weapons and would not hesitate to use them. That wasn't likely to change after bin Laden's death in 2011.

Rolf Mowatt-Larssen, who tracked nuclear proliferation for the CIA and Energy Department for nearly three decades, found that bin Laden and his followers were determined to get and use a nuclear weapon. "Al Qaeda's patient, decade-long effort to steal or construct an improvised nuclear device flows from their perception of the benefits of producing the image of a mushroom cloud rising over a U.S. city, just as the 9/11 attacks have altered the course of history," Mowatt-Larssen said in 2010. "This lofty aim helps explain why al Qaeda has consistently sought a bomb capable of producing a nuclear yield, as opposed to settling for the more expedient and realistic course of devising a 'dirty bomb,' or a radiological dispersal device."

The Mowatt-Larssen paper rebuts skeptics who suggest that al-Qaeda's assertions about using nuclear weapons are merely rhetorical. His chronology of al-Qaeda activities shows that the group has repeatedly tried to acquire a weapon or the materials to make one. Obtaining nuclear materials is not an implausible prospect. "Our number one concern is the acquisition of fissile material by a terror group," a senior American intelligence official said.

Iran, with its extensive terror connections, could become a source. It seems determined to develop its own nuclear weapons and has erected a series of nuclear installations capable of producing highly enriched uranium and plutonium. Iranian progress was temporarily slowed in recent years by an Israeli-American covert operation that employed a cleverly designed computer worm to disable Iranian centrifuges used to produce enriched uranium.

Before the worm was planted, American and Israeli intelligence officials said they thought Iran was just a year or two away from making a bomb. To do so, the Iranians would need to raise the enrichment level of the uranium they have already produced at their enrichment facility in Natanz. Unless they have a clandestine enrichment facility, which the officials could not rule out, on-site inspectors from the International Atomic Energy Agency (IAEA) would likely detect the additional steps required to generate bomb-grade fuel. Or Iran could first expel the inspectors, signaling it was moving to make nuclear weapons. By mid-2011, the Iranian nuclear program seemed to be recovering from the American-Israeli cyberattack and the clock started running again toward production of a bomb within a few years.

"If they are allowed to develop nuclear weapons, I think it will be very destabilizing in the whole region and, I think, probably spark a nuclear arms race in the region," Robert Gates said while serving as secretary of defense. He made the comment before the 2011 uprisings in the Arab world.

Gates said he did not favor a military strike against Iran, fearing it might unify Iranians against the United States while only temporarily disrupting their program. "My view all along has been that while we need to keep all of our options on the table, absent a decision by the Iranian government not to pursue nuclear weapons, virtually all tactics are delaying tactics," he said. Israel might be more inclined to use military force, but in a series of interviews in 2009, current and former Israeli officials were divided about whether Israel should—and could—take out the Iranian nuclear program with air strikes.

Pakistan is another unsettling nuclear trouble spot, much on the minds of Shultz, Kissinger, Perry, Nunn, and Drell. "Pakistan is the most dangerous country in the world," Perry told a London audience in 2011. It has all the elements needed for a terrorist nuclear weapons conspiracy. There is a large, active weapons program, including uranium enrichment plants. Osama bin Laden lived for years in a secure compound on the outskirts of Abbottabad, just steps away from the Pakistani military academy, before American commandos killed him there on May 1, 2011. It was hard to believe the government, at least some elements of it, was unaware of his presence.

Bin Laden was not the only terrorist to seek shelter in Pakistan. The country is home to several determined terror groups, and at least one international terror plot—the 2005 London Underground and bus bombings—was partly hatched there. Homegrown Taliban insurgents operate in parts of Pakistan, and Pakistan's intelligence service, the Inter-Services Intelligence directorate (ISI), has been allied with the Taliban in Afghanistan to ensure continued Pakistani influence there when American forces pull out. On top of all this, Pakistan's central government is weak and political chaos always seems close at hand.

Using Pakistan as a base to export nuclear materials is not a theoretical idea. A. Q. Khan, the Pakistani scientist, showed it was possible to operate a lucrative international black market in nuclear weapons technology for years before intelligence and law enforcement agencies caught up with him. He built Pakistan's weapons program by stealing uranium-enrichment technology from Europe and clandestinely acquiring bomb-making equipment from European and North American suppliers. He then sold bomb blueprints, expertise, and equipment to North Korea, Iran, and Libya. It is not clear he was put entirely out of business even after he was placed under house arrest in Islamabad in 2004 and his network was supposedly shut down.

American officials seem confident that Pakistan's nuclear weapons are well protected by the army, which has received American aid and technology to help secure its warheads. "Our view is as long as the army remains intact, the weapons will remain secure," Robert Gates said. "If the army should collapse, then obviously you've got a very different situation."

There is less confidence about Pakistan's nuclear materials, whether under military or civilian control. Gates said he was concerned because of the "size of the nuclear enterprise in Pakistan, and the worry about the technology or even materials falling into nongovernmental hands." He added that he was "less worried, probably, about a weapon per se than I am nuclear material and technology. I mean, they clearly played a role in the North Korean program."

North Korea, which built its weapons program with Khan's help, is another potential source of fissile material. While not located in a hotbed of Islamic extremism, North Korea is a madcap dictatorship with nuclear weapons and a desperate need for money to fund its large army and military industries. That makes for a dangerous proclivity to export nuclear technology and materials. "Whether it's drugs or arms, they sell anything they can get hard currency for," Gates said.

Perry agreed. "I doubt that they would be selling a bomb," he said, "but they might very well be selling fissile material. And that is something to worry about. I don't think they're going to be putting a bomb on an ICBM and firing it at the United States. . . . I'm concerned about one of their bombs ending up in the United States by freighter or a truck, not by a missile."

North Korea's cash-and-carry approach was evident not long ago in the clandestine construction of a North Korean–designed nuclear reactor in Syria. An Israeli air strike on September 6, 2007, demolished the reactor, but construction of the large complex had advanced for years in the Euphrates Valley before American and Israeli intelligence agencies spotted it and determined it was a nuclear project.

An American intelligence official who briefed reporters on the site eight months after the Israeli attack said the CIA suspected as early as 2003 that North Korea and Syria were collaborating on some kind of nuclear project, but the agency had no idea what they were doing. "We had no details on the nature or location of the cooperative projects," the official said. "We assessed the cooperation involved work at sites probably within Syria. But again, we didn't know exactly where. So we had this body of evidence, almost like a cloud of, boy, there's something going on here but we can't get a whole lot of precision on it."

Construction at the Al Kibar site began in 2001 but went undetected by American spy satellites for several years. That was probably due to a shortage of wide-area imagery satellites that scan broad swaths of the earth's surface and the high demand for satellite intelligence about Afghanistan and Iraq. When the Syrian site was spotted, the construction did not seem to include a cooling tower, power lines, security installations, and other facilities typical of a nuclear reactor. The building was disguised to look more like a Byzantine fortress, similar to several nearby fortresses that are open to tourists.

It was not until the spring of 2007 that the CIA and Israeli intelligence agencies definitively identified the project as a nuclear reactor, based on photographs taken at the site and shared by Israel. Photographs of the exterior and interior of the building convincingly showed that it housed a reactor. The design closely resembled a reactor in Yongbyon, North Korea.

Proliferation specialists said intelligence analysts from a variety of government agencies who were working the case were partly hampered by their own preconceptions. The analysts, for instance, figured Syria could not believe it could construct a North Korean reactor in the open without being detected, so why would it try? And since it was easier to make a bomb with highly enriched uranium rather than plutonium, it made no sense for Syria to make its own plutonium. These "barriers to analysis," as one official put it, led the CIA to presume that the Syrians were building a water treatment plant or some other benign industrial project.

If the United States, with all its powerful intelligence-collection systems, could not spot a nuclear reactor under construction in the open Syrian desert for several years, the odds are not encouraging that it can detect small amounts of highly enriched uranium smuggled across international borders—just the kind of operation terrorists might use to acquire enough fissile material to make a weapon or dirty bomb.

Georgia, the small, ancient nation wedged into the Caucasus Mountains, is ground zero for nuclear smuggling. Its location between Russia and Turkey, its mountainous terrain and criminal underworld make it a tempting pathway for anyone trying to smuggle highly enriched uranium from Russia, where it is plentiful, to the Middle East and South Asia, where terror groups are concentrated. To make matters worse, two separatist enclaves in

Georgia—South Ossetia and Abkhazia—are aligned with Russia and operate outside the control of the Georgian central government in Tbilisi. Since Soviet rule in Georgia ended in 1991, the country, with a population of 4.6 million, has been rocked by ethnic violence and political turmoil. Russian and Georgian military forces clashed in 2008 in a tug-of-war over South Ossetia. Mikheil Saakashvili, the American-educated president of Georgia since 2004, has been an erratic leader who has introduced elements of democracy and the rule of law. But Georgia, still plagued by corruption and lawlessness, remains inviting terrain for smugglers.

There have been several smuggling cases in Georgia in recent years involving highly enriched uranium. The amounts were small—less than 120 grams in each case—and an elite Georgian police team intercepted the shipments before they could be delivered to buyers, most likely in neighboring Turkey. But the cases are troubling because the enrichment level was 89.5 percent, well above the grade needed to make a weapon. In several instances, smugglers boasted in wiretapped calls that they had access to much larger amounts. In one case, the prospective buyer operated a trucking company in Turkey that delivered goods to Iran. The Georgians also seized small amounts of cesium-137, a highly radioactive isotope that would be ideal for use in a dirty bomb.

Archil Pavlenishvili, a 1996 graduate of the Georgian Technical University in Tbilisi, heads the Interior Ministry's nuclear enforcement unit. Pavlenishvili, thirty-six years old, is well regarded by American intelligence officials, who described his team as very competent and determined.

In 2006, Pavlenishvili and his team unraveled a clumsy but potentially serious smuggling scheme. One of the smugglers, Oleg Khintsagov, was carrying one hundred grams of highly enriched uranium in two plastic bags in his leather jacket. He claimed he could get two or three kilograms if a buyer was interested. The asking price: ten thousand dollars per gram. After he was arrested—Khintsagov remains in a Georgian prison today—he told investigators that the uranium came from Novosibirsk, a Siberian industrial and scientific center that includes a plant that produces highly enriched uranium. American forensic examinations of Khintsagov's purloined uranium indicated it almost certainly originated in Russia. Khintsagov later changed his story and denied that he knew the source of the uranium.

Pavlenishvili acknowledged that he lacks hard evidence about both the origin and destination of the nuclear materials he has intercepted in Georgia. That's unsettling. Russia seems the most likely source, but after initially cooperating with American and Georgian authorities, Russian law enforcement and intelligence agencies stopped providing assistance in 2006 as Georgian-Russian relations deteriorated. "In 2003, 2004, and 2005 there was cooperation. Suddenly every contact with Russia was terminated," Pavlenishvili said.

Turkish law enforcement and intelligence agencies can also be standoffish with Georgian authorities. The Turks looked into the trucking company that seemed the likely buyer of the enriched uranium in one case and reported they could find nothing suspicious about the firm. "Turkey is the main black market for radioactive materials," Pavlenishvili said.

The truth is, the Russians don't know precisely how much highly enriched uranium the Soviet Union produced during the Cold War, and how much might have slipped out of government control during the turbulent years after the collapse of the USSR. American intelligence officials who track nuclear materials call missing uranium "Material Unaccounted For," or MUF. One of the officials said, "Even in the United States, we don't know where every gram of fissile material is, or just how much we made."

In 2004, the CIA said of Soviet fissile material, "We assess that undetected smuggling has occurred and we are concerned about the total amount of material that could have been diverted or stolen." Porter Goss, the CIA director, told Congress a year later, "There is sufficient material unaccounted for so that it would be possible for those with knowhow to construct a nuclear weapon." Given the lack of precise information, it is impossible to know if there is sufficient fissile material on the black market to make a bomb. There is unquestionably some of the stuff in circulation, as the recent cases in Georgia show.

To cut off smuggling through Georgia, the United States has spent $37.5 million since 2005 to help Georgia install radiation detection devices and related equipment at most of its border crossings with neighboring nations and equip Georgian police with mobile detection vans and backpacks. One of the sites is the main border checkpoint at Sadakhlo, a rural village on the mountainous Georgian-Armenian frontier. The modern checkpoint complex, built by the U.S. Army Corps of Engineers, opened in 2007, replacing an outmoded post. All vehicles and pedestrians entering Georgia must pass through radiation detectors. Trains that run between the two nations also go through detectors as the tracks, on a riverbank, pass a few yards from the checkpoint. Yet for all the investment, and the conscientious effort of Georgian police forces to make good use of the gear, two Armenians successfully slipped seventeen grams of highly enriched uranium by the checkpoint on March 10, 2010, by storing it in a small lead-coated cigarette box they stowed aboard a passenger train. The men crossed the border in a taxi, while the container made its way to Tbilisi, the Georgian capital, concealed on the exterior ledge of one of the railcars. Fortunately, their scheme was disrupted by Pavlenishvili and his team after the men picked up the hidden cargo at the Tbilisi train station.

More troublingly, the most tempting Georgian smuggling routes remain largely unmonitored. They go from Russia through South Ossetia and Abkhazia, which straddles the Black Sea coast. Smugglers seeking to move fissile materials from Russia to the Middle East or South Asia could circumvent the Georgian radiation detection systems by carrying the material from southern Russia to the Abkhazian seaport of Sukhumi and from there by ship to Turkey.

Pavlenishvili is not confident he can permanently prevent the smuggling of fissile materials through Georgia. "Well, we think that right now we are controlling the situation more or less successfully," he said. "But of course on the other hand there is no hundred percent guarantee that nothing can happen. A good deal of our success is based on good intelligence, and this intelligence is successful just because this community is quite closed, and quite limited in number. But if there will be some new players on the field, which will deal separately, I don't know. We will need much more time to find them out."

Americans should not take comfort in thinking that terrorists could never get a nuclear bomb into the United States. A crude uranium weapon would be bulky—too big for a car, too hard to disguise as air cargo. But not too cumbersome to fit into a shipping container to be transported by sea, or to carry in a truck, if the vehicle could be brought across the border without attracting suspicion and inspection.

The threat bears an eerie resemblance to the scenario Albert Einstein described to Franklin Roosevelt in an August 2, 1939, letter informing the president about recent breakthroughs in nuclear physics that pointed to the possibility of creating an atom bomb. "A single bomb of this type, carried by boat and exploded in a port, might very well destroy the whole port together with some of the surrounding territory," Einstein said.

Today, the United States is working with foreign governments to prevent shipping containers with a nuclear weapon or the materials to make one from slipping through customs checkpoints at major international ports like Antwerp. Washington has helped to equip Antwerp with radiation detectors, gigantic X-ray machines, and other devices designed to screen the thousands of trucks that enter the busy port daily from distant sites in Europe, Asia, and the Middle East. The effort is expensive and requires close collaboration between the National Nuclear Security Administration, which manages the program, and foreign government agencies. Known as the Second Line of Defense Megaports Initiative, the $600 million program is designed to break up a terror plot before terrorists can get a bomb or bomb-making materials into the United States. Catching a bomb or nuclear materials before they reach American soil is essential since a bomb placed aboard a cargo ship could be detonated as the ship docked at an American port, before cargo containers were checked as they entered the United States.

The Antwerp operation is one small piece of a very large puzzle. Over 90 percent of global commerce moves by ship. Roughly speaking, 500 million twenty-foot-equivalent units—the technical term for shipping containers—move across the world's oceans annually, many millions of them entering America's main ports, including Los Angeles, Oakland, Seattle, New Orleans, Baltimore, and Newark. The United States hopes to equip one hundred seaports around the world with radiation detection devices by 2016, giving customs officials a look at about 80 percent of U.S.-bound container traffic.

The bright yellow radiation portal monitors installed at all entrances to the Port of Antwerp, located along the industrial banks of the Schelde River, can pick up small levels of gamma and neutron radiation, signaling the possible presence of bomb-making materials or a weapon. Every truck hauling a shipping container is routed through a pair of detectors located on each side of all the entrance roadways. Oversize rumble strips force drivers to slow to five miles per hour as they pass by the monitors. An average of one hundred containers a day set off radiation alarms, but none has involved nuclear weapons materials since the security system was installed in 2007. Suspect containers are brought to a modern customs complex, where they are put through an X-ray tunnel that allows the contents of the container to be closely examined without opening the container.

Port officials like Tanja Peeters, a customs supervisor, and Pascal Fias, a physicist, work with inspectors to determine if the cargo is a natural, radiation-emitting material like ceramics, hair dyes, black tea, and bananas, or something that requires closer scrutiny. A shipment of canned blueberries from the Chernobyl area in Ukraine, the site of the 1986 nuclear reactor explosion, lit up the Antwerp alarm system a few years ago. The berries turned out to fall within American radiation limits and were shipped on to the United States. One day in 2010, a truck hauling a container set off the alarm before the container itself passed through the portal monitor. Fias replayed a video of the truck as it moved past the monitor and looked at the radiation level on a computer screen as it spiked as the truck cab went by. "The driver is setting off the alarm," Fias said. "He is probably being treated with radioactive iodine for a thyroid condition." That proved to be the case, confirmed by medical papers the driver produced when questioned by customs agents.

The elaborate security systems in Antwerp and other ports may discourage terrorists from shipping bomb-making materials by sea, but the systems are far from infallible. There are numerous false alarms. Depositing nuclear materials in a lead-lined box prevents radiation leakage and would defeat the portal monitors. A diligent customs officer might note inconsistencies between the weight of the container and the materials it supposedly contains, which are declared on the cargo manifest, but there's no guarantee a lead-lined box would be spotted. Technologically advanced detection systems are being developed to overcome the problem, but it will be some years before they are ready.

Bypassing conventional shipping methods may be the simplest way to get a nuclear weapon to a target city. South American drug

cartels have developed an ingenious, semisubmersible vessel designed to elude U.S. Navy and Coast Guard surveillance. The
low-slung vessels, which look a bit like the USS *Monitor*, the Civil
War–era ironclad warship, can slip through the sea, barely visible
above the surface. The Coast Guard has seized a number of these
self-propelled craft carrying tons of cocaine. They were built to
travel from South America to the California coast without refuel-
ing. It is not hard to imagine one creeping undetected by night
into New York or Los Angeles harbor with a nuclear weapon nestled inside.

The variety of unorthodox nuclear threats was stunningly un-
derlined a few years ago when the U.S. Air Force lost track of six
nuclear warheads for thirty-six hours. During that time, the warheads, attached to cruise missiles, were flown across the country
from Minot Air Force Base in North Dakota to Barksdale Air
Force Base in Louisiana. Neither the munitions crew that loaded
the weapons on a B-52 bomber in North Dakota on August 29,
2007, nor the crew that unloaded them in Louisiana a few hours
later had any idea they were handling nuclear weapons.

A year earlier, the Air Force mistakenly sent Taiwan four electrical fuses for Minuteman missile nuclear warheads. After Pentagon investigations of the two incidents, defense secretary Gates
fired Michael Wynne, the Air Force secretary, and T. Michael
Moseley, the chief of staff. Gates said at the time, "I believe these
actions are required because, first, the focus of Air Force leadership has drifted with respect to perhaps its most sensitive mission.
Second, the performance standards in that sensitive area were allowed to degrade."

Gates said, "This had all happened so gradually over a fifteen or
so year period that I'm not sure the leadership of the Air Force really
was aware of how things had eroded. And frankly, the reason that
I took the dramatic action was not because the problem existed,

but it was that after the problem was discovered, they didn't take it seriously enough."

He went on: "The irony is that Congress and the American people were a hell of a lot more upset than the leadership of the Air Force about people flying nuclear weapons around the country and sending things to Taiwan and so on."

He agreed with the findings of a task force led by James Schlesinger, the former defense secretary: the government, starting at the highest levels, had neglected nuclear weapons policy and practices since the end of the Cold War.

"I would say the attention of the national leadership to the importance of the nuclear force as a deterrent eroded as well," Gates said. "I mean, the whole nuclear enterprise for the United States has been neglected."

Since the dismissal of Wynne and Moseley, the Air Force has initiated a number of changes, including the consolidation of all its strategic nuclear forces in a newly created unit, the Air Force Global Strike Command. Gates seemed satisfied with the reforms.

Still, if the U.S. Air Force could not keep track of its arsenal, imagine what might someday happen with nuclear weapons and fissile materials in Pakistan, North Korea, and Iran.

That is why George Shultz and his colleagues spend a lot of time pressing the United States and other nations to take short- and medium-term steps to keep nuclear materials from slipping into the hands of terrorists.

The material is frighteningly abundant and difficult to secure, as the United States recently found in Poland.

CHAPTER FOUR

This is the largest amount of spent highly enriched uranium
fuel we have ever removed, or ever will.
—ANDREW BIENIAWSKI

For years, Poland's Institute of Atomic Energy was the making of an American nuclear nightmare. Security at the decaying compound outside Warsaw was so lax that officials there might as well have posted a sign on the front gate directing a raiding party to the stockpile of highly enriched uranium. Building 19A, a compact, white brick structure not far from the front gate, contained enough enriched uranium to make eighteen nuclear weapons. The building's primitive security system consisted of a simple lock on an ordinary door and a flimsy wire-mesh fence. There was no alarm system, no electronic sensors, no security cameras. The gate to the institute compound in Otwock-Swierk, at the end of a country lane twenty miles southeast of the Polish capital, was haphazardly guarded.

It was exactly the kind of vulnerable stash that makes George Shultz, Henry Kissinger, Bill Perry, Sam Nunn, and Sid Drell fear that terrorists could turn up one day in London or New York with a homemade nuclear weapon hidden in the back of a van or in a shipping container.

The Polish Institute routinely transferred loads of highly enriched uranium to Building 19A from two research reactors at the compound. Instead of producing electricity, research reactors are used for scientific experiments or the production, among other things, of radioactive materials used in nuclear medicine. The spent or irradiated fuel at the Polish reactors—uranium that had exhausted its capacity to power the reactors—was stored in the same containers in which it was originally used, tubes known as fuel rods. The tubes were nestled in a tank of ultrapure water at the base of Building 19A. The water acted both as a barrier to nuclear reactions firing up between the tubes and as a radiation shield protecting anyone who came near or entered the building. As the years passed, the Poles deposited more than a thousand pounds of highly enriched uranium in Building 19A, known as the Spent Fuel Storage Building.

The only meaningful security came from "fission products" mixed with the uranium itself, some of which were highly radioactive and potentially lethal to anyone who handled them without protective equipment. As nuclear engineers like to say, they were "self-protecting," meaning only a fool would risk hijacking them. But over time, the radiation threat ebbed as short-lived but highly radioactive elements in the fission products decayed. Eventually, a good deal of the stored uranium became cool enough to be moved by someone intent on stealing it. Extracting the fissile isotope uranium-235, the critical ingredient for a bomb, would require chemical processing to separate the isotope from other materials in the fuel rods. A few chemical engineers with widely available laboratory equipment and supplies could do the work in a garage.

Even more tempting to terrorists, smaller amounts of fresh highly enriched uranium, which can be safely handled without protective gear, were stored in loosely secured vaults at the two reactors. The fresh material was awaiting use in the reactors and had not yet accumulated highly radioactive fission products. It was anything but "self-protecting." Someone can safely pick up a brick of fresh highly enriched uranium with bare hands without any health risk.

The hardest part of nuclear bomb making is producing enriched uranium. Until now, it has required industrial-scale operations beyond the resources of a terror group. That may change with the advent of laser enrichment technology. With only sixty pounds of highly enriched uranium in hand, a small team of engineers and technicians could construct a simple weapon. That amount could be smuggled across borders in several containers about the size of half-gallon milk jugs. The triggering mechanism that unleashes the nuclear energy is relatively elementary—one block of enriched uranium slamming into another block at high velocity. Such a device requires exact engineering, but the work is well within the capability of a technically savvy group. Detailed design information for a crude uranium bomb, known as a gun-assembly weapon, has been available online for years. Robert Oppenheimer and his colleagues in the Manhattan Project, the American wartime effort to develop nuclear weapons, were so confident the design would work that they didn't bother to test their gun-type weapon before it was dropped over Hiroshima on August 6, 1945.

A 1977 U.S. government study, completed well before bomb-making information appeared on the Internet, said: "A small group of people, none of whom have ever had access to the classified literature, could possibly design and build a crude nuclear explosive device. . . . Only modest machine-shop facilities that could be contracted for without arousing suspicion would be required."

The feeble security that long prevailed at the Polish Institute is disturbingly typical of research reactors around the world. Roughly 160 of some 200 research reactors built in more than forty nations during the Cold War ran on bomb-grade fuel, or close to it. Dozens still do.

Most of the research reactors outside the United States are relics from an age when the United States and Soviet Union rewarded allies by giving them reactors and the fuel to run them, gifts that promised to unlock the peaceful benefits of the atom in medical and scientific research. President Dwight Eisenhower called his program "Atoms for Peace." Over the decades, the United States shipped 3,000 pounds of highly enriched uranium overseas. The Soviet Union dispersed 5,200 pounds. Another ton of the material that did not originate in Russia or the United States is stored at sites around the world. Altogether, enough to make more than 170 bombs.

The reactors remain a source of pride and nuclear know-how for many nations, so many are unwilling to give them up. The Maria reactor in Poland—named after Marie Curie, the Polish nuclear pioneer—still produces medically useful radioactive isotopes and is likely to serve as a training center for a new generation of Polish nuclear engineers needed to manage the nuclear power plants the government hopes to build. Similar stories abound with research reactors in other nations like Pakistan, Kazakhstan, Uzbekistan, Jamaica, Mexico, South Africa, Belarus, Ghana, Vietnam, and Russia. Yet most reactor operators long neglected security considerations, never dreaming someone might try to steal the uranium fuel.

Now, more than a half century after Eisenhower kicked off Atoms for Peace, the United States and Russia are frantically trying to spirit home the enriched uranium they sent abroad. The effort is one of the practical steps that George Shultz and his colleagues have urged Washington and Moscow to take to reduce nuclear threats. The U.S. Energy Department set a goal of removing 10,000 pounds by 2016. By mid-2011, it had carted away or secured 6,800 pounds and cleaned out reactors in some twenty countries.

It isn't easy or inexpensive to get the material secured, safely shipped, and ultimately made harmless by blending it down— essentially the reverse of the enrichment process—to a point that it is no longer bomb-grade quality. Indeed, it is a multimillion-dollar job requiring a high degree of technical expertise, elaborate security precautions, and the cooperation of dozens of government agencies. President Obama put the American program, known as the Global Threat Reduction Initiative, on a fast track, setting a 2013 deadline to get the most vulnerable bomb-grade uranium safely secured.

Obama's threat reduction initiative is the latest in a long series of American efforts to secure fissile materials that date back to the disintegration of the Soviet Union in 1991. Sam Nunn proposed the first steps that year, including American-financed initiatives to upgrade security at former Soviet nuclear weapons complexes. The programs are not perfect. In a 2010 report, the Government Accountability Office, which examines the efficacy of federal programs for Congress, found the fissile material cleanup strategy suffered from a lack of coordination between the Defense Department, the Energy Department, and the State Department. As a result, the GAO said, the overall effort was hobbled by poor planning, unclear cost estimates, imprecision about the identity of vulnerable material sites and facilities, and inadequate foreign cooperation.

Despite the problems, the programs have done a great deal to reduce nuclear dangers since the end of the Cold War. The work in Poland—which has cost American taxpayers $60 million—is a tangible example of the extraordinary measures required to prevent terrorists from going nuclear. The American-led effort in Poland, initiated at a more leisurely pace in the mid-1990s, is an unusual amalgam of diplomacy, technology, and bribery. Not illicit bribery, but the abundant use of American money to persuade foreign governments that it's in their interest to get rid of their highly enriched uranium. Even to the point where Washington pays much of the bill for repatriating Russian-origin enriched uranium to Russia. To keep the research reactors going in places like Poland, Washington is prepared to supply the technology to convert them to run on a less potent form of lower-enriched uranium that is unsuitable for weapons.

The last of the spent fuel at the Polish Institute was removed in September 2010. It was an intricately choreographed operation akin to a complex military maneuver, requiring the precise coordination of hundreds of preparatory and operational steps involving Americans, Russians, and Poles. Originally planned to be a four-year operation, it was condensed into eight months to meet Obama's aggressive deadline. The National Nuclear Security Administration (NNSA), part of the Energy Department, directs the work. Andrew Bieniawski, an assistant deputy administrator at NNSA, was the point man for the Polish operation and the dozens of similar efforts that NNSA manages around the globe under Obama's order.

Bieniawski, an energetic manager and cheerleader, was a good fit for Poland. His father was born in the Polish seaport of Gdansk and lived in Poland until 1939, when he fled to Rhodesia after the Nazi invasion. Andrew was born in South Africa—his mother is South African—and resettled in the United States in 1978 when he was eleven. He also spent several years in Moscow managing U.S. Energy Department programs in Russia. While in Warsaw, Andrew took a few hours off one evening to get together with a Polish cousin he had never met. He brought along a thick, meticulously researched book chronicling the Bieniawski family history.

Bieniawski, a Penn State graduate, has been called the real Jack Bauer, the protean hero of the Fox television series *24*. He doesn't care for the comparison and, with his gentlemanly demeanor, boyish charm, and wire-rim glasses, hardly matches the rough-and-tumble Bauer. But the comparison is apt in one way—Bieniawski is the first line of defense against nuclear terrorism. On Russia-related matters, he relies heavily on Igor Bolshinsky, a round-faced Ukrainian, now an American citizen, who has a knack for arranging deals with the Russians, including the removal of the Polish uranium. Bolshinsky's cell phone seemed permanently attached to his ear while in Poland as he fielded calls in English, Russian, and Ukrainian. The duo have developed a productive partnership and give the Global Threat Reduction Initiative an appealing international face.

Bieniawski is the boss, Bolshinsky the negotiator and fixer. They, in turn, call on a stable of country directors to handle the nuts and bolts of the repatriation operations. Michael Tyacke, a specialist in orchestrating the work, took the lead in Poland. He calls himself a transportation technical adviser and is employed by Idaho National Laboratory. Tyacke, wiry and intense, set up shop at a Warsaw hotel and spent weeks there working on the arrangements for the fuel transfer.

Dealing with the Poles required a fair degree of diplomacy. The Americans could not barge into Poland, announce its nuclear facilities were dangerously outmoded, and expect local leaders to welcome Washington's help. Tyacke had to find a Polish counterpart to direct preparations and deal with the numerous government agencies that had to sign off on the shipments or provide logistical support. He ended up collaborating with Wlodzimierz Tomczak, a mild-mannered, English-speaking director of Poland's Radioactive Waste Management Plant. They worked with police, military and other security services, intelligence agencies, federal and regional environmental enforcement offices, customs officials, and hazardous materials specialists. Road, train, and sea lanes had to be secured. Special shipping containers were needed. A customs officer loaded down with a steamer trunk of paperwork had to accompany the enriched uranium by truck, train, and ship on its long journey from the Warsaw suburbs to the Soviet arctic port of Murmansk. From there it would be carried by train to Mayak, a nuclear complex deep inside Russia, where it would be blended down into low-enriched uranium.

The tasks at times seemed overwhelming. "This is the largest amount of spent HEU [highly enriched uranium] fuel we have ever removed, or ever will, under NNSA's programs to secure these nuclear materials," Bieniawski said. Security at Swierk had to be upgraded so the spent fuel would be secure until it could be shipped. A closed-circuit television system was put in place and electromagnetic locks were installed. Transferring the spent fuel from the Maria reactor to specially designed storage casks required rebuilding a section of the reactor building. Even the most prosaic things needed attention—an improvised snow guard was fixed above an exterior rail at Building 19A to prevent a buildup of ice from blocking the movement of fuel rods along the rail to trucks waiting outside. The reactor operators had to be assured that the reactor could be successfully converted to operate with a special blend of low-enriched uranium developed in the United States. The cost for the reactor work alone was expected to be more than $10 million, paid by Washington. The items went on and on, and all the steps had to be carefully sequenced so that the removal and transport of the fuel rods could be done without a hitch on a tight schedule.

The Russian end was equally elaborate. To ensure that the nuclear material could be safely stored on a cargo ship for the seven-day sea voyage to Murmansk, Bolshinsky contracted with ASPOL-Baltic, a Russian shipping company, to refurbish one of its ships. The vessel, built for the Soviet navy in 1990 by a Singapore shipyard, was originally designed to carry Soviet nuclear missiles. Nearly two decades later it was put in a drydock in Tallinn, Estonia, where it was equipped with several layers of radiation shielding, a sophisticated firefighting system, and other alterations. It was rechristened the *MCL Trader*. The United States picked up the $1.5 million renovation bill.

The enriched uranium was transferred back to Russia in five installments, starting in October 2009, six months after Obama's appearance in Prague. (Most of the more easily handled fresh nonirradiated highly enriched uranium at the reactor had been removed in 2006 and 2007.) The last shipment contained roughly ninety-six pounds, more than enough to make a bomb.

The Maria reactor was built with Soviet help. It opened in 1974. By 2010 it sported the latest surveillance and security gear, courtesy of Washington. Despite the upgrades, the reactor building was in disrepair, with peeling plaster and paint, roof leaks, and other signs of neglect and insufficient funding. A red and yellow radiation-monitoring machine in the lobby that checked visitors for contamination looked and sounded like a prop in a Buck Rogers movie. A thick, imposing door that separated the reactor itself from adjacent lab space and the control room creaked ominously as it was opened, leading to an inner air pocket just outside the reactor core.

Despite the antique equipment, the place was clearly a source of pride to Grzegorz Krzysztoszek, the institute director. The bearded, balding scientist, cloaked in a white smock atop a sporty blue blazer and checkered pink-and-white shirt, showed off the reactor core, the control room, and other corners of the reactor building. Maria may be Poland's small, obsolete piece of the nuclear age, but Krzysztoszek left no doubt that he and his colleagues plan to keep it going, even if they have to convert it to run on low-enriched uranium. "We are not so happy to convert our reactor," he told a group of American visitors.

The spent fuel first had to be removed and transferred to the shipping casks. It was a delicate exercise done in a "hot room," a thickly sealed chamber equipped with robotic arms and pincers remotely controlled from outside. The casks, in turn, were placed in seven bright blue shipping containers that were locked down on flatbed trucks. Each container held three casks, each cask housed four fuel rods, and each fuel rod contained about a pound of spent fuel. Diamond-shaped radiation warning labels attached to the sides of the containers listed the radioactive elements: U-238 (base uranium), U-235 (highly enriched uranium), Pu-239 (plutonium), Cs-137 (cesium).

At 4 p.m., as the sun settled low in the sky on an unusually warm fall afternoon, the convoy was readied. Police and special forces swarmed into the Swierk complex, taking up position near the exit gate where the trucks were forming a line. Fire trucks, an ambulance, and several other emergency vehicles lined up, too. Captain Gregori Trzcinski of the Polish State Police summoned the truck drivers for a final briefing. The beefy commander told visiting American and British reporters he did not expect any problems and knew of no threat to intercept the convoy. "Poland is rather a peaceful country," he said with a smile. A military helicopter swept into view, circling noisily above the waiting convoy. "I feel like we're prepared for everything, but you're just a little bit nervous," Bolshinsky said. Moments later, the trucks and their escorts bolted through the gate, roaring toward Warsaw and the train depot.

The next morning, after the three-hundred-mile train trip to Gdynia on the Baltic coast, the containers awaited transfer to the rust-red *MCL Trader* on a huge wharf, guarded by masked assault troops. A Polish technician checked each container with a sophisticated Geiger counter to be sure there was no radiation leakage. As Polish, American, and Russian officials watched, a giant crane lifted the blue containers one by one from the dock and lowered them into the cargo hold, where longshoremen locked them into place. Then thick metal plates, each weighing ten tons, were placed over the containers to create a radiation shield. When the first uranium shipment reached Gdynia in 2009, dockworkers refused to load the containers, wary of the radioactive cargo. They were reassured it was safe by Polish officials and handled subsequent shipments.

When the last plate was fixed in place, the deck, which had been folded back at the bow of the ship like a colossal accordion, was slowly unfurled until it scraped to a stop, sealing the cargo hold. Two tugboats steamed alongside the ship, gently coaxing it away from the dock and pointing it out toward the harbor and open sea. The *MCL Trader*'s engines started with a roar and the ship's foghorn bellowed as the helmsman set course for Murmansk.

Poland was the sixth country Bieniawski and Bolshinsky had tackled since Obama's Prague speech. The others were Romania, Libya, Taiwan, Turkey, and Chile. Many more awaited, including Ukraine, Serbia, Mexico, Vietnam, and Kazakhstan. Belarus joined the list of cooperating nations in late 2010, but suspended its agreement in 2011. In November 2010, Kazakhstan, with American help, completed the shipment of ten tons of highly enriched uranium and three tons of plutonium from a Caspian Sea port to a safe storage site 1,500 miles away in northeastern Kazakhstan. That was enough fissile material to make hundreds of nuclear weapons. A month later, Serbia, also working with the United States, shipped thirteen kilograms, or twenty-eight pounds, of highly enriched uranium to Russia.

As the *MCL Trader* disappeared from sight in the Gdynia shipping channel, Bieniawski, Bolshinsky, Tyacke, and their Polish and Russian partners gathered under a makeshift tent on the wharf for a buffet lunch and a round of toasts.

Bieniawski raised a glass of vodka to salute the completion of the job. "We have developed a special saying," he declared. *"Nevozmozhno—mozhno,"* he said in Russian. "The impossible is possible."

In Poland, yes, but not so far in Pakistan, the most alluring source of bomb-making material for any terrorist group. Confidential State Department cables made public in December 2010 by WikiLeaks disclosed that Pakistan has resisted American requests to repatriate highly enriched uranium it received for a research reactor under the Atoms for Peace program. Anne Patterson, the United States ambassador to Pakistan, told colleagues in Washington in a May 2009 cable that Pakistan was ignoring a 2007 agreement with Washington to give up the fissile material. Earlier in 2009 she wrote that "our major concern is not having an Islamic militant steal an entire weapon but rather the chance someone working in GOP [government of Pakistan] facilities could gradually smuggle enough material out to eventually make a weapon."

Patterson's fears were warranted, given Pakistan's open support of Taliban forces in Afghanistan and the government's indifferent efforts to locate and capture al-Qaeda leaders hiding in the mountains of Waziristan in northwestern Pakistan. It is not alarmist to imagine that a small group of Pakistanis with access to government stocks of fissile material might provide terrorists with enough highly enriched uranium to make several weapons.

PART II

Pathways to Power

CHAPTER FIVE

By the time we got to San Diego, the war was over.
—GEORGE SHULTZ

Twice a year, on the first Saturday in April and October, the birthplace of the nuclear weapons age is opened to the public. It is a solitary spot, unmarked on most tourist maps.

As Interstate 25 threads south of Albuquerque, New Mexico, it follows the Rio Grande through large swaths of uninhabited territory in the Rio Grande rift zone, a desolate landscape of wind-whipped valleys and high mountain peaks. As the river descends slowly toward Las Cruces, I-25 bisects a string of dusty communities, including Los Lunas, Belen, and Socorro. At San Antonio, a bare-bones settlement that advertises itself as the birthplace of Conrad Hilton, the hotel magnate, U.S. Route 380 cuts off to the east, toward Roswell, a mecca for UFO fanatics. Roughly twelve miles along Route 380, a scenic marker appears on the south side of the road, an apparition in the wilderness, anchored in the arid ground by thick wooden posts.

The marker reads: "TRINITY SITE. The nuclear age began with the detonation of world's first atomic bomb at the Trinity Site on July 16, 1945. The site may have been named Trinity by Robert Oppenheimer, director of the Los Alamos Nuclear Physics Laboratory, who said at the blast, 'Now, I am become Death, the destroyer of worlds,' quoting from the Bhagavad Gita. The detonation of the bomb marked the culmination of the Manhattan Project."

A few yards ahead, across a cattle guard, Route 525, a narrow state road, heads south into the Tularosa Basin, a remote area larger than Connecticut. It is the site of the White Sands Missile Range, a 3,200-square-mile military complex that is the largest piece of Pentagon real estate in the United States. At the time of the Manhattan Project, it was called the Alamogordo Bombing Range. There, in the nearly mile-high parched flatlands known as the Jornada del Muerto, or Dead Man's Trail, Oppenheimer and his team placed their virgin bomb atop a hundred-foot-high steel tower in the furnacelike heat of the summer of 1945.

At precisely 5:29:45 a.m. mountain time on July 16, the detonators fired, commencing an implosion of the spherical device that compressed the plutonium core, starting a chain reaction. In a few millionths of a second, it accelerated into a mighty burst of energy similar to the forces produced by the sun.

I. I. Rabi, one of the physicists working on the Manhattan Project, witnessed the birth of the nuclear age from a base camp not far from ground zero. "Suddenly, there was an enormous flash of light, the brightest light I have ever seen or that I think anyone has ever seen. It blasted; it pounced; it bored its way right through you. It was a vision which was seen with more than the eye. It was seen to last forever. You wish it would stop; altogether it lasted about two seconds. Finally, it was over, diminishing, and we looked toward the place where the bomb had been; there was an enormous ball of fire which grew and grew and it rolled as it grew; it went up into the air, in yellow flashes and into scarlet and green. It looked menacing. It seemed to come toward one.

"A new thing had just been born; a new control; a new understanding of man, which man had acquired over nature."

Trinity Site today is a curious blend of solemnity and gaiety. A black lava obelisk marks the spot, a desolate patch of dirt and scrub grassland flanked by distant mountains. From afar, it looks like any other nondescript corner of the Southwest—at once scenic and forbidding, the sort of wide-open space where only the hardiest settlers would try to scratch a living out of an unforgiving land. At closer range, the uniqueness of the place becomes apparent. Large black-and-white photographs of the test blast and mushroom cloud it produced hang along a chain-link fence that circles ground zero. At a cluster of small shacks by the entrance, books about the Manhattan Project are for sale, along with key chains featuring miniature models of the bombs dropped on Hiroshima and Nagasaki. On one of the visiting days not long ago, tourists gathered next to a large white bomb model resting on a flatbed truck at the heart of the site. It is the casing for the type of bomb dropped on Nagasaki on August 9, 1945. That plutonium device, similar to the one tested at Trinity Site a few weeks earlier, was called "Fat Man" because of its rounded shape. (The more elongated uranium bomb dropped on Hiroshima a few days earlier was known as "Little Boy.")

Hundreds of visitors, some who had come from as far away as Florida and Massachusetts, wandered around the site, reflecting quietly about the history that had been made there. For others, it just seemed another tourist site, an exotic destination in the high desert where they could get a snapshot of their children grinning beside an atomic bomb model before heading to the Grand Canyon, Las Vegas, and Disneyland.

The elemental forces unleashed at Trinity Site a half century ago shadowed the lives of George Shultz, Henry Kissinger, Bill Perry, Sam Nunn, and Sid Drell. With the exception of Nunn, who was six years old, they were just stepping out into the world when they learned that an atomic bomb had vaporized most of Hiroshima on August 6, 1945.

Shultz was a Marine captain aboard a troopship in the Pacific, heading back to San Diego, where he and his fellow Marines

expected to be mustered for an invasion of the main Japanese islands. "We're hardly out of port when we get word that something
called an atomic bomb had been dropped," he recalled. "Nobody
had a clue of what it was. But we thought, well, if it's been announced it must be something of importance. And the ship lum-
bers on. And then we hear another one was dropped, and by the
time we got to San Diego, the war was over.

"We all knew we were going back to the States to be re-formed
into the outfits that were going to go and assault the Japanese islands. And all of us had been involved in at least one landing, and
so we can imagine what landing on the Japanese islands was going
to be like, and the war's suddenly over. So you have to say, whatever the atomic bomb is, it probably has something to do with the
fact that we're not assaulting those islands."

Bill Perry, an engineering student at Carnegie Tech, was riding
the streetcar home to his fraternity house in Pittsburgh after a
differential equations class when he heard that a new weapon, an
atomic bomb, had been dropped on Hiroshima. He knew it meant
the war would soon end. "The main feeling was one of relief," he
said.

He was fascinated by the new bomb. "I was taking an engineering course among engineers, and we were all very much curious
as to what the hell the new technology was all about. And so the
chemists and the physicists were trying to figure out and explain to
us what this was all about. And of course the next day in class the
chemistry professors were trying to explain what it was all about.
Not that they were in the program, but they knew enough about
the nuclear discoveries of the previous ten years that they could
sort of piece together what had happened."

As he learned more about the explosive power of the bomb, he
figured "it would make war inconceivable" and that "the old calculus of using wars to solve political problems wouldn't work anymore." Too many civilian lives would be lost, too much property

destroyed, Perry thought. He was right that the destructive power of nuclear weapons would inhibit their use. He was wrong that the development of nuclear weapons would banish war.

Sid Drell was a Princeton undergraduate. He learned about Hiroshima while taking a study break in Fine Hall, the campus math and physics building. Solomon Lefschetz, the head of the math department, came barreling into the hall bearing news of the attack. Lefschetz instantly seemed to appreciate the polarizing impact the bomb would have in political and scientific circles.

"I heard they just dropped a nuclear bomb on Hiroshima," he informed Drell. "I hope they build two of them, and they take all the people who built the first one, put them on an island, and drop the second one on them."

Henry Kissinger got news of the bomb while serving as a young U.S. Army officer in recently defeated Germany, not far from his birthplace. "I knew it was a big event, but I was a staff sergeant at the time, in counterintelligence, and this being August '45, I was, weirdly enough, in charge of counterintelligence in a German county of a population of about two hundred thousand. So I was primarily concerned with de-Nazification, the aftermath, military government. I knew it was a big event but I was not yet even a foreign policy student."

At a distance of more than sixty years, it can be difficult to appreciate how profoundly the invention of nuclear weapons changed the calculus of warfare and statecraft in 1945. Conventional wars typically involved massive land armies, years of grinding ground combat, aerial bombardment, and naval battles. A nuclear war would be waged in a matter of hours with a small fleet of long-range bombers. The spike in firepower was mind-boggling. The bomb that leveled Hiroshima packed the equivalent of fifteen thousand tons of TNT. It would have taken two thousand B-29s, the workhorse American bomber of World War II, to deliver a similar blow with conventional bombs. The immense destructive power catapulted the concept of war to a new and unfamiliar plane. Tens of millions of people would be killed in the opening minutes of a nuclear war, with millions more facing death from radiation exposure.

The potential for such devastating consequences called for uncommon restraint in the management of international affairs. Owning nuclear weapons might deter attack, or put new muscle in coercive diplomacy, but actually using the weapons was such a sobering prospect they could only be employed under the most extreme circumstances.

As Shultz, Kissinger, Perry, Nunn, and Drell came of age during the early years of the nuclear era, the United States was seized by contradictory impulses—a desire to amass the power to destroy civilizations and a reluctance ever to use that power. The tension has been a recurring theme in their careers as the men struggled to find the right balance in their work, and in the nation's defense policies.

For a few years after Hiroshima—fewer than American officials expected—the United States maintained a nuclear monopoly. America was the sole superpower as the world began the long recovery from World War II. Yet even during this period of unparalleled power, Harry Truman and his administration recognized the limits of their nuclear arsenal. As did Joseph Stalin, the Kremlin ruler. Washington's nuclear weapons did not stop Moscow from imposing its will on the nations of Eastern Europe after the war. On March 5, 1946, less than a year after the German surrender, Winston Churchill, the British wartime leader, famously said, "From Stettin in the Baltic to Trieste in the Adriatic, an iron curtain has descended across the Continent."

Nor did America's nuclear weapons prevent Stalin from blockading Berlin in June 1948, forcing the United States, Britain, and France to airlift food and supplies to the Western-controlled zones of the city, which were locked deep inside East Germany.

As disturbed as he was by these developments, Truman never seriously contemplated the use of nuclear weapons to punish the Soviet Union for its aggressive conduct.

The American nuclear monopoly ended on August 29, 1949, when the Soviet Union tested its first fission bomb. Less than a year later, on June 25, 1950, the North Korean People's Army invaded South Korea, igniting a war that soon involved American and Chinese forces. Truman considered using nuclear weapons, and dispatched a bomber wing armed with atom bombs to Guam in August 1950. Asked at a news conference several months later about possible use of nuclear arms, Truman said: "There has always been active consideration of its use. I don't want to see it used. It is a terrible weapon, and it should not be used on innocent men, women, and children who have nothing whatever to do with this military aggression. That happens when it is used."

Truman's remarks brought Clement Attlee, the British prime minister, to Washington in a hurry to appeal to Truman not to use nuclear weapons. In the end, Truman held his fire, as did his successor, Dwight Eisenhower, who was elected president in November 1952. Eisenhower brought the war to an end in 1953.

By then Washington had added hydrogen bombs to its inventory. The new thermonuclear technology, successfully tested for the first time on November 1, 1952, was based on fusing atoms rather than splitting them. The Kremlin matched the breakthrough to a new order of nuclear magnitude on August 12, 1953. These weapons boosted the explosive force to new, almost incomprehensible levels. The first American hydrogen bomb was the equivalent of 10.4 million tons of TNT, nearly seven hundred times more powerful than the bomb dropped on Hiroshima.

The nuclear arms race was under way. At first, the only way to deliver nuclear weapons to targets halfway around the world was by ponderous propeller-powered bombers, but technological advances in the 1950s gave birth to high-speed delivery systems.

Jet engines led to a new generation of fast bombers, including the American B-52s. Then came intercontinental ballistic missiles, a technology that transformed the arms race. It became clear that the Soviet Union had mastered the new technology when Moscow successfully launched Sputnik I, the first earth-orbiting satellite, in 1957. Though the rocket science required to place a satellite in orbit differed somewhat from the missile science involved in spanning continents, the launch of Sputnik I fueled fears in Washington that the Soviet Union was leaping ahead in military technology and led to a sharp increase in spending on defense research.

Soviet and American intercontinental missiles, designed with the help of German rocket scientists who had developed V-2 rockets for the Nazi regime, cut the flying time between the two nations from ten hours to thirty minutes. The miniaturization of weapons—contracting bombs from the size of a small truck to the size of a small refrigerator—made it possible to bolt a warhead to the tip of an intercontinental missile. The two nations doubled down on their nuclear arsenals by adding nuclear-powered submarines outfitted with nuclear-tipped missiles that could be launched from undersea. The American nuclear arsenal grew from a handful of nuclear weapons immediately after World War II to 25,540 warheads by 1962.

There seemed to be no limit to the inventiveness of scientists and engineers. "There grew up a community of geniuses that once you turn them on, you can't turn them off," a retired senior American general said. "Armies of extremely bright, inventive people will come up with the next hot thing and they will find a way to instill it into the mind of strategists and Congressmen."

The new technologies, in turn, drove war planners to ever more grandiose war-fighting plans. "There is a kind of mad momentum intrinsic to the development of all new nuclear weaponry," Robert McNamara, defense secretary under John Kennedy and Lyndon Johnson, once observed. "If a weapons system

works and works well, there is strong pressure from many directions to procure and deploy the weapons out of all proportion to
the prudent level required."

From a twenty-first-century perch, the work of mid-twentieth-
century strategic thinkers seems outlandish, or as George Shultz
says, "insane." Washington's nuclear war-fighting plan in the
1950s assumed a nuclear exchange with Moscow would quickly
escalate and that the United States would respond to a Soviet
attack with an overwhelming retaliatory strike. The strategy
became known as the doctrine of massive retaliation. Kennedy
and McNamara developed a more graduated strategy known as
flexible response. It was designed, in part, to give NATO forces
in Europe war-fighting options short of employing nuclear weapons if they came under attack. McNamara later acknowledged
that his efforts did not produce a radical change in the Pentagon's
plans for waging all-out nuclear war.

Pioneering nuclear strategists like Herman Kahn engaged in
chilling debates about how many tens of millions of people would
be killed in the first and second assault waves of a conflict and
whether a nuclear war was winnable, in any familiar sense of the
word. Kahn, like Kissinger, favored a graduated war plan rather
than an all-out first strike. He once told a group of officers at the
Strategic Air Command (SAC), America's nuclear bomber force,
"Gentlemen, you don't have a war plan, you have a war orgasm."

Fred Kaplan, who chronicled the work of Kahn and other early
nuclear strategists, described one of Kahn's zanier propositions,
meant to mock the Air Force war plan. "Kahn proposed what he
called a 'Doomsday Machine.' It would be a vast computer wired up
to a huge stockpile of H-bombs. When the computer sensed that the
Soviet Union had committed an act defined as intolerable, the machine would automatically set off the Doomsday bombs, covering
the earth with sufficient radioactive fallout to kill billions of people.
Along with an engineer at RAND, Kahn had figured out on paper

that such a Doomsday Machine was technologically feasible." The
Soviet Union actually considered something similar, an automated
system, known as Dead Hand, that would launch a Soviet retaliatory strike without human involvement. The idea was abandoned,
but the Kremlin did develop a protocol that would give mid- and
low-level military officers the authority to launch a nuclear strike
absent explicit approval by national leaders in Moscow.

As Kahn and the others strategized, the United States and
Soviet Union invested heavily in underground shelters and other
civil defense programs designed to safeguard government leaders
and civilians during a nuclear strike.

With the weapons came the urgent need for better intelligence
about nuclear-armed adversaries. The next surprise attack would
make Pearl Harbor look like a bee sting. Instead of losing a naval
fleet, the United States could be enfeebled if not vanquished.
Absent reliable intelligence about the scale of the Soviet threat,
Washington might go broke paying for military forces to defend
against every conceivable threat.

President Eisenhower, alarmed by the pace of Pentagon spending, warned that America was in danger of becoming a garrison
state in which defense requirements overwhelmed social needs.
As a former general, Eisenhower knew effective spying was the
best way to ensure that American forces were properly sized and
equipped to defend against real rather than imagined threats. As
Edwin Land, the inventor of instant photography and an Eisenhower adviser, put it, "We simply cannot afford to defend against
all possible threats. We must know accurately where the threat
is coming from and concentrate our resources in that direction.
Only by doing so can we survive the Cold War."

This was the world that greeted Shultz, Kissinger, Perry, Nunn,
and Drell as they made their way to Washington.

CHAPTER SIX

He was born with a natural curiosity.
—ED PERRY

Bill Perry's interest in military matters was evident at an early age when he spent hours studying history and geography books at the public library in Butler, Pennsylvania, a blue-collar, steel-making town in the hills northeast of Pittsburgh. In 1939, when he was twelve years old, he closely followed the initial phases of World War II by listening to the radio and reading newspaper reports. "I still remember the names of the three ships that sank the *Graf Spee*—the *Ajax, Exeter,* and *Achilles*," he said with obvious pride in 2008, nearly seventy years after the December 1939 naval battle between the German battle cruiser, known as a "pocket battleship," and three British cruisers off the coast of Uruguay.

"I was deeply interested and followed all these events very, very closely," Perry said. "Not typical for a twelve-, thirteen-year-old." Or for the other members of his family. "I was the oddball," he said.

Indeed. Perry's older brother, Ed, remembers Bill studying geography books at the family's modest home on Locust Street in Butler. "That wouldn't be my first choice of something that I'd want to do on a nice summer day," Ed said. "But I couldn't get him away from that.

"I think he was born with a natural curiosity. And it was bent toward the world, a worldwide vision that he had."

Perry was born on October 11, 1927, in Vandergrift, Pennsylvania, like Butler, a small, industrial town northeast of Pittsburgh. He was the youngest of three children. His father, Edward, a coal miner's son, made a living initially as a crane operator at a local foundry. As Bill was growing up, the family moved to Indiana, Pennsylvania, not far away, and eventually settled in Butler. After a spell driving a bakery delivery truck, Bill's father started his own bakery. A few years later, with his brother, Ernest, he operated Perry Brothers, a small chain of neighborhood grocery stores, struggling to make ends meet during the Great Depression.

The family was Republican—at least the father was—and Presbyterian, though not always actively so. Bill's brother recalls their father never attending church, telling the minister one day that he had better uses for Sundays. "I work too hard. I'm too busy. I need the rest." To which the minister replied, "Ed, if you're that busy, you're too busy."

Bill's mother, Mabel, was a schoolteacher in Sewickley, a dozen miles northwest of Pittsburgh, before she married. Six years older than her husband, she appears to have been the calm anchor of a combustible home environment. Ed Perry, Bill's brother, recalled that their father, fearing he might harm one of the children in a tantrum, largely left disciplinary matters to Mabel. "He said he didn't trust his strength and what would happen if he got mad at us," Ed recalled. "And he never laid a hand on us, never."

Ed described their father as "hard to get close to," and said Mabel "was my source of inspiration, and I'm sure Bill's, too."

"Mother was not only his wife, but his mentor who would encourage and advise him with making career decisions. Dad was always very dependent on Mother and respected her opinion."

Lee Perry, Bill's high school sweetheart and wife since 1947, described the Perry family of Bill's childhood as close and caring. "Bill was very fond and respectful of his mother in particular, probably more so than his father," she said. "His father was maybe a little more authoritative. But his mother was very thoughtful."

Bill and Leonilla Green met in trigonometry class when they were juniors at Butler High School. They were also in the high school choir, and soon started collaborating in Bill's boogie-woogie band, the Two O'Clock Club: Bill played piano; Lee was the vocalist. They were accompanied by three trombones, three trumpets, and drums. Along with fellow band members, they would pile into the Perry Brothers delivery truck on weekends and travel to surrounding towns to perform at dances. "Bill and Lee could do a pretty good jitterbug," Ed recalled.

Lee, a bright, petite brunette, came from a more liberal, politically active Butler family than the Perrys. "Bill used to love to come and sit in on some of our discussions. He was very fond of my two brothers, who were very active in all kinds of political things."

After the Japanese attack on Pearl Harbor on December 7, 1941, Perry was determined to join the fight, even though he was not nearly old enough to enlist. "I wanted to be part of it," he said. "I was fourteen years old, which meant the war would have to last four more years if I was going to get in it."

On his seventeenth birthday, in 1944—still a year short of enlistment age—Perry headed for Pittsburgh to sign up for the Air Cadet program in the Army Air Corps. He was sworn into the Army and sent home to await an opening in the pilot training program. Perry later speculated that the Army accepted him despite his age because it may not have planned to call him to active duty until he turned eighteen. He left high school, where he was an academic star and had exhausted what the teachers could offer him intellectually, and enrolled at Carnegie Tech in Pittsburgh.

In early 1945, the Air Cadet program was disbanded and Perry received an honorable discharge notice. With the war still unabated, Perry immediately enlisted in the Navy Air Corps and was sent to

Philadelphia to be inducted. He was still shy of his eighteenth birthday. To his surprise and great disappointment, he failed the physical exam because of repeated high blood pressure readings. After completing a year and a half at Carnegie Tech, he enlisted in the Army Engineers. By then he was eighteen and the war was over.

The Army shipped Perry and his engineering company to postwar Japan to help plan reconstruction. When he got to Naha, the capital of Okinawa, he was stunned by the destruction left in the wake of the fierce fighting on the island in the spring of 1945. "You just couldn't believe it if you hadn't seen it," he said. "A city the size of San Jose and not a building left standing."

When his tour in Japan ended, Perry stopped in northern California on his way home. He was smitten by the mild climate and western landscape and decided to transfer from Carnegie Tech to Stanford within a year or two. Bill and Lee were married before an impromptu altar in the Greens' living room on Orchard Avenue in Butler on December 29, 1947. The following summer they drove to California and he enrolled at Stanford that fall. By 1952 they had four children, including twin daughters.

After graduating from Stanford in 1949, and collecting a master's degree in math there a year later, Perry spent nine months teaching math at the University of Idaho in Moscow, Idaho. Then the family headed to Seattle, where Bill took a summer job at Boeing working on the still-secret B-52 bomber program. As the summer wound down, the Perrys traveled by train back to the East Coast. In September 1951, Bill, aiming to become a math professor, enrolled in the math Ph.D. program at Penn State in State College, Pennsylvania, little more than one hundred miles from Butler.

The allure of Penn State was partly financial. In addition to the tuition aid he received, Perry worked half-time at Haller, Raymond & Brown, Inc., a State College think tank that did analytical defense studies. John L. McLucas, who went on to become director of the National Reconnaissance Office and secretary of the Air Force, was technical director of the firm while Perry worked there.

The Haller, Raymond & Brown job—program manager for an Army Signal Corps study—gave Perry his first serious taste of defense work. He was enthralled. "I found it very interesting," Perry said. "I was good at it." He found it so compelling that at age twenty-six, as he neared completion of the Ph.D. program in 1954, he abandoned his math teaching ambitions and accepted a job offer from Sylvania in California. The electronics company, eager to expand its defense business, was opening a new electronics lab in Mountain View, not far from Stanford, to do work for the Army. Soon the Perrys were back on the train, heading to California and a breakthrough job assignment for Bill.

SIDNEY DAVID DRELL was born in Atlantic City, New Jersey, on September 13, 1926. His father, Tully, emigrated from Ukraine to the United States fourteen years earlier, lived in Philadelphia, and attended Penn State, where he earned a pharmacy degree. At the time of Sid's birth, he was working as a pharmacist at Reliable Pharmacy, a neighborhood drugstore in Atlantic City. Sid's mother, Rose White, moved to America from Russia with her family around 1905. She attended Temple University in Philadelphia, and began a career as a schoolteacher. Rose and Tully met in Philadelphia and got married in 1920 in Atlantic City, where Rose's father operated a successful dry goods business.

The two-story, wooden Drell home was located on South Victoria Avenue, just off Oriental Avenue, not far from the boardwalk. "I always thought I was born on Oriental Avenue because that was on the Monopoly board," Drell said. "It was Depression time. We were never hungry for food or anything. But it was a life that was without a lot of frills. And it was a typical immigrant family. The thing that mattered was education. My sister and I were going to go to college, no matter what."

Tully Drell was a voracious reader, and passed the habit to his son and daughter, Thea. The house was filled with books. "My father was anything but a good businessman," Drell recalled. "Life for my father meant reading Plato, Aristotle, Emerson, Santayana—he read them all; I've got them all. . . . He was escaping, I mean he was reading or playing chess. But he had to earn a living." Sid grew especially fond of Conrad and Dickens, and fell in love with poetry. "I had a wonderful teacher in the Atlantic City High School, a man by the name of Clarence Dike. I remember him because I got introduced to Wordsworth, Shelley, Byron, Keats, the world of poetry, which my father loved, too."

Math was Sid's strongest subject in school. While other students were struggling with algebra and trigonometry, Drell taught a non-credit course for his schoolmates on how to use a slide rule. He loved Latin, too. He learned how to play the violin—he relishes playing chamber music to this day—and joined his boyhood friends roller-skating and biking around Atlantic City and playing basketball in backyards. The family never had a car. His parents were Jewish, but not practicing—"My father was against it," he said—and the family did not attend synagogue. Six months before Sid turned thirteen, his father relented a bit, promising his father that Sid would be bar mitzvahed. "It would mean a lot to my grandfather," Sid said. "So they found a reformed rabbi. I never knew what I said. I never knew what I did. I know I made a mistake because somebody in the temple corrected me while I was saying it, and to top it off, my grandfather died two weeks before I turned thirteen."

As his interest in math and literature deepened, Drell imagined he might concentrate on physics or classics in college. "I liked mathematics, but I didn't like pure mathematics for its own sake," he recalled. "I liked applying it to problems that I could figure out what was going on around me."

As a math whiz and top student, Drell would naturally have gravitated toward the University of Pennsylvania, the school of choice in those days for the best students at Atlantic City High School. Harvard seemed outside his universe. "Never thought that far away," he said. "I'd been once to New York. I'd been to Philadelphia once a year. In a school trip I got to Valley Forge. That's as far away from Atlantic City I'd ever been. . . . Washington, D.C., Boston—they were beyond the horizon."

He settled on Princeton as his first choice, sight unseen. "In my senior year, I read a lot about this guy Einstein," he said. Drell thought the renowned mathematical physicist was a Princeton professor, not realizing that Einstein's position at the Institute of Advanced Study put him in Princeton but not directly at the university. "It sounded great, so I said, why not apply?"

He did, and was admitted—at age sixteen. Just days after he unpacked his belongings at Princeton in July 1943, Drell got word that his father had been rushed to the hospital in Atlantic City with a bleeding ulcer. Severe postoperative complications led to the removal of one of Tully's lungs and a long convalescence that effectively ended his days as a pharmacist. A month after arriving at Princeton without need of financial aid, Drell had to apply for a scholarship and look for part-time jobs to help pay his way through college. He worked as a waiter, a mover, did some tutoring, and managed the parking lots around Palmer Stadium during home football games, which resumed after the war.

Wartime conditions had sanded down the tony sheen of Princeton, making it somewhat easier for Drell to fit in. The ritzy eating clubs were closed or turned into dining halls and the preppy, clubby side of Princeton life was less pronounced. Still, Drell, a brainy Jew with thick glasses from Atlantic City, was not exactly the classic Princeton type. For the most part, though, he found his own niche and settled into an intellectually bracing, personally gratifying time as a physics major. "There were always some prep school boys who looked upon me as a foreigner," he recalled. "That's really nothing."

Drell also took to the Princeton music scene, becoming concertmaster of the student orchestra. "The great discovery of my senior year was when the old Budapest Quartet came to Princeton and did the Beethoven Cycle. I was getting some sense in my head by that time in my life, because I went. And that just blew me away. That was a world I had never had any knowledge of. That's when my violin got serious."

Drell faced his own medical crisis in early 1945 when his appendix ruptured and he developed acute peritonitis. His induction notice arrived while he was in the hospital. By the time Drell had fully recovered, the war in Europe was ending. He enrolled in summer school at Princeton to make up for lost time, expecting to be drafted in the fall. The war ended abruptly that summer after the bombing of Hiroshima and Nagasaki.

As a physics major, Drell knew many of the university's leading physicists were absent from campus, but not that they were working on the Manhattan Project, the secret project to develop an atom bomb. "I had no idea why all the physicists were away when I was an undergraduate, and what they were doing," he said. "I had never heard the word *fission*." One of them was John Wheeler, an expert on nuclear fission, who worked at the government's secret reactor complex in Hanford, Washington, where plutonium for the Manhattan Project was produced. Wheeler became Drell's senior thesis adviser after returning to Princeton after the war. By his senior year, Drell realized that his passion for math and physics could best be pursued in theoretical physics. He said, "I was no good in the lab. When I did lab physics or chemistry labs, I didn't really enjoy it. I didn't do it very well. I broke things."

Drell did his thesis on radiation damping theory, an aspect of particle physics. A number of fellow Princeton students were working on particle theory issues at the time, including Richard Feynman, a grad student and Wheeler protégé, who later won a Nobel Prize in Physics. In June 1946, at age nineteen, after just three years at Princeton, Drell graduated with honors. His next stop was graduate school at the University of Illinois in Urbana-Champaign. He would have been welcome at Princeton, but could not afford the expense, and the University of Illinois offered him a teaching assistantship that would cover all his expenses as a Ph.D. candidate. Still largely unfamiliar with the world outside New Jersey and eastern Pennsylvania, Drell mistakenly bought a train ticket to Urbana, Ohio, about forty miles west of Columbus. He caught the miscue before packing up for his first trip to the Midwest.

Though the University of Illinois lacked the international stature of Princeton, its physics department was top rate. Drell quickly found an inspiring mentor in Sidney Dancoff, a theoretical physicist and former student at the University of California, Berkeley, of Robert Oppenheimer, who directed the Manhattan Project. Dancoff had worked during the war at the Metallurgical Laboratory at the University of Chicago, where Enrico Fermi and his colleagues in 1942 had built the world's first nuclear reactor and initiated the first successful nuclear chain reaction under the stands at Stagg Field, the university's football stadium. "He was a brilliant and wonderful person, and the experience of working with Sid Dancoff was just marvelous," Drell said.

One Sunday, a fellow grad student stopped by Drell's residence to invite him out for a beer at the one-room apartment where several female grad students had hosted a party the night before. "I said, 'Go away. I'm trying to finish my thesis.' But he bothered us enough that I went. We picked up a bag of jelly beans and went to drink some beers." And so Sidney Drell met Harriet Stainback, a smart, vivacious, no-nonsense German-literature grad student and Wellesley graduate from the hamlet of Minter City, Mississippi. Her father, Frank, was a cotton farmer. Her mother, also Harriet, came from the Midwest, with roots in the Northeast.

After a year as a postdoctoral student at Urbana–Champaign, Drell spent a few months doing theoretical physics at the government's nuclear complex at Oak Ridge, Tennessee, then headed to Stanford in September 1950 to be an instructor in the physics department. He had barely settled in when John Wheeler invited him to work on a secret project—development of a hydrogen bomb. Drell demurred. "I decided I was going to stay academic," he said. He and Harriet stayed in touch. After picking up her master's in Illinois, she returned to Mississippi, then took a job in Washington, D.C., at an Army security agency, using the Russian she had learned at Wellesley and Illinois. They would get together in Washington when Drell traveled to the East Coast to attend meetings of the American Physical Society.

In 1952, Drell decided to cut short his three-year appointment at Stanford to move to MIT and the hottest physics program in the nation. He and Harriet married in March 1952 in Minter City, a most improbable melding of North and South. "My parents would have preferred that I married a Christian," she recalled with a laugh in 2009. Persis Drell, their eldest daughter, said, "I just imagine their wedding in the living room of my mother's parents' house, with my father's parents there and my mother in a red wedding dress marrying a Jewish man in this tiny town in Mississippi. Wow!"

The next four years in Cambridge put Drell in touch with some of the rising stars of the field, including several future Nobel Prize winners, and Bud Wheelon, who had enrolled as a doctoral student at MIT after graduating from Stanford. Marvin "Murph" Goldberger, another fellow MIT grad student and Drell companion, went on to become president of the California Institute of Technology. Several times a week, Drell and Goldberger would hitch a ride with Wheelon along the Charles River to Harvard to attend a course in quantum electrodynamics taught by Julian Schwinger, a former assistant to Robert Oppenheimer at Berkeley.

Drell thought he was on course for a university career as a theo-retical physicist. He was, but only partly so. John Wheeler's invita-tion to work on the hydrogen bomb project turned out to be just the first of many opportunities to assist the government on defense matters. Before long, Drell was spending a lot of time in Wash-ington, dealing with some of the nation's most highly classified national security programs.

CHAPTER SEVEN

Every day I thought was going to be my last day on earth.
—BILL PERRY

The development of ballistic missiles during the 1950s opened a volatile new phase of the Cold War, and put Drell and Perry to work in common cause helping Washington track and gauge the Soviet missile threat.

The advent of the intercontinental ballistic missile (ICBM) made the prospect of surprise nuclear attack frighteningly possible. The oceans, America's natural barrier to military assault, afforded no protection against missiles. The United States might be able to blunt an attack by Soviet bombers that would be in the air for hours before reaching American airspace. But the warning time for a missile attack, if there were a warning, would be less than thirty minutes.

No Cold War threat was more alarming or destabilizing. Intercontinental missiles all but eliminated the margin of error in managing the nuclear balance of terror. For President Dwight D. Eisenhower, who sought to maintain American military strength while controlling defense spending, the Soviet missile threat was doubly vexing. As the Russians appeared to be making rapid advances in missile technology, Eisenhower came under withering political attack for letting the United States fall behind in the missile race. Democrats and conservative Republicans hammered him about the "missile gap." John Kennedy ran to victory in the 1960 presidential election partly by invoking the "missile gap" as he campaigned against Vice President Richard Nixon.

Despite the uproar, the limited intelligence that the United States had about Soviet missiles was ambiguous. Similar charges made about a "bomber gap" had been discredited in 1956–57, when the U-2 spy plane went into service. The exotic airplane, built and operated in secret by the CIA, penetrated deep into Soviet airspace, initially beyond the range of Soviet antiaircraft missiles as it cruised at an altitude of seventy thousand feet. Cameras aboard the U-2 snapped photographs of Soviet air bases, showing a far smaller fleet of bombers than feared.

Was the missile gap another mirage? An accurate answer was critical to American security. It required reliable intelligence about a host of issues, including the number of Soviet missiles, their range and accuracy, the location of missile bases, and advances in missile technology as time passed, just to name a few. Collecting the intelligence data, in turn, depended on the development of new spy technologies that would allow the United States, in effect, to reach deep into Soviet territory to steal the Kremlin's most valuable secrets.

Scientists and engineers like Drell and Perry put their expertise to work to invent and refine just such espionage systems. The 1950s and '60s were a time when American scientists, working in tandem with industry and the government, opened new frontiers in military and intelligence technology. During the Eisenhower administration, 1953–61, the United States developed nuclear-powered submarines and aircraft carriers, intercontinental missiles, nuclear warheads small and light enough to fit atop a missile, and spy satellites that could peer into the Soviet Union from space.

Not long after Bill and Lee Perry returned to California from Penn State in 1954, Bill was put to work on the Soviet missile puzzle. His problem-solving skills were soon apparent.

"Bill is a very pragmatic person," said Paul Kaminski, who worked closely with Perry over the years and managed the Pentagon's acquisition of new weapons systems during the Clinton administration. "When you present a problem to him, he'll always observe it from a top level and break it down into its fundamental parts. . . . A lot of people can see problems in a textbook and work the problems, but some of the real-world problems you deal with are very ill-posed. And Bill is very good at looking at ill-posed problems and getting at the root elements of the problem and then looking to see, can I attack the root elements and create a solution. . . ."

Perry's California base was Sylvania's Electronic Defense Laboratory in Sunnyvale, the heart of what later became known as Silicon Valley. The lab, known simply as EDL, was located in a complex of single-story buildings, including a central electronics lab, surrounded by orchards. Sylvania, like a number of other electronics companies, set up shop not far from Palo Alto in the early years of the Cold War to tap into research work at Stanford. The university was rapidly building one of the nation's top engineering schools and its professors and students were seeding the area with companies and labs that capitalized on new technologies they had developed at Stanford. Defense-related research was a natural complement.

Perry, a bow-tie-wearing easterner, didn't seem a natural fit for the casual culture and hard-core engineering work at EDL, but he had a knack for making conceptual leaps that opened new technological vistas and a confident, low-key leadership style that won the respect of colleagues. Lew Franklin, an electrical engineer who worked with Perry at EDL, said it is "a rare thing for a mathematician to jump the bridge to be respected as an engineer by engineers."

Perry, by his own account, brings a "cerebral approach" to electronics. "Ask Lee sometime how adept I am at repairing television sets," he joked.

During the first years of the missile race with the Kremlin, early-generation Soviet missiles were guided to targets by radio signals. EDL's initial assignment from the Army was to come up with electronic hardware that would disrupt, or jam, Soviet guidance systems, throwing Russian missiles off course.

Perry reasoned that the development of countermeasures would be futile until the Army, and by extension EDL, understood the intricacies of the Soviet guidance system. Put simply, you couldn't defeat the Soviet system until you understood how it worked. And to gain that understanding, Perry realized, you had to devise intelligence-gathering technologies that could pick up guidance signals for Soviet missiles during test flights as the missiles streaked across the sky to their intended targets. Since the United States had no on-site access to Russian missile bases and target zones, the collection would have to be conducted from far afield. The best sites were in Turkey and Iran, the American allies closest to Soviet missile testing bases near the Black Sea and Caspian Sea. Electronic listening posts in both nations offered a line of sight, in effect, down the critical powered flight path on the Soviet missile ranges.

As EDL and the Army started work, they learned Soviet missiles also transmitted data streams, or telemetry, by radio to Soviet ground stations during launch and flight. The data tracked the performance characteristics of the missiles—how fast, how far, how fair they flew. The data covered dozens of factors, including rocket thrust, acceleration, speed, engine shutdown, guidance system operation, fuel consumption rate, warhead separation, and so on. If the United States could intercept the telemetry radio signal and disaggregate it, or demodulate it, as engineers would say, Washington would know nearly as much about Soviet missiles as Soviet missilemen.

Perry saw the potential payoff for EDL, and more broadly, for American security. Intelligence collection was the key, first to capture and decipher missile test telemetry, and later to intercept a

wide range of Soviet weapons development data. He pushed hard
to redirect the lab from developing countermeasures to Soviet missiles to designing intelligence-gathering systems. He succeeded,
catapulting himself into a top management post at EDL and the
front ranks of the nation's defense contractors.

The first hurdle for EDL was making sense of the radio signals
from Soviet missile tests. The U.S. Army opened listening posts in
Sinop and Samsun, on Turkey's Black Sea coast. The first receivers
sent to Sinop picked up signals from Kapustin Yar, the southern
Soviet missile base used for short- and intermediate-range missile
tests, but the signals could not be demodulated. It was like trying
to tune in an AM radio station on an FM radio. The Jet Propulsion
Laboratory in Pasadena, California, which was devising telemetry
systems for NASA, had provided receivers tuned to pick up the
kind of frequency modulation, or FM, radio signals the United
States was using for telemetry.

Bill Perry had a suggestion: the Russians might be using pulse
position modulation, or PPM, which could be picked up with a
different kind of radio receiver and recorders. A new set of receivers was shipped to Sinop. They did the trick, making it possible to
pick up and demodulate the Soviet radio transmissions.

EDL soon set up another listening post for the Army on Shemya
Island, in the Aleutian archipelago, about 1,450 miles southwest of
Anchorage, Alaska. From there, radio receivers could tune in to telemetry transmissions from Soviet intercontinental missiles during
final stages of flight as dummy warheads homed in on target zones
on the Kamchatka Peninsula. To overcome the curvature of the
earth, which limited the range of ground-based listening posts,
EDL developed eavesdropping systems that were placed aboard
airplanes flying out of Turkey and Pakistan. From their flying altitude of 20,000–40,000 feet, the planes looked out over the Russian test ranges, affording access to a fuller set of telemetry data.

Eager to understand the telemetry, the National Security

Agency (NSA), the intelligence organization primarily responsible for intercepting communication signals, enlisted a small group of scientists and engineers from outside government, including Bill Perry, to study the missile data. The group was called the Telemetry and Beacon Analysis Committee. (Some members of the group, including Perry, had previously been recruited by the CIA and Air Force to examine each new batch of photographs taken by the high-flying U-2 spy planes. The intense four-day bursts of activity involving the U-2 photos were called "Jam Sessions.")

The intercepted Soviet telemetry data reviewed by the beacon analysis group was distributed to EDL and three other defense organizations to be deciphered and examined. Bud Wheelon, who worked on the project, said that untangling the puzzle of the Russian data was "one of the great breakthroughs of technical intelligence."

He compared the cooperative work of the science panel to solving a jigsaw puzzle. "It was very much like a family on Thanksgiving holiday getting out a picture puzzle and working on it. One person puts the piece in and then somebody else does, and pretty soon the whole picture begins to emerge."

By all accounts, it was painstaking yet exhilarating work for the scientists and engineers, with each new revelation leading to the next, ultimately giving policymakers in Washington a detailed picture of advances in Soviet missile engineering. At a time when Washington feared a surprise Soviet nuclear attack, the data showed both the strengths and weaknesses of the Russian missile program. It gave Eisenhower a more measured assessment of the Soviet threat.

Perry led the EDL team, and he and Lee periodically hosted representatives from the other groups for dinner at their Palo Alto home. Perry's leadership and manner impressed Wheelon. They had attended Stanford at the same time in the late 1940s—Perry majored in math, Wheelon in physics—but they had not met as students. Wheelon found Perry to be unusually good at bringing out the best in his colleagues.

"It was just clear that Bill had a kind of poise and sort of a judicious wisdom," Wheelon said. "He was right in the thick of these identifications, but he was always encouraging others under him, not taking credit, very much in his way, and trying to get to the deeper truths instead of the details."

Perry spent the summer of 1958 in Washington studying U-2 photography of Soviet missile sites. "The only people they had cleared to work at them were photo interpreters, who didn't know a damn thing about missiles or electronics," he said. "They asked me if I would come back for the summer and work with these photo interpreters and see if I could make any technical sense out of what they were seeing."

Perry's highly detailed report was the definitive work on Soviet missiles at the time. Between his work on telemetry and his examination of the U-2 photographs, the onetime mathematician had turned himself into one of the nation's top experts on Soviet missiles.

He was soon back in Washington on another sensitive missile assignment. In 1960, Allen Dulles, the director of central intelligence, appointed a task force to referee a heated dispute about a new Soviet missile. The prospect that the Russians were developing a new, powerful solid-fuel ICBM that might carry a blockbuster warhead fueled fears that American security was, indeed, threatened by a "missile gap."

With the Air Force and Navy demanding additional funding for their missile programs in light of the new Soviet missile, and the CIA and the Army skeptical about the new weapon, Dulles asked Pat Hyland, the president of Hughes Aircraft, to chair a panel of defense experts to determine which camp was right. Hyland invited Perry and Wheelon to join the group. They were both thirty-two years old, veritable newbies compared to the flag-rank military brass on the panel. But Perry and Wheelon were experts on Soviet missiles, unlike the other members. "We were the two kids that knew something," Wheelon said.

"I mean, this was really a hot potato," Wheelon recalled. "Passions were high; people's reputations were on the line; people had gone out on great limbs. . . . I was struck by how deliberative Perry was in terms of piling up the facts the way a good lawyer does, and then presenting them and defending them. There was none of the assertiveness that so often went with weekend warriors who show up in Washington and claim they're big experts. He went in in a problem-solving way, and essentially built the case that Hyland and our elders could endorse and then defend."

The verdict: the CIA and Army were right; the new missile was not a behemoth. "Unlike most panels, this one actually came to an unambiguous and unanimous conclusion," Perry recounted years later. The report added to the growing sense in Washington that there was, in fact, no missile gap with the Soviet Union. If anything the United States had a more advanced missile program. The limits of the Soviet missile threat were definitively confirmed by pictures of Soviet missile bases produced by America's first photo reconnaissance satellites in 1960 and early 1961. After President Kennedy and Secretary of Defense McNamara were informed about the findings in 1961, McNamara told reporters there was no missile gap and the issue soon faded away. "The United States was able to plan its defense programs based on facts, not fantasy," Perry said.

At Wheelon's instigation, Perry was thrown back into missile issues during the 1962 Cuban Missile Crisis. By then Wheelon was a deputy director of the CIA, running its science and technology operations, including the first-generation photoreconnaissance satellites. When the components of Soviet missiles were first spotted in Cuba in photographs taken by a U-2 plane, Wheelon was immediately drawn into crisis deliberations to direct daily intelligence evaluations of the missile threat.

The thirteen-day crisis brought Washington and Moscow perilously close to a military conflict that might have escalated swiftly into a nuclear exchange. President Kennedy viewed the introduction of Soviet missiles in Cuba as an unacceptable threat. He did not know at the time that Soviet nuclear warheads had also been secretly shipped to Cuba, but understood the arrival of missiles could be followed by warheads. His ultimatum to the Kremlin to withdraw the missiles and his order to block further missile shipments at sea, by force if necessary, brought the crisis to a combustion point.

As chairman of the Guided Missile and Astronautics Intelligence Committee, Wheelon supervised the nightly analysis of new intelligence data about the Soviet missiles that poured into Washington every day. He and the nation's top photo interpreter, Arthur Lundahl, briefed President Kennedy on their findings each morning.

Perry was urgently summoned to Washington to lend a hand. "I received a phone call asking me to come back to Washington to give some advice," he recalled. "I said, 'Fine, I'll change my schedule and be back next week.' They said, 'No, you don't understand. We want you to come right away.' So I took a night flight to Washington. The next morning I was taken into an analysis lab. I was stunned to be shown pictures of Soviet nuclear missiles being deployed in Cuba."

For Perry, the peaceful resolution of the missile crisis left an enduring sense that nuclear war was just one miscalculation away. "Every day I thought was going to be my last day on earth," he said.

DRELL'S INTRODUCTION TO the Soviet missile threat—and the larger world of defense technology—also began in California. After four years as a junior faculty member at MIT, Drell returned to Stanford in 1956 as an assistant professor, drawn back west, among other things, by the allure of working with Wolfgang K. H. Panofsky, another star in the physics firmament, who had recently moved to Stanford himself from Berkeley. Panofsky's primary job at Stanford was to design, build, and run a powerful new atom smasher, a two-mile-long linear accelerator that would use powerful beams of electrons to advance the frontiers of particle physics research.

Drell soon bonded with Panofsky, a diminutive man and towering intellect known as Pief to his friends and colleagues. The two men became partners in physics research and government service, as well as fast friends. Drell often refers to Panofsky as one of his heroes, along with Hans Bethe, another nuclear scientist. In Panofsky, Drell found a mentor who helped guide him through the realm of theoretical physics and introduce him to the world of arms control and high-level government scientific advising. Over time, Drell became Panofsky's top deputy at the Stanford Linear Accelerator Center (SLAC), and head of the SLAC theory group.

"Right from the beginning, when SLAC was no more than Project M housed in a warehouse on the Stanford campus, Sid left the more familiar and comfortable world of academe to join the adventure of creating a great new laboratory," James Bjorken, a Drell student and collaborator, recalled in 1998 when Drell retired from the lab.

Under Drell's direction, the SLAC theory group quickly developed a reputation for high-powered discussions, a mix of applied and formal theory, productive collaboration with experimental scientists, and an informal atmosphere that made sophisticated physics, in Bjorken's words, "not only deeply satisfying but also just plain fun to do."

Drell turned to Panofsky for advice in 1960 after receiving an invitation from another eminent physicist, Charles H. Townes, to join a new group of young physicists that was being set up to advise the government on scientific matters. Drell remembered the call vividly nearly five decades later. "I was upstairs in the evening after dinner and the phone rang in our bedroom. I picked it up. It's Charlie Townes. I knew who Charlie Townes was. I'd never met him."

Townes, who had done groundbreaking work in microwave radiation (he was awarded a Nobel Prize in 1964 for his pioneering work leading to the invention of the laser), was working with several other physicists to get a new generation of scientists involved in defense issues as the Manhattan Project generation was receding. The Soviet Union's successful 1957 launch of Sputnik, the world's first man-made satellite, stirred intense concern in Washington that the United States was in danger of falling behind the Soviet Union in science and defense technology.

Though Drell had earlier turned down John Wheeler's invitation to work on the H-bomb, he realized by 1960 that the acute dangers of the Cold War and nuclear weapons were rapidly intensifying. Panofsky, who had played a peripheral role in the Manhattan Project, was a veteran of several science advisory groups. After Robert Oppenheimer told a congressional committee in 1945 that the only way to detect whether a nuclear device was hidden in a shipping crate was to open the container with a screwdriver, the government asked Panofsky to help investigate how more advanced technologies might be used. The resulting study, dubbed the "Screwdriver Report," advised that radiation detectors would be useful, though only within close range of a nuclear device. By 1960, Panofsky had served on the Physics Panel of the National Science Foundation and the Science Advisory Board of the Air Force, and had chaired a panel of the President's Science Advisory Committee on detecting nuclear explosions in space.

Panofsky urged Drell to give the Townes group a try. He flew to Washington for a briefing, found the plans intriguing, and traveled that spring to Key West, Florida, with other physicists to review antisubmarine warfare defenses. He agreed to participate in a summer study group that would be convened in Berkeley. The new organization was called "Jason." It was not an abbreviation or acronym, but rather borrowed from the Greek myth about Jason and the Argonauts' search for the Golden Fleece. The Jasons, as group members still call themselves today, would be funded by the government and provided with classified information about government technology projects and challenges, but operate independently and render unfettered judgments about the issues they examined.

By chance, the puzzle Drell was assigned when he got to Berkeley was the perfect introduction to the intersection of science and defense policy. It turned out to be Drell's sweet spot and he spent the better part of the next four decades working problems at that crossroads. The question he faced that summer revolved around whether a satellite equipped with an infrared sensor could spot the launch of Soviet intercontinental missiles by detecting the heat, or infrared radiation, of the rocket exhaust plume. The warning time between launch and the arrival of a warhead over the East Coast would be short, but seconds counted if the president hoped to order an American counterstrike before Washington was vaporized. No less important, accurate launch intelligence could help avoid the terrifying prospect that the United States might fire off its missiles based on a false report of a Soviet attack.

Space science was still in its infancy, and Drell tackled the issue of whether the Soviet Union could blind an orbiting infrared sensor by detonating nuclear weapons in the atmosphere moments before firing its missiles at the United States. He worked with another Jason recruit, Malvin Ruderman, a theoretical astrophysicist trained at Columbia and Caltech. A nuclear weapon detonated in the atmosphere would produce an intense burst of X-rays that would temporarily alter the chemistry of the atmosphere by creating nitrogen oxide molecules. As the new molecules decayed, they would generate a blanket of infrared radiation, potentially enough to blind a satellite sensor. Drell and Ruderman set out to determine the strength, duration, and other characteristics of the "red-out" that a nuclear blast would produce. "We showed that it would take too many megatons and the clouds would be blown by the winds at high altitude, so that was not an effective way to blind it," Drell said.

Based partly on their findings, the Pentagon moved ahead with development of the satellite system, known as the Missile Defense Alarm System (MIDAS).

Drell and Perry crossed paths for the first time as the Pentagon was taking an initial look at the missile detection system. A new government office, the Arms Control and Disarmament Agency (ACDA), recruited both men as consultants on a variety of projects soon after it was established in 1961. Drell was based at Stanford, Perry at EDL. "Sid and I were both technical consultants," Perry recalled. "That's how we got involved in that kind of stuff. And we probably interfaced dozens of times during the sixties and seventies in our joint roles as consultants to intelligence agencies. But not in an organized way. We'd end up at the same meetings." The two men jointly organized an arms control conference at Stanford in 1962.

Bud Wheelon reinforced the interaction by inviting Drell and Perry to advise the CIA on new technologies. Perry said, "Bud and Sid and I worked very closely together. We all had a Stanford connection. We were all about the same age, and we all had a common interest . . . pushing the state-of-the-art technology."

Drell reengaged with the MIDAS project in 1961 when he was appointed to the Strategic Military Panel of the President's Science Advisory Committee (PSAC), an elite group of scientists that advised the White House on some of the nation's most important technology projects. The committee was chaired by Jerome Weisner, President Kennedy's science adviser, who later served as president of MIT. Drell was now operating in the most rarified of scientific circles, working alongside some of the nation's most distinguished scholars, advising the president, the secretary of defense, the director of central intelligence, and other top officials.

It was a seductive world. Years later, looking back at his early engagement with the government, Drell said, "Call it entrapment, commitment or whatever, but I have remained actively involved in technical national security work for the United States."

The same was true for Perry. His work on various aspects of Soviet missiles soon led to other government assignments, putting him in play in Washington as a rising star in the defense world and laying the foundation for his involvement in nuclear weapons policy.

Drell and Perry were perfectly positioned to play leading roles in a critically important Cold War field that was just starting to take shape—spying on the Soviet Union from space. The new technology, among other things, would make it possible to monitor and verify nuclear arms control agreements.

CHAPTER EIGHT

Given the Soviet Empire, its stated goals and existence,
we had to deter them.
—SID DRELL

By the early 1960s, Cold War tensions were escalating. Nikita
Khrushchev, the Soviet leader, tested American and Western resolve with the erection of the Berlin Wall in 1961, making it
all but impossible for East Germans to enter the British, French, and
American zones of the city. The same year Khrushchev bragged
that the Soviet Union had developed a one-hundred-megaton nuclear warhead—roughly six thousand times more powerful than
the bomb dropped on Hiroshima. The 1962 Cuban Missile Crisis
compounded fears that nuclear war might be unavoidable. Meantime, hundreds of aboveground nuclear tests by the United States
and Soviet Union through the 1950s had contaminated the earth's
atmosphere with toxic radioactive elements.

As tensions rose, it became ever more important for the United
States to monitor the strength and status of Soviet military forces so
that some false alarm would not ignite a nuclear war. Spying from
space was one answer. Vaulting America's espionage operations into
the heavens opened new Washington opportunities for Drell and
Perry. Both men were soon immersed in the new world of spy satellites. Once again, Bud Wheelon at the CIA was the catalyst.

Wheelon phoned Drell in late 1963. "He said he wanted to

show me something that was important, and he needed my help," Drell recalled. Wheelon urgently needed assistance to solve a technical problem that was crippling the nation's first fleet of photoreconnaissance spy satellites. The highly secret Corona satellites, introduced in August 1960 after a crash development program, had given the United States eyes in the sky that could freely photograph Soviet military installations, unimpeded by antiaircraft defenses. They had produced a bonanza of intelligence about the Soviet military, including missile forces. The satellites also opened the door to arms control agreements that could be verified by keeping tabs on Soviet missile forces from space.

Each satellite, which orbited the earth every ninety minutes in an elliptical orbit that ranged from 80 to 140 miles high, was a technological marvel. Equipped with a sophisticated camera system, it would circle the planet for several days, snapping moderately detailed images of ground sites, then jettison a large canister of exposed film. The canisters, coated with a heat shield to prevent incineration during the high-speed plunge through the atmosphere, were snared from the sky by specially equipped airplanes during the last, parachute-braked phase of descent over the Pacific, not far from Hawaii. Once developed at the Eastman Kodak plant in Rochester, New York, the photographs were rushed to Washington, where specially trained analysts, known as photo interpreters, would scour them for useful intelligence.

The torrent of new intelligence from Corona was disrupted early in 1963 when much of the film returning from the satellites turned up with white streaks, ruining many of the images. The cause was a mystery and solving it was exceedingly difficult because the cameras aboard the satellites burned up when the spacecrafts fell from orbit, leaving no hardware that could be recovered and examined. The satellites carried no instruments that could tell ground controllers what might be causing the problem. Wheelon said, "The streaks were the result of little lightning strokes, the kind that you get sometimes on a rug when you put a key in the lock and get a little spark. Well, that was what was going on in the cameras. It was a vacuum up there and sparks were created very easily, and they made a mess of the film.

"When the flashes went off, it was like having a flash camera in a darkroom. And these little lightning bolts would shed a hell of a lot of light just as the film was going through."

Wheelon figured Drell would be well suited to direct a Corona task force. "I asked myself who could lead and have the respect of a group of people, who could dig to the bottom of it, and then present it in a clear way, whatever they found, to [CIA director John A.] McCone and others, plus me."

When Drell showed up at CIA headquarters outside Washington—his first visit to the agency—Wheelon told him about the Corona system, showed him some of the streaked images, and asked him to run a technical group that would try to diagnose and remedy the problem. "I learned, to my amazement, that we could photograph the earth with fairly good resolution from satellites," Drell said. Wheelon had put together a team of scientists and engineers associated with the companies that built the satellites, including Lockheed, Eastman Kodak, and Itek. Drell added two physicists whom he knew well, Luis Alvarez from Berkeley, and Mal Ruderman, who had worked with Drell a few years earlier on the infrared sensor project. "The investigation was to be in a scientific realm that was new to me, and I wanted my two colleagues to add to my confidence that I would stay on track and not go off on useless tangents," Drell said.

Drell moved to Washington for four months, returning to Stanford on weekends. Wheelon recalled, "There was a list of hypotheses of what could be doing this, and each one of them had to be examined very carefully, because any one of them could have been it. . . . And meanwhile, we're going months and months with no coverage.

"They had to chase an awful lot of rabbits that could have been the problem, and figure out which one was really doing it, and then figure out how to fix it."

Examining suspected causes was tricky because test conditions on the ground were quite different from the satellites' operating environment in space, with zero gravity and a vacuum. "It was a heck of a job," Wheelon recalled. "It's like going over someone's tax return and trying to figure out where they made a mistake. It doesn't take a lot of brilliance; you just have to be very methodical, very penetrating, very patient, and very organized. And Sid's a very good guy to do that. Just sift through all the possibilities."

As Drell and his colleagues narrowed the possibilities, they found the streaking was caused by a buildup of electrostatic charges in the camera system. Electrical, thermal, and vacuum conditions, coupled with the material used in rollers that unspooled and spooled the film, led to electrical discharges as the ultrathin film sped across the rollers. The flaw was fixed primarily by switching to a different roller material.

The Corona project highlighted Drell's leadership style—a blend of scientific expertise, quiet confidence, warmth, and self-effacement. "He led not by domination," Wheelon recalled.

Drell's involvement in the Corona project led quickly to another assignment from Wheelon. This time Wheelon asked Drell to help gauge the future limits of the Corona system to determine whether a more advanced model or development of an entirely new system would produce better pictures. The answer was that a new system was needed, and before long, Drell was drafted to serve on the CIA's top technology advisory panel, a high-powered group of scientists headed by Edwin Land.

The Land Panel, as it was known, was an indispensable source of good advice to a series of CIA directors over several decades, beginning with John McCone in the early 1960s. Though Land was best known to Americans for his work in instant photography, he played a secret central role in the intelligence world, often tipping the decision-making balance in favor of cutting-edge technologies that government officials and defense contractors were hesitant to pursue. Eisenhower benefited from his advice in ordering development of the U-2 spy plane and the Corona satellites over the objections of the Pentagon and the doubts of Allen Dulles, Eisenhower's CIA director.

Drell joined the Land Panel as it was beginning to look ahead to the next generation of spy satellites. A key question, as Drell had discovered working on Corona, was how to improve coverage of broad areas of the earth's surface, the better to identify military installations and other sites of interest. Some photoreconnaissance satellites specialize in focusing on specific sites to show as much detail as possible. Others look at wider areas in search of facilities like missile bases, airfields, and radar complexes. The Itek Corporation, a Boston firm that had produced the Corona cameras, agreed to develop a new broad coverage system, then backed out of the CIA project, mistakenly betting that the Air Force, working on its own photoreconnaissance satellite, would end up developing the new satellites.

Wheelon turned to Perkin-Elmer, another optics company, to see what they could do. The company showed him a novel gadget called "The Twister," which the firm's engineers had devised and then put on a shelf, seeing no practical use for it. "It was just an incredible thing," he said. The Twister, which could precisely synchronize the movement of film and mirror systems in a camera, opened the way to the creation of a new, high-resolution, broad-coverage camera system. "When Din Land saw it, he just fell in love with it," Wheelon recalled, referring to Land by his nickname. "He said, 'This is a marriage made in heaven.'" The result was the Hexagon program, the successor to Corona, with cameras provided by Perkin-Elmer and the spacecraft built by Lockheed. The first Hexagon satellite went into service in 1971.

Drell's immersion in spy satellite work gave him a sense that he could make a difference on vital defense issues. As time passed, nothing seemed more important to Drell than controlling the nuclear arms race and reducing the risk of nuclear war. "Over time," Drell said, "I could not escape the reality that progress in nuclear science back in the 1920s and '30s had led to terrifying new dangers to the very survival of our civilization on a global scale. I am speaking of nuclear weapons capable of unimaginable destructiveness."

The growing threat made arms control a moral issue for Drell. "It is my personal conviction," he said of his thinking then and now, "that the scientific community—not each individual but as a whole—bears a responsibility, a moral obligation, to project the implications of the technological changes initiated by our scientific progress, and to help citizens and their governments shape their practical applications in ways beneficial to all society. This responsibility is most cogently manifest in dealing with nuclear weapons, whose enormous destructive potential leaves so little margin for error."

Reflecting in 2008 on the moral dimensions of nuclear weapons, Drell cited the thoughts of Father Bryan Hehir, a Boston parish priest and professor at Harvard's John F. Kennedy School of Government. Drell was particularly struck by these comments made by Father Hehir at a symposium in 1987: "For millennia people believed, but if anyone had the right to call the ultimate moment of truth, one must name that person God. Since the dawn of the nuclear age we have progressively acquired the capacity to call the ultimate moment of truth and we are not gods. But we must live with what we have created."

Though Drell is not religious, he was drawn to Father Hehir's statement because it addresses the unparalleled power that nuclear weapons place in the hands of the human species. "In the words of a religious person, that power can be simplified and summarized by the word *God*," Drell said. "Father Hehir's comment to me summarizes that we have assumed the power to do something that exceeds anything in our history—we can alter the conditions for existence on this planet. We can destroy our species. That is a profound idea."

To be a player on defense issues, Drell had to make his peace with deterrence theory and practice, the centerpiece of American Cold War nuclear strategy. At its essence, deterrence boiled down to a simple, brutal strategic balance of terror: the United States would maintain a massive nuclear arsenal, ensuring it could retaliate against a Soviet attack with sufficient firepower to destroy the Soviet Union. The policy was called mutual assured destruction, or MAD. At the height of the nuclear arms race in the mid-1980s, Washington and Moscow together had more than seventy thousand nuclear warheads.

In Drell's view, drawing on a 1983 pastoral letter about nuclear weapons issued by the United States Conference of Catholic Bishops, "Deterrence is acceptable not as an end in itself but only as a way of making progress toward getting rid of the weapons."

"I struggled like many people did with the idea of 'How could I accommodate the idea of deterrence?'" Drell said in 2008. "I never accepted the notion that these are weapons to use in war. I always quoted Eisenhower, saying, 'With these weapons, war is no longer the battle until exhaustion and surrender, but it has now become destruction and suicide.' . . . I believed that given the Soviet Empire, its stated goals and existence, we had to deter them. We had to be clear: these are not weapons we want to use, these are not weapons we plan to use, but they have to know that should they monkey around with us, they had to expect that we're going to use them against them. And at a degree that's unacceptable to them. I couldn't do better than that."

During the Cold War, Drell did not challenge Washington's refusal to forswear the first use of nuclear weapons. That position—still American policy today—means that the United States is prepared to strike first with nuclear weapons, rather than committing itself to use the weapons only in self-defense. Intense doctrinal debates over this issue have persisted for decades. Embracing what is known as a No First Use policy would de-emphasize nuclear weapons as the heart of American defense strategy, but opponents fear it would weaken American defense by removing an intimidating threat that may make enemies wary of tangling with Washington. Today, as he campaigns for the abolition of nuclear weapons, Drell is still not prepared to endorse No First Use. But he does say that nuclear weapons should be viewed as "the defense of last resort."

As DRELL, AT Stanford, was deepening his involvement in defense matters in the 1960s, Bill Perry was building advanced defense gadgets a few miles down the Bayshore Freeway in Sunnyvale. As EDL's government work grew, Sylvania promoted Perry to direct the lab division that handled systems-design work and eventually made him the head of EDL. Over time he grew impatient with Sylvania's corporate culture and business strategy and started to brainstorm with colleagues about establishing their own company to do defense work. They would gather periodically at Bill and Lee's home on Charleston Court in Palo Alto. One morning in the den they came up with a name for the company with an abbreviation that sounded a lot like EDL: Electromagnetic Systems Laboratory (ESL). Despite the similarity, or perhaps because of it, Perry told the group that the new company would make no effort to transfer contracts from EDL to ESL. The new firm was founded in January 1964. Its first offices were located in Palo Alto, then later in Sunnyvale. Perry was the chief executive.

Starting a new company to compete with established defense contractors was risky, but Perry and his team filled a vital niche—the collection and processing of electronic intelligence, or ELINT.

Soviet missile telemetry was just one piece. By the mid-1960s, advances in electronics opened up new communication channels, including microwave transmissions. Communication satellites were going into operation and the United States and Soviet Union were investing heavily in new defense communication systems.

Under Perry's leadership, ESL quickly became a highly profitable boutique defense contractor, specializing in exotic ELINT systems. He tapped into a growing stream of government spending on defense and intelligence technologies that helped make Santa Clara County a high-tech defense center, precursor to the growth of Silicon Valley in the same area.

Perry was not a conventional businessman. Gilbert Decker, who worked with Perry at ESL and later succeeded him as CEO, described ESL senior staff meetings.

"You know how staff meetings go. You sit there and argue with each other. Sometimes I would think Bill was sound asleep. He'd let some subject run its course and we'd yell at each other. 'You're full of baloney, you don't know what you're talking about.' And when it had run its course, you would realize he had digested everything he heard. . . . And he would put together a synthesis of what he thought ought to be done. And you'd look at him and you'd say, how the hell did he do that?"

Though little known outside the world of specialized defense contractors, ESL was right at the center of one of the Cold War's biggest intelligence coups—the creation of spy satellites that could vacuum up much of the Soviet Union's communications.

The idea of sweeping up electronic transmissions from a perch in space was alluring but wickedly difficult to accomplish. Airplanes, like those outfitted with eavesdropping gear by EDL, did not fly high enough, and could not stay aloft long enough, to provide a steady steam of data. Satellites orbiting several hundred miles above the earth revolved around the planet too fast to permit more than the momentary collection of electronic signals at any one place.

The solution was to put a spy satellite in orbit high enough that its position over the earth would remain constant. The technical term was geosynchronous orbit—the orbiting speed of the satellite, operating at an altitude of roughly twenty-two thousand miles above the equator, would match the rotation of the earth around its axis, allowing the satellite to stay over the same spot on earth. Bud Wheelon imagined the possibilities one morning in 1963 as he read about the first communications satellite placed in geosynchronous orbit, where it could relay telephone calls from one continent to another, dispensing with the need for transoceanic cables. A spy satellite in similar orbit could pluck off not only telephone calls but also a variety of other electromagnetic signals, including Soviet telemetry data and ground-based radar.

Bill Perry had a similar epiphany not long afterward. "I said, wait a minute. If they can pick up a communications signal in a geosynchronous orbiter, then we can put a telemetry receiver in that. So I went down to visit Pat Hyland, who was president of Hughes, and I said, 'Pat, why don't we put one of our little receivers in your synchronous communications satellite and we'll be able to pick up the telemetry signal one hundred percent of the time.'"

It wasn't that easy. Space was cluttered with electronic signals. Picking out the telemetry signals was like looking for a toothpick in a haystack. It would require a huge antenna, far larger than any previously employed in space, and a new, high-powered signal processor on the ground to separate the telemetry from the other signals.

The dish antennas common on satellites at the time were eight to ten feet in diameter. The new satellite needed a sixty-foot dish that would have to be compressed during launch, then unfurled in space, no easy engineering feat.

Once the antenna was in place, chances were good it would pick up a cacophony of signals coming from nearly a full hemisphere of the earth. Soviet military signals were transmitted at around 70 megahertz, which happened to be the same frequency as two of the main Soviet television channels. Absent a sophisticated system to filter out all the noise, the telemetry signals that Perry wanted to capture would be drowned out by the high-powered television signals. Since a satellite was too small to accommodate an advanced filtering system, the solution was to record all the signals and beam them back to earth, where a processing system could separate out the telemetry signals.

Secret development of the new spy satellite, code-named Rhyolite, turned into one of the most audacious, and successful, technological projects of the Cold War. Perry's new company, ESL, was not nearly big enough to handle most of the work, so TRW served as the prime contractor. ESL developed the critical processing filter design, as well as the antenna. The antenna when fully unfurled was seventy-five feet across yet compact enough when folded up to fit into a rocket nose cone. ESL also served as the system engineers, or technical managers, of the overall project for the government.

ESL handled a variety of other classified government jobs, including devising a plan to automate a series of hilltop listening posts along the border between West Germany and East Germany operated by the U.S. Army Security Agency. ESL then built a similar set of listening posts in Vietnam. In a deal with the National Security Agency, ESL outfitted a fleet of small airplanes with electronic intercept equipment for U.S. Army forces in Europe. Hardware for the system, called Guardrail, was manufactured at a new ESL fabrication plant in Sunnyvale.

The company also played a role in 1965 in assessing the nature of a powerful new Soviet radar installation at the Sary Shagan antimissile test range in Kazakhstan. The ESL team creatively suggested that the radar signal, which the United States was unable to monitor from conventional listening sites, might bounce off the moon and be picked up halfway around the world by the 150-foot radio astronomy telescope at Stanford. The hunch paid off when special ESL receivers at the radio telescope detected the signal, which was more than a million billion times weaker than it was just miles from the transmitter. The radar data helped the CIA determine that the radar, dubbed "Hen House" by the Americans, was one of the most powerful in the world and was part of a new ABM radar network designed to detect and track incoming missiles if war broke out between the United States and Soviet Union.

Perry was active both on the research and marketing sides of the company. "Bill was always a big proponent of maintaining a healthy R & D program, and making sure it was looking at things that we didn't know the solutions to yet," Gil Decker said. "And it was a good lesson, because eventually about half that work really paid off."

By the mid-1970s, ESL had annual revenues of about $100 million, nearly all from classified government projects, and had grown from the small group that had founded it in 1964 to more than 1,800 employees. Perry encouraged initiative, delegated authority, and attracted and retained top engineering talent by giving employees a share of the company. Long before stock options became a hallmark of successful Silicon Valley companies, Perry made his employees fellow owners of ESL.

When he founded ESL, Perry recalled, he had the example of Hewlett-Packard in mind, and its founders David Packard and William Hewlett. "Dave had a motto, he said, 'You don't need an MBA if you have an MBWA.' By that he meant 'management by walking around.' "

As Perry strolled around ESL offices and labs, he discovered that many of the written project reports he received from the staff were not accurate. "Sometimes because the people who wrote them didn't know, sometimes because they didn't want to let me know what was going on," he said. "By walking around, I was talking with the engineers, and manufacturing people. If there was a problem, they knew about it. Moreover, they were only too happy to talk about it. So I quickly learned that part of management by walking around is that a manager's ears are more important than his mouth."

ESL's successful work on highly sensitive defense projects, and Perry's rising reputation as a resourceful defense executive, made him a prime candidate for a top Washington post. The modest mathematician would soon become the nation's most powerful defense technology executive, setting research priorities for hundreds of companies from a Pentagon office.

CHAPTER NINE

The basic motivation was how to prevent nuclear war.
—HENRY KISSINGER

Louis and Paula Kissinger were not contemplating a move to America on May 27, 1923, when Paula gave birth to a son, Heinz Alfred Kissinger, in the Bavarian city of Furth. Louis was a local schoolmaster, Paula the daughter of middle-class cattle traders. The Kissingers were Orthodox Jews, subject to the anti-Semitic restrictions common in Germany at the time. Heinz, as Henry was known during his German childhood, was channeled into Jewish schools and sports teams by prohibitions against Jews attending the best state schools. But as Adolf Hitler and the Nazi Party gained strength and anti-Semitic indignities grew more virulent, Louis Kissinger was driven from his school post. The family fled to New York in 1938, joining the German diaspora in Washington Heights, in northern Manhattan.

Henry Kissinger has long insisted that his turbulent childhood and the anti-Semitism his family encountered in Germany were not major factors in shaping his views. He said, "That part of my childhood was not a key to anything." Kissinger's childhood friends wondered if that was so. Fritz Kraemer, a fellow German who migrated to America and served as Kissinger's mentor in the U.S. Army during the final years of World War II, said, "Kissinger is a strong man, but the Nazis were able to damage his soul. For the formative years of his youth, he faced the horror of his world coming apart, of the father he loved being turned into a helpless mouse. It made him seek order, and it led him to hunger for acceptance, even if it meant trying to please those he considered his intellectual inferiors."

Once resettled in upper Manhattan, Kissinger quickly mastered the American idioms of baseball and advancement through education by attending games at Yankee Stadium and excelling at school. Interestingly, though he seemed in a rush to assimilate, he retained the thick German accent that remains his linguistic hallmark to this day. His brother, Walter, who arrived in America speaking the same native tongue, learned to speak English without a trace of a German accent.

After graduating from George Washington High School, Kissinger enrolled at the City College of New York, an education escalator that thousands of New York kids, many Jewish, rode to successful careers in myriad fields. Kissinger hoped to become an accountant. That plan was short-circuited in early 1943 when he was drafted.

Kissinger's military service made a lasting impression. It exposed him to people and attitudes far different from anything he had experienced in Germany or New York. His fellow GIs came from varied corners of American life, including farming, manufacturing, and mining communities. The Army also offered an immersion in a patriotic cause that granted foreign-born inductees instant citizenship and unimpeachable identification as an American patriot.

By the fall of 1944, Kissinger was on his way to Europe, a member of G Company of the 335th Infantry Regiment. As Allied forces swept across the Western Front in the months after D-day, Kissinger was reassigned to Division Intelligence at the recommendation of his friend and Army patron, Fritz Kraemer. He was later shifted to the Counter-Intelligence Corps, which could make good use of his fluency in German and familiarity with his home-land after Germany surrendered.

In 1945, just seven years after he left Germany, Kissinger assumed the unlikely role of administrator of Krefeld, a Rhine port city. He eventually wound up as the chief of a counterintelligence unit based in Bensheim, not far from Frankfurt. It was a heady time for the young sergeant, whose authority over the area was virtually unlimited. A year later, again at Kraemer's instigation, Kissinger moved to the newly created European Command Intelligence School in Oberammergau in the Bavarian Alps. In 1947, at the age of twenty-four, he returned to the United States as a civilian and was soon admitted to Harvard, which welcomed returning veterans, to resume his studies.

Kissinger found his calling at Harvard as a political theorist and strategic thinker about international affairs, especially nuclear weapons. As with Fritz Kraemer in the Army, Kissinger found a compelling intellectual mentor and sponsor at Harvard in William Elliott, a charismatic professor in the government department. Under Elliott's tutelage, Kissinger produced a tombstone of a senior thesis, a 383-page treatise on political theory, focusing on the works of Immanuel Kant, the nineteenth-century philosopher, and two more contemporary thinkers, Oswald Spengler and Arnold Toynbee. Elliott also helped Kissinger launch the Harvard International Seminar, an annual summer program designed to give a taste of Harvard learning to young people from overseas engaged in government service. For Kissinger, it proved to be fertile ground for networking at Harvard and abroad. As did *Confluence*, a new periodical he founded that published articles by a roster of rising stars in the foreign policy world, including McGeorge Bundy, who became dean of Harvard College and was President Kennedy's national security adviser; Paul Nitze, a defense expert who served as a top official in several administrations; and Walt Rostow, later President Johnson's national security adviser.

Kissinger's doctoral dissertation about two nineteenth-century leaders, Prince Klemens von Metternich of Austria and Britain's Viscount Castlereagh, examined how France under Napoleon challenged the accepted world order at the beginning of that century. As Kissinger drafted the thesis, another outlier nation, the Soviet Union, was challenging the twentieth-century world order. As Walter Isaacson suggests in his biography of Kissinger, Kissinger's reflections on history seemed to have current application and captured Kissinger's own political philosophy. Kissinger wrote, "Whenever peace—conceived as the avoidance of war—has been the primary objective of a power or group of powers, the international system has been at the mercy of the most ruthless member of the international community." He favored a different approach, one that valued "stability based on an equilibrium of forces."

As Kissinger was pondering the concept of legitimacy and international order, his circle of Harvard colleagues was delving into some of the new issues generated by the advent of nuclear weapons. They discussed subjects like how to shape diplomacy in an era of weapons of mass destruction, how to design a nuclear weapons doctrine that would deter the Soviet Union from invading Western Europe or attacking the United States, and how nuclear arms could be controlled to prevent a costly, destabilizing arms race. As Kissinger later recalled, much of the discussion revolved around the Eisenhower administration's defense policies.

"At that time the conventional wisdom at Harvard—which now seems absurd—was that Eisenhower was screwing up our defense by being too soft. . . . The conventional criticism of Eisenhower was that he was too accommodating. And above all that his defense policy was inadequate. That also was what Kennedy was running on in 1960.

"I started getting involved because a seminar was developed at Harvard for faculty and junior faculty on arms control. It wasn't really arms control; that didn't exist then. It was on the implications of modern strategy. And the conventional argument then—we're talking about the early fifties—was that we were not doing enough for air defense. The basic motivation was how to prevent nuclear war. This is from which my thinking evolved."

The seminar led to the formation of an informal discussion association known as the Harvard-MIT Arms Control Group. The group's research papers and conversations formed the basis for a new Cold War field that provided a theoretical, and eventually practical, antidote to the escalation of the American and Soviet nuclear arsenals. Kissinger became an active member of the group, forging friendships with several scholars whom he would later call on for advice when he moved to the White House. Paul Doty, a Harvard physical chemist, was one.

One day, in a chance encounter in Harvard Yard, Arthur Schlesinger Jr., the historian and a Kissinger friend, asked Kissinger to critique a paper he had drafted on nuclear weapons. Schlesinger opposed the concept of massive retaliation, the Eisenhower plan to respond to a Soviet nuclear attack with a blizzard of nuclear weapons. Schlesinger favored a more flexible strategy of limited nuclear strikes, proportionate to the scale of a Soviet attack. Kissinger's critique, which also lamented the reliance on massive retaliation, was published in *Foreign Affairs*, the periodical of the Council on Foreign Relations. That, in turn, led to an invitation from the council to serve as staff director of an upcoming council study of nuclear weapons strategy that would culminate in a book to be written by the staff director.

The role immersed Kissinger in the world of nuclear weapons and put him in close touch with the financiers, businessmen, and other power brokers who populated the CFR. Kissinger could demonstrate his formidable intellectual powers to a world beyond the academy and Cambridge while simultaneously getting to know the members of the foreign policy establishment. It was, in short, an ideal springboard to the halls of power.

Kissinger did not squander the opportunity. He split the high-powered study group into two sections, making him the focal point of the project. The result, thanks largely to Kissinger's analytical powers, was a blockbuster book published in 1957, *Nuclear Weapons and Foreign Policy*. Not that anyone, including Kissinger, expected it to be a popular success. The densely written, 450-page book championed the idea of limited nuclear war and the need for the United States to prepare to use nuclear weapons in limited conflicts rather than planning only for an all-out nuclear exchange. "Given the power of modern weapons," he said, "it should be the task of our strategic doctrine to create alternatives less cataclysmic than a thermonuclear holocaust."

Despite the sober subject and thick prose, the book became a bestseller. And Kissinger became a star. The *New York Times* featured the book in a front-page article that reported, "For the first time since President Eisenhower took office, officials at the highest Government levels are displaying interest in the theory of 'little' or 'limited' war. The lead in the debate has been taken not by anyone connected with Government, but by a scholar of foreign affairs, Henry A. Kissinger, in his recently published book."

While Kissinger was far from the only scholar or military strategist at the time to challenge the policy of massive retaliation, his book helped popularize the notion of more limited warfare. More important, the book helped lay the groundwork for John Kennedy and his defense secretary, Robert McNamara, to try to replace the Eisenhower-era strategy with a more graduated war plan known as flexible response.

Kissinger himself came to doubt the feasibility of limiting a nuclear war with the Soviet Union. "That was sort of an attractive alternative until you started studying how you would go about limiting it and how you would go about having the other side understand what you were trying to do without getting into an escalation that got out of control," he said.

Kissinger served briefly as an outside adviser to President Kennedy, but their foreign policy views were not in alignment. About this time—in late 1961—Kissinger was introduced to Sid Drell at a dinner party in Israel. It was the beginning of an on-again, off-again friendship that endured despite myriad political and policy disagreements. A few years later, the two men would find themselves meeting monthly in the White House Situation Room, dealing with critical defense issues.

CHAPTER TEN

I'm wondering, where's Patton, and rushed over to where I thought
he went and said, "Where the hell is Patton?" "Patton's dead, sir."
—GEORGE SHULTZ

George Shultz made his Washington debut in 1955 as a
young staff economist on President Eisenhower's Council
of Economic Advisers, setting up shop in a plum office overlooking the White House South Lawn. He quickly got a taste of the
nuclear threats facing Washington when he took part in air raid
drills to prepare for the possibility of a surprise Soviet attack. Decades later, he still remembered President Eisenhower's admoni-
tion to the White House staff that the most carefully constructed
plans would quickly dissolve if war came. "He said, 'You're taking
part in a plan. But if something happens, remember the plan is
worthless. What's important is the planning process. And when
things happen, they never happen exactly the way you thought, so
your mentality has to be one of shifting. That's why planning and
looking at alternatives is so important.' It was a very interesting
statement coming from an experienced general."

Unlike Bill Perry, Henry Kissinger, and Sid Drell, Shultz did
not follow a national security road to Washington. His career was
grounded in labor economics and the academic study of it. That
was natural, given his father's expertise in the workings of Wall
Street.

George Pratt Shultz was born in midtown Manhattan on December 13, 1920. His father, Birl, grew up on an Indiana farm, one of seven children. Raised as a Quaker, Birl was the first member of his family to attend college. As far as George Shultz knows, the first Shultz in his line to come to America was a German mercenary who fought alongside the British in the Revolutionary War, was captured, and decided to settle in the United States after the war, probably in Pennsylvania. Birl was a scholarship student at DePauw University, and helped pay his expenses by working tables and doing other odd jobs at the Indiana school, a forty-five-minute drive west of Indianapolis. He played football for DePauw, setting an example George would follow, and then moved on to Columbia University as a Ph.D. candidate in history. Birl turned his dissertation on legislative history into a book that was coauthored by Charles A. Beard, one of Columbia's top historians. He seemed keen to become a history professor, but took a detour to Wall Street after completing his graduate work and settled there for several decades before accepting an appointment to the Columbia faculty. (After Birl's death in 1955, Shultz found numerous unpublished papers on the Dred Scott decision in the family attic.) "When I wound up teaching in the university, he was pleased by that, because that is something he wanted to do," Shultz said.

Birl Shultz made a comfortable but not lavish living as a student of the stock market. He wasn't a stockbroker or investment banker, but rather an educator about the securities markets. In 1922 he founded the New York Stock Exchange Institute (now known as the New York Institute of Finance). The institute started as a training center for Wall Street clerks and other support staff and expanded to become a leading education program for Wall Street traders, investment managers, and other financial workers. In 1942 he published *The Securities Market and How It Works*.

George's mother, Margaret Pratt, was the only child of a Presbyterian minister who moved west with his wife and established a church in Shoshone, Idaho. When the couple died, Margaret, age four, moved to New York, where she would spend the rest of her childhood with her uncle, George Pratt, an Episcopalian minister, and his wife, Margaret. The younger Margaret met Birl Shultz when he was a graduate student at Columbia. They married sometime around 1918. Birl, the Quaker, accommodated Margaret, an Episcopalian, by attending church services, and George was confirmed, but his father "was not enthusiastic" about the elaborate church services.

He was an only child—an older brother died at an early age. When George was still a toddler, the family moved from Manhattan to more spacious but still modest quarters in Englewood, New Jersey, just across the Hudson River from Manhattan.

Shultz attended the Englewood School for Boys, but midway through high school his parents decided he ought to spend his last two years at a boarding school and he was admitted to Loomis (now Loomis Chafee) in Windsor, Connecticut. George played football and basketball at Loomis and developed an affinity for tennis.

Though naturally competitive, he got a jolt on the tennis court one day from Frank Boyden, the longtime headmaster at Deerfield Academy, a Loomis rival. He recalled the scene: "I was playing against this guy from Deerfield, and I had him on the ropes. I was beating him. And so the headmaster comes by and watches for a while and he said something to me between changing sides. Trying to be pleasant, I said, 'Well, it's a good competitor you have over there.' He looked at me and said, 'You'll never win with an attitude like that.' And he walked away. Boy, do I remember that comment."

When the time came to apply to college in 1937, Shultz looked to Princeton "because it's in my backyard and my closest friend's father went to Princeton." Shultz was admitted, as was his friend Norman Cook, and they roomed together for four years. He loved Princeton—he is coy about whether he has a tiger tattoo on his butt to prove it—pursuing a growing interest in economics and football. He became a member of Quadrangle, one of Princeton's eating clubs. It was not one of the tonier clubs, reflecting Shultz's lack of aristocratic pedigree, but like Sid Drell, who attended Princeton a few years later, he didn't seem to mind Princeton's stratified social world. Quadrangle members tended to be more liberal than other Princeton students, but Shultz wasn't especially political, spending much of his time studying.

John Brooks, a Shultz roommate who went on to become a successful author and New Yorker contributor, told an interviewer in 1982: "Maybe he's brilliant now. He wasn't then. He had a steady, plodding intellect. We used to have endless discussions. Norman Cook and I would say sort of half-baked, wisecrack things and he would think a long time and take them very seriously."

Shultz found fellowship and spirited competition on the football team. His teammates called him "Dutch," after the Chicago gangster Dutch Schultz. Shultz played offense and defense, not uncommon in those days, as a blocking back and a linebacker. A few years ago he told attendees at a black-tie dinner in New York about the college game he knew and loved: No coaching from the sidelines, playing both offense and defense, the quarterback calls the plays on his own. "In this game," he said, "eleven guys on the field play eleven other guys on the field. That's football. That does not resemble what is called football today, where two organizations play against each other and the plays are called by some guy up in the press box with binoculars."

His gridiron ambitions were derailed by a knee injury his senior year. As a consolation, he was invited to serve as backfield coach for the freshman team. It proved to be an important experience. "Somehow it dawned on me that it wasn't about teaching, it was about learning. And so the job of a good teacher is to arrange it so that the people who are there, learn. You haven't taught anything if you lecture people and they didn't get it." The realization became the bedrock of a leadership style that has served Shultz well. He said, "If you can create an atmosphere around you where every-body there is learning, you're going to have a hot group. People love to learn. You're going to have to send them home at night. That's not usual, I discovered. Most people running things think that they should know everything and tell people what to do."

Shultz discovered another insight into human nature—and economic data—over the summer between his junior and senior years when he did field research for his senior thesis about the agricultural program administered by the Tennessee Valley Authority (TVA). The Roosevelt administration created the resource management agency in 1933 to develop electric power and work on flood control, malaria prevention, and other programs in the impoverished Tennessee River Valley region. Shultz spent a few weeks in Washington collecting data about the agricultural program before traveling to the TVA headquarters in Knoxville, Tennessee. From there he headed into the hills to spend two weeks living with a farm family.

"They had zero education," he said. "It gradually dawned on me they were smart as they could be. And they understood. And I somehow realized that the way to get to know them was to say nothing. . . . If you can be quiet and listen, gradually they accept you, which they did."

When they asked Shultz to help them fill out application forms for government aid, he saw they were slanting the information they provided so it would satisfy government requirements.

He recalled, "I got back to Princeton and I got all my stuff, and it dawns on me: all the statistics that I gathered were summations of reports like the ones that we filled out. So they weren't telling you the right story. And ever since then, whenever I look at a number, I say, where does this number come from?"

Shultz graduated cum laude in 1942, six months after the Japanese attack on Pearl Harbor and America's entry into the war. He was eager to join the fight. Impressed by the courageous performance of British and Polish pilots fending off German aerial attacks during the Battle of Britain, Shultz tried to enlist in the Royal Canadian Air Force, hoping to help defend Britain. He failed the eye test, and uncertain when and how he could become involved in the war, he applied to the Ph.D. program in industrial economics at MIT and was admitted. Then he put off enrollment to join the Marines, which were not deterred by his poor eyesight.

Curiously, Shultz makes only the briefest mention of his wartime service in the autobiographical chapter of his memoirs about his service as secretary of state. He reports only that he joined the Marines as American units in the Pacific were beginning to overcome Japanese forces at Guadalcanal, that he went through boot camp at Quantico, Virginia, and got artillery training in New River, North Carolina. "By April 1943, I was in Samoa, then on to a couple of battles in the Pacific islands." That's all he has to say about his military service.

The brevity is odd both because he served with distinction in several battles and because combat helped shape his character in ways that influenced his conduct as secretary of state and have a bearing on his present effort to abolish nuclear weapons.

Once he completed training, Shultz and his antiaircraft battalion, the 7th Defense Battalion, were shipped out to Western Samoa. From there they headed temporarily to Funafuti, an atoll that today serves as the capital of the island nation of Tuvalu. As American forces were arrayed in the area to launch an attack against entrenched Japanese soldiers on Tarawa, Shultz's unit was dispatched to Nonomea, a nearby island. Their assignment: take the island and secure it so that it could be used as an airfield for handling troops wounded during the invasion of Tarawa, which turned out to be one of the fiercest battles of the war.

The next combat zone for Shultz was the invasion of Palau, another bloody battle. He served as a beachmaster for invading American forces at Angaur, a volcanic dot that is part of the

Palauan Islands. On September 17, 1944, the 81st Infantry Division landed on the island, accompanied by Shultz's 7th Marine Defense Battalion. Shultz's job was to direct supplies and troops as they landed on the beach. It proved to be a lesson in taking command.

"I went in about the second wave into the landing in Angaur. It had this landing beach and there were cliffs on the other side of it. By the time I got there, everything was stalled because there were Japanese in caves beside the beach and they were taking potshots at our guys in the beach. . . . I remember just sort of telling people what to do. Go here, do that. And they did it. And we finally made headway in getting the Japanese out of the caves."

At some point in the invasion, Shultz looked for one of his most reliable compatriots, Sergeant Patton. He recalled the moment: "I'm in very active combat mode, and I had a wonderful sergeant named Patton, was a terrific guy. And you become close to people in these kinds of things, very close. He's a fine person and smart, and he was one of these guys that could do things, could get people to do things. So I relied on him a lot. And things are going and I'm wondering, where's Patton, and rushed over to where I thought he went and said, 'Where the hell is Patton?' 'Patton's dead, sir.'

"So the reality of war sinks in. I will never forget that moment. Because it says to you when you're secretary of state or you're part of making decisions about sending people into combat, that you'd better be careful and have a good mission that can be accomplished. Because people are going to get killed, and you owe it to them to look at it that way."

Shultz applied another piece of military experience to his service as secretary of state, one that Ronald Reagan incorporated into his own thinking. When Shultz went to Marine boot camp, he recalled, the sergeant who first handed him a rifle told him, "This is your best friend. Take good care of this rifle. And remember one thing, never point this rifle at anybody unless you're willing to pull the trigger. No empty threats."

Reagan liked the story. "I can remember times in the Situation Room," Shultz said, "where we would be talking about something that might happen and people were saying we should say it's not acceptable. I would get the president to stop and say, 'Well, okay. Suppose it happens and we've said it's unacceptable. Then what are we going to do? Let's decide now we're going to do something. What is it? If the answer is, we're not going to do anything, then let's not say it in the first place. No empty threats.' I think one of our problems in our diplomacy right now and in the world diplomacy, for that matter, is that words don't mean very much."

Shultz, by now a captain, was on his way back to San Diego to muster for the invasion of Japan when the atomic bombings of Hiroshima and Nagasaki brought the war to an end. He was reassigned to a post at the Boston Navy Yard. It had been three years since MIT had invited him to do graduate studies in economics. When he showed up at the Cambridge campus to say he was ready to enroll, a grumpy MIT official berated him for relying on the GI Bill to pay for his education. Shultz brushed off the sour lecture and started taking economics classes, including one taught by Paul Samuelson, who went on to win a Nobel Prize in the field.

He also attended public lectures about atomic weapons, curious to know about the science that had produced the new bombs. In retrospect, he realized the physicists and other scientists were not infallible.

"Physics, of course, was riding high," he recalled. "Physicists were gods and something called nuclear things were what everybody wanted to know. So whenever one of the physicists would give a public lecture, I'd always go and try to learn what I could about it. And among the things I learned is, these guys are smart as hell but they don't know everything about their subject. Because they were testing in the atmosphere and we all watched the test at Enewetak and the big mushroom cloud goes up. And then you learn, this is insane to be putting that kind of radioactivity in the air."

One thing Shultz was sure about was that he had found the right woman to marry. Helena O'Brien, or O'Bie as he called her, was a nurse in Hawaii when they met during the war as his unit was taking a break. She joined him in Boston after the war, and they married between MIT semesters in early 1946. A daughter, Margaret, the first of five children, was born in Concord, Massachusetts, in May 1947. They were an exceptionally happy and romantic couple until her death at age eighty in 1995. A thoughtful, modest, and warm woman, she traveled with Shultz on many of his foreign trips as secretary of state and always seemed to pick up his spirits after a hard day of diplomacy. Unlike many high-level men in government, Shultz made clear to colleagues that his wife was an indispensable part of his life. In 1981, when Shultz flew to Washington from London, where he had been visiting when Reagan invited him to become secretary of state, two government cars awaited him at Dulles Airport, one to take him to the White House, the other to take O'Bie wherever she wished to go. Shultz dismissed the second car, saying, "No, she'll come with me. We're a package deal."

Shultz completed his Ph.D. in 1949 and accepted an offer to join the MIT faculty. As a rising labor economist, he served on a number of arbitration panels, quickly gaining a reputation as an unflappable and effective negotiator, a skill that would serve him well in later years. He also heard about the work of a brainy young faculty member just up the Charles River at Harvard. "I would read these things that a guy named Kissinger said," he recalled. "He took on the big themes. Mostly when people take on the big themes, it's BS. But when Henry spoke there was a cutting edge to it. There was something special, so I always read whatever he put forward."

In 1955, the Shultzes moved to Washington so he could take the staff post at the Council of Economic Advisers, which was headed by Arthur Burns. Shultz described the move in his memoirs: "In the Nation's Service, the Princeton motto, was a favorite of my father's. He was never more thrilled than when I was appointed to the President's Council of Economic Advisers. When my family and I drove down to Washington, where I would begin that service, my mother and father drove down too, forming a little caravan of sorts. My father saw my office in the Executive Office Building, right next to the White House, and he beamed. Later that year he died. 'Whatever you do,' he told me, 'do what you think is right for you. Somehow, the material side of life will take care of itself.' I have always followed that advice."

When the University of Chicago Business School was looking for a labor economist, it offered the faculty post to Shultz. Professor James Lorie, a member of the search committee, asked Albert Rees, a labor economist, to help him identify the right person for the job. Lorie recalled, "I asked Al Rees to name the outstanding man in America in labor economics, someone who was senior but not old, and he said that man was George Shultz." Shultz took the Chicago post in 1957. Five years later he became dean of the business school.

It was a great training ground for the cabinet jobs to come. "I had to create an environment conducive to learning but could not order students to learn," he recalled in his memoirs. "I worked with faculty members who could be prima donnas (which was all right if they could sing), and who could become difficult when brought together in a meeting, somewhat like a congressional committee. . . . I had responsibility for the health of the organization, but my only real authority came from my persuasive powers. I learned early on that I must be able to persuade if I was going to be effective."

Handling the University of Chicago faculty would seem like child's play just a few years later when Shultz reported for duty in the Nixon administration and found himself on a cutthroat team that included Henry Kissinger and Nixon henchmen H. R. Haldeman and John Ehrlichman.

CHAPTER ELEVEN

*I knew that if I ever had a chance, I was going to go back
to Washington in some capacity.*
—SAM NUNN

In retrospect, Sam Nunn's life in politics seems almost preordained. He was to the congressional cloakroom born. Nunn's mentor was Carl Vinson, his great-uncle and fellow Georgian. Vinson served for years as chairman of the House Armed Services Committee, one of the most powerful posts in Congress. "Uncle Carl," as Nunn called Vinson, gave the young Georgian his introduction to Washington and inspired his lifelong interest in military affairs.

Samuel Augustus Nunn Jr. was born in Macon, Georgia, on September 8, 1938. His father practiced law for more than fifty years in Perry, at the time a small town of five thousand people in central Georgia. He also managed the family farm, raising purebred horned Herefords and growing an assortment of crops, including pecans, peanuts, soybeans, corn, and cotton. He was chairman of the Perry Federal Savings and Loan Association and a force in local and state politics, serving in the Georgia legislature, on the state board of education, and as mayor of Perry from 1938 to 1946. Sam Senior married Elizabeth Cannon from Cordele, Georgia, not far from Perry, in 1935. She was fifteen years younger than the groom. Elizabeth, a schoolteacher, was described by a local newspaper as "a most attractive and popular lady." Elizabeth was a graduate of Georgia State College for Women in Milledgeville.

Sam Senior earned his law degree by attending evening classes while supporting himself with a day job at a drugstore. He loved to read. "My father had a great influence on me," Nunn told an interviewer in 1983. "He was 47 when he got married and 51 when I was born. I remember him as an older man . . . it was not one of those relationships of going hunting with your father or playing sports with your father."

Sam Senior's passion for reading was evident when World War I ended. Nunn, who fought in Europe as a second lieutenant in the 82nd Division, decided to stay on after the armistice for a year to study economics and law at the University of Toulouse.

Though a Democrat, he grew disillusioned with Franklin Roosevelt and the New Deal. A tribute to Sam Senior prepared by friends in Perry when he died in 1965 reported: "In the early thirties he made a strong appeal in many addresses to civic clubs and political groups for the American people to begin to think seriously so as to become aware of and to stop the drift of government toward socialism and dictatorship." Sam Junior said his father was deeply disturbed by Roosevelt's failed scheme to expand the Supreme Court to fifteen justices to make it more amenable to his policies.

Sam Junior grew up in Perry. The town, a hundred miles south of Atlanta, grandly calls itself the "Crossroads of Georgia." It was a provincial community during Nunn's childhood, with all the mores of southern life, including rigid racial segregation and simmering racial tensions. Nunn was smart, studious, ambitious, and fiercely competitive. Despite a bookish demeanor, he was a gifted athlete who easily made friends. He was an avid Eagle Scout and excelled academically at the all-white high school and on the basketball court. The basketball team was a state powerhouse. Nunn, a small but nimble right-handed guard, led the Panthers to the 1956 state championship in its division, scoring twenty-seven points in the championship game. "Red–hot Sam Nunn erupted like Mt. Vesuvius from all angles," the *Atlanta Journal-Constitution* exclaimed the next day.

"He was a tremendous rebounder for his size," Eric Staples, the coach, recalled. "One of those who always seemed to know where the ball would be, a good shooter, ball handler and defender. Sam was one of the greatest competitors I ever coached."

Nunn was a shy but dedicated student from the start. His fifth-grade teacher, Dorothy Ayers, said, "He really knew what was going on because he was an avid reader. If he thought he was correct, and he was very fair in his thinking, he wouldn't give up or let anyone influence his thinking. Like his late father, he was kind, thoughtful, calm, not fiery."

He was a reluctant public speaker. "He said he'd be afraid to get up in front of people and talk," recalled Florence Harrison, who taught English and Speech at Perry High School. To ease his anxiety, she suggested Nunn devote his first appearance in speech class to a demonstration of golf. "He asked if he could be first he was so nervous. He also asked how long he had to speak. I said about two minutes. There were so many questions, he just forgot himself and was still going strong 25 minutes after he started, all without notes."

Nunn headed to the Georgia Institute of Technology in Atlanta, hoping to play big-time college basketball and enroll in the Naval ROTC program. Despite leading the freshman squad in rebounding and finishing second in scoring, he was not offered a basketball scholarship. He quit the program and went on to play competitive college golf. "If I had been six-foot-four or six-foot-five, I probably would never have been in politics. . . . I think I would have been on the bench in some minor basketball league," Nunn told an interviewer in 1983.

He flunked the Navy eye test, enrolled in Army ROTC, and served for the required two years. After three years at Georgia Tech, he joined the Coast Guard in June 1959 and spent the next

six months training and then teaching recruits. When he left the
Coast Guard, he enrolled at Emory University Law School in Atlanta. He collected a bachelor of arts in law in 1961, and thanks to
law school credits he earned during his senior year, he graduated
from Emory Law School a year later.

As Nunn was completing law school, Uncle Carl suggested he
come to Washington to work for a spell on Capitol Hill. Vinson's
advice carried weight. "I followed his career from about the time
I was in the eighth grade. I read everything that I could get my
hands on that he was involved in," Nunn said. Vinson offered
him a temporary staff job on the Subcommittee for Special Investigations of the House Armed Services Committee—after John
J. Courtney, a seasoned Vinson aide, vetted the young lawyer.
"Uncle Carl actually sent him down to interview my law school
professors before he would hire me. He was very conscious of the
nepotism business. And he said I had to pass the bar."

Nunn's nine-month stint on Capitol Hill was an intoxicating
introduction to Congress and the attractions of working in Washington. The capital was a world apart from the small-town ambi-
ence of Perry. He told his parents: "I have a great opportunity here
at my job. Mr. Courtney is one of the top administrative lawyers
in the Washington area. I am also being exposed to, and have
access to, most of the inside information concerning our defense
today. (I have to be cleared for top-secret classification.) I also have
an opportunity to read and study about the workings of the Congress. I intend to take advantage of these opportunities."

Nunn treated the job very seriously, quickly abandoning a noisy
group house and settling into his own apartment so he could concentrate on his work. "I like the boys I'm now living with, but its
[sic] just like living in a fraternity house, so far as getting anything
done," he wrote his parents. "There is always something to do and
somewhere they want me to go, and its always too noisy even to
read a newspaper."

The 1962 Cuban Missile Crisis was Sam Nunn's nuclear baptism. He was touring Europe with a group of fellow congressional aides as the showdown escalated. They all had security clearances and were briefed by American military commanders at the height of the crisis, with American and NATO forces set to strike the Soviet Union if war broke out. The tension, and possibility of nuclear conflict, stunned Nunn, who was twenty-four years old.

More than four decades later, Nunn still vividly recalled the crisis. He said an Air Force general at Ramstein Air Base in West Germany informed the group that he had less than a minute to get his combat aircraft launched so they would be out of harm's way if the base, as expected, came under attack in the first moments of a war. The jet fighters were assigned one-way missions to deliver nuclear weapons to targets in the Soviet Union. (The planes lacked the range to fly back.) To ensure that the planes could take off quickly, pilots were ordered on several evenings during the crisis to stand by in their aircraft.

"That made a huge impression on me," Nunn said. "I decided at that stage if I ever had a chance to get into public life, I would. I didn't know what capacity at that stage. And if I ever had a chance to try to do something to reduce nuclear dangers, I would, because I felt mankind was really at stake then. The future of mankind. So that was a formative experience for me."

During the summer of 1962, several months before the Cuban Missile Crisis, Vinson invited Nunn to stroll across the Capitol with him to the Senate side. "Uncle Carl was going over to make a presentation before the Senate Armed Services Committee," Nunn said. He sat behind Vinson as the congressman addressed Senator Richard Russell, a fellow Georgian who was chairman of the Senate committee. "I recognized pretty clearly that Georgia had substantial power at that stage in my career," Nunn said. "So my ambition was to be a member of the House."

Before Nunn left Washington, Courtney handed him a stack

of magazines dealing with domestic and foreign issues, including nuclear weapons. "He was sort of a hawk on defense issues, but very liberal on social issues. And so he gave me a whole wide array of reading materials and—I don't even remember what all of them were, but I took every one of the magazines and read all that stuff."

Nunn returned to Georgia in 1963, determined to get back to Washington someday. "It had a big effect on me. I knew that if I ever had a chance, I was going to go back to Washington in some capacity," he recalled.

Perry must have seemed a sleepy place after Capitol Hill. But on the advice of family friends, including Herman Talmadge, a former Georgia governor then serving as a United States senator, Nunn headed home. Talmadge advised him to settle down in Perry, practice law with his father, and run for election to the Georgia legislature. "I didn't tell him he'd be in the United States Senate in 10 years," Talmadge recalled.

The advice was sound, but Nunn remained ambivalent. "I really wanted to be in Washington," he said. But his father was ill, his mother needed his help, and there was family pressure to take over financial management of the farm.

Nunn joined his father's law firm, helped supervise the farm work, established his own law firm, joined the Perry Chamber of Commerce, and launched the political career that would propel him to the United States Senate. He married Colleen O'Brien, a young CIA employee he had met in Paris while traveling abroad during the Missile Crisis. O'Brien, who grew up in Olympia, Washington, was a graduate of Washington State University. A cheerleader with a knack for foreign languages, she had studied French and joined the CIA after college.

Perry in the mid-1960s was unsettled by racial tensions. The civil rights movement was rippling across the South. Many communities, including Americus, Georgia, not far from Perry, were convulsed by violence as the ruling white establishment fought to preserve segregation.

Nunn was a creature of his culture, accustomed to and uncomplaining about segregation, taking it as a given as he grew up as a member of the white aristocracy of Perry, attending all-white schools, worshipping at an all-white church, socializing only with whites. "My father would have done anything for the black people that worked for him," Nunn said. "But he did believe in segregation. That was the era of segregation. So that was the atmosphere I grew up in, but the N-word was never uttered by my father or my mother. They were not in that vein at all."

Nunn awoke to the inequities of segregation one day in the early 1960s when he was driving a black client across the state to a court hearing. "I took him because he didn't have a car. And I remember, he had to go to the bathroom, and we stopped. He couldn't go anyplace to the bathroom. And I said, good grief. It's been going on for years and it just hadn't crystallized in my own mind . . . it should have dawned on me a lot earlier, but it didn't. And so I said, this is intolerable."

The unfairness was underscored by a white client, an elderly man called Doc Bellflower. When Nunn told him about the bathroom episode, Bellflower sighed. "I don't believe in integration," he told Nunn, "but this whole thing is unfair. I've got a little restaurant over there and I let black people come in there. I have for the last ten years. They don't have nowhere to eat. It's ridiculous."

As racial strains in Perry grew and other towns were rocked by bloody confrontations between white policemen and peaceful black demonstrators, Nunn realized that the economic stability and growth prospects for Perry could be shattered if the town became a civil rights battleground. "From a pragmatic point of view, I concluded that Perry was about to explode. We had some people who were hotheads; we had some people who really were almost emotionally unbalanced on the subject of the racial protests and all the things going on."

In 1965 the Perry City Council imposed a curfew after blacks and whites nearly came to blows near the town center, and Richard Ray, the mayor, announced that he would establish a biracial committee to ease tensions. Members of the all-white council angrily denounced Ray's plan. One member moved to impeach Ray. Nunn, by then president of the Chamber of Commerce, supported Ray. Ray recalled the scene: "The only person who stood up to be counted was Sam Nunn, who pledged his support to the easing of critical racial tension. Without this support at this critical time, the bi-racial committee would have failed. . . . If this situation had not been resolved, much of the new industry and progress destined to locate in Perry would not be here today."

The committee met in Nunn's law office several times. The black committee members were not militant. "They basically weren't demanding to go to the white churches," Nunn said. "They weren't demanding to do this and that. They weren't even that concerned about school. They just wanted a fair shake. I realized that they were not the outside agitators that everybody was talking about. These are homegrown, good people. They wanted their roads paved. They wanted the schools. . . . I agreed with everything they wanted. It wasn't a big 'let's integrate everything now.' They wanted basic fairness."

With Mayor Ray's leadership and Nunn's help, Perry remained calm and slowly worked its way toward desegregation.

In 1968, with his reputation growing in Perry, Nunn ran successfully for a seat in the Georgia legislature. The election seemed a natural prelude to a congressional race, especially if the Third Congressional District could be redrawn to create a middle Georgia seat, moving the district's center of gravity toward Perry and away from Columbus, on the Alabama border. As a member of the Georgia House reapportionment committee, Nunn managed to get a reconfigured district approved by the House, but Governor Jimmy Carter opposed the plan and it died in the state senate. That left Nunn with the unattractive prospect of trying to unseat a popular Democratic incumbent, Jack Brinkley.

Then Richard Russell unexpectedly died in early 1971. Carter named David Gambrell, a lawyer and chairman of the Georgia Democratic Party, to the seat, pending an election the following year. Nunn saw the developments as his ticket back to Washington. It was an audacious calculation. He was just thirty-three, had served only a single full term in the Georgia legislature, was largely unknown outside the Perry area, and lacked a clear political agenda. Compared to Russell, a powerful committee chairman who had served in the Senate for nearly forty years, Nunn seemed to be a political pipsqueak. Uncle Carl told Nunn he was a "damn fool" to gun for the Senate seat instead of aiming first for the House. Ed Beckham, one of Nunn's closest friends and a teammate on the 1956 championship basketball squad, recalled folks in Perry saying, "Good gracious, what in the world? Has he lost his mind?"

Nunn figured he might as well go for broke and see if he could make the move to Washington in one leap rather than slowly working his way up the ladder. "I decided I either had to get in or out. And I thought the best way to do that was to run for the Senate and see what happens," he said. "I would rather run and be defeated, knowing that I had given it a try, than not run and sit back the rest of my life wondering what would have happened."

Nunn's primary campaign got off to a feeble start. No Atlanta reporters showed up in Perry the day he announced his candidacy, even though Nunn had hired a bus equipped with a hard-liquor bar to transport journalists from Atlanta to Perry. The primary field was crowded with more than a dozen contenders, but Nunn managed to win enough votes to get into a runoff with Gambrell.

The runoff campaign was vituperative, with Nunn trying to position himself as a man of the people, depicting Gambrell as a Harvard-educated elitist. Gambrell called Nunn an ineffectual state legislator. Nunn fired back, "I'm really worried about David's health. He is working harder than a Harvard man is accustomed to. I think he's been out in the sun too long . . . a contest to see if a poor Georgia educated boy can keep up with a Harvard graduate. It's going to be the state of Georgia versus the Ivy League." The two candidates held a series of televised debates, which raised Nunn's visibility. He handily defeated Gambrell to win the Democratic nomination, making him the second youngest Senate candidate in the nation.

Winning the general election, even in a predominantly Democratic state like Georgia in 1972, promised to be a challenge with Senator George McGovern, a liberal lawmaker, atop the national Democratic ticket. Richard Nixon was the Republican nominee, running for a second term in the White House. He was expected to run strongly in the South. Nunn's opponent, Fletcher Thompson, a conservative Republican, hammered away at the McGovern connection. Nunn railed against court-ordered busing schemes designed to integrate schools and called for a constitutional amendment that would require federal judges to face voters every six years. Echoing his father's warnings in the 1930s about the threat of tyranny, Nunn told Georgians his proposal would "end the dictatorship created by the lifetime tenure of federal judges."

In a move that he seems defensive about today, Nunn traveled to Montgomery, Alabama, to receive the endorsement of George Wallace. At the time, Wallace was a conservative martyr. After famously defying federal school integration orders as governor of Alabama, Wallace had launched surprisingly effective runs for the 1968 and 1972 Democratic presidential nomination. He cast himself as a populist, playing on the prejudices and grievances of white, blue-collar workers in the Rust Belt unsettled by economic problems and social unrest. He placed second in the 1972 Wisconsin primary and was rising rapidly in the polls when an assassin, Arthur Bremer, gunned

him down in a Laurel, Maryland, parking lot on May 15. The attack
left him paralyzed in both legs. The day after the shooting, Wallace won the Democratic primaries in Maryland and Michigan. He
dropped out of the race to heal his wounds.

The Wallace that Nunn wrapped himself around was still a
symbol of southern resistance to desegregation even though he had
broadened his appeal and proved popular with disaffected northern
voters. Nunn recalls his trip to Montgomery as a populist statement, not racial politics. On that day in Montgomery, he declared,
"George Wallace represents the real views of Georgians." It's hard
not to see the language as code words for an appeal to white Georgians unsettled by desegregation and as a way of separating himself
from the liberal Democratic national ticket. To be fair to Nunn,
his record on civil rights in Perry was constructive and he was endorsed by a number of black leaders, including Coretta Scott King,
Martin Luther King's widow; Julian Bond, a Georgia state representative and civil rights leader who would later serve as chairman of the National Association for the Advancement of Colored
People (NAACP); and Georgia state senator LeRoy Johnson.

When asked in 2010 what one should make of the Wallace
endorsement, he compared his trip to Montgomery to visits by
Jimmy Carter and Ted Kennedy after the assassination attempt on
Wallace. He said the visit was partly designed to counteract the
defection of Lester Maddox, a former Georgia governor and ardent
segregationist, who had initially supported Nunn but later worked
to elect Fletcher Thompson.

To spotlight his Washington connections, Nunn enlisted Carl
Vinson, who had retired from the House in 1965, to accompany
him to Capitol Hill during the fall campaign. The goal was to
secure promises from Senate leaders that, if elected, Nunn would
get a seat on the Armed Services Committee. Vinson was eighty-
eight but gamely took the overnight train to Washington with
Nunn. The two men met with several Senate barons, including

John Stennis and Russell Long. The ploy worked. It was another audacious move, putting Georgians on notice that Nunn, unlike Thompson, could ensure a continuation of robust funding for the state's numerous military bases and defense contractors. Nunn easily won the election with 54 percent of the vote. He pressed Mike Mansfield, the Senate majority leader, to deliver on Nunn's campaign pledge about the Armed Services Committee, and got the coveted seat.

PART III

Manning America's Nuclear Arsenal

CHAPTER TWELVE

What does that candyass think we sent him over there for?
—RICHARD NIXON

Richard Nixon's inauguration as president in 1969 marked the beginning of a twenty-seven-year period when Henry Kissinger, George Shultz, Bill Perry, and Sam Nunn, either individually or in some combination, worked in the wheelhouse of America's nuclear weapons. As they traded power back and forth across Republican and Democratic administrations, each of the men left a distinctive mark on nuclear weapons policy.

Throughout the period, Sid Drell exercised his own, considerable influence as a scientific adviser to the White House, the Congress, and the Central Intelligence Agency. Shultz's prime time on nuclear policy came during the Reagan presidency, but he got an early taste of Washington's brutish politics while working for Nixon. The experience steeled him for the intramural combat he encountered later as secretary of state as he battled for control of nuclear weapons policy and relations with the Soviet Union. He also got to know Henry Kissinger, a fellow cabinet member.

George Shultz and Richard Nixon were an odd pair. Nixon was a political knife fighter convinced that the Ivy League–educated elite was his enemy. Shultz was a member of that elite, a pipe-smoking intellectual who believed deeply in the rule of law and the honorable use of government powers.

Shultz could sense the gap when he met with Nixon in late 1968 in Los Angeles to discuss Nixon's invitation to Shultz to serve as secretary of labor. Shultz had accepted the offer, but asked to meet with Nixon before it was announced. "I wanted to be sure the president-elect knew my views on labor matters and saw what kind of labor secretary I would be," Shultz recalled in his memoirs. "I would get along with the unions, try to make collective bargaining work, play down high-level and White House intervention in strikes, work on retraining programs for displaced or disadvantaged workers, advocate equal employment opportunity."

He found Nixon radiated a sense of insecurity. "I was struck to hear an uneasy, defensive statement about why I, as a university man, would feel comfortable in his cabinet. Was he afraid of rejection from a person in the academic community? I had supported him during the campaign. I thought to myself, this man has just been elected president of the United States and yet he is selling himself to me."

Despite the differences, the president and his labor secretary collaborated on a number of enlightened policy initiatives, including revitalization of the Job Corps and a number of effective civil rights programs. When Nixon created the Office of Management and Budget in 1970 to bring some coherence to executive branch budget management, he appointed Shultz as the first director. Then in 1972, Nixon elevated Shultz to Treasury secretary. He took office on June 12, five days before the botched Watergate burglary.

As Nixon grew increasingly preoccupied with the Watergate cover-up and scandal it produced, he and his aides tried to enlist Shultz in various schemes to use the IRS and Secret Service, components of the Treasury Department, to rough up or spy on perceived Nixon enemies. Shultz rebuffed the entreaties, infuriating Nixon and his closest White House aides, John Ehrlichman and H. R. Haldeman. At one point, Nixon says in disgust, "What does that candyass think we sent him over there for?" Another time

Nixon says, "He didn't get secretary of the treasury because he's got nice blue eyes."

In one recorded 1972 Oval Office conversation, Ehrlichman complains to Nixon that the Pentagon initially resisted a White House request for the service record of George McGovern, the Democratic presidential candidate. Nixon, Ehrlichman, and Haldeman go on to talk about Shultz:

EHRLICHMAN: Yes and it's kind of interesting, the problem that you have with this. I sent to the Department of Defense for McGovern's service jacket . . . and I got it, but Jesus, the grief I took in getting it is unbelievable. . . . But guys like [Secretary of Defense Melvin] Laird, like Shultz, like [Attorney General Richard] Kleindienst, are just touchy as hell about cooperating with us on this kind of thing.

NIXON: Well I guess there's nothing we can do about this problem. But it's just so goddamn frustrating . . . what is it, Bob, the cabinet officers are afraid?

. . .

EHRLICHMAN: How could [George] Shultz be non-political?

NIXON: It's almost impossible.

EHRLICHMAN: It cuts both ways, because if we do this the press is going to be unwilling to blame him for it. If we can cause him to do it, it would be a cover.

NIXON: Everybody thinks Shultz is an honest, decent man.

. . .

EHRLICHMAN: Well why don't I have a chat with him.

. . .

HALDEMAN: Well, is there a way to cause him to do it externally, so that it isn't his initiative? . . . Can't we get an external tip that gives him a rationale for doing it, that he then says he orders the investigation because this information has come into his hands.

Later that day, Shultz's intransigence comes up again:

EHRLICHMAN: Well, I wouldn't wait. I'd kind of like to throw a little fear. I'm going to get Shultz tomorrow and sit down and I'm going to ask him to have the IRS go behind that entry in that report we got.

. . .

NIXON: That's what we're going to do, and just tell George he should do it. . . . George has got a fantasy. What is George's—what's he trying to do, say that you can't play politics with IRS?

EHRLICHMAN: I don't know.

NIXON: Or maybe he just doesn't understand [unintelligible].

Shultz's dealings with Kissinger were more congenial, though the two men were not close. When Shultz started work in the Nixon administration, he had little interaction with Kissinger, who started out as national security adviser and soon became secretary of state as well. "At first when I showed up," Shultz recalled playfully, "he didn't pay much attention because, after all, the field of economics doesn't matter. And then along came some stuff about oil-import quotas and Arab oil embargoes and so on, and he began to turn on. Then when the exchange system went wild, he decided economics was pretty good."

As Nixon became engulfed in the Watergate crisis, Shultz, Kissinger, and Arthur Burns, the chairman of the Federal Reserve, started meeting periodically to be sure the government remained on an even keel. Shultz said, "We had a little tripartite group. We weren't trying to usurp the president's functions, but we talked a lot together to be sure that if anything critical came up we would be able to evaluate it quickly and give the president good advice because he was in another world at that point. Henry, in this regard, showed something that has always been a trademark of his as I've watched him in operation. He is a deep patriot and he's looking out for the interests of the United States, defending them, thinking about them, arranging things on our behalf."

Shultz, worn out by five years of grinding work in three high-pressure jobs, resigned as Treasury secretary on May 8, 1974. Nixon, facing impeachment, resigned three months later.

Reflecting years later on Nixon's brass-knuckle politics, Shultz said, "When it came to anything of that kind where you are using the power of government, I think, and I held then and I stuck to it, that you have got to do it properly. I was being asked to do something improper and I wouldn't do it. Things like that had been done before . . . so maybe the president thought he was doing the same thing others had done, but anyway, not with me."

Shultz's attitude reflected his philosophy about high-level Washington jobs. "I think that in any of these jobs that people go into, you can't want the job too much. And you have to stand up for what you think is right. There are all kinds of issues where you don't get your way. But on issues of deep principle you have got to hang in."

During his stint in the Nixon administration, Shultz also learned he could govern and play golf at the same time. Dwight Eisenhower was his tutor. The incoming labor secretary and the former president met early in 1969 in Eisenhower's suite at Walter Reed Hospital, where Eisenhower was under care for heart problems. After talking about labor issues, the conversation turned to golf.

Shultz recalled the scene: "We had fun talking about golf. And then a doctor came in to say it's time for me to go. And all of a sudden this genial man got very stern. He shook his finger in my face like this and said, 'Young man, you're going to come down here and you're going to work fourteen hours a day, seven days a week, and you're going to think you're doing your job. Let me tell you something. If that's what you do, there's no way you can do your job. You'll just burn out. So I can see you like golf as much as I do. If you don't get out on some golf course at least twice a week, get your mind on something else, you won't be able to do your job.'"

Shultz would remember the advice when he returned to Washington in 1982 as secretary of state and soon found himself under fire from many of Ronald Reagan's other top aides. Not to mention Henry Kissinger and Sam Nunn.

CHAPTER THIRTEEN

Is this the best they can do?
—HENRY KISSINGER

Nuclear weapons policy became more than an academic matter for Kissinger when Nixon unexpectedly selected him as national security adviser. Though well known and well regarded as a defense and foreign policy theorist, Kissinger was closely allied with Nelson Rockefeller, a Nixon rival and presidential aspirant himself. Overnight Kissinger catapulted from the academy to one of the most powerful posts in Washington. Instead of reflecting about nuclear weapons strategy in books and essays, he was, in effect, managing America's nuclear arsenal.

Less than a week after Nixon's inauguration, the newly minted president and his national security adviser traveled across the Potomac for a visit to the Pentagon and a briefing in the tightly secured National Military Command Center about the Single Integrated Operational Plan, or SIOP, Pentagon lingo for America's nuclear war-fighting plan.

It was a sobering—and disturbing—encounter with the blueprint for Armageddon. As outlined by Colonel Don LaMoine of the Joint Staff's Strategic Operations Division, the latest version of the war plan offered few of the graduated escalation options that Kissinger had championed as a scholar. Instead it called for an all-out nuclear assault on the Soviet Union and China.

LaMoine told Nixon and Kissinger, "the fundamental concept [was] to maximize US power [and] to attain and maintain a strategic superiority which will lead to an early termination of the war on terms favorable to the United States and its allies." At the time, the United States had more than twenty-nine thousand nuclear weapons.

Favorable terms by some calculations meant the destruction of most Soviet military, industrial, and urban centers, with roughly 90 million people killed, and similar devastation in the United States, including 80 million American fatalities. If that wasn't chilling enough, Colonel LaMoine advised Nixon and Kissinger that in a rapidly unfolding crisis, the president might have no more than a few minutes to decide how to respond.

Reflecting on the briefing, Nixon later told a White House aide, "No matter what [the Soviets] do, they lose their cities. . . . What a decision to make."

Not long after the briefing, Kissinger consulted with Robert McNamara, who as secretary of defense in the Kennedy and Johnson administrations had pressed the military services to come up with a more nuanced war plan. "Is this the best they can do?" Kissinger asked. He later said, "to have the only option of killing 80 million people is the height of immorality."

Whatever Kissinger's moral qualms, his strategic concern was that the apocalyptic scale of the war plan would not seem credible to the Soviet Union. As William Burr, a research scholar who has studied declassified Nixon administration documents, reported, Kissinger "argued that massive nuclear threats to back up security guarantees were simply not believable." Kissinger remarked, "It's difficult to believe either side will launch everything."

But that possibility was all too real. For one thing, the velocity of decision making would be blindingly fast. It also seemed likely that communication links between military commanders and the president and his team in Washington would be disrupted by the first salvos in a nuclear war.

A retired senior general described the likely decision-making scenario if the Soviet Union had launched an attack: "In that excruciating interim, you can imagine the tension, the stress involved, the fate of not just our nation but the Soviet Union and possibly civilization as we know it is at stake. And so in the circumstance, all of those fine gradations and all those deterrents, theoretical notions, they just go out the window, and it really comes down to a scripted set of questions and answers. This is the attack we're anticipating; we now have a thousand incoming warheads. We have determined that the target is Washington, D.C., the so-called decapitation strike, therefore, Mr. President, we need your decision in one minute. So in that circumstance, when the president now is being told for an absolute fact that our country is about to be annihilated, the recommendation is driven toward full-scale response. And it's launch under attack, because once their attack begins to arrive, our response capability is so degraded that we can't guarantee that the objectives of a counterstrike can be achieved, right? You see where it goes?"

Looking back many years later, Kissinger acknowledged that his efforts to get a more modulated war plan fell short. Military leaders resisted, fearing that limited options would weaken deterrence rather than strengthen it.

As he took office, he said, he knew McNamara had tried to make the war plan more flexible. "I thought it was sort of agreed that massive retaliation would be modified," he said. "So when I became security adviser, I asked for the war plans. And I looked at them and, while an element of discrimination had been added, their definition of discrimination was to omit certain countries that were automatically part of the war plan even if they had nothing to do with the origin of the war. But in the meantime the weapons had increased in numbers and sophistication. The casualty estimates were higher than they were, so I called McNamara to come in and said, 'What are they hiding?' I showed him and he said, 'No, that's all there is.'

"So I'd like to tell you that I did brilliantly better. We ordered reconsideration. It took us five years to get it and it was still a rehash of the original discrimination. A little better, but no significant impact on my basic problem, which was how can you justify a war with such casualties in relation to any conceivable objective, or in fact in relation to any objective that I could imagine. And that was the dilemma all through my period and I'm sure George Shultz will tell you the same thing."

Several senior Cold War military commanders confirmed Kissinger's account. They said that despite repeated efforts to scale back the war plan, it remained a blueprint for all-out nuclear combat. "The mind-set that drove the prospective response to a nuclear war was almost invariably, when the war comes, it's going to become total," one retired general said. The war plan at one stage of the Cold War involved 12,000 targets in the Soviet Union and the use of 10,000 American nuclear warheads. It called for aiming dozens of warheads at a single radar site near Moscow that controlled the missile defense system for the Soviet capital. Target selectors didn't seem to appreciate the absurdity of the fusillade they planned.

Despite Kissinger's concerns about the war plan, he was not averse to using the American nuclear arsenal to try to muscle Moscow, short of starting a nuclear exchange. In his view, ratcheting up the alert status of nuclear forces was a powerful but peaceable way to intimidate the Kremlin. He saw it as an acceptable form of coercion that did not risk uncontrollable escalation and he used it several times to signal American resolve to Moscow. It was to him a sound middle ground between unleashing a nuclear exchange, which he could not morally justify, and forswearing the use of nuclear weapons, which he thought was untenable and would invite blackmail by enemies willing to use nuclear weapons. "We were in a number of situations where we employed very low-level nuclear threats," he said.

But the brandishing of American nuclear forces entailed serious risks that Kissinger may not have appreciated, including the possibility that bombers would inadvertently stray close to Soviet airspace, leading to a Kremlin miscalculation that the United States was on the verge of launching an attack.

The first episode came in October 1969, when Nixon and Kissinger used the tactic to press the Kremlin to lean on North Vietnam to make concessions at the stalled Paris peace talks. Nixon, hoping to bring the war to a quick end when he took office, considered a drastic escalation in American attacks if the peace talks remained moribund when an American bombing moratorium hit a one-year anniversary on November 1, 1969. The threat was secretly translated into a plan for an intense, four-day air attack called Duck Hook. Twenty-nine military and economic targets were selected, and plans were prepared to mine Vietnamese ports. Nixon sent word to Hanoi that absent a breakthrough in Paris, "I would regretfully find myself obliged to have recourse to measures of great consequence and force."

Kissinger appointed a special staff group to review the Pentagon plans. He told the group, "I refuse to believe that a little fourth-rate power like North Vietnam does not have a breaking point. It shall be the assignment of this group to examine the option of a savage, decisive blow against North Vietnam. You start without any preconceptions at all."

It is unclear whether Nixon and Kissinger seriously entertained the possibility of using nuclear weapons against North Vietnam. Seymour Hersh reported that Kissinger did not exclude the use of a nuclear device to sever the critical Northeast Rail Line to China, even though Kissinger told an aide that administration policy precluded the use of nuclear weapons. Two declassified National

Security Council memos show that the nuclear option came up in planning discussions, though not necessarily as a live possibility. In one memo, two top Kissinger aides, Roger Morris and Anthony Lake, told a Navy captain involved in Duck Hook planning that the president would need to think in advance about how far he would go. "He cannot, for example, confront the issue of using nuclear weapons in the midst of the exercise," Morris and Lake said in a memo to Captain Rembrandt Robinson. "He must be prepared to play out whatever string necessary in this case."

The other document, a Kissinger memo to Nixon about initial Duck Hook planning, included a series of "Important Questions" that Kissinger attached to the memo. One was, "Should we be prepared to use nuclear weapons?"

The plan is cast in a way that would seem to preclude the use of nuclear weapons. It talks about "effective military action" that would impel the North Vietnamese to accept compromises at the peace talks, but rules out action that would invite intervention by the Soviet Union or China. Certainly, a nuclear attack, even the use of just a few small weapons to destroy rail lines, would have invited Soviet or Chinese intervention.

Ultimately, Nixon and Kissinger shelved the Duck Hook plan, wary of escalating the war at a time when antiwar fever was rising in the United States and many Americans assumed Nixon was genuinely eager to seek a peace agreement with Hanoi rather than prolonging the war. The two men also faced resistance to the plan from Secretary of Defense Melvin Laird and Secretary of State William Rogers.

But giving up on Duck Hook did not mean giving up on trying to leverage the Kremlin to push North Vietnam toward an agreement in Paris. Nixon and Kissinger decided to use America's nuclear arsenal to sway the Kremlin. The exercise was one of the most bizarre and dangerous foreign policy episodes of the Nixon presidency.

The concept itself was dubious, and its execution fraught with risks. The idea was to make Soviet leaders think Nixon was unstable enough to start a nuclear exchange. With the benefit of historical hindsight, it seems a precursor of later reckless Nixon conduct. Nixon believed that Eisenhower had successfully used the threat of a nuclear attack to bring an end to the Korean War in 1953. Add the nuclear dimension to the impression of presidential unpredictability, and you would have an effective strategy, or so Nixon thought. "If the adversary feels that you are unpredictable, even rash, he will be deterred from pressing you too far," Nixon wrote his in memoirs. "The odds that he will fold will increase and the unpredictable president will win another hand."

Nixon and Kissinger put the "madman" strategy to work in October 1969 by putting American nuclear forces on heightened alert, initiating a series of nuclear force maneuvers designed to unsettle Soviet leaders. As scholars Scott Sagan and Jeremi Suri showed in a 2003 reconstruction of the events, the secret exercises were quite provocative and could have led to Soviet miscalculation.

Sagan and Suri described the operation: "On the evening of October 10, 1969, Gen. Earle Wheeler, the chairman of the Joint Chiefs of Staff (JCS), sent a top secret message to major U.S. military commanders around the world informing them that the JCS had been directed 'by higher authority' to increase U.S. military readiness 'to respond to possible confrontation by the Soviet Union.' The Strategic Air Command (SAC) was ordered to stand down all aircraft combat training missions and to increase the number of nuclear-armed B-52 bombers on ground alert. These readiness measures were implemented on October 13. Even more dramatic, on October 27 SAC launched a series of B-52 bombers, armed with thermonuclear weapons, on a 'show of force' airborne alert, code-named Giant Lance. During this alert operation, eighteen B-52s took off from bases in California and Washington State. The bombers crossed Alaska, were refueled in midair by

KC-135 tanker aircraft, and then flew in oval patterns toward the Soviet Union and back, on eighteen-hour 'vigils' over the northern polar ice cap."

Though General Wheeler's message informed commanders that military actions "should be discernible to the Soviets, but not threatening in themselves," they turned out to be more provocative—and in some cases careless—than intended. Strategic Air Command (SAC) bombers flew toward Soviet airspace over the Arctic Circle before turning back and operated without the aid of ground-based navigation stations in Alaska that would normally have helped keep the planes from straying off course. Some SAC safety measures were suspended during the exercises and some B-52s followed routing vectors that put the nuclear-armed bombers dangerously close to other bombers.

Partly because of the risks and doubts about the effectiveness of the gambit, Defense Secretary Laird was dubious about the nuclear operations and pushed back against Kissinger's orders. General Andrew Goodpaster, the Supreme Allied Commander in Europe, also was unenthusiastic about the exercise and made his view known.

In the end, the nuclear card did not produce a winning hand. Kissinger mistakenly thought it might lead to a breakthrough on Vietnam when Soviet ambassador Anatoly Dobrynin unexpectedly requested a meeting with Nixon. H. R. Haldeman, Nixon's chief of staff, noted in his diary that "Kissinger has all sorts of signal-type activity going on around the world to try to jar the Soviets and NVN [North Vietnam]—appears to be working because Dobrynin has asked for early meeting—which we have set secretly for Monday. K thinks this is good chance of being the big break— but it will come in stages. . . . P[president] is more skeptical."

Nixon's skepticism proved prescient. Dobrynin offered no concessions on Vietnam in his October 20 meeting with Nixon and Kissinger, and made no mention of the increased American military activity. To this day it is unclear how much Dobrynin and his Kremlin colleagues knew of the nuclear exercises, or what they made of them.

Four years later, Kissinger played the nuclear card again, this time to discourage the Kremlin from sending military forces to the Middle East to prevent Israeli troops from routing the Egyptian Third Army before a cease-fire was put in place to end the October 1973 war. This time Kissinger acted with little, if any, involvement by Nixon, who was swamped by the confluence of Watergate and Vice President Spiro Agnew's resignation in a bribery scandal just as the Mideast war commenced. It was a perilous moment in a faltering presidency.

The Israelis were caught by surprise on Yom Kippur when Syrian tank units rolled across the Golan Heights while Egyptian troops simultaneously attacked on the Sinai Peninsula. The Israelis absorbed heavy losses of both troops and weapons and quickly pleaded with Washington to airlift tanks, ammunition, and other equipment. With Nixon preoccupied, Kissinger essentially took over national security policy.

Once the Israelis recovered and took the offensive, driving back Syrian and Egyptian forces, Washington and Moscow grappled over how to achieve and secure a cease-fire. Kissinger was determined to manage the crisis in a way that would enhance American influence in the Mideast and marginalize the Soviet role in the region in the years ahead. His hopes seemed in jeopardy when Leonid Brezhnev sent a message to the White House on October 24, proposing a joint military intervention to secure a cease-fire. Brezhnev warned that he would dispatch Soviet forces to Egypt if Washington refused. Brezhnev's threat was partly aimed at preventing Israeli troops from assaulting the Egyptian Third Army, which was cut off in the Sinai and in desperate need of water, food, and medical supplies. Soviet military intervention was the last thing Washington wanted—it could not only put the United

States and Soviet Union on a collision course as the war continued, but also likely give Moscow an enduring military presence in the region. Unsure how quickly he could prevail on Israel, Kissinger ordered American nuclear forces to the highest stage of alert, short of a war footing, to keep the Kremlin at bay. "We were determined to resist by force if necessary the introduction of Soviet troops into the Middle East regardless of the pretext on which they arrived," Kissinger recalled.

The decision to apply nuclear pressure was made at a meeting of top national security officials that began late on the evening of October 24 and ended well after midnight. Kissinger initially planned to hold the emergency meeting at the State Department—by this time he was secretary of state as well as national security adviser—but General Alexander Haig, who had replaced H. R. Haldeman as White House chief of staff in May, urged a shift to the White House to lend a sense that Nixon was involved. In fact, Nixon was upstairs, in the residential quarters, during the meeting, and may have been asleep. "Should I wake up the President?" Kissinger asked Haig a few minutes before 10 p.m. Haig said no. Thirty minutes later Haig asked Kissinger, "Have you talked to the President?" Kissinger answered, "No, I haven't. He would just start charging around. . . . I don't think we should bother the President."

Kissinger's doubts about Nixon's state of mind were probably warranted. Nixon was still reeling from the political firestorm and calls for impeachment that he had ignited just a few days before when he fired Archibald Cox, the Watergate special prosecutor. Elliot Richardson, the attorney general, had refused to carry out Nixon's order and immediately resigned, as had the deputy attorney general, William Ruckelshaus. Robert Bork, the solicitor general whose later nomination to the Supreme Court was rejected by the Senate, executed the Nixon order. The bloodbath was quickly dubbed the Saturday Night Massacre.

Midway through the National Security Council meeting, the group decided to raise the alert level from Defense Condition or DefCon IV to DefCon III. That meant, among other things, that American nuclear forces around the world would increase operations, including nuclear-armed bomber flights. Soviet intelligence-gathering systems were bound to detect the burst of communications traffic generated by the intensified operations. To underscore the signal, the State Department at dawn sent a stiff diplomatic note to the Soviet embassy in Washington saying the United States considered Brezhnev's "suggestion of unilateral action as a matter of the gravest concern involving incalculable consequences."

It didn't take long for word of the alert to make it to news organizations; the worldwide acceleration of American military operations was publicly visible at airfields and other military installations, including NATO bases in Europe. Kissinger gingerly addressed the alert at an October 25 news conference at the State Department. He noted that Washington was "opposed to the unilateral introduction by any great power, especially by a nuclear power, of military forces into the Middle East in whatever guise those forces should be introduced." He added, "And it is the ambiguity of some of the actions and communications and certain readiness measures that were observed that caused the President at a special meeting of the National Security Council last night, at 3 a.m., to order certain precautionary measures to be taken by the United States."

Asked if he had recommended the alert, or if Nixon had initiated it on his own, Kissinger said, "I may say that all of the President's senior advisers, all the members of the National Security Council, were unanimous in their recommendation, as a result of a deliberation in which the President did not himself participate, and which he joined only after they had formed their judgment that the measures taken—that he in fact ordered—were in the essential national interest."

The next day, Nixon said at his own news conference that he had acted after "we obtained information which led us to believe that the Soviet Union was planning to send a very substantial force into the Mideast, a military force." He was apparently alluding to the Brezhnev message, plus American intelligence reports that Soviet forces might be preparing to ship out to the Middle East. "When I received that information, I ordered, shortly after midnight on Thursday morning, an alert for all American forces around the world. This was a precautionary alert. The purpose of that was to indicate to the Soviet Union that we would not accept any unilateral move on their part to move military forces into the Mideast."

Several accounts of the crisis concluded that Nixon was not consulted about the nuclear alert. The transcripts of Kissinger-Haig conversations leave little doubt that Nixon was not involved in the NSC meeting and may have slept through it. Those conversations also suggest that the recommendation to go to a higher alert was not as unanimous as Kissinger asserted. "You and I were the only ones for it," Kissinger said to Haig the following day. "These guys were all wailing all over the place."

Kissinger's discussions with Haig at midafternoon on October 25 seem to show that Nixon did not order the alert. Recounting how he had fielded questions at his news conference that day, Kissinger told Haig, "[I] said it was [a] combination of the advice of all of his advisers—that the President decided to do this. I think I did some good for the President." Haig replied, "More than you know." Absent the alert, Kissinger said, "we would have had a Soviet paratroop division there this morning." Haig agreed. Then Haig asked, "Have you talked to the Boss?" Kissinger replied, "No. I will call him. Let's not broadcast this all over the place otherwise it looks like we (cooked) it up."

After Nixon's news conference the next day, Kissinger told Haig, "The crazy bastard really made a mess with the Russians." Kissinger was unhappy that Nixon's comments made it seem as if he was "taunting Brezhnev. . . . This guy will not take this. This guy over there is a maniac also."

Kissinger bristled at the idea he had acted on his own when asked about the incident in a 2009 interview. "That's irrelevant to the problem we're discussing," he said. "That's also not exactly true . . . there's so many things, what was allegedly done, either the president was aware of, or that the president had given different orders. Then the question is, why did I survive? How can you survive as national security adviser unless the president has total confidence in you? That's the absolute precondition."

He later told a California audience, "I cannot think of a single occasion when we took measures that were moving consciously toward nuclear war. There were two occasions which are often described as having gone on nuclear alert, which is basically nonsense. . . . DefCon I is nuclear war, so DefCon III has basically very little to do with nuclear weapons. We went out of our way not to threaten with nuclear weapons."

Brent Scowcroft, Kissinger's top aide during the October war, said, "I can't honestly say that I know he [Nixon] signed off on it. But Al Haig, who was chief of staff at that time, was communicating with the president in and out of the meeting."

Asked if the alert was a promiscuous use of a nuclear threat, Scowcroft said, "No. No. No. No. This was solely a way to tell the Russians, we're serious this time. That's all."

Brezhnev backed off and Soviet military forces were not dispatched to the Mideast. It is not clear whether the Kremlin was influenced by the nuclear alert. Israel's decision to refrain from attacking the Egyptian Third Army was more likely the decisive factor. Kissinger viewed the nuclear move as a judicious, well-calibrated use of American power.

"We were much more interested in the communications traffic that would result from DefCon III than in threatening nuclear war," he said.

Yet even as Kissinger wielded nuclear weapons as a form of coercive diplomacy, he made arms control negotiations with Moscow a top priority of the Nixon administration. The arms talks were part of a foreign policy strategy devised by Nixon and Kissinger that attempted to link together different elements of U.S.-Soviet relations. The prospect of nuclear arms agreements, for instance, might induce Soviet cooperation in bringing the Vietnam War to an end. Or so the theory went. At the same time, Nixon and Kissinger tried to exploit the rivalry between China and the Soviet Union to put pressure on the Kremlin. The geostrategic concept, called triangular diplomacy, led to Nixon's 1972 trip to China.

The arms discussions between Washington and Moscow covered both offensive and defensive systems. The Strategic Arms Limitation Talks (SALT), the first effort to halt the growth in Soviet and American strategic nuclear arsenals, opened in November 1969. Lyndon Johnson's effort to initiate negotiations had died in 1968 when Soviet military forces invaded Czechoslovakia to crush the democracy movement there.

Nixon and Kissinger revived the idea, and once talks began, Kissinger directed American negotiators. One of the major issues overhanging the talks was whether to limit or ban multiple-warhead clusters atop missiles. The new technology was one of the most momentous and contentious issues facing Kissinger. In the end, Nixon and Kissinger brushed off the advice of Drell and other scientists, acceding to Pentagon pressure to move ahead with the new system, known as a multiple independently targetable reentry vehicle (MIRV). The technology complicated the arms race just as Kissinger and Nixon were trying to slow it.

The idea of exchanging a single warhead for half a dozen or more on each ICBM was a game-changing development. More warheads meant more targets could be hit simultaneously, giving an attacking country a significant advantage. Multiple warheads could even knock out hardened missile launch sites, potentially crippling the retaliatory power of a nation under attack. That, in turn, might make it more tempting to strike first. All told, MIRVs threatened to make the nuclear balance of terror more volatile and unstable.

The issue came up soon after Nixon and Kissinger took office. Research and development work on a multiple-warhead system had begun in the early 1960s. By 1969 the Pentagon was preparing to move ahead with installation of MIRV clusters on land- and submarine-based missiles.

In the end, Kissinger chose not to block the use of multiple-warhead systems. After several years of grueling negotiation over a host of other highly technical weapons issues, Washington and Moscow agreed to limit, but not to reduce, the number of nuclear-armed missiles, submarines, and bombers they could maintain, but set no ceiling on warheads. The two sides also agreed to limit antiballistic missile systems. The accords were sealed in Moscow in 1972 when Nixon and Brezhnev signed the ABM Treaty and the interim agreement on strategic offensive arms, known as SALT I.

Kissinger's handling of the negotiations was uneven. With Nixon's blessing, he often operated outside normal State Department channels, dealing directly with top Soviet officials. The back-channel conversations infuriated Gerard Smith, the lead American negotiator, and his colleagues. Kissinger's lack of technical expertise led to several damaging blunders that more knowledgeable officials had to untangle.

The ABM Treaty limited the construction of antimissile systems to two American and two Soviet cities. The number was soon dropped to one apiece. Absent the accord, Moscow and Washington would likely have engaged in a very expensive defensive arms race.

As part of the interim agreement, Washington and Moscow agreed to continue negotiations, hoping to work out a comprehensive, long-term treaty to limit the nuclear arms race. Negotiations on a SALT II treaty began in November 1972. Nixon, swamped by the Watergate scandal and impeachment proceedings, was unable to complete an agreement before he resigned in August 1974. But President Gerald Ford and Kissinger, who remained in place as secretary of state after Nixon's departure, set the framework for an accord when they met with Brezhnev in the Soviet Pacific port city of Vladivostok in November 1974.

Looking back on his handling of nuclear weapons in a 2009 interview, Kissinger said, "I tried to introduce an element of discrimination into nuclear strategy. Secondly, I tried to reduce reliance on nuclear strategy. Thirdly, I wanted to use the fact that the Russians and we had these big stockpiles of weapons as a means of negotiation with the Russians to induce restraint in the conduct of international relations. And even more restraint in the use of nuclear weapons."

And how did he judge his performance?

"In some respects, whether it is possible to introduce discrimination is a question of American war plans, and that seems to have proved almost impossible to solve in a succession of different administrations with totally different personnel. I think on the dialogue with Russia, our performance achieved many of its objectives. On restraint in the use of nuclear weapons, there was no situation in which we were involved, in which we ever made a plan for using nuclear weapons. I mean other than the war plan, the general war plan, but in no local situation."

Viewed from a twenty-first-century perspective, the arms accords that Kissinger engineered look like modest steps—they set ceilings and slowed the pace of growth of the American and Soviet arsenals. They did not require reductions. But at the time, any steps to decelerate the nuclear arms race were significant. James Goodby, the longtime American arms negotiator, aptly described

SALT I this way: "The first strategic arms limitation agreement was important because it broke the ice. A precedent was set for more important agreements later. But it did little to halt the nuclear arms race."

After twenty years of breakneck growth in nuclear arms, some restraint was urgently needed. It would take a different president and secretary of state—Ronald Reagan and George Shultz—to plot a more radical course.

CHAPTER FOURTEEN

The insider goes into the centers of power and tries to work the levers from the inside. The outsider goes outside and protests.
—JAMES BJORKEN

By the time Nixon and Kissinger moved into the White House, Sid Drell was well established as a White House science adviser, and well aware that his high reputation in the academic world was taking a beating because of the Vietnam War. Whether it was fair or not, some of Drell's fellow scientists thought he was lending his good name and advice to help prosecute the increasingly unpopular war. Drell was unmoved by the criticism. He did not consider himself a war supporter but felt an obligation to give his government unvarnished advice on technical defense issues. And so, despite a growing uproar over the role of the Jason group, Drell re-upped as a member of the President's Science Advisory Committee (PSAC) under Nixon, and agreed to serve as a shadow adviser to Kissinger.

He certainly knew what he was getting into. Drell's work on the science committee during the Johnson administration had propelled him into the politically charged arena of the Vietnam War. As American involvement in the war rapidly escalated, PSAC increasingly turned its attention to the battlefields of Southeast Asia. The panel's monthly, two-day meetings in Washington in the mid- and late 1960s, while still largely devoted to a range of scientific and strategic nuclear issues, were often dominated by Vietnam. In March 1968, for example, committee members were notified that the regular meeting later that month would be replaced by a two-day session on Vietnam. A month later, David Beckler, the White House aide who coordinated the committee's work, notified members that the next meeting would deal principally with the report of the ad hoc Vietnam group. During these years, agendas included items like "Use of Science and Technology in Support of Operations in Vietnam," "CIA Briefing on Vietnam," and a study of the effectiveness of the air campaign against North Vietnam. Drell agreed to sit on the committee's ad hoc Vietnam group, which was chaired by Charles Townes, the Berkeley physicist who had recruited Drell to join the Jasons. Drell also founded and chaired the PSAC Ground Warfare Panel and was a member of the Strategic Military Panel.

Richard Garwin, a fellow physicist and government adviser, described the PSAC role in Vietnam this way in a 1969 memo: "From the beginning of the Vietnam War, the PSAC Military panels have been active in their two traditional roles: (a) to provide for the President an informed view of the nation's military capabilities, and (b) to aid the decision process, the Defense Department, the Bureau of the Budget, etc., in maintaining and creating the most effective and efficient military force. PSAC members and panels were heavily involved in the provision of electronic warfare apparatus for the aircraft flying in Vietnam, in the initiation and conduct of the 'barrier' to infiltration, and in studies of the means and possible effectiveness of various aspects of the bombing of North Vietnam and of a possible blockade of North Vietnam."

Drell struggled with the clashing cultures of the university and the White House as he traveled back and forth across the widening divide. He was disturbed by the war, opposed to the indiscriminate bombing of North Vietnam, yet unwilling to break publicly with the government and openly align himself with other scientists in the antiwar movement. His hesitation seemed driven partly by a conviction that his scientific advice was primarily devoted to arms control issues and other long-range matters unconnected to the war. He also had a natural aversion to ideological causes and the intellectual and political conformity they often command.

Drell's ambivalence was evident in a letter he dispatched to the White House in the waning days of 1967. "I am always amazed to find upon returning home from my Washington trips that events generally, but especially the Viet Nam news, appear in so different a perspective when I get distant from the White House," he wrote Donald Hornig, Lyndon Johnson's science adviser, a few days after Christmas.

Drell was disturbed by the punishing bombing raids on North Vietnam and the estrangement of many young Americans from their government. He strongly favored a halt to the bombing, though not for military or moral reasons. He told Hornig, "I urge that the government take this step because, without jeopardizing our military position, it can improve domestic support of and confidence in its policy objectives and methods particularly among the vitally important younger generation." He added that a temporary suspension could reaffirm American intentions to seek a negotiated resolution of the war.

James Bjorken, a close colleague and friend of Drell's, surmised that Drell made a conscious choice during the Vietnam era to work on the inside to influence decisions rather than protesting from afar. "Sid's an insider type," Bjorken said. "It's clear that Sid has a huge amount of idealism. He wants to change things for the better. And the insider goes into the centers of power and tries to work the levers from the inside. The outsider goes outside and protests."

Serving as White House insiders, including occasional meetings with presidents Johnson and Nixon, made the scientists a target of antiwar critics. Some scientists quietly extricated themselves from government service; others broke publicly, denouncing the war. Drell chose to remain engaged, and took a lot of heat for it, especially when war critics learned about Jason and pounced on its members for abetting the war effort. The most attractive target was a 1966 Jason study and recommendations about building an electronic barrier or battlefield across the Ho Chi Minh Trail to detect and help prevent the infiltration of munitions and other supplies from North Vietnam to South Vietnam. The study was disclosed when the *New York Times* and other newspapers published the Pentagon Papers in 1971. Though the barrier was proposed, in part, as a preferred course to bombing, the Pentagon Papers references to the Jason study cited the use of mines and cluster bombs to prevent infiltration, red flags for antiwar critics. Jason also studied the potential consequences of using nuclear weapons in Southeast Asia, another inflammatory issue.

Drell later said, "Many people who got involved in the electronic barrier went in with the best of motives, and saw some of the technical contributions they made used in ways they feel quite unhappy about. But that's inevitable. The laws of physics are fixed. The laws of politics change. And you're supping with the Devil in a difficult way. It's to be expected. It's unavoidable. And you have to keep your guard up."

Drell ran into heavy antiwar flak in Italy in July 1972, when he tried to deliver a physics lecture at the Guglielmo Marconi Institute at the University of Rome. Drell rebuffed demands from protesters to denounce the war and Jason, but talked for ten minutes about Jason and government advising. That seemed to satisfy the protesters, but when they returned a few minutes later with a bullhorn and resumed their verbal attack, he scooped up his papers and walked out. Several weeks later he ran into protests at the Institut d'Etudes Scientifiques de Cargèse in Corsica. Once again Drell refused to denounce Jason and the war, but offered to talk about Jason after giving the first in a series of lectures he planned. Only a small group of students agreed, forcing the school to postpone the lecture. When institute authorities were unable to resolve the standoff the next day, they abruptly ended the summer program a week early.

Exposure of Jason's Vietnam studies led to publication in December 1972 of a passionate critique, "Science Against the People." The subtitle: "The Story of Jason—The Elite Group of Academic Scientists Who, As Technical Consultants to the Pentagon, Have Developed the Latest Weapon Against Peoples' Liberation Struggles: 'Automated Warfare.'" That was a reference to the electronic barrier proposed by Jason.

The report was prepared by the Berkeley chapter of Scientists and Engineers for Social and Political Action. The group was led by Charles Schwartz, an MIT-trained physicist who had come to Stanford for postdoctoral work at Drell's invitation. He later moved to Berkeley. Schwartz was familiar with Jason, having participated in a Jason summer study in 1962.

"We feel that we make up a community of shared work and common understanding—students, teachers and researchers," the report said. "Can it be a matter of indifference to us that some members of the community—even some of its leaders—serve a military adventure that most of us regard as criminal?"

The report was contemptuous about the Washington access of Jason members. "The Jason people are 'insiders,'" it said. "They have access to secret information from many government offices and they expect their advice to be at least seriously considered, if not followed, by top-level policy-makers. Those who engage in criticism of government policies without the benefit of such inside access are termed 'outsiders.'

"When a debate arises between insiders and outsiders, invariably the argument is used that only the insiders know the true facts and that therefore the outsiders' positions should not be taken seriously."

The report singled out Drell, recalling a visit he made to Berkeley in October 1972. Drell had given a physics lecture at the Lawrence Radiation Laboratory and agreed to discuss his government work afterward. Charles Schwartz quizzed him aggressively about his association with Jason.

An account of their confrontation in the campus newspaper, the *Daily Californian*, captured the fraught exchange.

SCHWARTZ: I am very concerned with the role of science and its effect on warfare. Science helps the warfare. Science helps the war go on. How do you feel about the structure of science and the Vietnam War? Do you contribute to the electronic battlefield?

DRELL: The organization I work for—Jason—is accused of this and that. Jason is a very secretive organization. I know very little about it. Since I've been in Washington, I've seen the government do things I like and things I dislike. We need to have critics not just on the outside, but on the inside, too.

SCHWARTZ: What do you work on exactly?

DRELL: I don't feel obliged to tell you. Look at the record though. If one has any confidence in one's government, one must do something, I think.

SCHWARTZ: There's a problem, though: there is no record of what you do in Jason. Oh, excuse me, there is about a one percent record. It's nice to say, Sid, that the responsibility rests with the president, but that's not all true. We have to ask about our scientists who advise the president.

DRELL: There's a system in which all scientists are involved: some are on the outside, some are on the inside. I am on the inside, and you and other scientists are on the outside. I like this system of critics in and out of the government.

SCHWARTZ: Explain why you feel you must support
Nixon.
DRELL: Mr. Nixon is our president, and I will do any-
thing, within reason, to support him. Take, for example,
the SALT talks.
SCHWARTZ: The SALT talks aren't really the point. When
you say, "Support the president" does that mean you'd kill
Vietnamese?
DRELL: Oh, Charley, why don't you debate someone else?
I thought this would be serious.

Recalling the incident decades later, Drell said he was infuri-
ated by the headline in the *Daily Californian*, which he said was
"Drell Supports Nixon." The actual headline was "Jason Physicist
Backs War Role."

Asked in 2009 how he reconciled his political and moral views
with his science advising on matters related to the Vietnam War,
Drell said, "I was obviously troubled by Vietnam, but I was de-
coupled, really, from Vietnam. We weren't there looking at Vietnam, so I had no difficult moral decision to face."

Pressed to talk about whether his involvement with classified
projects and information was inimical to the values of the academy
and how he felt about walling off his government work from his
work at the university, he said he felt uncomfortable. Drell said
he did not try to hide his concerns about Vietnam and other defense issues, but adhered strictly to government restrictions about
the handling of classified information. "It was my responsibility to
draw a line," he recalled. "It was a time of a built-in strain."

Reflecting on his role, Drell emphasized the importance of
ensuring that government leaders be exposed to diverse scientific views when considering defense matters. He cited the example of Winston Churchill's reliance on the misguided advice
of his top science adviser, Lord Cherwell, who overestimated the

morale-breaking potential of bombing civilian centers in Germany. C. P. Snow, the British physicist and writer, lamented Lord Cherwell's dominant role in *Science and Government*, his thoughtful book about the role of scientists in government. Drell recalled Snow's account, saying it underscored the need for independent science advisers.

"I convinced myself that a strength of the United States was that it tolerated people like me, people like Panofsky, people who said we are contributing but we're not part of the government. We are independent. . . . If the government didn't approve of what I was doing, then they should tell me to go home. But I didn't feel like I had to hide my political views."

He went on: "So to me there was no conflict, but I chose my problems, first through the reconnaissance business, then in the arms control business, where it was quite clear to me that technical people had something to contribute that was in our healthy, national security interests, and I was going to do it."

Murph Goldberger, Drell's friend and Jason colleague, looked back with greater regret.

"We should have told Mr. McNamara to take his war and we didn't want any part of it," he said. "But we didn't. We thought we were doing good. We thought that we had some ideas about how you go about lowering the temperature of the war, thought that we were being very noble. And it turned out . . . we were being lied to by the national security adviser. All my friends outside the system, they were all over me about being such a fink. And I realize in retrospect that they were right, and just because you're inside, you really can't be sure that other people don't have some wisdom to offer you."

CHAPTER FIFTEEN

*There was no weapon that the human mind could
imagine that they would approve.*
—HENRY KISSINGER

Sid Drell doubled down on his insider status when he accepted
an invitation to join a small group of scientists advising Henry
Kissinger on defense technologies.

The existence of the group was not secret, but it operated
largely in the shadows, dealing frequently with sensitive security
issues. Paul Doty, a Harvard physical chemist who organized the
group at Kissinger's request, had befriended Kissinger as a faculty
colleague when they worked together on a Harvard–MIT arms
control seminar in the early 1960s. The two men attended several
Pugwash Conferences, gatherings of eminent scholars, scientists,
and public officials that were inaugurated in 1957 in Pugwash,
Nova Scotia, to explore the dangers posed by nuclear weapons.
As Kissinger set up shop in the West Wing of the White House in
1969, he asked Doty, who had worked on the Manhattan Project
and studied later at Columbia with Enrico Fermi and other eminent physicists, to assemble a small group of scientists to advise him
on technical defense issues.

Doty recruited a high-powered team: Sid Drell, Richard
Garwin, and Pief Panofsky; Jack Ruina, an MIT electrical engineer; George Rathjens, an MIT political scientist and physical

chemist; and George Kistiakowsky, a Harvard chemist and former Eisenhower science adviser. Doty and his colleagues playfully called themselves the Mafia.

Kissinger was not well versed on scientific and technological matters. Though he had written trenchant essays and a bestselling book about nuclear strategy, he was unfamiliar with much of the military hardware of the nuclear era. At one point, realizing Kissinger was ignorant about the fundamentals of radar, Drell prepared a basic primer for him that read like a high school text. It began, "Radar is an electronic device for detecting and determining the position of objects located at a distance. The term radar is an acronym derived from the phrase 'radio detection and ranging.' Radar was originally developed to provide warning of approaching aircraft, but has since evolved into a general sensor technology with diverse applications."

As Kissinger and Nixon escalated American combat operations in Southeast Asia, Kistiakowsky quickly withdrew from the group, followed by Rathjens. "George dropped out pretty early because he really couldn't tolerate what he felt was hypocrisy and double-dealing on the part of Henry and the Nixon administration," Garwin said. "We had a lot of dispute over—it wasn't our business, we were only there to answer questions, do studies for Henry, mostly on things like MIRVs and missile defense and dealing with arms control, but providing some understanding of the technology and the threat."

Garwin recalled that Kissinger was uncomfortable with the larger, established President's Science Advisory Committee, headed by Lee DuBridge, a former president of Caltech. Early on in the Nixon presidency, Kissinger scrawled in the margin of one PSAC report that made its way to the Oval Office, "We must get PSAC out of strategy." The report, prepared by the Strategic Military Panel, had been drafted by Drell. "Henry was national security adviser, so the first thing he did was try to reduce the influence of the president's science adviser," Garwin said. "He didn't like rival power centers. PSAC was unpredictable." Doty thought Kissinger was wary of the DuBridge panel because it had its own access to the president and he didn't know most of the members. "I felt he wanted something independent," Doty said.

Drell described the origins of the Doty group in talking points he prepared in September 1970 for a meeting with DuBridge's successor, Edward E. David Jr., a Bell Laboratories electrical engineer.

"Inform David that origin of Mafia grew from our worry that Kissinger and NSC badly need science advice at the Presidential level for SALT and it should not come from DDR&E or ACDA [Director of Defense Research and Engineering, Arms Control and Disarmament Agency]. We impressed upon Kissinger that we felt he badly needed technical support and that without independent advice such as PSAC should provide he was a captive of DDR&E. This we thought was dangerous. Therefore, in an informal way we became an end-run around PSAC because of the breakdown of communication between Kissinger and DuBridge. Everything we said was done with the full support, knowledge and blessings of Lee."

The Doty team got along well. Their expertise ranged across a broad array of fields, including physics, chemistry, biochemistry, nuclear weapons, intelligence, and military technologies. Panofsky, a prolific writer with an eye for detail, churned out many of their papers. Drell was knowledgeable about a lot of technical issues and had good political instincts and an ability to see the big picture. Everyone respected Garwin's intellectual brilliance. "Garwin was the smartest and the most original, but totally unperceptive as to whether a good idea could be sold," Doty recalled. Ruina, always practical and pragmatic, helped forge consensus on difficult issues, and Doty brought years of arms control experience to the discussions.

Kissinger faithfully kept his appointments with the group, meeting with them almost every month, often in the White House Situation Room. The meetings usually took place in the evening, when Kissinger's busy schedule lightened and the men could slip into the White House with less chance of being spotted by reporters and staff members. Sometimes they would return early the next morning to continue the conversation. The men surmised that Kissinger, working to earn the trust of Nixon and his inner circle, was not eager to be seen conferring with a group of Cambridge and California intellectuals. "We just knew that our continuation depended on us being off the screen," Doty said.

Garwin was troubled by Kissinger's machinations. "I was dead set against the secrecy with which he and Nixon were running the government. I was appalled. One time I said, 'This is very dangerous. If the president would die, the people in the Defense Department and the State Department would have the wrong idea of your goals. They're just spinning their wheels.' And he said, 'I want it that way, so they don't get in the way of what I am trying to do.'"

Whatever secrecy the group maintained was shattered one morning in early November 1972 when Kissinger walked into the White House room where they had gathered, trailed by Oriana Fallaci, the Italian journalist, and her camera crew. The footage of Kissinger with Doty and company was not broadcast in the United States but was seen in Europe, where several of the scientists were well known and easily recognized. "So Henry himself revealed the existence of the group," Garwin said.

The scientists, all cleared to handle classified information, prepared dozens of detailed papers for Kissinger. The studies explored a wide variety of arms control issues, including the Strategic Arms Limitation Talks with Moscow and whether the Pentagon should revise its plans for waging nuclear war. In a cover letter to his fellow scientists that accompanied a draft paper on arms control matters, Ruina wrote wryly, "The name of the enclosed song is 'Why Not Give SALT A Chance?'"

The Doty group offered technical counsel on all these fronts, almost always coming down on the side of more arms control. The group spent a great deal of time studying the multiple-warhead technology and its implications. The scientists urged Kissinger to seek an immediate moratorium on MIRV testing with Moscow or make a MIRV ban part of the nuclear arms agreement Washington was negotiating with the Kremlin. Kissinger was reluctant to engage the technological issues associated with MIRVs, Doty recalled. In the end, Kissinger punted on the question and both the United States and Soviet Union invested heavily in arming their missiles with multiple warheads. Garwin's impression was that Kissinger did not want to tangle with the Pentagon on MIRVs just months after he had resisted military efforts to expand ballistic missile defenses. Kissinger himself later regretted his acquiescence on MIRVs. "I would say in retrospect that I wish I had thought through the implications of a MIRVed world more thoughtfully in 1969 and 1970 than I did," he told reporters at a 1974 background briefing.

By and large, Kissinger seemed indifferent to many of the Doty group's recommendations. When asked many years later about the group, he said the members' acute disdain for Nixon prevented them from fairly evaluating new weapons systems. "There was no weapon that the human mind could imagine that they would approve," he said with bemusement. "The mood was not the same one that characterized the Harvard [arms control] seminar, where we said, 'Here's the common problem.' They had the attitude—I may be unfair to them—that this administration was not what they wanted and that the basic attitude of Nixon, which was to link issues together, not separate arms control out as a separate problem, to continue defense efforts while you're negotiating, none of this was palatable to them. Then there were issues like Cambodia, so that it became uncomfortable for them and for us.

"I always said, the fact that I didn't agree, or we didn't agree, didn't mean that I didn't respect them. It was an outstanding group."

When told about Kissinger's comment about the group's implacable hostility to new weapons, Drell laughed. "That's a Henryism. That's Henry at his best."

Despite the differences between Kissinger and the Doty group, Drell remained engaged with Kissinger. "I felt that he gave us an opportunity, and it wasn't just talk," Drell said.

The access to Kissinger proved critical on one of the most significant defense technology decisions made during the Nixon presidency. It involved development of a new spy satellite that could give Washington nearly instantaneous pictures of Soviet military sites. Unlike cumbersome film-based systems that took several days to deliver images from space to the light tables of photo interpreters, the novel technology could electronically transmit pictures to ground stations just seconds after they were recorded. It exploited a breakthrough made at Bell Labs in New Jersey, where two scientists had created the basis for digital imaging by developing semiconductor devices that turned light energy into tiny electrical charges that could be stored, measured exactly, and converted into digital data that could be relayed electronically. At the CIA, Bud Wheelon recognized the potential spy satellite applications. He figured correctly that the Bell Labs invention, later known as charged-couple devices, could be married to an advanced optical system to create an electro-optical satellite.

The Air Force and its Pentagon benefactors had other ideas. They favored development of an updated version of a conventional, film-based satellite, code-named FROG. The Air Force system would allow ground controllers to periodically activate a readout mechanism aboard the spacecraft that would transmit a copy of the film image to the ground. In a June 4, 1971, meeting with the president, Edwin Land, speaking on behalf of the

President's Foreign Intelligence Advisory Board, described FROG as "the cautious choice" that would "utilize existing hardware and technology." He said the electro-optical system was "the adventurous choice, and one which would be a quantum technological advance." He urged President Nixon to intervene in the intramural battle over which system to fund.

Nixon said he would take "a hard look" at the issue, but with Defense Secretary Melvin Laird siding with the Air Force, the issue remained unresolved. To break the deadlock, Drell and Garwin went to Kissinger. "Sid and I carefully drafted a top-secret, code-word handwritten letter that was personally delivered to Kissinger at what seems to have been the last possible moment to obtain a favorable decision for the electro-optical system," Garwin recalled. The two scientists then talked Kissinger through the issue at a meeting in the Situation Room. Their presentation was persuasive. On September 23, 1971, Kissinger notified Laird and other top officials that Nixon had approved development of the CIA system and was terminating funding for FROG.

The new satellite system, developed by the CIA and Lockheed, gave the United States a powerful new tool for spying on the Soviet Union from space. Officials in Washington could view images of Soviet military installations, factories, and other sites moments after the satellites orbited over the Soviet facilities. The first images were given to Jimmy Carter on the day he was inaugurated as president. The pictures showed him being sworn in on the Capitol steps.

Over time, differences over the Vietnam War corroded relations between Kissinger and the Doty group. Doty, who had the longest-standing friendship with Kissinger when the group was formed in 1969, grew disillusioned as Nixon's first term wound down in 1972. "What really broke my close relations with him was when it became clear that he essentially prolonged the war for four years," Doty said. Doty and Kissinger have rarely spoken since. "I've only seen him once of late," he said in May 2009, sitting in his Cambridge apartment, overlooking the Charles River. "He's always asked me to stop in New York if I'm going through, but I don't travel anymore."

Neither Kissinger nor Drell would have guessed that they would be reunited one day in pursuit of a world free of nuclear weapons.

CHAPTER SIXTEEN

This time I want to write you not an "open" letter but a most ordinary one, and to thank you with all my heart.
—ANDREI SAKHAROV

As the Nixon presidency was imploding during the summer of 1974, Sid Drell traveled to the Soviet Union to attend a physics seminar organized by the Soviet Academy of Sciences. It turned out to be a pivotal moment in his career.

In Moscow, he met and befriended Andrei Sakharov, the distinguished Soviet physicist, nuclear weapons architect, and human rights campaigner. The two men were natural allies, drawn together by their common interest in physics and the dangers of nuclear weapons. Their friendship, bolstered by Drell's unflagging defense of Sakharov during the years of his internal Soviet exile from 1980 to 1986, reinforced Drell's concerns about nuclear weapons.

Neither man was prepared at the time to call for the unconditional elimination of nuclear weapons, but they both believed the growth of nuclear arsenals was racing out of control and that new arms control agreements were desperately needed. "What is necessary," Sakharov wrote to Drell, "is to strive, systematically though carefully, for complete nuclear disarmament based on strategic parity in conventional weapons." When Drell reread that 1983 statement in 2011, he smiled. "He's saying exactly what we're saying now," he said.

Before traveling to Moscow, Drell had admired Sakharov from afar. Though one of the designers of the Soviet H-bomb, first tested in 1953, Sakharov grew estranged from the government as he questioned the repression of dissent and wrote about the dangers of nuclear war. Drell was especially impressed by the Russian's eloquent essay "Progress, Coexistence and Intellectual Freedom." Sakharov wrote in the 1967 epistle (published in the West in 1968), "The unchecked growth of thermonuclear arsenals and the build-up toward confrontation threaten mankind with the death of civilization and physical annihilation. The elimination of that threat takes unquestionable priority over all other problems in international relations. This is why disarmament talks, which offer a ray of hope in the dark world of suicidal madness, are so important."

As Sakharov's disagreements with the Kremlin became more acute, he helped establish the Committee for Human Rights in Moscow in 1970. In 1973 he issued a public appeal to support Kremlin critics who had been forcibly committed to psychiatric hospitals. In a society where even mild dissent was discouraged, Sakharov's outcry was tantamount to a declaration of war with the Kremlin.

Drell and Sakharov liked one another immediately when they got together in Moscow. Beyond their common interest in science and nuclear weapons, they shared an affection for music, read widely, were actively engaged with the world around them, and were determined, each in his own way, to hold science to a high moral standard.

Sakharov invited Drell to his apartment for a family dinner. Drell never forgot the occasion, not least because it was preceded by a visit by the police to Sakharov's residence, the latest example of government harassment. The neighbors, the police reported, had complained about a noisy party hosted by Sakharov the night before. Sakharov told Drell the "noise" was a private operatic recital performed by two stars of the visiting La Scala opera of

Milan, who had unexpectedly dropped by the apartment to show their admiration for Sakharov. The best way they could do so, they said, was to sing—and they did.

Two years later, Drell and Sakharov met again at a scientific conference in Tbilisi, the Georgian capital. They talked for hours about physics, arms control, human rights, and literature over a series of informal lunches, dinners, and teas. Drell noted in a private travelogue that Sakharov and his wife, Yelena Bonner, "think Faulkner is America's greatest author; 'One Day in the Life of Ivan Denisovitch' is Solzhenitsyn's best work; 'Cancer Ward' comes next: and the Gulag [*The Gulag Archipelago*, by Solzhenitsyn] is most important for history."

Drell agreed to carry some dissident papers to the West, and packed them with his own notes in his luggage, concealed, among other places, in his socks. "It took me close to an hour to find the various letters and documents buried among my other papers and on me that I was carrying out because I had hidden them so well," he noted.

For Drell, Sakharov was a saintly figure—a scientist and man of conscience and courage prepared to challenge the Kremlin. He once called him "a great scientist, and eloquent and brave spokesman for human rights, an indomitable and unflinching figure of courage and reason, a stirring example of the freedom and dignity of the human spirit."

Sakharov was awarded the Nobel Peace Prize in 1975 but was barred by the Kremlin from traveling to Norway to accept it. In 1980 the KGB secret police hauled him from his Moscow apartment and took him to Gorky, an industrial city closed to foreigners, where he was confined for the next six years. Though virtually under house arrest and without a phone line, Sakharov managed to relay messages and papers to the West through a network of family and friends. Drell took up his cause with a passion. In a barrage of letters and petitions to fellow scientists, the White House,

Congress, and the Kremlin, and appearances at international conferences, Drell became one of Sakharov's most faithful defenders. On one occasion, in December 1981, he showed up uninvited at the Soviet consulate in San Francisco with Paul Flory, a Stanford colleague, to deliver a statement supporting Sakharov. His entreaties outside the gate were so intense the Russians finally invited him inside for a brief but futile conversation.

Sakharov, who engaged in several debilitating hunger strikes in Gorky to protest his confinement, gratefully employed the Drell connection to reach foreign scientists and leaders. In 1983, he produced an essay titled "The Danger of Thermo-Nuclear War," which was presented as an open letter to Drell and reprinted in *Foreign Affairs*.

The two men did not always agree on arms control matters. In the *Foreign Affairs* article, Sakharov offered a qualified endorsement to the American plan to build the MX missile, seeing it as a step that would ultimately encourage nuclear arms negotiations. Drell disagreed, believing the new weapons would add a new element of instability to the Soviet-American nuclear standoff because they would be vulnerable to a Soviet strike. He told Sakharov so in a letter.

Sakharov followed Drell's campaign on his behalf via Radio Free Europe broadcasts that he could barely make out in Gorky over the static of Soviet jamming towers. He was very thankful for the support. In a letter dated June 1, 1981, and smuggled to the West by friends, he wrote:

Dear Sidney,

This time I want to write you not an "open" letter but a most ordinary one, and to thank you with all my heart.

Lyusya [Yelena] and I continue to feel that in that infinitely distant world which our children have wandered off to and where they now live, there are some people (a tiny few) who have not forgotten them or us, you being one of the few. I sense this almost physically, seeing you in my mind's eye in your checkered suit (though you may dress differently now).

We do not know what will happen next, and we are very worried. Since the theft of my briefcase, I have not been doing any science. I lack the strength and time for it. Somehow I have to make up for what was stolen, and I have the feeling I must hurry. So long for now. Stay well.

Despite all the obstacles, the two men continued to compare notes about physics, too. "In Tbilisi, incidentally, you (perhaps thinking aloud) asked me the memorable question, why is the charge of the proton exactly equal to that of the positron," Sakharov wrote in a smuggled note late in 1981. Sakharov went on to explore the issue in detail, including several complex mathematical equations.

Drell was thrilled when he got word in December 1986 that Mikhail Gorbachev had decided to free Sakharov and let him return to Moscow. He wrote Sakharov later that month, "It was marvelous news to hear that you have now returned to your apartment in Moscow and are ready and able to resume a normal existence again. It is the best news in a long while for your many friends." Drell was pleased to receive an invitation to visit Moscow from the Soviet Academy of Sciences not long after Sakharov's liberation and was reunited with his friend there in May 1987. The two met again at Stanford in August 1989. By then Sakharov had become an outspoken member of the Soviet parliament, openly challenging Gorbachev and the Communist Party. The rapid transformation of Sakharov from muzzled dissenter to politician and public scold was a powerful signal of the change that Gorbachev was encouraging in Soviet society. Sakharov died just a few months after his Stanford sojourn.

Drell, to this day, remembers Sakharov with great warmth and affection. He will sometimes recall the lines he penned for a memorial tribute. "Andrei Sakharov is one of those very rare figures in history of whom it may be said, as did Anatole France in his eulogy at Emile Zola's funeral, noting his persistent and effective pursuit of justice in the Dreyfus case: 'His destiny and his courage combine to endow him with the greatest of fates. He was a moment in the conscience of humanity.'"

He was also the man who pointed Drell toward the goal of nuclear disarmament.

CHAPTER SEVENTEEN

I'm not sure whether our tactical nuclear weapon policy frightens the Soviets, but it sure scares the hell out of me.
—SAM NUNN

Not long after taking his place in the Senate in January 1973, Sam Nunn encountered a nuclear weapons issue that terrified him. It was the hair-trigger status of American nuclear weapons in Europe.

Senator John Stennis, who had succeeded Richard Russell as chairman of the Armed Services Committee, was seriously wounded by gunfire during a mugging outside his Washington home in 1973. Unable to travel, he dispatched Nunn in his stead to Europe in February 1974 to review the readiness of NATO forces. He told Nunn he wanted him to "to be his legs and eyes, in effect, in Europe." Stennis assigned Frank Sullivan, one of the committee's senior staff members, to work with the freshman senator. The two men spent hundreds of hours preparing for the trip—a level of painstaking advance work that became a Nunn trademark whenever he tackled a major issue.

During their two-week trip, Nunn and Sullivan were startled to find that NATO and American military commanders in Western Europe considered the use of nuclear weapons a first rather than last resort. Their reasoning was simple: "Use them or lose them," as Nunn recalled.

If a European war started, defense analysts at the time assumed, it would begin with a massive ground attack by Warsaw Pact tank divisions through the Fulda Gap, along the border between East Germany and West Germany. The invasion route would put the Warsaw Pact forces quickly within striking distance of Frankfurt and several large American military bases.

NATO forces, despite the presence of more than 150,000 American troops in West Germany, would be badly outnumbered, possibly by three to one. To avoid defeat, NATO and American commanders might have no choice but to respond with nuclear weapons. While that might be militarily effective, it could ignite a devastating nuclear exchange, or short of that, would put NATO in the untenable position of using nuclear weapons in its own territory to blunt an invasion.

The military-political equation was unsustainable—the greater the imbalance in forces, the more NATO needed nuclear weapons; the more it relied on nuclear weapons, the more it risked waging a war that would consume all of Europe and quite possibly lead to a global nuclear confrontation between the United States and Soviet Union.

"I felt it was imperative we move away from relying on the early first use of nuclear weapons," Nunn recalled. "I was both surprised and disturbed to find how much our frontline commanders relied on tactical nuclear weapons and . . . how deteriorated we were in terms of conventional capability and how terrible morale was."

Several tactical commanders met Nunn and Sullivan for a beer one evening and told them they were likely to seek Washington's approval to use nuclear weapons as soon as fighting started. Nunn said: "Their theory was—and this was never written down, and people in Washington didn't realize this—that it was going to take any president four, five days to give them release authority to use tactical nuclear weapons. So they were going to ask at almost the beginning of any kind of conflict, even if it was inadvertent. And that was a warning to me. I said to Frank as we were coming back . . . 'I'm not sure whether our tactical nuclear weapon policy frightens the Soviets, but it sure scares the hell out of me.' "

If NATO forces didn't use battlefield nuclear weapons in the first hours of battle, they would probably retreat westward with the weapons, setting the stage for an equally unappealing scenario— firing nuclear arms at targets in West Germany. Nunn compared it to a Marx Brothers routine he had seen. "Groucho held the pistol up to his—he was standing by the window, and the thugs were coming toward him, and he said, 'Take one step closer and I'll pull the trigger.' He had it on his own head."

Even plans for handling the families of American troops in wartime concerned Nunn. He said: "We were not going to be able to evacuate the dependents. That was a joke. . . . Nothing affected me more than the realization that you couldn't get the women and children out, and they were going to be right in the middle of the battle, and the soldiers who were supposed to be fighting were going to be worrying about their families."

Nunn was also shaken to find that NATO nuclear weapons were poorly secured. "One of the last stops we made was to a tactical nuclear weapons storage place," he recalled. "As I was leaving and had gotten briefed by the generals and they were walking along with me, I shook hands with a sergeant on the way out and I felt a note crumpled up that he handed me. I looked at it while I was still there, and it said, 'Senator Nunn, this is all b.s.'—except spelled out. He said, 'If you'll see me and my buddies after you can shake your escorts, I'll tell you what's really going on.' "

Nunn and Sullivan slipped their escorts later that day. The troops warned them that nuclear arms stored at the base were so poorly secured that a small group of terrorists could easily break into the base and steal them. The soldiers also described widespread drug use among the men guarding nuclear weapons. "This was after Vietnam," Nunn said. "There was a huge deterioration of morale in the military. So there were people guarding nuclear weapons that were hooked on drugs."

"That had a huge effect on me," Nunn said. When he returned to Washington, he went straight to see James Schlesinger, the secretary of defense. "Jim took it very seriously," Nunn recalled. "The Defense Department took a lot of corrective steps. We didn't have good electronic wiring. We didn't have good perimeter fencing. We did not have a good emergency relief capability. We could have held off three or four terrorists. We couldn't have held off ten or twenty. The guards didn't have adequate clothing for perimeter patrols in wintertime. It was a mess."

The visit convinced Nunn that NATO needed to build up its conventional forces. "We were so complacent, and so dependent on nuclear weapons. We were going to just basically blow up the world."

Nunn prepared an unclassified trip report for the committee that was made public in early April. "The nuclear threshold in Europe is quite low," Nunn reported. "There is a considerable danger that tactical nuclear weapons would be used at the very outset of a war, leading to possible, or even probable, escalation to strategic nuclear war. Our plan to use tactical nuclear weapons 'as soon as necessary' is heavily emphasized—but 'as late as possible' does not get enough emphasis. I believe that much more emphasis should be given to the latter."

He warned that some West German leaders saw the presence of American conventional forces in their nation as a "big bell" that would sound in the first hours of a land invasion, leading American commanders to use nuclear weapons along the East German border, thereby preventing West German cities and industrial centers from becoming "a nuclear wasteland, or a conventional battleground."

"Some military commanders may tend to exaggerate the need and accelerate the request to use nuclear weapons because they fear that political decisions to use nuclear weapons would take so long that all conventional forces would be destroyed."

The report gave Nunn his first taste of national attention on defense issues. It immediately established him as an authority on NATO affairs, and put his fellow senators on notice that Sam Nunn was going to be a formidable force on military matters, an important step toward assuming the powerful role Richard Russell had played in the Senate, and that Uncle Carl had exercised in the House.

In the wake of the report, Nunn sponsored three legislative measures related to NATO that profoundly altered the makeup of NATO forces and the alliance's strategy for use of nuclear weapons. One measure beefed up American forces in Europe by permitting the Army to cut support troops on the continent and convert them to combat units, which became known as the Nunn Brigades. A second measure required the Pentagon to examine tactical nuclear weapons in Europe—plans for their use, where they were based, how they were secured, and so on. The legislation led to an overhaul of American and NATO policy governing the handling and potential use of the weapons. The third action forced NATO to improve planning for American and allied forces to fight together.

NATO was just one of many military issues that Nunn tackled as he settled into the Senate. The Vietnam War was a national preoccupation, and he devoted a good deal of time to getting up to speed on the conflict. That quickly brought the new senator to the attention of Henry Kissinger, who was helping Richard Nixon prosecute the war and manage the peace talks with North Vietnam aimed at ending it.

Nunn headed to Vietnam in January 1975—five months after Nixon resigned and Gerald Ford became president—to assess the war and how much money Congress should appropriate for it. While he was there, Kissinger summoned top aides to the White House Situation Room to go over war funding plans. He reported that Ford wanted "to take a forward-leaning position" and "wants to do as much as possible to restore the situation in South Vietnam and Cambodia." When William Clements, the deputy defense secretary, informed the group that Nunn was in South Vietnam, Kissinger said, "I don't know if that's a plus or a minus." Clements, a Texas oilman, assured Kissinger, "Overall, I think it's a plus. He's a pretty good guy." Kissinger replied, "Yes, Nunn is a good fellow."

Unhappy with congressional meddling in Vietnam, Kissinger complained to Clements and the other officials that budget cuts in 1974 "resulted in a deterioration of the situation and that is their god-damn fault." To overcome congressional resistance to a supplemental funding request, Kissinger urged his colleagues to go on the offensive. He told them, "You have to make it clear to Congress that they have to take full responsibility for the fact that 50,000 men died in vain. That they understand."

Later in the discussion, he said, "They are not going to give us the money if we act like a bunch of pacifists."

After the three-week trip, Nunn put together a report on American aid to South Vietnam for the Armed Services Committee. It described the war as "a series of misjudgments, political and military mismanagements and tragedy."

Nunn recommended, among other things, that the United States limit military and economic support to South Vietnam to a level comparable to the military and economic aid North Vietnam was likely to receive from the Soviet Union and China, and that Washington not recommit American forces to South Vietnam. By 1975 the South Vietnamese military was handling combat operations. He noted that if his recommendations were followed, "our nation would have to be willing to accept the possible fall of South Vietnam without reentering the war." Given a reasonable level of aid, Nunn said, "South Vietnam does not appear in imminent danger of capture of its significant population centers or decimation, and has some chance of economic development." North Vietnamese forces captured Saigon less than three months later.

Nunn returned to Europe in November 1976 for another look at NATO forces, accompanied by Senator Dewey Bartlett, an Oklahoma Republican. This time the focus was a growing imbalance between NATO and Warsaw Pact conventional forces. Nunn and Bartlett issued a public report on their trip in late January 1977. "It is the central thesis of this report," the two senators said, "that the Soviet Union and its Eastern European allies are rapidly moving toward a decisive conventional military superiority over NATO. This trend is the result of NATO's failure so far to modernize and maintain its conventional forces in response to the Warsaw Pact's buildup and modernization of conventional forces."

The timing was fortuitous. A week earlier, Jimmy Carter had succeeded Gerald Ford as president. His new defense secretary, Harold Brown, selected Bill Perry to run the Pentagon's research and engineering programs. Nunn and Perry were soon working together to modernize American and NATO forces.

Carter's election also brought an end to Henry Kissinger's dominant role in shaping American foreign and defense policy, but it did not silence him. Far from it. Though battered by the Vietnam War and unflattering accounts of his role in the Nixon administration, Kissinger remained visible, outspoken, and influential. He opened a successful consulting firm in New York, capitalizing on his fame and unparalleled access to foreign leaders, and produced two formidable books about his service in the Nixon and Ford administrations. He also launched a nationally syndicated column, a megaphone that he energetically employed to critique Jimmy Carter's foreign policy—and later unexpectedly turned against a fellow Republican secretary of state, George Shultz.

CHAPTER EIGHTEEN

We must make the most effective use of the superior technology in the United States and the stronger industrial base we enjoy.
—BILL PERRY

Bill Perry was the natural candidate to manage Pentagon research and engineering for Jimmy Carter and Harold Brown, both of whom were familiar with the worlds of science and engineering. Carter had studied nuclear engineering at the U.S. Naval Academy before taking over his family peanut business in Georgia and running for office. Brown, a physicist, former director of the Lawrence Radiation Laboratory in Livermore, California, and former president of the California Institute of Technology, was the first scientist to serve as defense secretary. He had directed Pentagon research and engineering himself from 1961 to 1965, when Robert McNamara was defense secretary.

Brown and Perry had met during the Kennedy administration but had not talked much since then. Eugene Fubini, a physicist and electrical engineer who had worked closely with Brown at the Pentagon and was renowned as an R & D dynamo, urged Brown to hire Perry.

The post seemed a perfect fit for Perry. He could direct billions of dollars in Pentagon spending and build a new generation of high-tech weapons. To Brown's surprise and dismay, Perry declined. Lee Perry recalled, "He got the call from Harold Brown.

And I was out trimming my roses. We have this wonderful property in Los Altos, and he said, 'I just got a call from Harold Brown,' and he explained what it was. And he said, 'I'm inclined to say no.' And so he did. And I said that's fine with me. I mean, he had his company going. We were very happy with what we were doing. And the company was successful and really engaging him."

But the calls kept coming. Fubini, deflated by Perry's rejection, told him it was the wrong decision and asked him to fly to Washington to talk it over. When they met, Perry outlined his reasons for staying at ESL. Fubini told him, "Weigh that against the job itself, what it will mean to you. . . . It's like being the chief defense technologist and senior design engineer of the entire defense community of the entire country. All the technology and most gifted scientists in the world will be available to you, and you'll have the power to set the agenda for their work."

By then Brown had unsuccessfully offered the job to other candidates. "I said, now I'm down to number five or six. I think I'll go back to Bill Perry and try to convince him. . . . What I told him was that he had no idea of what this could lead to, and that I could assure him that he would not regret taking it. So there is a story around that he was my sixth choice, which he was, but he was also my first." Perry accepted the post.

Like Sam Nunn, Perry was troubled by the appearance of increasingly robust Soviet and Warsaw Pact military forces, especially in Eastern Europe. "This was probably at the peak of the Cold War in terms of our concern that the Russians may be achieving military superiority," Perry said in 2008. The Pentagon estimated that the Soviet Union had achieved a clear numerical superiority in conventional weapons. "All during the fifties and sixties, we said, never mind, we have substantial nuclear superiority," Perry recalled. "By about the midseventies, that wasn't so clear anymore, and most estimates were that the Russians were approaching us or perhaps equal to us in nuclear weapons. Some were alleging that they were pulling ahead of us."

Perry came to the job with two primary objectives: maintain nuclear parity and offset the Soviet advantage in conventional weapons with superior American technology. He saw the twin goals as essential to a greater purpose: preventing a nuclear war.

Nuclear parity, including offensive systems like missile-equipped submarines that were resistant to surprise attack, would discourage the Kremlin from launching a nuclear strike against the United States. And robust conventional forces in Europe would prevent Soviet leaders from thinking that they had sufficient advantage to invade West Germany, an assault that might quickly escalate into a nuclear conflict.

One way out of the strategic box was to overcome the Warsaw Pact advantage in manpower and conventional firepower with a revolutionary new generation of smart, nonnuclear weapons and intelligence systems. In effect, if you can't outshoot them, outsmart them.

"We didn't have any serious consideration of trying to equal them in numbers," Perry recalled in 2008. "The cost would have been just absolutely prohibitive, not to mention the problem of where do you get all the soldiers to man all this equipment. So the challenge was to try to find a way of offsetting their numerical superiority with a qualitative advantage."

Perry briefly alluded to the concept when his nomination came before the Senate in March 1977. "I believe that this is a dangerous time for our country," he told the Armed Services Committee. "We are being challenged by the Soviet Union, which is conducting what I believe is an unprecedented buildup in military capability." America's response, Perry suggested, should include new weapons systems designed with "clever applications of technology and in particular in the technology of computers and electronic systems."

Sam Nunn was a committee member at the time. Perry recalled, "I can still remember being grilled by him in my confirmation hearing. And I thought, this is one smart cookie. He really knew what he was talking about."

Perry returned to the smart-weapon theme later in 1977, when Brown upgraded the Perry post and the promotion brought Perry back before the Armed Services Committee for confirmation to the new post. This time, having refined the idea with Brown and other Pentagon officials, he was more explicit about his objectives.

He told the committee, "We must make the most effective use of the superior technology in the United States and the stronger industrial base we enjoy. In order to get the advantages of the superior technology, we have a challenge in the Defense Department to get that technology out of the laboratories and into the field."

He cited three specific areas: reconnaissance, smart weapons, and improved munitions.

Brown dubbed the approach the "offset strategy." Years later, in describing the approach, Perry said the goal "was to offset the Soviet numerical advantage in conventional weapons by upgrading American tactical forces with modern technology, with special emphasis on information technology." The three primary elements were "improved sensors that would allow American troops to detect and locate targets on the battlefield," "precision-guided weapons that could destroy those targets with a single shot," and "stealth technology to protect American aircraft from Soviet air defense systems."

The Pentagon had been tinkering with smart weapons for years, without great success. "There was a long history of development of some of those things," Brown recalled. "I'd been in the Pentagon from 1961 to '68. I had started the idea of precision munitions in the early 1960s, and it actually took until the end of the '70s and thereafter before they came into inventory in a way that made them really effective."

The Brown-Perry plan, strongly supported by Jimmy Carter, was a logical extension of Perry's signature approach at EDL and ESL—developing conceptual breakthroughs, then producing technologically advanced hardware to achieve the audacious objectives. The two men made the effort a centerpiece of their tenure at the Pentagon, though the development work at the time was done in secret and received little public notice or credit.

The stealth aircraft program was quintessential Perry, employing the traits that made him a successful engineer and businessman. Brown, explaining Perry's success, said he was "careful, analytical, low-key but very determined. Planned carefully."

At Gene Fubini's suggestion, Perry recruited Paul Kaminski, a well-regarded young Air Force officer studying at the National Defense University in Washington, to be his special assistant and gave him wide latitude to examine the feasibility of designing and building radar-evading aircraft. To make communication as easy as possible, Perry assigned Kaminski to a small office adjacent to his office located on the Pentagon's E Ring, overlooking the Potomac River. Harold Brown had used the compact, inner office as a private retreat where he could read and write when he ran the Pentagon's research and engineering operations.

Kaminski recalled Perry's initial approach to the stealth project: "He got some early pieces that looked kind of interesting to him. He thought, this might be feasible. . . . One of the special assignments he gave me one day was to say, 'Here, go out and look at this. Do you think in practice in the field you could really get this to work and maintain the airplanes?' . . . I would take two or three weeks and look into some of these things and when we came back, we'd put our feet up and talk. And then he would integrate all of it together. That's the way he came to the conclusion that we ought to go make a big push."

Airplane designers had long dreamed of building a radar-evading aircraft, or in more technical terms, an airplane minimally visible as measured by its radar cross section (RCS). The very idea was electrifying. A stealth airplane would render traditional air defense systems obsolete, giving pilots virtually free run of the skies. Few new technologies could do more to reorder the rules and mores of war than fighter planes and bombers that the enemy could not detect. But the goal had proved elusive, as many development efforts ran up against theoretical and practical problems. Planes with design features and radar-absorbing materials that would reduce their radar signature, for instance, proved too heavy, too slow, too ineffectual, or just plain too unaerodynamic to be of much use. The obstacles led to other solutions, like the U-2, which defeated Soviet air defenses for four years by flying at 70,000 feet, outside the range of Russian surface-to-air missiles, and the SR-71, which traveled at three times the speed of sound as high as 93,000 feet. Both were reconnaissance aircraft, not combat airplanes.

The holy grail was a nearly radar-invisible combat aircraft—a warplane that radar systems would mistake for a bird in flight. Perry and Kaminski found soon after taking office that the Defense Advanced Research Projects Agency (DARPA), the Pentagon's over-the-horizon research unit, had been studying the feasibility of stealth technologies, some of which looked promising. The "Skunk Works," Lockheed's advanced aircraft unit in Burbank, California, had come up with a way to compute how visible different aircraft design features would be to radar. The technical term was computing the radar cross section. This was no easy trick relatively early in the computer era. The new computer program was based, in part, on the work of a Russian scientist that had been published in the Soviet Union in an unclassified technical journal in 1962 but not translated into English by the U.S. Air Force until 1971. Engineers at the Skunk Works figured that a combination of flat, angular surfaces could deflect radar signals better than a streamlined conventional shape. Ben Rich, who ran the Skunk Works at the time, described the proposed airplane design as "a diamond beveled in four directions, creating in essence four triangles." It looked like an Indian arrowhead when viewed from above.

Perry thought the Lockheed project, code-named "Have Blue," was encouraging enough to make stealth a top Pentagon goal and put it on an exceedingly fast track by Defense Department standards. He wanted an operational aircraft—the F-117 fighter—in three or four years. He also initiated work on a stealth bomber, the B-2. That contract was awarded to Northrop Corporation by the Reagan administration in 1981.

Perry, known for his whimsical humor, ambled into a stealth planning meeting one day with an empty model airplane stand and announced, "Here's the stealth bomber."

Without Sam Nunn's support, the Air Force might have ended up with just a token fleet of the new planes. He learned about the development program by chance during a 1977 visit to Georgia, when a Lockheed executive mentioned the top-secret project. Later, he was formally briefed during a visit to the RAND Corporation, the Santa Monica, California, defense think tank that was created by the Air Force in 1948. As a member of the Armed Services Committee, Nunn made an annual January visit to RAND to catch up on the latest thinking about defense policy and technology, and to spend a few hours in the California sunshine playing golf with Don Rice, the RAND president. On one of those visits in the late 1970s, Ben Rich picked up Nunn and took him to the Lockheed plant to tell him about the stealth plans. The project was so closely held that a Senate aide who had accompanied Nunn to RAND was not permitted to go with him to Lockheed.

Nunn liked what he saw and returned to California several times in ensuing years to check on progress; one trip included a visit with Paul Kaminski to a heavily shielded Nevada airfield where he could see the planes in action. He became an enthusiastic supporter of the program.

Despite the obvious advantages of stealth warplanes, the Air Force was ambivalent about buying a large fleet of either the F-117 fighter or the B-2 bomber. As the Air Force trimmed funding for the planes during their manufacturing phase in the 1980s, Nunn insisted that the Air Force budget cover the cost of fifty-four fighters and twenty-one bombers.

In addition to the stealth projects, Perry thought it essential to give military commanders on the ground better intelligence about the battlefields on which they operated. Earlier administrations had developed an airborne radar system that gave American and allied forces a detailed picture of aerial operations in the skies for hundreds of miles around the mobile radar system. It greatly enhanced the management of air battles and air strikes. Perry wanted a similar system for ground commanders that would show them the location and movement of all forces on the battlefield, or in military parlance, provide a comprehensive order of battle.

"That was a tough development," he recalled. "You're looking at a ground background, which is a very cluttered environment. So you had to develop a radar which was capable of picking up a target as small as a tack in a noisy background environment. It was a very difficult technical problem." The program led to development of the Joint Surveillance and Target Attack Radar System, or JSTARS.

The hardware Perry launched is by now well known. The stealthy batlike F-117 fighter and the B-2 bomber, which looks more like a boomerang than a conventional airplane, rewrote the rules of airpower by giving the United States airplanes invisibility to conventional radar. Precision-guided munitions like laser-guided bombs permitted pinpoint targeting. And an array of new air-based sensors gave American commanders an instantaneous, detailed picture of the battlefield and the forces, weapons, and buildings on it.

While at the Pentagon, Perry saved a vital defense project that was headed for the garbage bin—the space-based global navigation technology known as the Global Positioning System, or GPS. Even though the system promised great advances in navigation by using satellites to determine the precise location of places and objects on earth, Pentagon budget cutters axed the project in an early stage of development. Perry persuaded Harold Brown to reinstate it after witnessing a demonstration of the system's accuracy. GPS technology proved critical to the development of high-tech weapons systems and is widely used today in everything from combat operations to commercial navigation devices and cell phone apps that guide users to their destination.

Perry also initiated research on unpiloted aircraft. The work led to development of the pilotless drones that now roam the skies over northwestern Pakistan, tracking and sometimes firing Hellfire missiles at suspected al-Qaeda terrorists hiding in the mountainous area. The aircraft are also used to hunt down suspected terrorists in Yemen and other locations in Africa and Asia. Unlike conventional airplanes, the missile-equipped drones can circle unobserved over a target site for several hours. One version, the Global Hawk, which does not carry missiles, can stay aloft for days, supplying an unbroken stream of intelligence.

The drones in many cases are operated by pilots based in Nevada who maneuver the planes from afar by remote control. The pilots use high-powered cameras aboard the unmanned planes to identify targets. When a suspected terrorist is spotted, and the identity is confirmed by the CIA, the pilots launch Hellfire missiles. While the drones have proved to be very effective, their use has raised questions about whether targeted individuals can be accurately identified and whether the missile attacks constitute a legally questionable form of assassination.

Looking back at his partnership with Perry, Brown said, "I

think that we essentially provided the technology that both contributed to convincing the Soviets that they were in a losing game, and served as the basis for subsequent U.S. military success, where there's been success."

While Perry was revolutionizing conventional military technology, he was also immersed in America's nuclear armory, discovering how unsettling it could be.

CHAPTER NINETEEN

My work has always been motivated by the fear—by the clear understanding of how dangerous nuclear weapons were.
—BILL PERRY

During the summer of 1980, late in his tenure as undersecretary of defense, Perry was awakened at 3 a.m. by a frightening phone call from the watch officer at the North American Air Defense Command (NORAD), the Pentagon nerve center for tracking a missile attack against the United States. The general reported that computers at the command center's heavily fortified underground complex near Colorado Springs, Colorado, showed two hundred Soviet missiles streaking toward the United States. "I still remember the general's words as if that call had been yesterday," Perry said.

The computer alert was a false one, but for a few terrifying minutes NORAD officers feared World War III might be starting. The malfunction proved to be a faulty computer chip that led to a simulation of a Soviet attack.

"That call is engraved in my memory," Perry said. "The danger of a nuclear war, the danger of a nuclear holocaust was not academic to me."

As the Pentagon's chief of research and engineering, Perry played a pivotal role in maintaining American nuclear parity with the Soviet Union, which was rapidly increasing its arsenal of warheads.

Along with Nunn, he also had to address the use of nuclear weapons to counter a feared Warsaw Pact invasion of Western Europe.

One potential response to the Warsaw Pact threat was the neutron bomb, a nuclear weapon variant designed to kill people rather than to destroy property. The explosive power, or yield, of the device would be less than a normal nuclear weapon, minimizing the lethal blast and heat generated by detonation. But it would generate an intense burst of neutrons that would kill people while leaving buildings intact. In theory, the weapon could be used on European battlefields to repulse invading ground forces without destroying nearby communities and their civilian populations. Samuel T. Cohen, a physicist and bomb designer at the Lawrence Livermore National Laboratory, invented the bomb in 1958, and a prototype was tested in 1963 at the underground test site in Nevada. "It's the most sane and moral weapon ever devised," Cohen said. "It's the only nuclear weapon in history that makes sense in waging war. When the war is over, the world is still intact."

Jimmy Carter and his defense team initially favored the weapon and included funding for it in their first budget plan. But opposition to the neutron bomb spiked after the *Washington Post* disclosed the secret budget item in 1977. Senator Mark Hatfield, an Oregon Democrat, called it "unconscionable" because it could be directed at civilian populations. As the Carter administration wavered, Sam Nunn stepped in to defend the bomb when the Senate debated the weapon in a rare closed session on July 1, 1977. The public and press were barred from the Senate chamber. Early in the debate, Senator Hubert Humphrey, the former vice president whom Richard Nixon defeated in the 1968 presidential election, opposed the bomb, but later in the day said he had changed his mind after Nunn's presentation during the floor debate.

Nunn recalled that he supported the neutron bomb because it was a battlefield weapon that the United States was more likely to use against Warsaw Pact forces than ordinary nuclear arms. "I had come to the conclusion that our nuclear weapons were not useable, and therefore were not a deterrent and didn't have the psychology of helping prevent war. . . . I felt like a more credible posture, with fewer tactical weapons, was essential." The Carter administration eventually turned against the weapon and moved to cancel warhead production in 1978. Henry Kissinger, like Nunn, disagreed with the decision and castigated the administration for "inconsistent pronouncements and unpredictable reactions that may have confounded and possibly encouraged Soviet leaders."

For Perry, the neutron bomb debate was just a preview of a volatile national donnybrook over whether the Soviet Union was on the verge of gaining nuclear superiority, and what Washington should do about it. Perry spent endless hours examining the enhanced Soviet threat and going over the issues in excruciating detail with congressional committees. One multiday set of Senate hearings in the spring of 1978 covered "Strategic Force Management," "ICBM Survivability," "Theater Nuclear Forces," "Sea Based Deterrent," "Strategic Bomber Force," and "Strategic Programs." Some of the most arcane discussion involved matters like silo hardness—the ability of underground missile silos to survive a nuclear attack—and "physics of fratricide." Fratricide, in nuclear terms, dealt with whether a reentry vehicle, the part of the missile carrying warheads, could withstand the detonation of warheads from a nearby reentry vehicle.

The catchphrase for America's perceived new weakness was "window of vulnerability." It captured the rising fear that a surprise Soviet nuclear attack could wipe out most of America's land-based intercontinental missiles before they could get off the ground. The idea seized Washington in the mid-1970s, driven by advances in Soviet missile and warhead technology.

From the time that the "missile gap" was debunked, in the early 1960s, to the mid-1970s, there was rough parity between American and Soviet nuclear forces, if not an American advantage. Soviet strength in land-based intercontinental missiles was counterbalanced by American bombers and submarine-launched missiles. But as the Russians built more powerful and accurate missiles, and armed them with multiple warheads, some exceedingly destructive even by nuclear bomb standards, American defense planners grew concerned that Moscow might calculate that it could launch a disabling first-strike attack against America's ground-based missiles, housed in underground silos in Missouri, Montana, Wyoming, South Dakota, and North Dakota. To counteract the threat, the United States needed its own new generation of ground-based ICBMs and a plan to shield them from Soviet attack. Planning for both had begun during the Nixon and Ford administrations.

Perry, as the Pentagon's chief weapons buyer, quickly found himself at the vortex of the debate. Looking back at the arguments today, they seem surreal, the ultimate expression of a world contorted by visions of nuclear Armageddon. There was general agreement in Washington that the United States needed a new intercontinental missile, the MX, to replace its aging fleet of Minuteman missiles. The heat was generated over where and how to base the MX, in particular how best to shield the missiles from attack. The greater potency and accuracy of Soviet missiles, in theory, meant that they might destroy or disable even heavily reinforced underground launch sites. The answer, or so it seemed, was to hide the missiles, or move them around, making it difficult for Soviet spy satellites to spot them and for war planners in Moscow to target them.

That gave rise to a variety of elaborate, costly, and outlandish basing schemes, all taken quite seriously at the time. One proposed the construction of gigantic oval railroad "racetracks" on federal lands in Utah and Nevada. Two hundred MX missiles would be shuttled among several thousand hardened shelters along the tracks, changing location from time to time. Under a variation, a Strangelovian shell game known as "multiple aim point," thousands of extra missile silos would be built, leaving Moscow guessing which sites actually housed weapons. Another madcap scheme, known as "mobile highway," called for putting the missiles on huge trucks, which would wander about the Interstate Highway System to keep the enemy mystified about their location. Advocates were undaunted by the fact that each vehicle, with a missile aboard, would weigh enough to crumble most highways. Other proposals included basing the missiles aboard small submarines operating in coastal waters, which was a more sensible plan, and stowing them aboard giant airplanes, which was not. The debate was fodder for countless editorial cartoons. One sly suggestion was to put the missiles on Amtrak trains, thus ensuring that no one would ever know where they were.

Tom Wicker, the *New York Times* columnist, ridiculed Perry in June 1980 for assuring Congress that the oval track design had been replaced by a simpler, less expensive straight-line track plan and that "no further changes beyond 'fine tuning' would be needed."

As the basing arguments escalated, Bill Moyers assembled a panel of experts in Salt Lake City on May 13, 1980, to debate the issue on a nationally televised PBS broadcast. Perry and Sid Drell were two of the combatants.

It was a politically charged event that Perry would probably prefer to forget. As the senior government official present, he took the lead in defending the plan. The audience at Symphony Hall, the debate site, frequently interrupted the discussion to applaud critical comments about the racetrack design. Moyers didn't disguise his own doubts about the plan. And Perry's comments at times unwittingly reinforced the perception that the plan was implausible. Here's a sampling:

MOYERS: Given that so much is going to be at stake for the Soviets, won't they go all-out to penetrate the location of the MX, and how can you be sure, in an open society such as ours, that you're going to keep the location of that particular missile secret?

PERRY: We have two different ways of preserving the security of the system, Bill. One of them is maintaining the secrecy of where the missile is located, and we have very elaborate ways of planning to do that. But in addition to that, even if the Soviet war planner were to believe that he had penetrated, even if he were to believe he knew where those missiles were located, he still could not launch an attack against the system, because even if he knew where they were located when his missiles were launched, he could not be sure that our ICBMs were in the same shelters when he arrived, and that is because we have designed the system so that the missiles could be moved quickly from shelter to shelter in an emergency.

MOYERS: If the MX takes direct hits, won't the fiber optics melt, and won't the radioactivity disturb the microwave and electromagnetic communications, making it very difficult for our controllers to communicate with the missiles and give them orders?

PERRY: We have three or four different redundant ways of communicating with the missiles, Bill.

MOYERS: Alternative ways?

PERRY: Alternative ways, any one of which is sufficient to communicate. The one which probably will survive all of these different moves you're talking about, would be a launch command given from our airborne command and control stations, and medium-frequency radio signals. This would not be susceptible to the nuclear blast and would not be concerned with lines being destroyed on the ground.

MOYERS: You mean we would have an alternative command center, airborne at all times?

PERRY: Yes, we will.

MOYERS: But I thought the Air Force had rejected the airborne MX because of the vulnerability of aircraft.

The audience erupted at that point with cheers, laughter, and applause.
Drell got a gentler reception.

MOYERS: Sidney Drell, you're a member of the President's Science Advisory Committee, and executive head of theoretical physics at Stanford University's Linear Accelerator Center. Do you have an alternative to the land-based MX?
DRELL: Yes, I do. I do believe it's important to the survivability of our forces. . . . We have studied other basing schemes and have proposed as an idea the deployment of the MX missile on small submarines moving in near coastal waters.

Looking back on the basing proposals a few years ago, Perry said drily, "We had a very convoluted development program trying to come up with different ways of basing the MXs so that they would not be subject to a disarming attack. . . . We finally ended up just putting them in silos."

Drell keeps two artifacts from the debate in his Hoover Institution office. One is a *New Yorker* cartoon picturing two men at a bar, one saying to the other, "Ordinarily, I lean toward a landbased MX system. But when I have a few drinks, I lean toward those little submarines."

The other is a miniature spoof model of one of Drell's favored mini-submarines, made by several of his graduate students during the MX basing battle. It's a bulbous vessel with a missile attached to either side and a tiny Drell doll in the wheelhouse. "USS Drell" is stenciled on the front.

Perry's work on the nuclear front was not confined to the MX missile or B-2 bomber, both of which were designed to carry nuclear warheads. He also set in motion, or accelerated, development of several other weapons systems that could deliver a nuclear blow against the Soviet Union, including the Trident submarine, Trident missile, and a variety of cruise missiles.

"At the time," he sometimes tells his students, "I saw all too clearly the risks in building such deadly weapons systems, but I believed it was necessary to take those risks, given the very real threats we faced during the Cold War."

In his mind, the new weapons were designed less to wage war than to prevent one. "All of these things I've described to you were designed to prevent a nuclear war," he said. "We did not want the Soviet Union to believe that it had such a military advantage over us that they might be tempted to attack.

"My work has always been motivated by the fear—by the clear understanding of how dangerous nuclear weapons were. And the fear that they were going to be used, and also a clear understanding of how catastrophic the results would be if they were used. I don't think people understand that, even today."

Though Perry was not directly involved in nuclear arms negotiations with the Soviet Union, the weapons work he initiated had potential implications for any agreement that limited delivery systems for nuclear weapons. The Carter administration inherited the unfinished second phase of arms talks, SALT II, from Gerald Ford and Henry Kissinger. After recalibrating the American bargaining position, Jimmy Carter sent Cyrus Vance, his secretary of state, to Moscow in March 1977 to present the new American proposal. It called for a lower ceiling on nuclear arms than Ford and Brezhnev had set as a target in Vladivostok in late 1974. The Kremlin brusquely rejected the new proposal, saying it was not consistent with the earlier agreement.

Over the next several years, Washington and Moscow narrowed their differences and eventually reached agreement on a new treaty that Jimmy Carter and Leonid Brezhnev signed in Vienna on June 18, 1979. The agreement set an initial limit of 2,400 on strategic nuclear delivery vehicles—long-range land- and sea-based missiles, heavy bombers, and air-to-surface missiles. The ceiling would drop to 2,250 by 1981. It also covered a variety of other matters, including a ban on mobile missile systems like some of the MX basing schemes, and a limit on the number of warheads a missile could carry—ten per missile for a new missile that could be developed under the treaty, fourteen per submarine-based missile. Carter sent the treaty to the Senate for ratification four days after the signing ceremony in Vienna.

Sam Nunn, dissatisfied with the Carter administration's commitment to strengthening American military forces after the Vietnam War, informed the White House that the Senate was unlikely to ratify the treaty unless the administration proposed a large increase in defense spending. Henry Kissinger, not long out of office and still an influential voice on arms control matters, also said ratification should be delayed until Carter pledged to bolster the Pentagon budget.

Ratification became a moot issue after the Soviet invasion of Afghanistan in late 1979. Carter asked the Senate to suspend consideration of the treaty, one of several retaliatory moves he ordered. He later announced the United States would comply with the treaty as long as the Soviet Union did so. The Kremlin said it would. The Reagan administration reaffirmed the commitment when it took office in 1981.

With Ronald Reagan's election as president in 1980, Bill Perry looked westward once again. Rather than resuming his career as a defense contractor, he joined a San Francisco–based investment banking and venture capital firm, Hambrecht & Quist, which specialized in technology companies. Eventually he set up and managed a spin-off venture, Technology Strategies and Alliances. It forged partnerships between established technology companies and Silicon Valley start-ups. He eventually recruited Paul Kaminski, his right-hand man on the stealth airplane programs and later the Pentagon's chief weapons acquisition officer, to serve as chief operating officer.

In 1988, Perry joined the Stanford faculty as codirector of the Center for International Security and Arms Control, the organization that Sid Drell had cofounded in 1983. He kept lines open to Washington by serving on numerous defense task forces and commissions, including the Packard Commission, which led to an overhaul of Pentagon management and weapons procurement practices. It was headed by David Packard, one of the founders of Hewlett-Packard and a former deputy defense secretary.

Despite the Washington assignments, Perry had no intention of returning to Washington, and no expectation that he would be handed the opportunity to dismantle some of the nuclear weapons he had helped build.

CHAPTER TWENTY

They all thought Reagan was out of his mind,
and I was out of my mind.
—GEORGE SHULTZ

When George Shultz accepted Ronald Reagan's unexpected invitation on June 25, 1982, to become secretary of state he did not know that the elimination of nuclear weapons would be high on his diplomatic agenda. As an economist who had served Richard Nixon in three domestic policy posts and then retired to California to help run the Bechtel Corporation and teach at Stanford, he was a nuclear weapons novice. The atom bombs dropped on Japan may have saved his life by ending the war before Shultz and his fellow Marines were ordered to invade Honshu, Japan's heartland, but the Cold War nuclear arms race that followed crossed Shultz's desk primarily as an economic and budget matter rather than a defense issue. "It's a fair statement that I wasn't thinking about defense issues in any deep way," he said.

With the abrupt exit of Alexander Haig as secretary of state, Shultz stepped into the arcane but critical realm of nuclear weapons like a rookie quarterback starting his first game in the National Football League. His views about nuclear weapons were relatively conventional, but not deeply embedded. He understood and accepted their central role in America's defense strategy, but as a domestic policy specialist, he was not a keeper of the nuclear faith or hidebound defender of the concept of nuclear deterrence.

As he soon discovered, his new boss was a nuclear heretic. After some hesitation, Shultz became one, too, though he continued to harbor doubts that nuclear weapons could really be abolished.

Shultz's tenure as secretary of state was a tumultuous time, and much of his attention was devoted to other issues, including Soviet and Cuban efforts to expand their influence in Central America. Shultz spent countless hours trying to restrain administration colleagues, like William J. Casey, the director of central intelligence, who were eager to counter Soviet and Cuban moves with covert American intelligence and paramilitary operations in the region. Instability in the Middle East was also a consuming concern. Devastating suicide terrorist attacks in 1983 against the American embassy in Beirut (seventeen Americans died) and the U.S. Marine Corps barracks in Lebanon (241 American servicemen were killed) stunned Shultz and the world. They proved to be the opening shots in a new era of suicide terror attacks. The carnage haunts him to this day. "The worst day of the Reagan administration, particularly for me, being a Marine, was when our Marine barracks were taken out in Beirut," he said. "They were there on a peacekeeping mission, and I've second-guessed myself on that mission more than any other thing I've ever been involved in in my life." But as the Reagan years passed, Shultz's attention turned increasingly to Moscow and arms control issues.

The origins and passion of Ronald Reagan's nuclear apostasy have been much examined and debated. Some acolytes see Reagan as a visionary leader who decisively cut through the nuclear orthodoxy of his day. Other observers view Reagan as an unsophisticated thinker who naively and recklessly challenged America's reliance on nuclear weapons as the ultimate deterrent to attack. There's some truth to both depictions. Reagan abhorred the idea of nuclear war, and came to office determined to replace the nuclear balance of terror with some saner strategy, up to and including the elimination of nuclear weapons. But he lacked a nuanced strategy to achieve that goal. He ended up embracing the Strategic Defense Initiative (SDI), a misconceived, overdrawn scheme to build a space-based antimissile shield. His faith in the plan ultimately undermined his dream of abolishing nuclear weapons. Shultz was skeptical about the project—as were Bill Perry, Sam Nunn, and Sid Drell—but he eventually embraced it.

Reagan's doubts about nuclear weapons can be traced back to the beginning of the nuclear era. In December 1945, just four months after the destruction of Hiroshima, the future president signed up to speak at an antinuclear rally in Hollywood. Reagan dropped out after Warner Bros. advised its movie star that the appearance would violate his contract with the studio. Reagan was a liberal Democrat in those days, but even after making a hard turn to the right and becoming Republican governor of California in 1967, he remained dubious about nuclear weapons. Several Reagan advisers in Sacramento, who later served as his top White House aides, recalled that as governor, Reagan often expressed doubts about the heavy American reliance on nuclear weapons. Reagan told them he thought a nuclear war could not be won and should never be fought, a line that he would repeat many times in the years ahead.

At the 1976 Republican National Convention, Reagan addressed the party faithful after they had nominated Gerald Ford. Straying from the usual boilerplate for such moments, Reagan talked about the danger of nuclear war and how future generations would know whether "we kept our world from nuclear destruction."

Reagan did not campaign in 1976 or 1980 as a nuclear abolitionist. If anything, his strident anti-Soviet comments and repeated calls to strengthen American military forces suggested he would build up America's nuclear arsenal. Rather than easing fears of a nuclear confrontation with the Kremlin,

Reagan's hot rhetoric fueled concern that he might be quick to pull the nuclear trigger.

His confrontational stance masked a genuine dread of nuclear war. "The decision to launch nuclear weapons was mine alone to make," Reagan wrote in his autobiography. "We had many contingency plans for responding to a nuclear attack. But everything would happen so fast that I wondered how much planning or reason could be applied in such a crisis. The Russians sometimes kept submarines off our East Coast with nuclear missiles that could turn the White House into a pile of radioactive rubble within six or eight minutes.

"*Six minutes* to decide how to respond to a blip on a radar scope and decide whether to unleash Armageddon!

"How could anyone apply reason at a time like that?

"There were some people in the Pentagon who thought in terms of fighting and *winning* a nuclear war. To me it was simple common sense: A nuclear war couldn't be won by either side. It must never be fought. But how do we go about trying to prevent it and pulling back from this hair-trigger existence?"

The Reagan team that moved into Washington's top defense and national security posts in January 1981 was filled with defense hard-liners. They included Secretary of Defense Caspar Weinberger and his aides at the Pentagon, Bill Casey at the CIA, and the White House national security staff. Secretary of State Alexander Haig, a retired Army general who had been a Kissinger aide and later White House chief of staff for Nixon, was less ideological than his colleagues but shared their conventional views about the Kremlin and nuclear weapons.

Reagan led the charge against the Kremlin in the first years of his presidency. Just days after his inauguration, he said of the Kremlin, "they reserve unto themselves the right to commit any crime, to lie, to cheat." Addressing members of the British Parliament in London in June 1982, he talked of "the march of freedom and democracy, which will leave Marxism-Leninism on the ash heap of history." And most memorably, he told a gathering of the National Association of Evangelicals in March 1983 that the Soviet Union was "an evil empire."

He matched his tough talk with a series of hard-edged policy decisions that went well beyond the long-standing American strategy of trying to contain the Soviet Union. Rather than checking the Kremlin, Reagan seemed intent on checkmating it. One pivotal policy document, National Security Decision Directive 75, adopted on January 17, 1983, called for reversing Soviet expansionism. The White House backed up the decisions with a spike in defense spending and covert operations designed to counter Soviet weight in Poland, Afghanistan, Central America, Africa, and other areas.

Yet, even as Reagan squeezed the Kremlin, he quietly looked for ways to open arms control negotiations. Unlike his predecessors, he set his sights on reducing, then eliminating American and Soviet nuclear arsenals, rather than settling for a ceiling on delivery systems. His defense buildup, at least in his mind, was designed in part to induce the Kremlin to make such a deal. His determination to rid the planet of nuclear weapons only seemed to grow stronger after he barely survived an assassination attempt on March 30, 1981.

To the great dismay of Haig and top White House advisers, Reagan decided in April 1981 to respond to a pro forma letter from Leonid Brezhnev, the Soviet leader, with a personal letter that he drafted by hand. Reagan wrote of the desire of people everywhere to live in peace and freedom and reminded Brezhnev that a decade earlier, during a visit to California, the Soviet leader had warmly gripped his hand and assured him he understood the universal yearning for peace. Haig later told Lou Cannon, a *Washington Post* reporter and Reagan biographer, "I found myself astonished by [Reagan's] attitude when I measured it against the backdrop of what he was saying publicly, and what was attributed to him as a classic Cold Warrior." Richard Pipes, a Harvard historian serving as the top Soviet affairs specialist at the White House, found the draft "mawkish." He recalled, "I could not believe my eyes . . . it was written in a Christian turn-the-other-cheek spirit sympathetic to the point of apology, full of icky sentimentality."

After several days of skirmishing with his aides, Reagan produced a muted version of his letter. He instructed the State Department to deliver it to Brezhnev, along with the more standard diplomatic boilerplate Haig and his aides had prepared.

Reagan's arrival in the White House coincided with and energized a wave of antinuclear sentiment that threatened to undermine American and NATO plans to base a new fleet of intermediate-range Pershing II missiles in Western Europe to counter similar Soviet weapons. Intermediate-range missiles have a range of 500–5,500 kilometers (300–3,400 miles). In the mid-1970s, the Kremlin had added hundreds of new intermediate-range missiles to its arsenal, most based in Western regions of the Soviet Union. The weapons, SS-20 missiles, were within easy striking distance of all Western European capitals. Each could carry three nuclear warheads.

The nuclear freeze movement, as the campaign was called, swept through Europe and the United States. The goal in Europe was to block the placement of the Pershing II missiles in Western Europe. But the movement's appeal extended well beyond the immediate issue of European missiles. It tapped into decades of Cold War anxiety about the prospect of nuclear war and a growing sense among many citizens that the nuclear balance of terror was morally and politically unacceptable. Jonathan Schell gave voice to the alarm in a series of *New Yorker* essays in 1982 that he expanded into a book, *The Fate of the Earth*. In June 1982, nearly a million people gathered in New York's Central Park to call for freezing the production of nuclear weapons. Numerous demonstrations erupted in Western Europe.

While the movement's aims, broadly speaking, were aligned with Reagan's antinuclear views, he was not prepared to let it undercut his resolve in dealing with Moscow. His administration deftly countered the freeze movement with what became known as the "zero-zero" proposal. If Moscow removed its intermediate-range missiles from the European theater, Reagan said, Washington would cancel its Pershing II basing plan. Looking back at the decision in his memoirs, Reagan saw the "zero-zero" plan "as the first step toward the elimination of all nuclear weapons from the earth." Moscow rejected the proposal and the United States installed its missiles in Western Europe in late 1983.

George Shultz leaped aboard the fast-moving Reagan express in June 1982 without a great deal of experience handling relations with the Soviet Union. Though he had served as an informal Reagan adviser during the presidential campaign and headed an economic advisory committee for the new administration, he was preoccupied with Bechtel business during the first months of the Reagan presidency. Reagan had passed over Shultz in assembling his cabinet. Richard Nixon pushed for the appointment of Haig, telling Reagan, "George Shultz has done a superb job in every government position to which I appointed him. However, I do not believe that he has the depth of understanding of world issues generally and the Soviet Union in particular that is required for this period."

What Shultz did have was a commonsense philosophy about how relations between nations should be conducted, and a conviction, based on his experience mediating labor-management disputes, that disagreements could be bridged by patient negotiation. He also had a firm but collegial management style. Over time he forged a close working relationship with Ronald and Nancy Reagan that helped him overcome fierce opposition and infighting within the administration. The First Lady, concerned about her husband's legacy, also favored improving relations with the Soviet

Union and encouraged the president to do so. Once he grew conversant with defense policy, Shultz put all these tools to work on behalf of Reagan's arms control agenda.

As Nixon's Treasury secretary, Shultz had dealt with numerous foreign economic leaders, including the Soviet minister of foreign trade, Nikolai Patolichev. He was impressed by the Russian's toughness and pragmatism, and touched by Patolichev's veneration of the millions of his countrymen who had died defending their nation during World War II. In his memoirs, Shultz noted: "I also learned that the Soviets were tough negotiators but that you could negotiate successfully with them. In my experience, they did their homework and had skill and patience and staying power. I respected them not only as able negotiators but as people who could make a deal and stick to it."

As he took office, Shultz was troubled by the breakdown in high-level communication between Washington and Moscow that followed the 1979 Soviet invasion of Afghanistan and the American boycott of the 1980 Summer Olympics in Moscow. Not long after Shultz became secretary of state, Helmut Schmidt, the German chancellor, told Shultz at a dinner at Shultz's California home, "George, the situation is dangerous, there is no human contact." When he returned to Washington, Shultz discussed the problem with Reagan and they agreed Shultz should start meeting regularly with Anatoly Dobrynin, the Soviet ambassador. Shultz emphasized the importance of keeping lines of communication open in September 1983 when the Soviet military shot down a Korean Airlines Boeing 747 carrying 269 passengers and crew after it inadvertently strayed into Soviet air space. The incident put a chill in relations with Moscow as Reagan and Shultz denounced the brutal attack, but Shultz pointedly did not cancel an upcoming meeting with Andrei Gromyko, the Soviet foreign minister. With Reagan's approval, he also resisted calls from Weinberger and other Reagan aides to suspend arms control talks with the Kremlin.

As Shultz waded into world affairs, he surrounded himself with knowledgeable, confident advisers, including Paul Nitze, a defense expert who had advised presidents since the beginning of the Cold War. Shultz said, "From a half century of involvement, he was a walking history of the Cold War as well as one of the creators of the doctrines by which the alliance of democracies had proven able to contain Soviet power. . . . He was just the man to help me master the incredibly complex issues of arms control."

Shultz's self-confident management style tolerated strong personalities like Nitze. He welcomed debate and dissent, but expected his staff to adhere to policy directives, once deliberations ended and presidential decisions were in place.

Giving his staff a sense of ownership was critical, he said. "If you listen to people and give some room for people to use their own discretion on the things within their span of work, you're going to be much further ahead. There is a saying that summarizes it in an odd way: 'Nobody ever washed a rented car.'"

Jim Goodby, who considers Shultz the best of the ten secretaries of state he served, said, "He encouraged people. He gave them a sense of their worth. He gave them a sense of the potential that could be realized. That's very unusual in a high-level person like that." On one occasion, Shultz arranged an Oval Office meeting with Reagan and Goodby. When they arrived, Shultz steered Goodby to the chair next to the president, the spot normally reserved for the ranking visitor. Goodby keeps a photo of the encounter on his wall to this day.

As Shultz started to engage nuclear weapons issues, he found Reagan bedazzled by the idea of a missile shield. Exactly how Reagan lighted on the notion remains unclear. It may have been during a 1967 visit as California governor to the Lawrence Radiation Laboratory. Edward Teller, the lab director at the time, had championed development of the hydrogen bomb and later became a leading proponent of the missile shield concept. The lab visit included a two-hour briefing on missile defense technologies. In 1979, presidential candidate Reagan visited the North American Air Defense Command, based in an underground complex at Cheyenne Mountain, Colorado. When commanders told him they could track but not stop incoming Soviet warheads, he said, "There must be something better than this."

Early in his presidency, Reagan asked the chiefs of the armed services to tell him about the consequences of an all-out nuclear war with the Soviet Union. They delivered the answer at a meeting of the National Security Council in the Cabinet Room at the White House on December 3, 1981. "The JCS [Joint Chiefs of Staff] estimates that if the Soviets evacuate their cities prior to a nuclear attack, their losses would be 15 million, a number less than they lost in the Second World War or in the purges. The U.S., on the other hand, would lose some 150 million people. An effective civil defense program can cut that down to less than 40 million."

Shultz was not yet secretary of state, but he heard about the briefing later. He said it reinforced Reagan's view that a defense strategy premised on the extermination of millions of people was intolerable.

Reagan set his sights on a technologically audacious plan to protect the United States with an array of new weapons that, in theory, would intercept incoming Soviet missiles in flight. Scientists like Edward Teller were excited about the potential of powerful X-ray lasers, kinetic energy devices, particle beams, and other exotic technologies that might someday be turned into space-based weapons. The technologies were largely untested. Intercepting a single missile in midflight was hard enough. Knocking out a barrage of them accompanied by dozens of decoy warheads, the likely problem during a Soviet attack, seemed impossible.

Shultz first learned of Reagan's interest in missile defenses at an unscheduled private dinner with the Reagans on February 12, 1983, but didn't really understand the import of what Reagan said.

When a snowstorm prevented the Reagans from traveling to the presidential retreat at Camp David for the weekend, they invited George and O'Bie Shultz to supper in the family quarters at the White House. "During the course of the discussion," Shultz recalled, "he was telling me about the importance of learning to defend ourselves against ballistic missiles. I didn't get it until later."

That would be a month later, as it turned out—just days before Reagan planned to unveil his vision of a missile shield in a nationally televised address. In principle, Shultz thought "learning how to defend ourselves from ballistic missiles was a good idea." But he had serious doubts about the Reagan plan. Though not a technical expert, he suspected Reagan's advisers, including Teller and George Keyworth, the White House science adviser, were overselling the futuristic technologies. "We don't have the technology to say this," he told his State Department aides.

He also realized that work on a missile shield would likely run up against the 1972 ABM Treaty, upset allies, and effectively overturn decades of American nuclear strategy. It would, as he said, break the nuclear balance by giving the United States a huge advantage. If the Pentagon could shield America from a Soviet attack, Washington could deliver a deadly blow to the Soviet Union without fearing a retaliatory strike. Moscow would have to react to that terrifying prospect by coming up with its own shield, and before long, the two nations would be spending furiously on a defensive arms race.

On Capitol Hill, Sam Nunn had similar worries. As far as he was concerned, the ABM Treaty set strict limits on development, testing, and deployment of defensive systems. When the administration later asserted that it read the treaty and its legislative history differently, Nunn blew a gasket. He led an exhaustive Senate review of the negotiating and legislative record. When it was completed, he informed Reagan and Shultz that the Senate had approved the treaty on the clear understanding that it limited testing and development of defensive systems. Nunn wasn't opposed to all research, but thought it essential that the work conform with treaty restrictions. Nunn warned that "a unilateral executive branch decision to disregard" the Senate view "would provoke a constitutional crisis of profound dimensions." In his view, the White House was brazenly challenging the Senate's authority under the Constitution to review and ratify treaties. He threatened to slash funding for the missile shield program.

Shultz confronted Reagan with his own doubts about the missile shield plan and the wording of Reagan's planned speech. He recalled the White House scene in his memoirs: "I found great resistance to any change in the words for the speech. 'This paragraph is a revolution in our strategic doctrine,' I told President Reagan. He had Keyworth called in. I asked him, 'Can you be sure of an impenetrable shield? And what about cruise missiles? What about stealth bombers? Your language is sweeping. I'm not objecting to R and D, but this is a bombshell. What about the ABM Treaty? What about our allies and the strategic doctrine on which we and they depend? You don't say anything about those questions.' His answers were not at all satisfactory to me."

Despite Shultz's objections, Reagan went ahead with the announcement, adjusting the speech slightly to reflect some of Shultz's concerns. Speaking from the Oval Office in prime time on March 23, Reagan said, in part:

Let me share with you a vision of the future which offers hope. It is that we embark on a program to counter the awesome Soviet missile threat with measures that are defensive. Let us turn to the very strengths in technology that spawned our great industrial base and that have given us the quality of life we enjoy today.

What if free people could live secure in the knowledge that their security did not rest upon the threat of instant U.S.

retaliation to deter a Soviet attack, that we could intercept and destroy strategic ballistic missiles before they reached our own soil or that of our allies?

. . .

Tonight, consistent with our obligations of the ABM treaty and recognizing the need for closer consultation with our allies, I'm taking an important first step. I am directing a comprehensive and intensive effort to define a long-term research and development program to begin to achieve our ultimate goal of eliminating the threat posed by strategic nuclear missiles. This could pave the way for arms control measures to eliminate the weapons themselves. We seek neither military superiority nor political advantage. Our only purpose—one all people share— is to search for ways to reduce the danger of nuclear war.

Critics instantly dubbed the Reagan plan "Star Wars," after the popular George Lucas movies.

Shultz was not happy, but he publicly supported the initiative. He admired Reagan's instinct to embrace visionary ideas and to stand his ground. But he saw a downside to Reagan's boldness. As Shultz put it, Reagan had "a tendency to rely on his staff and friends to the point of accepting uncritically—even wishfully— advice that was sometimes amateurish and even irresponsible."

Many scientists, including Sid Drell, thought the scheme was fanciful. Among other faults, it seemed to run up against a basic principle of modern warfare, namely that any defense, no matter how clever, could be defeated by developing new and better offensive weapons. And in the nuclear arena, the sheer number of incoming Soviet warheads during the opening minutes of an attack—5,000 to 10,000—would overwhelm any defensive shield.

Drell considered ballistic missile defenses the equivalent of "quack medicine." He compared bold assertions about the missile shield to "invoking magic in a fashion reminiscent of the claim by

Glendower, in Shakespeare's *Henry IV, Part I,* 'I can call spirits from the vasty deep,' to which Hotspur responds, 'Why, so can I, or so can any man, but will they come when you do call for them?'"

Before long, Drell and two Stanford colleagues examined the Reagan plan in detail and pronounced it unworkable and ill-advised. "Our analysis raises grave doubts, on technical and strategic grounds, that substantial acceleration or expansion of ABM research and development is warranted or prudent," they said. "We do not know how to build a strategic defense of our society that can render nuclear weapons impotent and obsolete as called for by President Reagan."

Bill Perry was also unimpressed. He had initiated research work on laser weapons and particle beams while at the Pentagon during the Carter administration, and thought the technologies might someday prove workable, but he realized they could be effectively countered. He said: "The problem with Star Wars is that, unlike the Manhattan Project or the landing on the moon, we're not just competing with nature. We're competing with an opponent who can change the rules of the game and can invoke technology to try to defeat the system."

Perry and Brent Scowcroft, Gerald Ford's national security adviser, questioned the missile shield in a bipartisan report sponsored by the Aspen Institute for Humanistic Studies. "We see virtually no prospect of building a significant and effective population shield against a responsive enemy inside this century, and there is great uncertainty about the long term," they said.

Henry Kissinger, opining frequently about foreign policy issues from his new base in New York, viewed the Reagan plan more favorably. "President Reagan's Strategic Defense Initiative is the most recent attempt to overcome the military dead-end," he wrote in a 1985 *Washington Post* op-ed article. "I support the concept, but I fear that the plethora of explanations offered on its behalf may turn it into a slogan in search of a mission."

The missile defense plan was wedded to Reagan's vision of a world without nuclear weapons. In his prime-time address, Reagan alluded several times to his desire to free the world from the threat of nuclear war. He explained that the defense initiative could "pave the way for arms control measures to eliminate the weapons themselves."

None of Shultz's nuclear weapons tutors at the State Department thought abolition was plausible. Richard Burt, an arms control expert, called it a "pipe-dream." White House and Pentagon aides were equally dismissive. Whenever Reagan slipped the goal into the draft of a letter to the Soviet leader, or proposed embracing it in a speech, administration officials would try to take it out. Shultz initially questioned the goal himself. Reagan dug in.

In late 1983, Shultz told several State Department arms control specialists, "The president has noticed that no one pays any attention to him in spite of the fact that he speaks out about the idea publicly and privately. We owe him an answer. The president believes this is the way to go. If we disagree, we have to demonstrate why."

Shultz once again raised his doubts directly with Reagan. "I told the president I shared his dissatisfaction with our dependence on the threat of nuclear annihilation as the means of keeping the peace. 'But nuclear weapons cannot be uninvented,' I said. 'The present structure of deterrence and our alliances depends on nuclear weapons and the best approach is to work for large reductions in nuclear arsenals.' I made no real impact on the president with this argument. I gave him a paper with my line of reasoning, but he stuck with his own deeply held view of where we should be heading."

The president and his secretary of state continued to debate the merits of Reagan's approach over the course of several months. "He was annoyed with me for expressing my reservations," Shultz recalled.

In late November 1983, at a meeting in the Cabinet Room with Reagan and his top national security advisers, Shultz supported a

Weinberger plan to proceed with missile shield research and development work. But Shultz again voiced doubts. "We should go easy on throwing out a deterrence strategy that has worked well in favor of something new and immature," he said. Echoing Perry's analysis, he went on, "Military history teaches that the best defense is a good offense. We should not become confident that we can develop a defense that could not be countered."

Shultz seemingly surrendered in 1984. Reagan's landslide election to a second term that November reinforced Shultz's growing sense that he and his colleagues should defer to Reagan on nuclear policy, however unconventional his views. Lower-level administration officials were baffled by his shift. "They all thought Reagan was out of his mind, and I was out of my mind," Shultz said. He told one group of skeptical officials, "If you win 48 out of 50 states, you, too, can talk about eliminating nuclear weapons."

Shultz underscored his support in a showcase article in the Spring 1985 issue of *Foreign Affairs*. The article was titled "New Realities and New Ways of Thinking." On nuclear weapons, Shultz said: "During the next ten years, the U.S. objective is a radical reduction in the power of existing and planned offensive nuclear arms, as well as the stabilization of the relationship between offensive and defensive nuclear arms, whether on earth or in space. We are even now looking forward to a period of transition to a more stable world, with greatly reduced levels of nuclear arms and an enhanced ability to deter war based upon an increasing contribution of non-nuclear defenses against offensive nuclear arms. This period could lead to the eventual elimination of all nuclear arms, both offensive and defensive. A world free of nuclear arms is an ultimate objective to which we, the Soviet Union, and all other nations can agree."

If the new Reagan-Shultz collaboration on nuclear weapons was going to amount to anything more than wishful thinking, the men needed a partner in the Kremlin. They unexpectedly got one on March 11, 1985, when Mikhail Gorbachev was installed as Soviet leader.

By the time Gorbachev took office, Reagan had dealt with three increasingly feeble Kremlin leaders: Leonid Brezhnev, Yuri Andropov, and Konstantin Chernenko. Andropov, a former head of the KGB, might have turned into an unorthodox Soviet interlocutor for Reagan, but his tenure was cut short by kidney disease. Chernenko, a Communist Party apparatchik, lasted only fourteen months before dying. Sputtering U.S.-Soviet relations during these sclerotic times in the Kremlin were not helped by intramural battles in Washington, as Shultz wrestled with Weinberger, Casey, and other hard-liners over control of American foreign policy.

Gorbachev's arrival broke the logjam in Washington and opened new vistas in U.S.-Soviet relations. Gorbachev, age fifty-four, was clearly a different kind of Kremlin leader—younger, more dynamic, and more open to new ideas than his predecessors. Even before taking office, he had impressed Margaret Thatcher, the no-nonsense British prime minister. After meeting him in London in late 1984, Thatcher said, "I like Mr. Gorbachev. We can do business together." But the constant question during Gorbachev's first months as Soviet leader was whether he was simply a more appealing face for a familiar ideology, or a true reformer prepared to refashion the Soviet system and Soviet foreign policy.

The CIA advised Reagan and Shultz not to get swept up in the Gorbachev euphoria. The new Soviet leader might be more appealing than his predecessors, but nothing fundamental had changed in the Soviet Union, the agency said in a series of analytical reports. From the outset, Shultz had a different take. After meeting Gorbachev for the first time when world leaders gathered in Moscow for Chernenko's funeral, Shultz told Vice

President George H. W. Bush, "In Gorbachev, we have an entirely different kind of leader in the Soviet Union than we have experienced before."

Shultz was right. The CIA was wrong. Shultz, more open-minded and less dogmatic than his colleagues, correctly sensed a sea change might be brewing in Moscow. His positive reading of Gorbachev may well be the signal achievement of his long government career. Bucking an army of doubters in Washington, not to mention clangorous objections from Henry Kissinger, he recognized the historic opportunities inherent in Gorbachev's leadership and encouraged Reagan to work with the Soviet leader. The result was a tectonic shift in international relations and a turning point in twentieth-century history.

A quarter century removed from that time, it is easy to underrate Shultz's role in the transformations that followed Gorbachev's arrival as Soviet leader. Reagan was the leading protagonist, and it was Reagan who reached for improbable goals like the elimination of nuclear weapons. But without Shultz at his side, Reagan could not have taken full advantage of the possibilities presented by Gorbachev. The overwhelming consensus in Washington at the time was to stick with the Cold War script, to see the Soviet Union as an implacable enemy bent on world domination. Almost all of Reagan's most senior national security aides shared that view and the initial thrust of Reagan's defense policy reflected that outlook. Weinberger, Casey, and other top administration officials questioned Shultz's judgment about Gorbachev and repeatedly attempted to block or sabotage his efforts to work with the Kremlin.

It would have been natural for Reagan to side with the skeptics. No one was more militant toward Moscow than the president. But unlike his administration colleagues, Shultz understood that Gorbachev offered Reagan the unexpected opportunity to act on his desire to reduce the threat of nuclear war and even to abolish nuclear weapons. Shultz stubbornly and skillfully pressed the case.

After meeting Gorbachev, Reagan agreed with Shultz's judgment and the two men plowed ahead in an effort to work with the Kremlin despite setbacks in U.S.-Soviet relations and the sustained objections of many Reagan aides. As the Iran-Contra scandal engulfed Reagan during his second term, the prospect of historic accords with the Soviet Union became the best way for Reagan to steady his presidency and enhance his legacy. In the end, Shultz outlasted his opponents and prevailed in the most significant national security debate of the Reagan presidency.

Shultz got an assist from an unexpected quarter when Reagan befriended Suzanne Massie, an expert and author on Russian culture who offered the president a more benign view of the Soviet Union than most of his advisers and tutored Reagan on Russian history and culture. She met with Reagan more than twenty times following their first encounter in 1984.

Reagan's admirers like to say that he engineered the end of the Cold War and that his military buildup led to the collapse of the Soviet Union. Both assertions greatly overstate the case. The Soviet Union imploded. American pressure may have speeded its demise, but it was not the primary factor.

By the time Gorbachev took over, the Soviet Union was rotting from within. Its economy was in a stupor, weighed down by decades of heavy-handed central planning. Agricultural production was becalmed by cumbersome collective farming practices, the political life of the nation frozen by totalitarian rule. The Soviet army was bleeding in Afghanistan. Nationalism, long repressed by Moscow, was quietly on the rise in the Baltic republics of Estonia, Latvia, and Lithuania, and other places that Stalin had forcibly lashed together to create the Soviet Union. The Soviet empire in Eastern Europe was restless as Solidarity, the anti-Soviet trade union federation in Poland, gained support and dissent escalated in other nations.

Gorbachev understood that the Soviet Union was in decline

and set out to reverse course. His goal was not to dismantle the communist state, but to revive it in a gentler, more productive form. He failed for a host of reasons, perhaps most important by underestimating the powder keg of nationalism. The more Gorbachev opened Soviet society and politics, the more he loosened the Kremlin's grip on the republics. His courageous decision to let the Berlin Wall fall and allow the nations of Eastern Europe to break free undermined the Kremlin's control at home.

Gorbachev's domestic initiatives proved to be insufficiently bold. The policy of glasnost, the catchphrase for efforts to make society and the press more transparent, unleashed a good deal of ferment and reopened closed chapters of Soviet history, but fell short of creating a truly open society. Perestroika, his campaign of political and governmental reform, ended up undermining the power of the Communist Party and rallying Gorbachev's opponents, without substituting a different political system.

Gorbachev's America strategy was pragmatic. Dispensing with much of the ideology that had long disfigured Kremlin foreign policy, he set out to stabilize relations with Washington and to reposition Moscow as a force for peace and arms control. A lot of what he said and promised was hyperbolic and laced with propaganda, but he moderated Soviet behavior in numerous areas. He advanced far-reaching arms control proposals. He recognized that the political and economic costs of forcibly maintaining an empire in Eastern Europe were unsustainable. Over time, he pulled out of Afghanistan and lowered tensions in other places like Angola and Central America.

Reagan's first chance to take the measure of Gorbachev came in Geneva in November 1985. Though not much of substance was accomplished, Reagan and Gorbachev spent several hours talking privately, including an extended conversation beside a roaring fire in a pool house by the lake. They agreed on future reciprocal visits: Gorbachev to Washington, then Reagan to Moscow. And the two sides issued a joint statement at the end of the meeting that, among other things, said they "agreed a nuclear war cannot be won and must never be fought."

Shultz thought the most important outcome was the good chemistry between Reagan and Gorbachev. "Personally, I thought the big story was that they hit it off as human beings," he said. Shultz also took the measure of the new Soviet foreign minister, Eduard Shevardnadze, who had served for many years as Communist Party chief in the Soviet republic of Georgia. He immediately liked the gregarious, undogmatic Georgian. Over time, the two formed a highly productive working relationship and warm friendship.

The surprisingly upbeat spirit of the Geneva meetings did not immediately translate into improved relations between Washington and Moscow. Diplomatic wrangling continued over the American missile shield program and ABM Treaty limits on the development and testing of defensive weapons. The two sides quarreled about global hot spots like Afghanistan, Angola, Cuba, and Nicaragua. And they bickered over human rights issues as Shultz and Reagan pressed the Kremlin to address abuses in the Soviet Union, such as the incarceration of political and religious dissidents and the refusal to let Jews immigrate to Israel.

Gorbachev shattered the status quo on January 15, 1986, by unveiling a grandiose plan to go to zero nuclear weapons and ballistic missiles by the year 2000. On one level it was a dazzling propaganda ploy, a blockbuster announcement that captured headlines around the world. Even though Reagan had been talking for years about eliminating nuclear weapons, he had never translated the concept into a detailed proposal. Gorbachev did just that.

"This is our first indication that the Soviets are interested in a staged program toward zero," Shultz advised Reagan. "We should not simply reject their proposal, since it contains certain steps which we earlier set forth." Reagan agreed. With Reagan's approval, Shultz organized an arms control task force to review Gorbachev's plan and come up with a counterproposal that could be presented by American diplomats in Geneva who were handling arms control negotiations with their Soviet counterparts. Though internal squabbling persisted, Weinberger reshaped the debate by proposing that the United States and Soviet Union eliminate ballistic missiles. The idea seemed far-reaching, but would have reinforced the American advantage in delivery systems like long-range bombs and cruise missiles while undermining the Soviet Union's heavy reliance on ballistic missiles.

By late summer 1986, Shultz, Weinberger, Casey, and other top advisers came up with a new American proposal that called for an initial 50 percent reduction in strategic, or long-range, nuclear weapons and the eventual elimination of all ballistic missiles. It also included a compromise of sorts on missile defenses. Under the plan, Moscow and Washington would agree not to withdraw from the ABM Treaty for seven and a half years and for five years would limit missile defense work to research, development, and testing. After that, if Washington or Moscow decided to build missile defenses, it would offer to share the technology with the other.

As the summer months slipped by without tangible progress at the Geneva arms talks, Gorbachev grew impatient. One day in August, while vacationing at his Black Sea dacha, Gorbachev instructed Anatoly Chernyaev, his national security adviser, to draft an urgent letter to Reagan proposing that the two men hold a quick one-day meeting in September or early October in London or Reykjavik, the Icelandic capital. When Chernyaev questioned the choice of Reykjavik, Gorbachev replied, "It's a good idea. Halfway between us and them, and none of the great powers will be offended."

A few days later, events in Moscow suddenly intervened. On August 30, Nicholas Daniloff, the Moscow bureau chief of *U.S. News & World Report*, was arrested near his Moscow home and charged with spying. The charge was false, but Daniloff had been lured into a KGB sting operation that made it seem as if he had been trading in sensitive information. The KGB move seemed designed to give the Kremlin a bargaining chip to negotiate the release of a Soviet diplomat who had been arrested by the FBI in New York just days before. The arrests threatened to throw relations into a deep freeze. As Washington and Moscow struggled to resolve the crisis, they hit on a plan that included the snap summit meeting that Gorbachev had suggested. Instead of trying to set a date for Gorbachev's promised visit to Washington—a step that had proved elusive because the two sides were not close to any agreements—Reagan and Gorbachev would hold an interim meeting in Iceland once Daniloff and the Russian diplomat were freed.

The complicated deal held. Daniloff left the Soviet Union on a Lufthansa flight on September 29, and the Soviet diplomat was allowed to return home. The Kremlin also released Yuri Orlov, a prominent dissident, from prison and let him and his wife leave the Soviet Union. The White House announced Reagan and Gorbachev would meet in Reykjavik on October 11 and 12.

Arms control would be on the agenda, but the meeting had been so hastily arranged that the American side doubted much would be settled, beyond possibly fixing the date for a Gorbachev visit to Washington. Gorbachev himself said in a September 15 letter to Reagan that the meeting "would not be a detailed one." In a classified memo to Reagan examining Gorbachev's likely goals and tactics, Stephen Sestanovich, a top National Security Council aide, said, "We go into Reykjavik next week with very little knowledge of how Gorbachev intends to use the meeting." Shultz advised Reagan not even to think of the meeting as a full-fledged summit but rather as a modest step toward a Washington summit. Eight time zones to the east, unbeknownst to the Americans, Gorbachev had much grander expectations.

CHAPTER TWENTY-ONE

I don't know when we'll ever have another chance like this.
—RONALD REAGAN

Reykjavik was a wild-card summit. The impromptu nature of the meeting and unconventional location stripped the talks of the formality and carefully scripted character of most summit sessions. There were no prenegotiated agreements, no pre-baked communiqué ready to hand out to reporters from dozens of nations who flocked to Iceland to cover the event.

Iceland's barren volcanic landscape and bubbling hot-sulfur springs lent an otherworldly aura to the setting. Reagan and Gorbachev left their usual battery of aides outside the conference room, inviting only Shultz and Shevardnadze to join them at the table. (A Russian and an American translator and one note taker from each side were present as well.) Hofdi House, the two-story seaside wooden building where Reagan and Gorbachev conferred, gave an added air of simplicity and informality to the discussions. "Here we can discuss everything calmly," Reagan told Gorbachev. The whole scene seemed to give the leaders license to think outside the usual bounds.

That they did. "That's what alarmed people so much about Reykjavik," Shultz recalled. "You get two leaders there without being controlled by their respective bureaucracies."

To a remarkable degree, Reagan and Gorbachev followed their

core instincts rather than their briefing books. Reagan, the dreamer, wanted nothing more than to make deep cuts in nuclear weapons while protecting his cherished missile shield. Gorbachev, more the pragmatist, sought a landmark agreement to reduce nuclear weapons so he could concentrate on domestic political reforms, but he was unwilling to accept Reagan's missile defense plan.

Reykjavik is remembered primarily as the moment when the world's two nuclear superpowers put the elimination of nuclear weapons on the negotiating table. It hadn't happened before, and hasn't happened since. It unquestionably left an indelible impression on George Shultz, and helps to explain his current effort to abolish nuclear weapons.

But the Iceland talks were far more multidimensional than the signature minute when Reagan and Gorbachev momentarily agreed that they should abolish nuclear arms. For two days, Reagan and Gorbachev ranged over an astonishing array of defense and diplomatic issues and came very close to reaching an historic accord that would have drastically cut their nuclear arsenals and eliminated ballistic missiles by 1996. The deal collapsed when the two men could not find common ground on Reagan's missile shield plan.

With just days to prepare for the snap summit, both sides scrambled to come up with negotiating game plans. Gorbachev's impatience to break the deadlock at the Geneva arms talks, the impetus for his August offer to arrange a brief meeting with Reagan in London or Reykjavik, was still palpable as he strategized with top aides in early October, just days before heading to Iceland. Instead of sticking to his stated notion of a quick, broad-based discussion with Reagan, Gorbachev hastily put together an audacious set of proposals calling for deep cuts in nuclear arms.

He rejected incremental proposals suggested by senior diplomatic, defense, and Communist Party officials. What he wanted, as Anatoly Chernyaev, his national security adviser, recalled, was "to sweep Reagan off his feet with our bold, even risky approach to the central problems of world politics."

The propaganda value of advancing bold ideas was clear, but Gorbachev had his sights on more important matters. He understood the sagging Soviet economy could not support ever-increasing defense spending and a costly new missile defense system. If a defensive arms race began, there was no guarantee that the Soviet Union could keep pace with American technology. And managing his ambitious reform agenda at home would be easier if Cold War tensions subsided.

Gorbachev outlined his thinking at a meeting with Kremlin leaders the day before he departed for Reykjavik. "Our goal is to prevent the next round of arms race," he told them bluntly. "If we do not do this, the threat to us will only grow. And if we do not compromise on some questions, even very important ones, we will lose the main point: we will be pulled into an arms race beyond our power, and we will lose this race, for we are presently at the limits of our capabilities. . . . If the new round begins, the pressure on our economy will be inconceivable."

Gorbachev doubted Reagan would be as daring. Describing his sense of the American political environment, Gorbachev told the Politburo, the inner circle of Kremlin leaders, "The right[-wing politicians] are concerned about Reykjavik, they are intimidating Reagan."

Noting that anti-Soviet rhetoric was flaring anew in Washington, he said, "From all this, it follows that the meeting will be very difficult. We should not exclude a possibility of a failure."

Gorbachev informed the Politburo that he was prepared to make concessions on intermediate-range missiles and deep cuts in strategic weapons but would not compromise on Reagan's missile defense scheme. And he told them he would not hesitate to cite the prevalence of poverty, drug abuse, and criminal violence in the United States if Reagan brought up human rights issues in the

Soviet Union. "Let's unload all this during the press conference at the end," he promised them. His pugnacious presentation may have been partly intended to reassure more conservative Politburo members that he would be resolute in Reykjavik.

It is hard not to wonder what impact the Chernobyl nuclear disaster had on Gorbachev's thinking as he prepared for Reykjavik. The April 26, 1986, explosion of a nuclear power reactor not far from Kiev was a turning point on many fronts. "The accident at the Chernobyl nuclear power station was graphic evidence, not only of how obsolete our technology was, but also of the failure of the old system," Gorbachev noted in his memoirs. "At the same time, and such is the irony of history, it severely affected our reforms by literally knocking the country off its tracks."

Reagan, for one, thought Chernobyl surely had changed Gorbachev's attitude. "Chernobyl has altered Gorbachev's outlook on the dangers of nuclear war," he told his aides six weeks after the accident—months before the Reykjavik summit.

The gruesome death from radiation exposure of plant workers and emergency responders who were dispatched to the reactor in the hours after the explosion was a grim reminder of the dangers of the atomic age. The spread of a radioactive cloud across a large swath of the western Soviet Union, Eastern Europe, and Scandinavia gave Gorbachev a glimpse of the grave health risks that would come with nuclear war. Japan experienced a similar awakening in 2011 when radioactive particles and gases leaked from damaged reactors at the Fukushima nuclear plant, contaminating food and water supplies and forcing the evacuation of hundreds of thousands of people from the danger zone.

The American preparations for Reykjavik, based on the assumption that the meeting would be devoted primarily to clearing the way for the long-delayed Gorbachev visit to Washington, were less improvised than the planning in Moscow. Months of deliberation in Washington had produced a far-reaching American

arms reduction plan, including the elimination of all offensive ballistic missiles. Reagan was willing to consider compromises that
might lead to an agreement on intermediate-range missiles. He was
also open to sharing missile defense technologies with the Soviet
Union, but he was not prepared to abandon research and development work on a missile shield.

A week before the meeting, Shultz put together a memo to
Reagan outlining his expectations for Reykjavik. To prepare the
ground for a Washington summit, Shultz said the discussions in
Iceland should reaffirm the importance of the Geneva arms talks,
settle most of the remaining issues on intermediate-range missiles,
and give Gorbachev a better understanding of his thinking about
missile defenses. Shultz also emphasized the importance of pressing Gorbachev on human rights abuses in the Soviet Union. He
told Reagan, "Gorbachev must go home with a clear sense that
Moscow's continuing insensitivity to the humanitarian dimension
of the relationship will assume greater significance as prospects
open up in areas of mutual concern."

Reagan got to Iceland first, arriving aboard Air Force One on
Thursday evening, October 9. After a brief welcoming ceremony
at the airport, Reagan, who was not accompanied by his wife,
headed by motorcade to the American ambassador's residence in
Reykjavik, a forty-five-minute drive from the airport. The residence would be his base for the next three days.

Gorbachev arrived on Friday, October 10, with his wife, Raisa,
and a small army of Soviet officials who soon fanned out around
the compact capital to pitch reporters on the virtues of Gorbachev's
domestic and defense policies. The Gorbachevs were escorted to a
Soviet ship anchored in the harbor that was to serve as their temporary home.

On Saturday morning at precisely 10:30, as planned, Reagan
and Gorbachev arrived at Hofdi House. They posed briefly for
news photographers, then got down to work in a small, spare

conference room overlooking the sea. After some initial conversation, Gorbachev suggested that they invite Eduard Shevardnadze, the Soviet foreign minister, and Shultz to join the meeting. They did. Reagan and Gorbachev sat at opposite ends of a small rectangular table, Shultz and Shevardnadze settled into seats facing one another on either side of the table.

Reagan and Gorbachev jockeyed briefly about human rights—Gorbachev was clearly irritated that Reagan had raised the issue so early in the discussion—but the conversation soon turned to nuclear arms. Drawing on a large stack of papers he had laid on the table, Gorbachev outlined the latest Soviet proposals. He offered a 50 percent cut in strategic, or long-range, weapons, including intercontinental ballistic missiles, submarine-based missiles, and heavy bombers. He also said he was ready to eliminate Soviet and American intermediate-range missiles in Europe, though he was not ready to give up similar Soviet missiles based in Asian areas of the Soviet Union. He was less forthcoming on missile defense, suggesting that the development and testing of new space-based technologies be limited to laboratory work, accompanied by a ten-year period during which both nations would promise not to withdraw from the ABM Treaty. All told, the package was a striking shift from Moscow's bargaining stance in Geneva and put the Kremlin much closer to the American proposals.

Reagan said he was encouraged by the Soviet proposals but noted continuing differences and urged Gorbachev to consider the American proposal to replace the ABM Treaty with a new agreement that would impose few constraints on the development of missile defenses. Reagan reiterated his desire to rid the world of nuclear weapons and spoke passionately of how a missile shield could open the door to that goal by making missiles obsolete. He assured Gorbachev that if the United States succeeded in developing a missile shield, it would share the technology with the Soviet Union and other nations.

Gorbachev, miffed that Reagan was not more welcoming to his new offers, said, "We will view your statements as being preliminary. I have just presented entirely new proposals and they have not yet been discussed at any negotiations. Therefore, I ask you to give them proper attention and to express your reaction later."

Despite the skirmishing, the first round of discussions vaulted the meeting to an improbable plane where Soviet and American leaders were talking seriously about radical cuts in their nuclear arsenals. "This is the best Soviet proposal we have received in twenty-five years," Paul Nitze said. Shultz realized that "the whole nature of the meeting we had planned at Reykjavik had changed." The participants sensed history might be in the making.

When the talks resumed after lunch, Reagan walked Gorbachev through the American plan, which called for the total elimination of offensive ballistic missiles over a ten-year period and an overall reduction of 50 percent in strategic offensive arms. Reagan proposed extensive verification measures to ensure that both sides were adhering to agreed limits. The men debated aspects of an intermediate-missile accord. But the deadlock over antimissile work remained frozen. As the weak northern daylight receded, Gorbachev told Reagan he couldn't take his technology-sharing offer seriously. "You are not willing to share with us oil well equipment, digitally guided machine tools or even milking machines. Sharing anti-missile technology would be a second American Revolution. Let's be realistic and pragmatic."

"He and I had at it all afternoon," Reagan later said. Reagan wondered again about the influence of Chernobyl. "As the day wore on," he recalled in his presidential memoirs, "I began to wonder whether the Chernobyl accident and a fire that had occurred aboard a Soviet nuclear submarine just a few days before our meeting was behind Gorbachev's new eagerness to discuss abolishing nuclear weapons. The radiation emitted at Chernobyl had made it impossible for thousands of people to live in their homes, yet it had been less than the amount of radiation released by a single nuclear warhead; as we talked, I wondered: Has Chernobyl made Gorbachev think about the effects of a missile with ten nuclear warheads?"

Before recessing for the day, Reagan and Gorbachev instructed their aides to break down into two working groups, one on arms control, the other on human rights, and work through the night to narrow differences and sketch out agreements.

The overnight marathon produced agreement on deep nuclear arms cuts, including a breakthrough on arcane counting rules for bombers. The human rights group reached a milestone with Soviet assent to treat human rights issues as a normal subject of discussion, breaking with long-standing assertions that internal matters were not open to outside influence. But the two sides were still at odds over elements of a European missile accord and far apart on the development and testing of missile defenses.

Twenty-five years on, it is heartbreaking to read the transcript of the final negotiating sessions on Sunday afternoon. It is clear both men understood they were on the brink of historic agreements as the discussions unfolded. "George and I couldn't believe what was happening," Reagan later said. "We were getting amazing agreements. As the day went on I felt something momentous was occurring."

Yet frustration mounted as the minutes ticked by without resolution of the missile defense impasse. "You could feel the tension rising as it deadlocked," recalled Tom Simons, the State Department note taker at the last Sunday meeting. Reagan would not yield on his defense initiative and Gorbachev would not accept the rest of the arms deal that was on the table without some concession from Reagan on the development of a missile shield.

The idea of totally abolishing American and Soviet nuclear weapons came up almost accidentally as the two leaders jousted over deep arms cuts. Reagan raised it. Simons thought Reagan was "fleeing forward out of an uncomfortable box."

Here's the critical exchange:

REAGAN: Let me ask this: Do we have in mind—and I think it would be very good—that by the end of the two five-year periods all nuclear explosive devices would be eliminated, including bombs, battlefield systems, cruise missiles, submarine weapons, intermediate-range systems and so on? It would be fine with me if we eliminated all nuclear weapons.

GORBACHEV: We could say that, list all the weapons.

SHULTZ: Then let's do it.

REAGAN: If we agree by the end of the 10-year period all nuclear weapons are to be eliminated, we can turn this agreement over to our delegations in Geneva so they can prepare a treaty which you can sign during your visit to the U.S.

GORBACHEV: Well, all right. Here we have a chance for an agreement. What I am seriously concerned about is another factor. What we are talking about is to comply strictly with the unlimited ABM treaty for the purpose of pledging not to exercise the right to withdraw from the treaty for 10 years. We are doing this under conditions of reducing nuclear weapons. We don't understand, then, why the American side does not agree to having research development and testing be restricted to the confines of the laboratory.

A few moments later, Gorbachev said, "If you will agree to restricting research work to the laboratory, not letting it out into space, I will be ready in two minutes to sign the appropriate formulation and adopt the document."

Sensing that breakthrough agreements were within reach, Shevardnadze appealed to the men to overcome their differences. "Let me speak very emotionally, because I feel we have come very

close to accomplishing this historic task. And when future generations read the record of our talks, they will not forgive us if we let
this opportunity slip by."

Reagan would not budge, insisting that he had to keep his
promise to the American people to proceed with development of
a missile shield. Gorbachev would not give ground on limiting
development of missile defenses.

Reagan scribbled a few words on a piece of paper and slid it
across the table to Shultz. The note said, "Am I wrong?"

"No, you are right," Shultz whispered to Reagan.

Reagan almost pleaded with Gorbachev to soften his stance.
"Let me say frankly that if I give you what you ask it will definitely
hurt me badly at home," Reagan said.

Moments later, after Gorbachev rebuffed the appeal, Reagan
made it seem even more personal. "After our meeting in Geneva
I was convinced that you and I had established personal contact of
the kind the leaders of two countries never had before. You and
I understood each other very well. But now, when I have asked
you a personal favor which could have enormous influence on our
future relations, you have refused me."

The impasse was insurmountable.

"It's too bad we have to part this way," Reagan said as the men
brought the talks to an inconclusive end. "We were so close to
an agreement. I think you didn't want to achieve an agreement
anyway. I'm very sorry."

Gorbachev replied, "I am also very sorry it happened this way.
I wanted an agreement and did everything I could, if not more."

Reagan said, "I don't know when we'll ever have another
chance like this and whether we will meet soon."

Gorbachev said, "I don't either."

With that, the men collected their coats and stepped into the
cold Icelandic night. Reagan's grim visage, caught by photographers, telegraphed his dejection as he bade farewell to Gorbachev

outside Hofdi House. As Reagan approached his armored limousine, Gorbachev made one last appeal. "There is still time Mr. President," he said. "We would go back inside to the bargaining table. I don't know what more I could have done."

"You could have said yes," Reagan replied. Reagan then settled into the backseat of his limousine and a Secret Service agent firmly closed the door. Within minutes, word flashed around the press center that the talks had collapsed in failure.

Later, in his memoirs, Reagan described his feelings. "I was very disappointed—and *very* angry."

In Reagan's view, Gorbachev had brought him to Iceland "with one purpose: to kill the Strategic Defense Initiative." Reagan said, "He must have known from the beginning that he was going to bring it up at the last minute."

Ironically, Reagan could probably have accepted Gorbachev's demand to limit missile defense research work to the laboratory without gravely impairing development of missile shield technologies. In 1986, most of the newfangled technologies were in their infancy and it might well have taken five to ten years of laboratory work to get them to a point where they could be tested in space.

Shultz looked depressed and emotionally drained when he appeared before dozens of reporters who had gathered in Reykjavik. His words came slowly, at times haltingly, as he stood before a simple microphone stand. "The President's performance was magnificent and I have never been so proud of my president as I have been in these sessions and particularly this afternoon," he said.

"The President, hard as he had worked for this extraordinary range and importance of agreements, simply would not turn away from the basic security interests of the United States, our allies and the free world, by abandoning this essential defensive program. He had to bear in mind, and did bear in mind, that not only is the existence of the Strategic Defense Program a key reason why we were able, potentially, to reach these agreements, but undoubtedly its continued existence and potential would be the kind of program you need in the picture to ensure yourself that the agreements reached would be effectively carried out.

"And so, in the end, with great reluctance, the President, having worked so hard creatively and constructively for these potentially tremendous achievements, simply had to refuse to compromise the security of the US, of our allies and freedom by abandoning the shield that was held in front of freedom."

A few blocks away, Gorbachev also looked somber as he spoke to hundreds of reporters, but he described the meetings as a potential turning point. "My first, overwhelming, intention had been to blow the unyielding American position to smithereens, carrying out the plan we had decided in Moscow," Gorbachev later recalled. "I had not yet made up my mind when I suddenly found myself in the enormous press conference room. About a thousand journalists were waiting for us. When I came into the room, the merciless, often cynical and cheeky journalists stood up in silence. I sensed the anxiety in the air. I suddenly felt emotional, even shaken. The people standing in front of me seemed to represent mankind waiting for its fate to be decided."

Looking back, Tom Simons sees the brief exchange about abolishing nuclear weapons as a sideshow. "This exchange," he said, "now looks like the core twenty years later, now that you're in a nuclear abolition mode. But at the time, it was not the key to Reykjavik. The key to Reykjavik was those massive reductions in offensive weapons, and the breakdown over SDI."

Confusion about the talks reigned in the hours and days after Reykjavik, and Reagan and Shultz came under heavy fire from all sides. In the absence of a transcript, which was not made publicly available at the time, incomplete and distorted accounts swirled through world capitals. America's closest European allies feared Reagan had been on the verge of undermining NATO security by pulling intermediate-range missiles out of Western Europe without addressing the Soviet and Warsaw Pact advantage in conventional military forces in the region.

As word spread that Reagan and Gorbachev had actually discussed the elimination of all Soviet and American nuclear weapons, Reagan and Shultz were castigated in Washington for entertaining the thought. Arms control proponents, for their part, were aghast that Reagan had given up a deal to make deep cuts in nuclear weapons in favor of a missile shield plan they considered half-baked. When the American party returned to Washington, Margaret Thatcher soon appeared and summoned Shultz to the British embassy. "She handbagged me," he recalled, describing how Thatcher figuratively whipped him with her handbag for failing to restrain Reagan.

Sam Nunn assailed the summit in an appearance on the Senate floor five days after the meeting: "I may be wrong—and indeed I hope I am wrong—but based on my discussions this week with President Reagan, Secretary Shultz and other senior administration officials, there would appear to be a genuine question as to whether on Sunday, October 12, 1986, the president of the United States of America reached a verbal agreement with the General Secretary of the Communist Party of the Union of Soviet Socialist Republics to eliminate all, I repeat, all strategic offensive nuclear arms by 1996."

After running through a litany of complaints, Nunn said, "I do not raise these matters with any sense of pleasure. I think it obvious that these proposals have not been thought through. I think it is obvious that they have not been really studied adequately in terms of where they are leading us."

He went on: "I think they need to go back to the drawing boards in terms of what our real goals are in arms control. I believe the total elimination of nuclear weapons is a laudable objective. I, too, can dream of a day in which the world is free from the nuclear menace. However, there are significant conditions precedent to that day. There are a number of things that have to be done, fundamental matters, perhaps very expensive, before we contemplate going to zero strategic nuclear weapons."

Nunn's concerns were widely shared. At the time, the overwhelming impression was that Reykjavik had been a train wreck. As Shultz put it, "The reality of the actual achievements at Reykjavik ironically never overcame the perception conveyed by the scene of Reagan and Gorbachev parting at Hofdi House and my own depressed appearance at my press conference."

He said, "Sometimes people asked me why I looked tired and disappointed and I said, 'Well, because I was tired and disappointed.' But I should have taken a deep breath and thought more carefully about it and projected a different image. I don't think I did a good job in that press conference, because I said how I felt, and I said what happened."

A few days after the meeting, Shultz was more upbeat. He compared the public disappointment to the fifteenth-century perception that Christopher Columbus failed in his first voyage because "he only landed on a couple of islands and didn't bring any gold back to Spain." Recalling that people eventually realized Columbus had discovered a new world, he told Reagan, "In a way, you found a new world this weekend."

A few weeks after Reykjavik, Shultz pulled together his thoughts about nuclear weapons in a speech he delivered at the University of Chicago, just steps away from a squash court under Stagg Field where Enrico Fermi had generated the first self-sustained and controlled nuclear chain reaction forty-four years earlier.

It was a striking address, both for what Shultz said about the future of nuclear arms control, and what he did not say.

Speaking of the Reykjavik talks, he said, "In years to come, we may look back at their discussions as a turning point in our strategy for deterring war and preserving peace. It has opened up new possibilities for the way in which we view nuclear weapons and their role in ensuring our security."

But in the wake of the uproar over Reagan and Gorbachev's talk about abolishing nuclear weapons, Shultz pointedly did not reaffirm that goal. Instead, he told the audience: "The nuclear age cannot be undone or abolished; it is a permanent reality. But we can glimpse now, for the first time, a world freed from the incessant and pervasive fear of nuclear devastation. The threat of nuclear conflict can never be wholly banished, but it can be vastly diminished—by careful but drastic reductions in the offensive nuclear arsenals each side possesses."

When asked about the speech in 2011, Shultz acknowledged that he had backed away from the abolition language used at Reykjavik. "I struggled with that speech," he said. "This was basically Paul [Nitze] and I working on this to put the effort to get nuclear weapons way down into a framework that would be more acceptable to people."

To explore that new world Reagan had discovered in Reykjavik, John Poindexter, the national security adviser, recommended that Reagan ask the Joint Chiefs to examine how the military services could transition over ten years to a world without offensive ballistic missiles. Reagan signed off on the Poindexter proposal, which was translated into National Security Decision Directive 250 and signed by Reagan on November 3, 1986. It did not mention that Reagan and Gorbachev had discussed the elimination of nuclear weapons altogether.

"I want to ensure that we are prepared to exploit, fully and safely, our proposal, should the Soviet Union be willing to join us in its pursuit," the directive stated, referring to the ten-year goal of eliminating offensive ballistic missiles. "In order to do so, the necessary foundation of detailed, careful planning must be laid now. Therefore, I request the Joint Chiefs of Staff, under the direction of the Secretary of Defense and drawing upon other agencies as necessary, to provide a plan which would permit the US to safely transition to the alternative future I have proposed."

A senior general who was based in Washington at the time recalled that the military response to Reykjavik was "tantamount to panic." The formal response from the Joint Chiefs to Poindexter's assignment was blunt: eliminating missiles would lead to an unsustainable increase in the Pentagon budget as the armed services added manpower and weapons to fill the gap. Alton G. Keel Jr., executive secretary of the National Security Council, summarized the Joint Chiefs' initial reaction in a memo to Reagan on December 19, 1986. "They will probably present the view that the Army will need more divisions, the Navy more anti-submarine warfare capabilities and sea-launched cruise missiles, and the Air Force greater bomber/ALCM [Air Launched Cruise Missile] penetration and air defense capabilities. In very gross terms, they will indicate that these additional capabilities will cost more than the current projection for defense budgets for the future." Keel estimated the additional cost would come to roughly $40–50 billion a year.

By the time the Joint Chiefs delivered their message, Reagan was foundering in the Iran-Contra typhoon that slammed Washington just days after Reagan signed National Security Decision Directive 250. His presidency was imperiled by the revelations that, contrary to long-established American policy, the Reagan administration had secretly made arms deals with Iran to secure the release of American hostages held in the Middle East. Money raised from the arms sales was, in turn, covertly funneled to pro-American paramilitary forces based in Honduras who were operating inside neighboring Nicaragua, trying to dislodge the leftist Sandinista regime in Managua. The forces were known as the Contras. The diversion of money appeared to be a brazen violation of the Boland Amendment, a congressional ban on American military assistance to the Contras.

At first, it looked as if Reagan might not survive the affair politically. He did, barely, but never fully recovered his footing. Shultz was not directly implicated in the scandal, but the turmoil and backstabbing in the White House grew so intense that he considered quitting several times. In Reagan's weakened state, wholesale nuclear arms reductions were no longer a tenable prospect. Yet, as the turbulence subsided, Reagan and Shultz were eager to come up with a few foreign policy achievements to offset the damage. Improving relations with the Soviet Union and reaching agreement to eliminate intermediate-range missiles would fit the bill nicely.

Gorbachev conveniently complied on February 28, 1987, by renewing his offer to eliminate all intermediate-range missiles in Europe. This time he was ready to detach that issue from other nuclear weapons matters, including the missile defense debate that had scuttled the Reykjavik talks. The path now seemed open to negotiating the first Cold War agreement between the United States and Soviet Union that would eliminate an entire class of nuclear weapons.

Henry Kissinger supported the Reagan missile defense plan. "As for SDI, I consider the so-called 'Star Wars' program one of the seminal decisions of the Reagan presidency," Kissinger said a few days after the Iceland meeting. "SDI provides at least a partial way out of a nihilistic strategy based on mutual extermination. At a minimum, it would complicate the calculations of an attacker. Those who blame Reagan for letting SDI abort Reykjavik should remind themselves that it was SDI that brought the Soviets back to the conference table and produced whatever concessions have since been offered."

But Kissinger was not happy with Reagan and Shultz's overall handling of relations with Moscow. Richard Nixon, whose views on the Soviet Union still commanded attention, felt the same way. The two men thought a European missile accord would leave Moscow and its Warsaw Pact allies with an overwhelming advantage in conventional military forces in Europe, and no way for the United States to counter a Soviet land invasion of West Germany, short of launching a global nuclear war.

In April, Nixon and Kissinger agreed to record their views in a joint op-ed article, the first they had written together since Nixon's resignation in 1974. It was a cannon shot aimed directly at Reagan and Shultz. Referring to the possibility of an intermediate-range missile treaty, they wrote, "If we strike the wrong kind of deal, we could create the most profound crisis of the NATO alliance in its 40-year history—an alliance sustained by seven administrations of both parties." They also warned against falling for "the Soviets' disingenuous fantasies of a nuclear-free world."

A few days after the article appeared, Nixon slipped into the White House for an unpublicized meeting with Reagan. They met in the residential quarters on the second floor, seated in matching armchairs separated by a coffee table and ottoman. Nixon walked Reagan, Howard Baker, the new chief of staff, and Frank Carlucci, the new national security adviser, through his worries about an intermediate-range missile accord. He then took aim at Shultz, who was not present. "I got in one shot at Shultz, which I thought was quite effective," Nixon later noted in a memo he wrote for his records. "I said he had been a great Secretary of the Treasury, a great Secretary of Labor and a great director of OMB [Office of Management and Budget], and said he did an outstanding job of negotiating with [AFL-CIO chairman George] Meany for a period. But I said negotiating with Meany was much different from negotiating with Gorbachev."

Nixon's verdict on Reagan was roughly the same, though he didn't say so to the president. Noting that he found Reagan looking "far older, more tired and less vigorous in person than in public," Nixon said in his memo, "There is no way he can ever be allowed to participate in a private meeting with Gorbachev."

Kissinger kept hounding Shultz. When Shultz called him in September to inform Kissinger that the two sides had reached an agreement in principle on an intermediate-range missile agreement, Kissinger warned that it "undoes forty years of NATO."

In a *Newsweek* opinion piece, he belittled Reagan and Shultz by comparing their policies to the antinuclear protesters. He wrote, "The most conservative U.S. administration of the postwar era stigmatized nuclear weapons with arguments all but indistinguishable from the Committee for Nuclear Disarmament."

American and Soviet negotiators completed the European missile treaty that fall and Gorbachev made a triumphant visit to Washington to sign it on December 8, 1987. Washington greeted him like a rock star. Crowds instantly gathered on the sidewalk when he stopped his motorcade to step out and shake hands with Washingtonians. American intellectuals flew into town to meet with him. The capital hadn't seen anything like it in years, never with a Soviet leader.

But the political sniper shots at Shultz kept coming, especially from Kissinger. After attending a state dinner for Gorbachev at the White House, Kissinger sourly opined in *Newsweek* about the "euphoria" at the dinner and the "near ecstasy" of American officials. "I could not shake a melancholy feeling as I watched the leaders of the country whose nuclear guarantee had protected free peoples for forty years embrace Gorbachev's evocation of a nuclear-free world—a goal put forward, if with less panache, by every Soviet leader since Stalin."

A month after Gorbachev's visit, Kissinger denounced the Reagan administration for abandoning a balance-of-power approach to Moscow. "The most conservative U.S. administration of the postwar era is preoccupied—almost obsessed—with arms control and personal appeals to the Soviet leadership," he declared in a *Washington Post* op-ed piece that appeared under the headline "Arms-Control Fever." "Agreements are called historic because they abolish two categories of nuclear weapons but are then schizophrenically justified as safe because all necessary military missions can be performed by the remaining nuclear arsenal. Agreement has become its own reward.

"The euphoria of the Gorbachev visit may in retrospect appear as an escapism that dealt with symptoms, not causes. The underlying political crisis may in fact be accelerated by the gradual deterioration of America's leadership role and the danger that the Soviet Union may be tempted by the West's yearning for tranquility, however temporary, to tip the global balance of power in its favor."

Kissinger outlined what he thought American leaders should be telling Gorbachev. Among his points: "Conventional deterrence rarely works. Unfortunately, Reykjavik devalued the nuclear deterrent by producing agreements on the zero option on medium-range missiles, and on the totally unrealistic objective to abolish all nuclear weapons with the destruction of strategic missiles as a first step. Thus, the resolution of political conflicts grows correspondingly more urgent because it is unlikely that they can be contained by conventional deterrence alone. True, lip service is being paid to the objective of a political dialogue. But it has yet to receive appropriate high-level attention or negotiating priority."

Shultz, who had been quietly smoldering about Nixon's and Kissinger's repeated attacks, fired off an angry letter to Kissinger after reading the *Post* article. "It is one thing to criticize the Administration if you disagree with it; it is something else to attack us for failing to do what we in fact are doing. The dialogue which you say has not occurred has in fact taken place at all our key meetings with Gorbachev, and in depth.

"Incidentally, I don't sense any Gorbachev euphoria around here. It is all in a day's work."

Relations between the two men were strained enough that Kissinger thought it wise to reassure Shultz that their foreign policy arguments would not spill over into their annual July outing in the Bohemian Grove, the rustic retreat north of San Francisco where influential financiers, academics, and artists gathered every summer. "I notice that we will be at Mandalay together next month," Kissinger wrote, referring to one of the Bohemian Grove camps. "It goes without saying that whatever marginal disagreements we may have had about this or that aspect of foreign policy, Mandalay will not be the place to air them. I will do my best to ensure you a restful and relaxing weekend. It will be nice to see you again."

"Marginal disagreements" hardly captured their fundamental differences over the future course of relations with the Soviet Union. As it turned out, Kissinger's ominous commentary about Gorbachev and his intentions proved to be mistaken. But Shultz was not one to carry a grudge. "His basic principle in life is to be inclusive," Jim Goodby said of Shultz. Alluding to Shultz's willingness to look beyond Kissinger's irritating complaints, Goodby said, "I wish I had that self-control."

Kissinger eventually called for Senate ratification of the intermediate-range missile treaty. While he remained dubious about the accord, he said failure to ratify would itself damage the NATO alliance and probably lead to the withdrawal of American missiles from Western Europe.

Nunn, for his part, insisted that the administration stipulate that the treaty was final and official before the Senate voted. He wanted no repeat of the battle over interpretation of the ABM Treaty. Shultz provided the necessary assurances. The Senate voted 93–5 to approve the treaty on May 28, 1988. It stipulated extensive verification measures, including on-site inspections that gave American technical experts access to Soviet missile sites and missile factories, and vice versa.

Reagan landed in Moscow the next day for a capstone meeting with Gorbachev. There were rumblings of unrest in the Soviet empire by then, but neither man could have suspected that the Berlin Wall would fall eighteen months later and that the Soviet Union would cease to exist by the end of 1991.

While touring Red Square with Gorbachev as his guide, Sam Donaldson, the ABC News correspondent, asked Reagan, "Don't you still think you're in an evil empire, Mr. President?"

Reagan replied, "No, I was talking about another time and another era."

To Shultz's dismay, the election of George H. W. Bush as president in November led to a pause in relations with Gorbachev. He indirectly alluded to his disappointment in his memoir, noting that President-elect Bush did not seem to welcome the chance to meet with Gorbachev in New York on December 7. Gorbachev was there to address the United Nations and Reagan was pleased to fly up to see him.

Bush, concerned about the pell-mell pace of Reagan's dealings with Gorbachev, decided to put relations with the Kremlin on hold so he and his national security team could take stock of the relationship. Brent Scowcroft, Bush's choice to be national security adviser, had suggested the idea.

"I was very upset," Shultz said in 2010. "They felt Reagan and I were all wrong in the way we were approaching the Soviet Union, that it couldn't change and wouldn't change," he said, referring to Scowcroft and Kissinger. "They couldn't have been more wrong. They really were wrong, deeply, deeply wrong. But Brent had this idea and he persuaded Bush to do a review, so everything was put on hold."

Shultz sensed Bush's coolness as Gorbachev, Reagan, and Bush met on Governor's Island in New York Harbor. "Reagan says to me, 'What's the matter with George?' He acted like he didn't want to be there." When Bush paused the relationship, Shultz phoned James A. Baker III, his successor as secretary of state. He told him, "Jim, come on, you're losing time, and the momentum was there, that's slipping away from you."

In retrospect, Reykjavik was an arms control aberration. Washington and Moscow never again seriously discussed the elimination of offensive ballistic missiles. The abolition of nuclear weapons reappeared in recent years, thanks largely to Shultz and his allies.

If Reagan and Gorbachev had agreed on abolition that autumn

afternoon in Iceland, it seems doubtful that the Senate would have ratified such an agreement. Gorbachev's Kremlin colleagues might have balked, too. "The world was not ready for a world free of nuclear weapons," Shultz agreed.

Except for Ronald Reagan. Not quite a year after Reykjavik, he told Shultz and his other top aides: "If we could just talk about the basic steps we need to take to break the logjam and avoid the possibility of war. I mean, think about it, where would the survivors of the war live? Major areas of the world would be uninhabitable. We are about bringing together steps to bring us closer to the recognition that we need to do away with nuclear weapons."

But, in truth, Reykjavik marked the end of Ronald Reagan's pursuit of a world without nuclear weapons. He may still have dreamed of that day, but the moment when that goal seemed within reach had come and gone in a flash. The only president to seriously embrace that goal during the Cold War was undone by his own quixotic quest to build a missile shield.

When asked in 2011 if he had any regrets about Reagan's unyielding stance, Shultz paused for a moment. Yes, he said a bit wistfully, he wished he had thought to ask Gorbachev a simple question: "What exactly do you mean by a laboratory? Is space a laboratory? When you say the word *laboratory*, you think of a little room and people in white coats. But maybe we could have found out how to define *laboratory* in a way that would have been acceptable, but I didn't think of that and we didn't do that."

CHAPTER TWENTY-TWO

Count me out. . . . That's never going to go in Illinois.
I will never get re-elected.
—SENATOR ALAN DIXON

S am Nunn immediately knew something had to be done about the Soviet nuclear arsenal and the scientists and engineers who maintained it. It was just days after the August 1991 coup attempt in Moscow that briefly left Mikhail Gorbachev under house arrest at his Black Sea dacha and threatened to undo his reform efforts. When the coup collapsed on August 21, Nunn scrapped plans to fly home from Budapest, where he was attending a conference, and instead headed to Moscow at the invitation of a Russian official who thought the senator should see for himself that the Soviet Union was beginning to unravel.

Nunn was amazed by the convulsions in Moscow, and unnerved by Gorbachev's failure to give him a clear answer when asked who controlled Soviet nuclear weapons during the coup. "I've seen him answer questions a lot of times and I've known him to be very forthright," Nunn recalled. "He clearly was evasive in his answer on this one and clearly he was very uncomfortable."

If the Soviet Union disintegrated, which looked increasingly likely, at least four pieces of the USSR—Russia, Ukraine, Kazakhstan, and Belarus—would wind up with large stockpiles of nuclear weapons.

After talking with Gorbachev, Nunn realized that the "pro-liferation of weapons, the whole question of the nuclear risk and accidents and miscalculations was going to be the top thing that we were going to be faced with . . . in the breakup of the Soviet Union, and it was apparent it was going to break up."

So began one of the most enlightened American defense pro-grams of the last two decades. Initiated by Nunn and Senator Rich-ard Lugar, an Indiana Republican, with a powerful assist from Bill Perry, it was, in effect, a mini–Marshall Plan for the nuclear weap-ons complex left adrift by the disintegration of the Soviet Union. Like the Marshall Plan, which helped to rebuild Europe, including West Germany, after World War II, the Nunn-Lugar program was designed to strengthen American security not by amassing new arms at home but by preventing the rise of new threats abroad. Working with American financial aid and technical assistance, the new governments that emerged from the ruins of the Soviet Union were able to strengthen security at their nuclear weapons facilities. Over time, Ukraine, Kazakhstan, and Belarus transferred back to Russia or destroyed the nuclear weapons they had inherited. The program, and others like it that followed, did not provide an iron-clad guarantee against the theft of nuclear weapons and fissile ma-terials, but they unquestionably reduced the danger.

While Nunn was working on the Soviet arsenal, Sid Drell was applying some of the same safety considerations to American weapons. Though there seemed little, if any, danger that American warheads and fissile materials could escape tight security controls, concern was rising about potential accidental detonations and other problems.

In an influential report prepared for the House Armed Ser-vices Committee, Drell and two prominent fellow physicists, John S. Foster Jr. and Charles H. Townes, examined the safety of America's nuclear arsenal. The report recommended a series of steps to optimize warhead safety—measures to minimize the risk that weapons would accidentally explode or scatter plutonium over a wide area if they were mishandled or exposed to a severe electrical storm that caused a nonnuclear detonation. The findings involved everything from warhead design and components to operational procedures and management. The broad objective was to prepare the weapons laboratories and warhead stockpile for the post–Cold War era when new technologies and procedures were likely to be in demand to upgrade the safety of the American arsenal.

Two decades later, the Drell and Nunn programs look farsighted. But when Nunn first suggested his plan for Soviet weapons, it was a startling idea. Sending American aid to help secure Soviet nuclear weapons and materials seemed like giving aid and comfort to the enemy. After more than four decades of fearing Soviet aggression, the United States was going to help Soviet military forces and nuclear weapons scientists? Bill Perry called it "defense by other means" and "preventive defense," but the reassuring sobriquets did little to quell the doubts.

When Nunn returned to Washington after his conversation with Gorbachev, he met with Representative Les Aspin, the chairman of the House Armed Services Committee, who was proposing to take $1 billion out of the defense budget to provide food, medicine, and other humanitarian aid to Russia and other pieces of the Soviet Union. They worked out a deal to include funds to help maintain control of nuclear, chemical, and biological weapons on Soviet territory.

"All hell broke loose," Nunn recalled. Senator Alan Dixon, an Illinois Democrat, foreshadowed the reaction when he burst into Nunn's Senate office suite one day. As a Nunn aide recounted, Dixon said, "Sam, I just heard your press statement about giving money away to Russia. Count me out. . . . That's never going to go in Illinois. I will never get re-elected."

Nunn withdrew the measure and looked for a better way to

sell the idea. He found it a few days later at a briefing in his Senate office arranged by David Hamburg, an arms control advocate who was president of the Carnegie Corporation, one of the nation's largest foundations. Ashton Carter, a Harvard professor, led the November 19 briefing, describing a study he had recently completed for Carnegie, titled "Soviet Nuclear Fission: Control of the Nuclear Arsenal in a Disintegrating Soviet Union."

The dimensions of the problem were staggering. The breakup of the Soviet Union would create fifteen newly independent states. Four of them—Russia, Ukraine, Belarus, and Kazakhstan—would wind up owning just about everything in the Soviet nuclear arsenal. Ukraine alone would house some 1,600 strategic warheads, as well as a fleet of modern, nuclear-armed bombers, plus a large military-industrial complex. Overnight it would become the world's third most powerful nuclear state, trailing only the United States and Russia.

The Soviet Union's command and control system for nuclear weapons was elaborate and well managed, but there was no guarantee it would hold together as the country came apart. Nuclear warheads, especially smaller, tactical weapons, might be susceptible to theft. Large stockpiles of highly enriched uranium and plutonium could become inviting sources of illicit revenue for workers with access to them. The scientists and engineers who designed and built nuclear weapons might be tempted to sell their knowledge to countries or groups eager to produce their own nuclear weapons.

"The study predicted that the breakup of the Soviet Union posed the biggest proliferation threat of the Atomic Age and outlined a new form of 'arms control' to stop it: joint action by the two former Cold War opponents against the common danger," Carter recalled.

Everyone at the briefing was braced by Carter's report, including Bill Perry and Senator Lugar, who was already alarmed by the potential hazards. Perry, based in California at the time, had been looking at how the state-owned military-industrial enterprises of the Soviet Union might be converted to civilian uses to help power a post–Cold War Soviet economy.

Nunn and Lugar invited twenty fellow senators to meet with Carter two days later at a working breakfast. The sixteen senators who attended came away as concerned as Nunn and Lugar. Nunn and Lugar and their staff members quickly drafted a new legislative measure called the Soviet Nuclear Threat Reduction Act. Lugar's weight as a cosponsor, coupled with the alarming picture painted by the Carter study, transformed the political equation. On November 26, the Senate overwhelmingly approved the Nunn-Lugar program.

The program provided $400 million to dismantle Soviet nuclear and chemical weapons, and $100 million for the kind of humanitarian aid Les Aspin favored. It was not a great deal of money, given the scale of the problem, but it opened the door for more ambitious efforts. On the diplomatic front, Secretary of State James Baker took the lead in working with the new governments to encourage cooperation among them to ensure that the Soviet arsenal did not become the hub of an international nuclear black market. The diplomatic challenges were daunting as Russia jockeyed with Ukraine, Belarus, and Kazakhstan over control of their nuclear inheritance.

Baker's efforts were part of a White House strategy to reduce overall nuclear threats as the Cold War came to an unexpected end in 1991. It was a momentous year for George H. W. Bush's administration, beginning with the successful American-led military campaign to evict Iraqi forces from Kuwait. Thanks to Gorbachev, the Kremlin did not oppose the military operation. Only a few months later, Gorbachev's rule was imperiled by the coup attempt. In September, President Bush ordered a significant drawdown in American nuclear forces. Many tactical nuclear weapons—items like nuclear artillery shells and nuclear-armed cruise missiles carried aboard ships—would be withdrawn. The long-range bombers of the Strategic Air Command, a symbol of Cold War tensions, would no longer remain on twenty-four-hour alert, ready to take off at a moment's notice. Bush also instructed the Air Force to take missiles off high alert that were already destined for dismantlement under an arms accord with Moscow, and said he would try to work out a deal with the Kremlin to eliminate long-range missiles with multiple warheads.

To keep the arms control momentum going, Nunn led a Senate delegation to Russia and Ukraine in March 1992. Perry, Carter, and Hamburg accompanied the group. Perry recalled, "We were all concerned with what was happening in nuclear weapons in Russia, which was in a state of turmoil, and the Ukraine, which was in a state of turmoil." The men were troubled by what they saw. On the long flight home, they drafted a more expansive plan for a cooperative threat reduction program. Congress approved the bill, the Freedom Support Act, in the summer of 1992. It provided another $400 million for a variety of steps, including safeguarding and dismantlement of nuclear, chemical, and biological weapons and the establishment of science and technology centers to keep weapons scientists and engineers engaged.

When congressional support for the program softened over time, Nunn smartly defended the initiative by highlighting domestic and global threats involving weapons of mass destruction. Under his direction, the Senate Permanent Subcommittee on Investigations held a series of splashy hearings in 1994 about a chemical weapons attack on the Tokyo subway system earlier that year. With support from Richard Lugar and another Republican, Pete Domenici of New Mexico, Nunn won congressional approval not just to continue the program, but to expand it. "It just shows you," he said, "what you can do if you use a legislative committee and an investigative committee together."

With the inauguration of Bill Clinton as president on January

20, 1993, Bill Perry and Ashton Carter took ownership of the Nunn–Lugar program, Perry as deputy secretary of defense and Carter as an assistant secretary. Indeed, Nunn helped to persuade Perry to take the Pentagon job. Perry was attending an Aspen Institute meeting with Nunn and Hamburg when Les Aspin, Clinton's choice to be secretary of defense, asked him to serve as deputy secretary. "I told Sam and David about it and said I was going to turn it down, and the rest of the week they spent twisting my arm saying you'd better do this. So when I finally went into that job I invited them to come and speak at my swearing-in. I blamed them for being in the job in the first place."

Perry and Carter were eager to advance the Nunn–Lugar program. Gloria Duffy, who worked closely with them, said, "Perry took this as his mission, one of his missions, and really pushed it forward. He owned it."

Perry and Carter put it this way: "When we took office in 1993, it seemed to us entirely unlikely that Ukraine, Kazakhstan and Belarus would all stay on the path to become nuclear-free states; that Russia would continue to safeguard and dismantle weapons amidst its titanic social upheavals; that somewhere, sometime, there would not be a sale, diversion, theft, or seizure of these weapons or nuclear materials by disgruntled military officers or custodians somewhere across the eleven time zones that had been the Soviet empire. Every morning we would open the daily intelligence summary fearing to read that nukes had broken loose and hoping that at least U.S. intelligence sources would have detected the break."

Perry set up a new Pentagon office to manage the program and put Carter in charge of it. The management team they recruited included four women. The four—Gloria Duffy, Elizabeth Sherwood, Susan J. Koch, and Laura Holgate—were all defense specialists familiar with nuclear proliferation issues. At Perry's first meeting with senior Russian military officers, the Russian generals at the table seemed to assume the three women accompanying him were unimportant sidekicks.

"They assumed they were my consorts or something," he said with a laugh. Realizing there would be a problem if the Russians did not take the women seriously, he found a moment to make clear they were senior officials. At the first substantive question from the top Russian general, Perry said, "I don't know the answer to that." He turned to Elizabeth Sherwood. "Liz, would you tell me what we should do?" As he recalled, "She gave a very good answer to the question. That surprised the Russian. And then I said, 'Dr. Sherwood is my expert in this area, and I've authorized her to do this job. She will have my full support in doing everything she needs to get it done.'"

Several years later, as they were wrapping up work on a project, Perry returned to the general's office. As a photographer prepared to snap photos of Perry and the Russian officer, the Russian motioned to Sherwood to join them. Perry described the moment with relish years later. "The general said, 'Wait a minute. Liz, get over here. She should be in this picture, because she's the one that made it all happen.'"

Making Nunn-Lugar work was hard. Diplomatic deals had to be struck among newly created nations deeply suspicious of one another. For instance, getting Ukraine to give up its nuclear weapons required negotiation of a three-way treaty between Russia, Ukraine, and the United States. The money authorized under the early Nunn-Lugar legislation was already designated for other Pentagon programs. During the Bush administration, Secretary of Defense Dick Cheney and his colleagues were not enthusiastic about reprogramming, or transferring, the money. In one instance, the Pentagon comptroller told Gloria Duffy he couldn't release funds because the money was needed to refuel Navy ships. Even with a powerful nudge from Perry, the Pentagon bureaucracy was inherently wary of doing anything to help the remnants of the

Soviet Union handle weapons that were still aimed at the United States. Building housing for Russian or Ukrainian troops seemed almost surreal to longtime Pentagon officials.

"There was a lot of mentality changing necessary," Duffy said. As she recalled, the attitude of Pentagon officials was "This is the enemy. We don't do things to assist them. We're opposing them. It's a zero-sum relationship."

As a result, the Nunn–Lugar initiative got off to a rocky start. Much of the original $400 million down payment never materialized. Bureaucratic and logistical impediments slowed progress. Tensions among the newly independent nations disrupted negotiations. Congressional objections swelled. Still, Perry, Carter, and their colleagues managed to get a lot done, with a good deal of help from Vice President Al Gore and Bill Clinton's top Soviet adviser, Strobe Talbott, who became deputy secretary of state in Clinton's second term. Jim Goodby served as lead negotiator for many of the treaties that were required to assure the cooperation of the new states.

The most striking achievement was eradication of the nuclear arsenals in Ukraine, Kazakhstan, and Belarus. Perry made denuclearization of the three countries one of his top priorities and had the muscle to move the Pentagon when he became secretary of defense in 1994, after Les Aspin resigned.

In March 1994, as the pace picked up with Ukraine, Perry and Carter visited Pervomaysk, site of a large missile base. The Ukrainian defense minister, General Vitaly Radetsky, escorted them into an underground chamber, where two young Ukrainian officers controlled seven hundred nuclear warheads perched atop the intercontinental ballistic missiles housed in silos at the base. "Across one wall of the command center stretched a map of the United States," Perry and Carter recalled later. "Another map showed Europe. Small lights dotted across the maps indicated targets of the nuclear warheads controlled from this center. A few of the lights had been turned off, but most were still lit."

As the two Ukrainians simulated a countdown, Perry and Carter couldn't take their eyes off the map. "We watched the countdown and stared at the targets highlighted on the maps—cities in Germany and England, in Kansas and Oregon. We had known from the U.S. intelligence, collected laboriously over decades of Cold War, that facilities like this one would control the launch of Soviet nuclear-armed ICBMs aimed at the United States. We had both done analyses and papers on how to maintain the uneasy balance that constituted nuclear deterrence. But never had the 'balance of terror' seemed as real and as terrible to either of us as it was at that moment."

Perry and his aides returned to Pervomaysk three times after that first visit. The second time, in April 1995, they watched as a large crane lifted an SS-19 long-range missile from its silo, the first step on its journey to a dismantlement center, where it would be turned into scrap metal. They also toured a new housing complex, built with American aid. The prefabricated homes would house dozens of Ukrainian officers who were losing their jobs and homes as the missile base closed. During their next visit, in January 1996, they witnessed the destruction of one of the silos that had housed a Soviet missile. On the final trip on a summer day later that year, they returned to see the last set of warheads shipped off to Russia, where they would be dismantled. By then much of the base had been restored to farmland. "In place of nuclear missile silos and weapons control bunkers and barbed wire, a beautiful and lucrative crop of sunflowers now bloomed," Perry and Carter said. Accompanied by the Russian and Ukrainian defense ministers, Perry planted sunflower seeds in the dark soil.

During the same period, Perry escorted the Russian defense minister, General Pavel Grachev, to an abandoned Missouri missile base, where the men blew up an Air Force silo that had once housed a nuclear-tipped missile. The base, spread across 5,300 square miles of farmland, had been home to more than one hundred intercontinental missiles. Grachev said that future generations would someday consider history and wonder "what kind of madmen, on our side and on the U.S. side, could sit down and plan such weapons of mass destruction."

Another sign of progress came in Kazakhstan, home of the Soviet Union's primary underground nuclear test site, outside Semipalatinsk. As the new Kazakh government took control of the country after the fall of the Soviet Union, it discovered that approximately 600 kilograms, or 1,300 pounds, of highly enriched uranium was stored in a poorly secured warehouse at the Ulbinsky Metallurgy Plant, located twenty miles from the city of Ust-Kamenogorsk in eastern Kazakhstan. That was more than enough uranium to make twenty nuclear weapons. When they inspected the storage site, Kazakh officials found empty shipping canisters bearing addresses in Tehran. Kazakhstan notified the United States about the uranium in August 1993, setting in motion an elaborate plan, called "Project Sapphire," to pack up the material and transport it to the United States.

On October 8, 1994, acting with President Clinton's authorization, a team of thirty-one American nuclear specialists headed to Kazakhstan to prepare the highly enriched uranium for shipment. By the end of November, the fissile material was on its way to Dover Air Force Base in Delaware, where it was placed on a truck convoy for transfer to the Energy Department nuclear complex in Oak Ridge, Tennessee.

As the years rolled by, the Nunn-Lugar program and related American operations inspired by it played a significant role in the denuclearization of Ukraine, Belarus, and Kazakhstan. Equally important, the work helped Russia secure its sprawling nuclear weapons complex, including tons of bomb-grade highly enriched uranium and plutonium.

The results are impressive. As of December 2010, the cooperative threat reduction effort had led to the deactivation of 7,599 strategic nuclear warheads, the destruction of 791 long-range missiles and 498 missile silos, and the elimination of hundreds of submarine-launched missiles and dozens of submarines and bombers. The program also upgraded security at two dozen nuclear weapons storage facilities.

By 1995, Nunn thought he had accomplished about as much as he could in the Senate. "The Cold War was over," he said. "We were moving into another, a different, era. I'd gotten some major legislation passed. . . . So I just felt like it wasn't that we didn't have a continuing set of problems, but I'd sort of done a major part of what I thought I could do at that stage."

He was also mindful of exiting before Georgians started pressing him to outdo Richard Russell's thirty-five years of Senate service, and before business opportunities dwindled. "I'd been in politics from the time, if you count the state legislature, from the time I was twenty-eight," he said. "I knew that if I stayed until I was beyond fifty-eight, if I stayed one more term, I would be getting to the stage where I would not be very valuable to either boards or law firms, and it would be very hard at sixty-five to have the kind of runway in terms of number of years left to do other things."

So, at age fifty-eight, Nunn left the Senate in January 1997 and went to work as a partner at King & Spalding, an influential Atlanta law firm. He intended to remain active in the public policy arena, telling his new law partners he would split his time between firm work and outside interests. "I told them I wasn't going to go cold turkey," he said. He made several trips to Russia with Senator Lugar to track the evolution of the Nunn-Lugar program and became chairman of the Center for Strategic and International Studies, a highly regarded Washington think tank.

Perry retired as defense secretary the same month. Weary of the increasingly partisan battles over the defense budget and programs in Congress, and worn down by crises in North Korea, the Balkans, Haiti, and other hot spots, he headed back to California. He set up shop at Stanford as a professor and codirector, with Ashton Carter, of a joint Stanford-Harvard project on preventive defense. In addition he became a senior adviser at Hambrecht & Quist, the investment bank and venture capital firm where he had worked in the 1980s.

For Perry, the Nunn-Lugar program was a critical effort to deal with the new world order that developed after the Cold War and the new nuclear threats it presented. Looking back at the work in 1999, Perry and Carter wrote: "At Pervomaysk, a new and unfamiliar danger—an unprecedented surge of nuclear proliferation in the heart of Europe—took the place of the familiar military threat. . . . It might have taken some years and several turns of the wheel of history and social revolution in the former Soviet Union for these missiles and nuclear warheads to fall into the hands of those who might once again use them to threaten American lives and interests. But if the danger had been ignored and allowed to fester and grow, the resulting threat would be as fearsome as the Cold War's balance of terror."

Two years after they wrote those words, al-Qaeda struck New York and Washington.

PART IV

Going to Zero

CHAPTER TWENTY-THREE

If those planes had carried nuclear weapons,
Washington would have been destroyed.
—MAX KAMPELMAN

The thought of abolishing nuclear weapons was not much on the minds of policymakers in Washington or other capitals as the new millennium opened. With the Cold War receding into history, American and Russian nuclear weapons stockpiles were diminishing. Despite the nuclear ambitions of India, Pakistan, and North Korea, the threat of a global nuclear war seemed all but inconceivable.

As Shultz, Kissinger, Perry, Nunn, and Drell turned their calendars to 2000, the idea that the five men would band together to call for the elimination of nuclear weapons seemed far-fetched, to put it mildly. That the men could give new life to the dormant concept and galvanize world leaders would have sounded even more improbable.

"Going to Zero," cognoscenti shorthand for nuclear disarmament, was a red flag for nuclear weapons sophisticates. To them it bespoke a flaky idealism and profound ignorance about the realities of the nuclear age and the centrality of nuclear weapons in American defense doctrine. Ronald Reagan and George Shultz had been pilloried for discussing the abolition with Mikhail Gorbachev in Reykjavik. Most Reagan aides thought their boss's repeated allusions over the years to a world free of nuclear weapons were daffy and not to be taken seriously.

The United States continued to rely on its nuclear forces as the ultimate guarantor of its security. While the nation might no longer need to keep Russia at bay by threatening to pulverize it if it ever attacked the United States, defense planners still relied heavily on nuclear weapons to deter aggression, especially aggression involving weapons of mass destruction—nuclear, chemical, or biological. America's allies in Europe, Asia, and the Middle East, the theory went, depended on Washington's "nuclear umbrella" to deter attack by erratic nations like North Korea and Iran and to be able to forgo the development of nuclear weapons themselves. The nuclear gospel held that nuclear arms had helped preserve the peace after two convulsive world wars. Speaking realistically, opponents of zero said, there was no way to erase the knowledge of how to make nuclear weapons, so it was futile to try. Even moving toward zero would be reckless because the balance of power would become much more unstable as nations gave up their weapons, giving any country with just a handful of warheads a potential advantage over its adversaries.

Beyond all those factors, skeptics of zero like Harold Brown, a former defense secretary, and Brent Scowcroft, who served two presidents as national security adviser, feared it would undermine more concrete steps that could be taken to reduce nuclear threats. They thought it would distract attention from measures that might actually make a difference and, worse, equate such steps with the agenda of radical antinuke campaigners.

Scowcroft put it well. "I would not absolutely rule out that the day would come when nuclear weapons would be outlawed. But to me the basic problem is that you cannot disinvent nuclear weapons. And a world without them is likely to be a much more tense and alarming world than we can imagine, because in that world a country that cheats and develops them immediately becomes a superpower, comparatively. And human nature being what it is, it's hard to imagine a world where that wouldn't happen."

For Scowcroft, the emphasis should be on preventing the use of nuclear weapons rather than banishing them. "The right question is, what steps can we take so that nuclear weapons are never used? And to me zero is not that. But it is numbers of weapons, it is the character of the different weapons."

Kissinger, Perry, Nunn, and Drell wrestled with similar doubts, and even Shultz, who threw his arms around zero at Reykjavik, knew that eliminating nuclear weapons would be a devilishly difficult matter. "I didn't know how to get to zero," Perry recalled. "I couldn't imagine quite how you would get there or how you would function once you were there."

Kissinger couldn't, either. Skeptical about the Clinton administration's nuclear weapons policy, he said in 1998, "The national security strategy of the United States is built around nuclear weapons. Yet the rhetoric of the administration stigmatizes them in such absolute terms as to come close to undermining that policy. The administration is right to resist nuclear proliferation but it must not, in the process, disarm the country psychologically. Nuclear weapons cannot be abolished; no inspections system could account for them all."

Then came September 11, 2001, and suddenly terrorists with nuclear weapons vaulted from the realm of Hollywood thriller to plausible threat. Notebooks and other materials found at al-Qaeda hideouts in Afghanistan suggested that Osama bin Laden and his followers had been trying for years to obtain nuclear weapons or the means to make them. The prospect of a nuclear 9/11 hit Washington like a thunderbolt. For all their Cold War bluster and fearsome nuclear arsenals, the United States and Soviet Union were governed by leaders who understood the suicidal consequences of using nuclear weapons. Not so with untraceable terrorists, who would like nothing better than to vaporize New York or Washington.

It took the musings of Max Kampelman, an aging, all-but-forgotten Cold War diplomat, to revive the idea of eliminating nuclear weapons and make it part of a credible plan to blunt the threat of nuclear terrorism. He was the catalyst. As Sam Nunn told him in 2007, "You were the inspiration for the Shultz-Perry-Kissinger-Nunn Op-Ed, and you should be very proud of the discussion you have stimulated." Nunn said, "Max was on George's State Department team, and the two of them are close friends and Max enjoys great confidence with George. So I think his huge effect was on George. But Max also had an effect on me and on a lot of other people around town, even some who have never agreed with where we are now, because of his obvious dedication and his sincerity and the fact that he was absolutely committed to this and felt it was a moral mission."

Kampelman was an unlikely figure to relaunch a somnolent cause. By the early 2000s, he had long since retired from government service as Ronald Reagan's chief arms control negotiator. He was in his early eighties, living quietly in Washington, reporting daily to the Pennsylvania Avenue offices of Fried, Frank, Harris, Shriver & Jacobson, the law firm where he had worked. His spacious but remote corner office at the back of the building reflected his status as a respected but inactive figure at the firm. "I don't even know most of the lawyers here," he said. To Cold War historians, he was a secondary player, a Democrat and Hubert Humphrey associate who supported the Vietnam War and later crossed party lines to work for Reagan and George Shultz.

Yet anyone who entered Kampelman's office, filled with photographs of him cheerfully greeting presidents from Kennedy to Clinton, could see he was still engaged with international affairs, eager for a star turn on the world stage. "I came here with the knowledge that I would not practice law; I would practice public affairs," he said. He welcomed speaking invitations and, despite his advancing age and frail appearance, worked out most mornings at the gym at the Kennedy Warren, the apartment complex in north-west Washington where he lived.

Kampelman was shaken by the terror attacks of September 11, 2001, especially the frightening prospect that al-Qaeda might strike Washington or New York next time with a nuclear weapon. "I read in the *New York Times* that if those planes had carried nuclear weapons, Washington would have been destroyed," he recalled. "That piece really scared the hell out of me." He invited some of his former State Department and Pentagon aides to a series of meetings to discuss ways to reduce the chances that terrorists might obtain a nuclear weapon or the materials to make one. As the discussions unfolded over the course of many months, he realized the surest solution would be to eliminate nuclear weapons altogether.

It resonated for Kampelman, harking back to Ronald Reagan's conviction that nuclear arms ought to be abolished. Unlike most Reagan advisers, Kampelman had enthusiastically embraced his boss's thinking about nuclear weapons and was thrilled when Reagan and Gorbachev entertained at Reykjavik the notion of abolishing the weapons.

Kampelman's openness to Reagan's approach wasn't surprising. He became a pacifist in college, and served in a number of home-front roles during World War II after being granted conscientious objector status by his draft board. He described his background to an interviewer in 2006: "The rabbi who advised Jewish students at NYU, whom I got to know quite well, was a pacifist, and my discussions with him led me to read extensively in the literature of pacifism. I also had the occasion one summer, as the result of a scholarship, to join a Quaker work camp recommended to me by one of my professors. . . . As I look back on that period, I believe I was also greatly influenced by my mother, whose only brother was killed in the First World War and who insisted that I never wear a uniform or join the Boy Scouts because it reminded her of her brother."

Like Shultz, he came to the world of nuclear weapons policy-making for the first time in the 1980s with little background and few preconceptions. He was not a captive of Cold War thinking. He likes to recall the moment when Reagan asked him to head the American delegation at the arms control negotiations: "I said, 'Mr. President, I don't know the first goddamned thing about nuclear weapons.' I'll never forget his response. He said, 'Max, neither do I. We'll learn it together.'"

Seized anew by the idea of abolition after 9/11, Kampelman wanted to get it back into public discussion, even put it before the George W. Bush administration and United Nations for consideration. He knew getting President Bush's endorsement was a long shot, but as he followed policy debates in the months after September 11, he saw other arms control specialists proposing various schemes to keep nuclear weapons out of the hands of terrorists. All stopped well short of calling for nuclear disarmament.

While Kampelman was pondering his next step, Shultz, Kissinger, Perry, Nunn, and Drell were independently growing more alarmed about nuclear threats.

Several years after Nunn left the Senate, Ted Turner, the swashbuckling Atlanta billionaire and founder of CNN, approached Nunn about setting up and directing a nonprofit organization dedicated to reducing nuclear, chemical, and biological weapons threats. Nunn agreed to study the idea but was not charmed by Turner's desire to champion the abolition of nuclear weapons.

"I said, 'Ted, I'm not sure that you and I are on the same wavelength,' because he said even back then he wanted to rid the world of all nuclear weapons, and I felt like going on that mission with Ted was not going to be productive, if that's the way we started out the mission."

Turner and Nunn put together a small group to explore the idea for a new organization. In January 2001, well before the 9/11 attacks, they launched the Nuclear Threat Initiative (NTI). Turner was still eager for NTI to endorse the elimination of nuclear weapons, but the more cautious Nunn vetoed the idea, arguing it would hinder the organization's work and its ability to attract a politically diverse board of directors from the United States and abroad, including Republican senators Richard Lugar and Pete Domenici. "I felt like at that stage we'd be like a hound dog hollering at the moon," Nunn said, speaking of abolition.

"I wasn't ready. I didn't think the country was ready. I didn't think that I could put together a board. I thought it would end up being a left-wing movement and quickly be seized by the left wing, and I thought it was going to be totally counterproductive. . . . I believed that back then if you were ever going to do something and announce that, you had to have a track record of understanding first of all how tough it was going to be and how complicated, and how much you have to do on securing the material, setting up verification, setting up enforcement—the groundwork just hadn't been laid for this."

In December 2001, three months after the terror attacks, Nunn and Perry took the first step on the path that would ultimately lead to the *Wall Street Journal* article. In collaboration with senators Lugar and Domenici, and David Hamburg, the former foundation president long active on the arms control front, they proposed a joint American-Russian initiative against catastrophic terrorism. They sent the proposal to President Bush, recommending, among other things, that Bush and President Vladimir Putin of Russia "catalyze a global coalition against nuclear terrorism." The two leaders were scheduled to meet a few months later.

The proposal, in effect, would have expanded work already under way in Russia under the Nunn-Lugar program to secure Russian nuclear weapons and materials, and extended the effort to other nations. It said, "Many nations around the world have unsecured nuclear weapons and nuclear materials, harboring 'cells' of potential nuclear terrorism. Containing and securing nuclear materials worldwide, unlike controlling terrorist motivations worldwide, is a finite challenge—we can define it and specify precisely what it would take to meet it—so we should be able to meet it."

Nunn could not recall precisely how the White House responded to the proposal, but said, "It wasn't 'let's engage on this issue.' It was, 'thank you very much for your thoughts and we'll consider them in time,' something polite."

Nunn and Perry returned to the issue of nuclear terrorism in 2003, this time with an important new ally who was close to President Bush—George Shultz. With Sid Drell serving in the wings as a Shultz counselor, this joint effort during the summer of 2003 marked the beginning of a four-way collaboration that would eventually enlist Henry Kissinger and evolve into the campaign that is officially called the Nuclear Security Project.

Kissinger was not involved during this early stage. He seemed an unlikely ally to Nunn and Perry and his doubts about abolishing nuclear weapons were well known. In 1999 he had objected to the Comprehensive Nuclear Test-Ban Treaty, an accord that would bar the testing of nuclear weapons. While supporting the administration's efforts to combat the spread of nuclear weapons technology and materials, Kissinger said, "For the foreseeable future, the United States must continue to rely on nuclear weapons to help deter certain kinds of attacks on this country and its friends and allies."

Drell's relationship with Shultz, though unheralded, was critical as Nunn and Perry approached Shultz in 2003. When Shultz left government service in 1989 at the end of the Reagan presidency, he returned to the Bay Area, which had been his base of operations from 1974 to 1982, when he served as a senior executive and eventually president of the Bechtel Corporation, the global construction company. During that period, he had taught part-time at the Stanford Business School and bought a campus home. Shultz and Drell did not meet at the time. But as Shultz was preparing to exit Washington in early 1989, Paul Nitze suggested he get together with Drell at Stanford. Shultz invited Drell to lunch and they soon forged a mutually respectful friendship.

"I knew about Sid but I had never met him when I was in office," Shultz said. "People were constantly quoting him. So when I came back here, we got together . . . we started having lunch together, and enjoyed it. And then when anybody interesting came to town, and I was going to have the person for lunch, I'd invite Sid and vice versa. I can remember a wonderful evening with Sakharov."

Drell was tickled by the new friendship. "I clearly didn't call George up. I'd never met him. I knew he was a great man, but we had regular lunches and as time goes on, one of the issues we talked about clearly was nuclear weapons and the dangers."

Superficially, the two men could hardly have been more different. Shultz was a stalwart Republican, a wealthy four-time cabinet member, and an accomplished golfer welcome at Augusta National and other elite clubs. He was also a prominent summer denizen of the Bohemian Grove, the rustic retreat north of San Francisco where industrial titans, bankers, and other establishment figures gather for an annual encampment in the redwood forests. Drell was content just to be a member of the Stanford Faculty Club. He was a longtime Democrat, a man of modest means, and an occasional softball pitcher at the Stanford Linear Accelerator Center's annual field day.

But Shultz and Drell shared a love for Princeton, their alma mater. They are both apt to wear garish orange sports jackets and other Princeton attire when the occasion warrants. They liked to swap stories and talk policy and both had devoted a great deal of time to government service. They soon found they agreed about the need to de-emphasize the role of nuclear weapons in American defense strategy and make drastic reductions in American and Soviet nuclear arsenals.

Drell's scientific expertise and detailed command of nuclear weapons technology matched up nicely with Shultz's diplomatic instincts and big-picture perspective. "George has enormous confidence in him," Nunn said. Absent Drell's support, Shultz might have lacked the confidence on nuclear issues to propose audacious new initiatives. "He's a comfort blanket for Shultz," said one nuclear weapons expert who knows Shultz. "If you pull out the comfort blanket, I don't know that Shultz is ever there." Absent Shultz's vision and visibility, Drell's views might never have gained an audience outside the scientific community.

As Shultz put it, "Sid is very knowledgeable. He knows the physics from the inside out. It is always comforting to have somebody aboard who really understands the nature of this animal we're talking about. And he's wise and thoughtful and fun, so he's a great colleague. . . . People know that if they're going to work with him, they know that they're on their mettle."

Nunn and Perry were also comfortable with Drell. Perry and Drell, of course, had known each other for years and collaborated on several defense matters. Nunn had come to know Drell during Drell's appearances before the Senate Armed Services Committee. "I've always admired him. . . . I've always felt he was a brilliant scientist and had a real way of putting things, like Perry, in a way people can understand."

When Nunn and Perry approached Shultz in July 2003, they were primarily interested in cutting American and Russian nuclear forces and adjusting the launch status of the thousands of missiles still targeted on each other's territory. The two Democrats figured Shultz would be sympathetic to the cause and could get their proposals a hearing in the Bush White House. Shultz had been an early Bush supporter as the Texas governor was gearing up for a presidential run in the late 1990s. For Bush, a candidate short on defense credentials, Shultz's endorsement represented a powerful blessing from the Republican foreign policy establishment.

Though Shultz sought no role in the Bush administration, he served as an informal adviser to the president during his first years in office. (Shultz later grew disillusioned with the policies pursued by Bush and Vice President Dick Cheney.)

Working with a RAND Corporation study on Russian and American nuclear forces commissioned by NTI, Nunn and his staff assembled a brief list of recommendations for steps to reduce the risk of an accidental or unauthorized missile launch. Nunn flew out to California to go over them with Shultz and Perry. The trio met for dinner at Shultz's Stanford home on July 29. Nunn described his acute concern about the American and Russian missiles that remained on high alert, meaning they could be launched on short notice, even as Washington and Moscow were drawing down the total number of missiles.

The last item on Nunn's agenda opened the door to a wider array of nuclear weapons issues. The NTI talking points prepared for the dinner said, "Would also like to explore your willingness to become engaged in a broader discussion on further steps that can be taken to reduce the danger posed by our strategic force postures."

Though Nunn, Shultz, and Perry didn't realize it at the time, the discussion that evening was the start of a series of conversations that led to the 2007 *Wall Street Journal* op-ed article. "That's where it started," Nunn said.

In the days following the dinner, Shultz condensed the highlights of the discussion into a memo that he circulated to Perry, Nunn, Drell, and Charles Curtis, the president of NTI. On August 14, after incorporating their suggestions and revisions, Shultz sent the group's recommendations to Condoleezza Rice, the national security adviser, with a request that she bring them to Bush's attention.

The memo opened with a set of proposals involving the American and Russian nuclear arsenals, or as the memo put it, "Removing unnecessary vestiges of Cold War confrontation—reducing the risks of accidental or unauthorized launch of nuclear weapons." The proposed steps included standing down, or taking off high alert, all the forces scheduled for reduction under the Treaty of Moscow, the arms reduction accord Bush and Putin had signed on May 24, 2002.

A second set of recommendations, which hinted at the direction that the four men, plus Kissinger, would take in the next few years, dealt with "preventing terrorists from acquiring a nuclear weapon." The memo called for accelerating security upgrades for vulnerable nuclear materials in the former Soviet Union and an effort to remove all bomb-grade materials from research reactors and facilities around the world.

The memo concluded with an exhortation to Bush: "An announcement that advances progress in these two key areas would be of historic dimension—the strongest sign yet that the two largest nuclear powers are committed to reducing the nuclear legacy of the Cold War and are working together to prevent the emergence of new nuclear states and the acquisition of these weapons by terrorists."

In a cover letter to Bush, Shultz wrote: "I feel a little presumptuous in sending this note to you since you have already made such headway on nuclear matters in your dealings with President Putin." After explaining that the recommendations reflected the work of Nunn and Perry as well as himself, Shultz offered to make their bipartisan support publicly known if Bush thought that would be helpful.

Bush, preoccupied with the invasion of Iraq and burgeoning debate about the absence of weapons of mass destruction there, never acknowledged receipt of the memo and ignored its recommendations.

Nunn found the response hard to explain. "I was disappointed and I was surprised, frankly, because I thought that President Bush, when you look at what he said in the campaign, had been on that wavelength. And we quoted some specific statements he made in the campaign. . . . I don't know what happened, but you have to say, was the staff on the same wavelength as the president? And my answer to that is, probably not."

Shultz was miffed. In his understated way, he said, "I remember being disappointed that I don't think we got any response at all. None. I didn't know what to make of it. I had a good relationship with Condi, of course, and some with George Bush—so they'd always take my phone calls, but they were not easy to have a conversation with. They'd listen, thank you. It was a very self-sufficient administration."

Even though the memo to Bush hit a dead end, Nunn and his colleagues at NTI thought that collaborating with Shultz offered the best chance of influencing the Republican White House. In late 2004, after Bush's reelection, a group of NTI staff members noted the potential benefits of reengaging with Shultz. "We first engaged Secretary Shultz on these issues in August 2003," the NTI staff noted in a memo in early November 2004. "He was supportive of taking a bold approach, and—along with Secretary Perry and Senator Nunn—sent a memorandum to the President through Condi. While nothing came of this, Shultz may still be our best way to directly access the President, and could provide advice on how best to navigate the shoals of the transition (depending on who ends up where)."

As Bush's second inauguration approached in January 2005, NTI's primary interest remained the volatile launch status of Russian and American missiles and related strategic weapons issues. But as work proceeded on those matters, Max Kampelman entered the picture, initiating a series of conversations that unexpectedly introduced the idea of abolishing nuclear weapons into NTI discussions.

Kampelman had a grand concept, however irresponsible it might seem to most defense analysts, but knew it needed refinement and

a corps of powerful supporters to have any hope of getting traction
in Washington. He turned to Steve Andreasen at NTI for advice.
Andreasen was a good choice. He was one of Washington's top
nuclear weapons experts. He started out as an intern to Paul Nitze
and an aide to Senator Al Gore and worked his way up the government ranks to become the top nuclear weapons and arms control
aide in the Clinton White House. By the time Kampelman reached
out to him in 2005, Andreasen was serving as a consultant to NTI
and a lecturer at the University of Minnesota's Humphrey Institute
of Public Affairs. In addition, he was a friend of Sid Drell, which
turned out to be a fortuitous connection in the months ahead.

Kampelman got in touch with Andreasen after reading a letter
from Andreasen and Drell that appeared in March 2005 in *Foreign
Affairs*. "It was a good and informative letter and it leads me to ask
whether you have published anything dealing with President Reagan's efforts to abolish all nuclear ballistic missiles," Kampelman
wrote to Andreasen in late March. Andreasen, in turn, notified
Drell a few weeks later that Kampelman seemed to be intrigued
with Reagan-era ideas about getting rid of ballistic missiles.

Kampelman and Andreasen knew one another, but had not
talked since 1989. After receiving Kampelman's letter in March,
Andreasen sent Kampelman an op-ed article and a long essay he
had recently published that made the case for eliminating ballistic
missiles. The Andreasen essay in *Survival*, a periodical published by
the International Institute for Strategic Studies, was titled "Reagan
Was Right: Let's Ban Ballistic Missiles." The two men agreed to
meet for lunch.

"When I went to see him for lunch, the Friday before Memorial Day," Andreasen recalled, "I thought we were going to
talk about Reagan's ZBM [Zero Ballistic Missiles] proposal. And
I was surprised that he expanded the conversation and made very
clear that what he was interested in was the proposal regarding
elimination."

Andreasen, like Nunn, was more interested in concrete steps to reduce nuclear threats, like taking missiles off high alert, than grand gestures, but Kampelman was insistent about eliminating nuclear weapons. "He's much more focused on the vision than he is on the steps," Andreasen recalled. "I agreed that I'd be happy to work with him to try and develop a set of ideas as to how that might make sense. I also tried to focus him on what can be done practically to try and advance towards that goal. He was very focused on the goal."

Andreasen and several senior NTI staff members, including Joan Rohlfing, recognized that American and international threat reduction initiatives were stalled and that a bold stroke might kick-start some discussion about addressing urgent nuclear weapons issues. "I thought it was very interesting," Rohlfing recalled, "because we were clearly coming up against a brick wall in terms of trying to move the debate on even more modest changes to our nuclear posture, and so the idea of something bolder was appealing."

Nunn himself was growing increasingly concerned that the United States and other nations were not giving nuclear threats the urgent attention he thought they demanded. In a speech to the National Press Club in Washington in March 2005, Nunn said, "Increasingly, we are being warned that an act of nuclear terrorism is inevitable. I am not willing to concede that point. But I do believe that unless we greatly elevate our effort and the speed of our response, we could face disaster. We are in a race between cooperation and catastrophe, and the threat is outrunning our response."

Andreasen and Kampelman traded ideas and in July, Andreasen prepared several memos identifying the key elements that might be included in a no-nuclear initiative. One of the memos opened by saying, "The only way to decisively address the nuclear threats of the 21st Century—i.e. the threat of deliberate nuclear use or nuclear blackmail; nuclear proliferation; nuclear terrorism;

accidental, mistaken or unauthorized nuclear use—is to eliminate all nuclear weapons globally." It went on to outline a series of steps that would produce a phased drawdown of nuclear arsenals by the nuclear weapons states.

By this time, Kampelman and Andreasen were also talking to Drell about their joint effort. On July 4, Andreasen sent Drell copies of the memos he had drafted. Kampelman liked Andreasen's papers but worried that they required too many steps and international conferences to get to zero. "My own hesitation," he told Andreasen, "is based on my belief that the political process slows up and sometimes gets swallowed up in 'steps,' 'conferences,' and 'conditions' as well as ambiguities. People lose interest and power with delays which also run the danger of getting lost in nitpicking and irrelevance."

That might have been said of Reagan and Gorbachev. Their preoccupation with Reagan's missile defense plan, particularly whether testing could be confined to the laboratory, derailed the grand arms reduction treaty that seemed within reach at Reykjavik.

As they massaged the issues, Kampelman and Andreasen decided they would try to compress their thoughts into an op-ed piece. Just before Thanksgiving, Andreasen sent the first draft to Kampelman. It said, "The United States should make clear that we are prepared to eliminate all of our nuclear weapons if the world joins us in that program and if the United Nations Security Council develops an effective regime to guarantee total conformity with a universal commitment to eliminate all WMD." A few days earlier, Andreasen had dispatched a memo to Nunn about his work with Kampelman. "I couldn't buy into that," Nunn said. "I told Max I couldn't."

As Kampelman recalls it, Nunn encouraged him to go public with the zero option. "But I have to say he was not optimistic about it at all," Kampelman said.

Impatient to get his idea a hearing at the White House, Kampelman cornered Dick Cheney at a dinner party and asked the vice president if they could get together. They did on the morning of November 16. Kampelman gave Cheney a copy of the latest Andreasen/Kampelman disarmament memo. "I found his reaction was one of keen interest and he quickly understood the virtues of our proposal," Kampelman reported in a summary of the encounter. He also noted that Cheney had recalled that Sam Nunn opposed Ronald Reagan's goal to abolish nuclear weapons.

It is hard to imagine Cheney seriously considering the Kampelman plan; more likely, he was being courteous to a man who had served Reagan with distinction. Kampelman seemed to sense an implicit brush-off when Cheney told him he would consult with the State Department, noting in his summary that "I suspect they will be skeptics."

Undeterred, Kampelman got in touch with a gaggle of other high-level Bush aides, including Condoleezza Rice, by then secretary of state, and two of her senior advisers, Robert Joseph and Nicholas Burns, as well as Eric Edelman, undersecretary of defense. He eventually got an audience late in 2006 with Josh Bolten, the White House chief of staff. He presented Bolten with the text of a speech he thought the president should deliver. President Bush dropped by while the two were talking in Bolten's office, but didn't engage Kampelman on the issue. In the end, Kampelman whiffed with the Bush administration.

While Kampelman was barnstorming in Washington, Shultz and Drell were conferring in California about what could be done to reduce nuclear threats. In Drell's view, negotiated arms cuts were not getting the job done. "Between 1990 and 2005 I look at the progress and everybody says, 'Well the numbers are coming down,' but they're not coming down in a meaningful way. To have twenty thousand instead of seventy thousand is still insane. . . .

What matters is the technology getting out in the hands of other countries, and that we still have an order of magnitude more than we know what to do with."

Shultz understood that terrorists would not fear retaliation: "If you think of the people who are doing suicide attacks, and people like that get a nuclear weapon, they are almost by definition not deterrable. And if you have terrorists get something, then you don't even know the return address. So, I think it's a very dangerous moment."

Over lunch at Shultz's home on December 20, 2005, they hit on the idea of organizing a conference in late 2006 to mark the twentieth anniversary of the Reykjavik summit meeting and to consider how the spirit of the Reagan-Gorbachev talks might be rekindled and applied to current nuclear issues.

Drell recounted the conversation a few years later. "We said, we're not getting anywhere. The danger is growing. The danger of proliferation is serious. . . . Maybe we should revisit Reykjavik and see what led to it. What implication did it have? But most important, what's its relevance for today?"

Shultz said, "Our idea was not to second-guess Reykjavik, 'If only they had done this, if only they had done that,' but rather to say, 'Well what are the implications of this for us today?' "

Jim Goodby, the former arms control negotiator, said Shultz had considered doing something to coincide with the tenth anniversary of Reykjavik in 1996, but had not reengaged the idea of abolishing nuclear weapons until Drell suggested the twentieth-anniversary conference. Shultz confirmed that the notion of doing something in 1996 never got off the ground.

Drell himself hadn't thought seriously about elimination, according to Goodby. "As I look back over the things that he and I have written together, I cannot tell you that either he or I were dedicated to the idea of eliminating nuclear weapons, because we were focusing more on the first steps in things that we wrote together. . . . I think he said, 'Yes, eliminating nuclear weapons is a noble idea but it's for the future.'"

"He seems to be a kind of genial scientist, benign," Goodby said of Drell, "but he could get a black belt in bureaucratic infighting in Washington. He's really very clever at it. And so I give him a lot of credit for getting the whole thing started."

Perry, though not party to the Shultz-Drell conversation, was equally worried that steps taken during the 1990s to reduce and secure nuclear stockpiles were giving way to a more dangerous time. "My conclusion," he said, "was that business as usual wasn't working. People are not enough concerned about the danger, and we were heading towards a much more dangerous situation. So I thought something dramatic, some dramatic change was needed to reverse that trend."

As 2005 ended, the core pieces were in place to generate a major new arms control initiative. Kampelman and Andreasen were developing the big idea—abolishing nuclear weapons. NTI and Nunn were coming to the realization that an audacious move was needed to advance their threat reduction agenda. They also recognized that a cross-party alliance with Shultz might be very helpful. And in California, Shultz, Drell, and Perry were mulling over what could be done to reduce nuclear arsenals, prevent the spread of nuclear weapons, and stop terrorists from getting their hands on a nuclear warhead.

Even so, turning the momentum into an antinuclear manifesto authored by Shultz, Perry, and Nunn seemed unlikely. Enlisting Henry Kissinger to the cause sounded inconceivable. That would soon change.

CHAPTER TWENTY-FOUR

You are in the heavy cream as far as I am concerned.
—GEORGE SHULTZ

The breakthrough came in 2006, gradually rather than in a single dramatic stroke. Until the last moment, it was not clear that Shultz, Kissinger, Perry, and Nunn could overcome political and policy differences to produce a startling call for nuclear disarmament.

Shultz, oddly enough, was the first to hesitate. In mid-February, Kampelman sent Shultz a copy of the op-ed article he and Andreasen had cobbled together, with the suggestion that Shultz serve as coauthor, or even take solo ownership of the article. It called for the abolition of nuclear weapons. "This message is not designed to rush you into a decision you are not yet prepared to make, which is why I'm sending this to you via Sidney," Kampelman said in a message, referring to Drell as the conduit. "The substance of the attached Op-Ed article reflects an almost yearlong effort by me and a bipartisan group of experts. During that time, we have been unable to find any compelling argument against our objective. . . . I believe an op-ed piece by you alone would wake us up, but if you wanted me to cosign it with you, it would be a honor."

Shultz responded at the end of March. "He called me and said, 'Max, I'm not ready for that,'" Kampelman said. But Shultz assured Kampelman that the elimination of nuclear weapons would be raised at the Reykjavik anniversary conference he and Drell were organizing. "I welcome any suggestions from you about possible things to advocate and write," Shultz said in a subsequent letter. "You are in the heavy cream as far as I am concerned." Referring to the conference agenda, Shultz reported, "We think of the penultimate meeting as dealing with your proposal and we count on you to lead the charge."

To prepare for the meeting, Shultz asked Martin Anderson, a Hoover Institution colleague who was working with Reagan's papers for a book project, to pull together a set that dealt with Reagan's desire to abolish nuclear weapons.

When asked in 2010 why he had been hesitant to lend his name to Kampelman's article, Shultz said, "I thought, just out of the blue from me an op-ed somewhere would not go anywhere. I didn't have in mind what ultimately happened, but I felt it had to have a better springboard than just me, and that turned out to be right."

Kampelman's article was published in the *New York Times* on April 24, 2006, under the headline "Bombs Away." It said, in part:

"At the age of 85, I have never been more worried about the future for my children and grandchildren than I am today. The number of countries possessing nuclear arms is increasing, and terrorists are poised to master nuclear technology with the objective of using those deadly arms against us.

"Unfortunately, the goal of globally eliminating all weapons of mass destruction—nuclear, chemical and biological arms—is today not an integral part of American foreign policy; it needs to be put back at the top of our agenda."

The article ended with a peroration about the world that "Is" and the world that "Ought" to be, a theme that Kampelman would return to in the months ahead with great conviction, impressing and inspiring Shultz. The next day, Drell messaged Andreasen, "Max's column was fine. And George liked it."

Despite Kampelman's impassioned appeal to eliminate nuclear

weapons, Shultz, Nunn, Perry, and Drell were not quite ready to take the plunge. In late spring and early summer 2006, the NTI staff pondered how best to expand its nuclear goals beyond a threat reduction agenda aimed primarily at American and Soviet nuclear forces and the fissile materials needed to make weapons. In mid-June, looking ahead to a Nunn meeting with Shultz and Perry in California later that month, Andreasen prepared a memo exploring how a goal of zero nuclear weapons might be linked to more concrete steps to reduce nuclear threats.

This was not just a semantic exercise. Nunn was still wary about embracing zero, though his thinking about it had evolved to the point where he was prepared to consider it. He still worried about drawing attention away from the specific steps promoted by NTI and muddying the threat reduction dialogue with grandiose concepts. Whenever Ted Turner brought up abolition at NTI board meetings, it failed to attract much support. As Nunn recalled, "He'd say, 'How many people around here want to abolish all nuclear weapons?' I didn't object to him asking the board. Well, about three people would hold up their hands, and he was one of them. And the rest of our board, international and otherwise, including Bill Perry and me, would never hold up our hands."

But with the global threat reduction agenda stagnating, Nunn was open to fresh ideas. Charles Curtis, president of NTI at the time, recalled, "I think it became increasingly clear to Sam that we had gotten to a point that we could no longer reduce nuclear dangers without broad international cooperation, and we couldn't get that international cooperation unless we linked the steps to reduce nuclear dangers with purposeful work on eliminating nuclear weapons.

"We had run the string. We had gotten as far as we could. . . . So it was his understanding that we need to change the vocabulary. We need to change the way we postured ourselves in the world on this matter."

The Andreasen memo outlined a "parallelism" strategy that would meld interim steps and long-term goals. It centered on a "commitment to pursue measures that are designed to get us to a world without nuclear arms . . . and a process that includes a set of actions that taken in parallel will move us in the direction of a world without nuclear arms."

On June 27, 2006, Nunn and Curtis gathered in Shultz's conference room at the Hoover Institution. They were joined by Shultz, Perry, and Drell and a number of Stanford colleagues, including David Holloway, an expert on nuclear weapons history and policy, and Harry Rowen, a former president of the RAND Corporation and assistant secretary of defense who had played a leading role in the development of nuclear deterrence strategies.

The windowless Shultz conference room, located on the second floor of one of two Hoover Institution office buildings at the base of Hoover Tower, was filled with Shultz memorabilia. Photographs of Shultz with U.S. presidents and foreign leaders covered the walls, along with the seals of the four cabinet agencies he had headed: OMB, Labor, Treasury, and State. Overlooking the group from the walls as they took their seats around the rectangular conference table were several photographs of Shultz and Gorbachev at the negotiating table in Moscow.

Shultz welcomed the group and the discussion soon turned to whether concrete steps to reduce nuclear dangers would be hindered or enhanced by attaching them to the goal of eliminating nuclear weapons. Kampelman's op-ed article came up. And as the discussion progressed, a consensus developed that going to zero was an aspirational goal that could well galvanize support for interim steps.

"We sat around talking, and we found ourselves drifting toward a world free of nuclear weapons," Shultz said.

Curtis recalled, "Shultz, I think it fair to say, was much more the vision man, and that comes out of Reykjavik and Ronald Reagan's ambition for a world free of nuclear weapons. And Sam Nunn was very much the steps man, the hard, pragmatic, but urgent work to reduce nuclear dangers. . . . It was one of the more remarkable meetings I've ever been in."

As the meeting neared an end, Shultz summoned his assistant and dictated a memo summarizing the discussion. When Shultz finished, Nunn thought, "It was just brilliant. He really nailed it; he captured it."

Shultz framed the summary as a memo to President Bush. His wording about eliminating nuclear weapons was deliberately opaque, calling for an American-led effort to de-emphasize nuclear weapons, but the drift was clear. Shultz, Perry, Nunn, and Drell no longer seemed fearful that the grand goal might distract attention from concrete steps. Indeed, they were coming around to the idea that the goal would attract support for the steps. They weren't quite prepared to call explicitly for the abolition of nuclear weapons, but they were edging closer.

This is what Shultz dictated:

THE NUCLEAR OUTLOOK AND WHAT CAN BE DONE ABOUT IT

You have taken important steps toward nuclear non-proliferation with the Moscow Treaty, the reduced emphasis on the role of nuclear weapons, and the Bratislava Summit at which you and President Putin took personal responsibility for nuclear security. But the nature of the nuclear threat in the twenty-first century has changed fundamentally from the Cold War period. This change presents both tremendous challenges and dangers, but also great opportunities. They are the reason for this memo.

The nuclear issue requires U.S. leadership. That leadership must take the world to the next stage—the stage of de-emphasizing nuclear weapons.

Nuclear weapons, once thought of as part of the solution to security concerns because they were a means of deterrence, have now become a threat to security. Their usefulness as deterrents had eroded by the end of the Cold War, and the threat of proliferation, particularly in an age in which terror is used as a weapon, has turned them into a threat. Also associated with the large-scale inventories of nuclear weapons in Russia and the United States is the threat of accidental launches of devastating consequences. What can be done?

Article VI of the Non-proliferation Treaty envisages the end of nuclear weapons. It provides that states that do not have nuclear weapons will agree not to obtain them, and states that do have them will agree to divest themselves of them. The meeting between President Reagan and General Secretary Gorbachev in Reykjavik 20 years ago was exhilarating to some but was shocking to most experts in the field of nuclear weapons. The leaders of the two countries with the largest arsenals of nuclear weapons were in the process of agreeing to abolish them and to abolish the ballistic missiles that constitute the greatest delivery threat, particularly now, in an age when mistaken or unintentional launchings are possible. Can the promise contained in the Non-proliferation Treaty and the possibility of the agreement registered in Reykjavik be brought to fruition?

Max Kampelman, a man who has been around this track many times, has put himself on record as answering this question in the affirmative. (See the attached *New York Times* article.) I propose that the achievement of this goal could be brought about by an identifiable series of subsidiary actions, some of which would take place sequentially, but most of which could take place simultaneously. Each of these actions is important in its own right, even if not attached to the others. These actions include the following:

1. A large amount of potentially dangerous bomb-quality material exists at 100 research reactors scattered around the world in 40 countries. Research can be conducted with proliferation-resistant low-enriched uranium, so one project would be to persuade countries with research reactors to sign an international

agreement to convert from highly-enriched to low-enriched uranium.

2. There are known places around the world where uranium is enriched for the purpose of nuclear power. An agreement could be reached that these locations would be put under international supervision to ensure that they would not escalate enrichment to produce weapons-grade uranium. Then all countries would agree to forego any further enrichment capability with the understanding that any country that wanted enriched uranium for nuclear power purposes would be able to obtain it at a reasonable price first from the Nuclear Suppliers Group and then from back-up reserves under the control of the IAEA or other suitable international assurance. This arrangement would be combined with an agreement that spent fuel would be collected and disposed of or be reprocessed.

3. Weapons that are now deployed and on hair-trigger alert would have their alert status changed, perhaps in steps, but perhaps more permanently. The present alert time is 30 minutes or less. You could encourage increasing the warning period to, say, an hour, a week, or longer.

4. The process would probably start with steps taken by the United States and Russia, who would have reached an understanding. The deterioration of Russian satellite and radar capability means that their warning time and their confidence in the capability of their early warning system is much worse than it was during the Cold War. It is in the interest of the United States to assist the Russians with their early warning system and to advance the cooperation that has begun but has not been making substantial progress.

5. The United States and Russia should reduce operationally deployed forces to the minimum essential numbers, which would be substantially lower than the current level and those levels contained in the Moscow Treaty.

6. Tactical nuclear weapons are the most likely weapons for terrorists to either steal or buy. We should seek transparency with the Russians beginning on a bilateral basis in terms of numbers and locations with the goal of getting rid of all tactical weapons over time. Before we could reach that goal, other countries would need to join in.

7. Review the Comprehensive Test Ban Treaty and get it into shape so that the Senate will be receptive to consenting to its ratification.

8. Work on verification procedures, as difficult as they may be, for a biological treaty as well as a fissile material cutoff treaty.

Looking back at the meeting and memo, Nunn said it was the moment when Shultz, Perry, and he realized that they were largely in agreement. "I would say that's when we had an understanding that all three of us really were generally in the same frame of mind. We had a meeting of the minds. I would call it a merger of the vision and the steps."

Before the meeting broke up, Shultz said he might show the memo to Henry Kissinger. The idea of enlisting Kissinger was a pivotal suggestion. His support could give added weight to the Shultz memo and bring aboard another former secretary of state and another Republican powerhouse. The quartet of Shultz, Kissinger, Perry, and Nunn would give a bipartisan or nonpartisan sheen to the memo. Given the rock-solid defense credentials of the four men, anything they jointly favored would instantly command attention in Washington and abroad.

Over the next several days, Shultz refined the memo, incorporating suggestions from other discussion participants. On July 13, Nunn sent Shultz a list of proposed changes and additions, reflecting his thoughts and those of the NTI staff. Nunn wanted to add a new final paragraph that said action on the points would "rightly be perceived as a bold initiative—consistent with

President Reagan's vision and America's moral heritage—that would have a profound impact on future generations in every corner of the globe."

Nunn also seconded Shultz's proposal to show the memo to Kissinger. "I think you are right in pursuing a direct and personal approach to the President, and I agree that sounding out Henry Kissinger on these issues could lead to a productive and powerful collaboration," Nunn wrote.

Nunn was not close to Kissinger but had long admired his intellectual firepower. Nunn had been new to the Senate during Kissinger's run as Nixon's national security adviser and secretary of state. Kissinger, he said, "was dealing with Scoop Jackson, he was dealing with Stennis and Symington, and those people, and so my direct contact with Kissinger one-on-one was limited in that period of time."

Shultz took a copy of the memo with him to the Bohemian Grove a few days later. "Henry, who has become a great friend, he's in the same camp I am. I said, 'Henry, take a look at this.' And he looked at it and he said, 'I have to think about this, this is important.' And I said, 'Well, keep it. And think about it.'" Shultz was surprised and delighted by Kissinger's response.

Would Kissinger play? The odds seemed long. Though he had taken the lead over the years in questioning American plans to unleash the full force of its nuclear arsenal against the Soviet Union, he had never favored the abolition of nuclear weapons. To Kissinger, the ultimate hardheaded foreign policy realist, the elimination of nuclear weapons was a fairy-tale fantasy.

But Kampelman, for one, thought Kissinger might not be a lost cause. Kissinger had been a featured speaker at a State Department ceremony at the end of 2005 when the American Academy of Diplomacy presented Kampelman with an award. He praised Kampelman as a man who had found the right balance between realism and idealism in his diplomatic career. When Kissinger turned to the issue of nuclear weapons, Kampelman was stunned by his comments. Kissinger said: "When I was in office, the problem that bothered me the most was the dilemma that as one of the people who would be asked if nuclear weapons were to be used, I had concluded that no one had the moral right to kill that many people. But as a practical operator of foreign policy, I also felt we had no moral right to turn the world over to potential genocide. Now in a two-power world you could navigate through this dilemma, but as nuclear weapons spread, that is an unmanageable problem, and therefore nonproliferation is in many ways the key issue of our time."

To Kampelman, Kissinger was endorsing the abolition of nuclear weapons. "He came out for zero," Kampelman recalled. "I quickly let Shultz know because George was deeply involved in this."

The text of Kissinger's remarks does not support Kampelman's interpretation. Saying nonproliferation was the key issue of our time wasn't the same as calling for the elimination of nuclear weapons. But Kampelman was right to surmise that Kissinger might consider the proposition. Kissinger's initial reaction to the Shultz memo seven months later at the Bohemian Grove reinforced the impression.

For Kissinger, the loss of control over nuclear weapons and materials as the technology spread was unnerving. As he later said, "In the Cold War period, and even in the possession of the well-established industrial countries, the amount, the kind of control that needs to be established against unorthodox use, or accidental use, or seepage into unorthodox hands are conceivable and worked out. But as technology spreads, that will become more and more difficult. And we have seen already in a country like Pakistan, which is a reasonably well developed country, that a whole system of proliferation was either possible or tolerated that spread nuclear technology to Libya, North Korea and some other rogue states."

The cast of characters was also a factor for Kissinger. Shultz, Perry, Nunn, and Drell were heavy hitters in the national security field. Whatever they said in unison about nuclear weapons was likely to command attention because of their standing and the novelty of Democrats and Republicans finding common ground on a pivotal defense issue. Kissinger also enjoyed good relations with each of the men. Had a different group approached him, he might not have engaged the matter as seriously.

Kissinger's encounters with Shultz at various international gatherings and in the informal camps of the Bohemian Grove seemed to soften old animosities. "George Shultz and I, as you have seen, are close friends, and we try to act in concert with each other," Kissinger said. "We write joint articles, we read each other's papers, we talk all the time." Shultz confirmed that they talk frequently.

Kissinger said his relationship with Nunn was "not that close, but close enough." He had few dealings with Perry, but thought well of him. "I have been historically less close to Perry but I'm fundamentally comfortable with him when we meet and work together. It's just that the first person I'd call is Sam Nunn when I'm going into this area of my thinking. But still, I think we're pretty well much on the same wavelength. He's technologically much more skilled than I am, and he has less of a strategic interest than I do."

Of all the men, Kissinger had known Drell the longest, dating back to their first meeting at a dinner party in Israel in 1961. "I've always respected Drell," Kissinger said.

While Shultz and Kissinger were conferring under the Bohemian Grove redwoods in July 2006, planning was moving ahead for the Reykjavik conference at Stanford in the fall. Shultz and Drell, who were managing preparations, invited a diverse cast of Cold War figures, including Perry, Kampelman, Admiral William Crowe, chairman of the Joint Chiefs of Staff from 1985 to 1989; Jack Matlock, American ambassador in Moscow, 1987–91;

Richard Perle, assistant secretary of defense, 1981–87; and James Timbie, a veteran arms control negotiator.

Shultz and Drell, drawing on Hoover funds, commissioned ten papers about the Reykjavik summit and its implications that were distributed to conference participants before the gathering convened. Nunn was invited to the conference but could not attend because the NTI board was meeting at the same time. Kissinger also had a scheduling conflict.

The participants gathered on the morning of October 11 in the Annenberg Room, an elegant, two-level conference space that Hoover officials had renovated for meetings just like this one. A large round table equipped with microphones and Ethernet connections rested in the center, surrounded by eighteen or so Aeron chairs. A second tier of seats circled the table on an elevated platform, giving the room the appearance of a mini–U.N. Security Council chamber. Shultz, Perry, and Drell sat at the inner table.

As the morning neared an end, Kampelman addressed the group. His gaunt appearance and faint voice gave his remarks unexpected poignancy and power. Shultz would later refer to the speech as "the most eloquent moment of the conference."

Kampelman called his presentation "The Power of the Ought." Recalling that the principles enunciated in the Declaration of Independence conflicted with the realities of the time like slavery, inequality of women, and property qualifications for voting, he said the "Ought" inherent in the Declaration ultimately overcame the imperfections of the new nation. "The political movement of the 'Is' to the 'Ought' has made our American democracy the country we cherish today," he said.

"What is needed today is a Reagan-esque initiative designed to enlarge the diplomatic canvas so that all nations can be convinced that the global elimination of nuclear weapons is in their national interest. The elimination of all nuclear arms is an 'Ought' that must be proclaimed and energetically pursued. It is time for us to get behind that essential 'Ought' and shape it into a realistic 'Is.'"

Kampelman, despite his earlier doubts about a multistep process, proposed a series of measures to go along with what he hoped would be a UN General Assembly resolution to abolish nuclear weapons.

As Shultz waited in the buffet line after the presentation, he told Kampelman, "That was a masterful speech, and I support it." That evening, during a panel discussion with Kampelman and several other conference participants, Shultz complimented Kampelman on his morning presentation. He told the group he, too, favored abolishing nuclear weapons. It was the first time since the Reykjavik summit itself that Shultz had publicly endorsed the idea.

Perry also turned the corner to nuclear disarmament at the conference. "Ordinarily, you can't point to a single event for changing your view," he said. "But in this case it was a single event. All of my concerns had been brewing the few years before that. I could see the dangers evolving. I could see nobody doing anything about them. And I knew that something needed to be done. And as I sat through the Reykjavik conference, it became clear to me that this is the catalyst we need to move."

After the conference ended on October 12, Andreasen started drafting a paper summarizing the conference discussions. The expectation, shared by Shultz and from afar by Nunn, was that the paper would be circulated to conference participants and that Shultz would either privately brief President Bush or present the paper in some public forum. Andreasen produced the first rough draft on October 13. There was no plan to turn it into an op-ed article.

The three-page paper was divided into three parts: "The Problem, The Vision, The Steps." It recapitulated points made at the conference, incorporated some of Kampelman's language, and included ideas that had been percolating for months among Nunn and his colleagues at NTI, and Shultz, Drell, Perry, and their colleagues at Stanford. It joined an expansive vision of a nuclear-free world with concrete steps to get there, combining the approaches favored by Kampelman and Nunn. Its emphasis on the elimination of nuclear weapons, at least on paper, restored that elusive goal to a marquee role it had not enjoyed among veteran foreign policy experts since Reagan and Gorbachev discussed it at Reykjavik in 1986.

As Andreasen and Drell were working on the draft, Shultz came up with the idea that it be turned into an op-ed article that might be offered to the *Wall Street Journal*. He got in touch with Paul Gigot, the editorial page editor of the *Journal*, who was receptive. Shultz figured the newspaper would be the ideal outlet in which to launch the initiative. "We thought that would be a good place to put it because the natural resistance would be rather conservative people," he said. Drell started cranking out drafts. It soon became clear that the best approach might be to weave together the more broadly cast op-ed drafts and the more detailed conference paper that Andreasen had been refining. The result was an op-ed version that captured both the long-term vision of a world free of nuclear weapons and a set of more immediate steps to reduce nuclear dangers.

Two critical questions were how explicit the article should be in endorsing the zero goal and who would sign it. Perry, who had attended the conference, seemed likely to sign. Shultz was hopeful that Nunn would, too, and thought Kissinger might.

Nunn's position seemed uncertain—he was moving toward abolition as a goal, but was he ready to put his name behind the idea?

His NTI colleagues thought he was. Over the summer he had privately told Joan Rohlfing and Charles Curtis that he had overcome his misgivings about zero and understood the advantages of endorsing the goal. As Rohlfing recalled their conversation, "He thinks the only way we're going to build the cooperation we need is to work toward the vision. And I remember pausing when he

said that, because for me this was—we'd clearly crossed a threshold. It was an important moment in time. And there had been
some internal debate about whether this was a politically wise area
to stake out. And so I remember asking him, 'Senator, this is what
I heard you just say. Is that really where you are? Are you comfortable?' The answer was yes."

Nunn later said his views had evolved. "I have come to the
conclusion over the last several years that without the vision, you
aren't going to get the steps done. But I always had the view that
without the steps, the vision wasn't realistic. And I still have that
view. Where I have evolved is that a vision of a world without
nuclear weapons has a lot more importance in terms of getting the
cooperation we need on the steps."

Even so, Nunn's intentions remained unclear in the days following the conference. In mid-November, after reading a version
of Andreasen's conference paper, Nunn sent Shultz a letter that
seemed to assume that the vision of a nuclear-free world required
further consideration before the men would openly endorse it.

Shultz gave his blessing to the draft op-ed at the end of November and Drell messaged Andreasen, "Our good efforts have
succeeded. George has adopted the attached version."

In early December, after extensive discussions with his staff,
Nunn sent Shultz a two-page letter with proposed revisions. The
most significant came on the last page of the draft. Nunn said, "I've
added a very short paragraph that makes the point that without the
bold vision, the actions will not be perceived as fair or urgent; and
without the actions, the goal will not be perceived as realistic or
possible. . . . This formulation is essential from my point of view
to bring the pragmatists and the idealists together so that progress
can be made in this vital area." Nunn sent copies of his letter to
Perry, Kissinger, and Drell. Shultz quickly accepted all of Nunn's
suggestions.

Perry read the working draft and sent word to Shultz on

December 11 that he concurred with it. That meant that Shultz and Perry were ready to sign the article. Two down, two to go.

As the op-ed article was being revised, Charles Curtis, the NTI president and a close friend of Nunn, feared the grandiose goal would undermine NTI's more immediate agenda. Curtis himself thought the goal was too sweeping. He was more comfortable with working toward a world "free from the *threat* of nuclear weapons." He supported an alternative option, the origins of which remain murky: that the article note that Nunn subscribed to its aspirations but that Nunn not join Shultz and Perry in signing the piece. As Rohlfing recounted it, "This was a suggestion Charlie supported to try and square the circle between where he thought NTI needed to be and where he saw the piece moving."

On December 14, Nunn sent word to Shultz and Drell that he had decided to sign the article. "I didn't like that idea," Nunn said, alluding to the proposal that he endorse the principle but not sign the article. "I entertained the idea because I had such respect for Charlie, but I felt it was too clever. I mean, I thought either you're for it or you're not. I didn't know what it meant, and I didn't think people would know what it meant, and I didn't think I could explain it."

Kissinger was the remaining holdout. Nunn and Shultz set to work to convince him. Kissinger, like Nunn, was concerned that the draft op-ed opened with a reference to Reykjavik. They feared the allusion would give the essay an anachronistic feel rather than grounding it in the here and now. Nunn said: "Kissinger was more forceful about it than I was. . . . Kissinger talked about the need to revamp the opening part so that the Reykjavik part came much later in the op-ed. George had led it off with Reykjavik."

Nunn and Kissinger spoke several times by phone. Nunn told him, "Henry, I know you've been thinking about saying we agree in principle without completely endorsing it. I've thought about that, but I think I'm just going to endorse it, because I agree with it now."

Looking back at the discussions in 2009, Kissinger recalled he was hesitant to sign because he was dubious about calling for the elimination of nuclear weapons. "I don't think anyone knew how to do it, then or now," he said.

But, in the end, he agreed to set the goal as an objective. He described his thinking at the time.

"I'm willing to state it as an objective because I believe that, first of all, if nuclear weapons are used, it will be a fundamental transformation of the world. And it will produce impulses that will be almost impossible to contain. And it will wind up with enormous catastrophes, which will end up with the hegemony of some group of countries over the world to control the nuclear problem. That I think is inherent in the nature of the threat.

"Secondly, I believe stopping proliferation is one of the key issues, maybe the key issue of our period.

"Thirdly, it is not possible for the United States to say nobody else can proliferate or build up nuclear arsenals while we continue to rely entirely on nuclear weapons. So we owe to ourselves and to the world a reduction of our reliance on nuclear weapons, at a minimum. And to push them into a situation in which their use occurs only under the most extreme circumstances of national survival."

Alluding to his friendship with Shultz, Kissinger went on. "George was doing this thing and he had heard me speak about my notions of the international system, and so he wanted to marry his approach to my approach. And at first I was only willing to say that we approve the general concept but not link ourselves to specific proposals. And we had found a formulation for that."

Kissinger also thought that embracing the goal, however unfeasible it might seem, would help spur new thinking about nuclear weapons that could reduce arsenals and even set the stage for their eventual elimination.

Kissinger transmitted his specific editing suggestions to Shultz on December 26. His cover letter outlined the points he was addressing in the draft article, a copy of which had been sent to Gigot at the *Journal* on December 19.

"I send you my edits. You will see most of them are stylistic. I have taken out some sentences or phrases that seem to me too much like special pleading. . . . I also think the word 'vision' is used far too much; we should not claim it for ourselves. . . . I have moved a paragraph to focus more on Reagan and to fit into the sequence of other leaders. Above all, we should separate Reagan and Gorbachev somewhat. Reagan is far more respected, and it will help our statement's acceptability in Russia. . . . For the rest, I have tried to reduce repetition. The case is weakened by repeating the same phrases over and over. I have not touched the recommendations."

Shultz readily accepted the changes, but thought Kissinger was still apprehensive. "Henry was always a little bit of a problem at the end," Shultz said. "He would know exactly how he wanted to express some things, so I generally went along with whatever he wanted. But he was nervous. Sam was not nervous. Bill was not nervous. I was not nervous."

Nunn said, "I'd say Shultz was the vision leader. And Perry and I were the steps. I think Kissinger made a big input into the way the whole article was structured. And he brought with it, of course, years and years of writing on this subject.

"If there was ever a group project, that was really a group project," Nunn said. "George was the quarterback, clearly. There's no question about it. Probably nobody else would have had the patience he did to do it. I give him immense credit."

Shultz thought Drell should sign the article, too, but Drell demurred, saying the piece would have more power if it came from the four more prominent men.

A revised version of the article, incorporating Kissinger's suggestions, was shipped off to the *Wall Street Journal* at the end of December. The authors thought it might stir some comment in foreign policy circles, but nothing more. How wrong they were.

CHAPTER TWENTY-FIVE

The breakthrough would be a new president
that says, "I'm going to do this."
—GEORGE SHULTZ

Americans were just getting back to work after the holiday season when the *Wall Street Journal* slotted the nuclear disarmament article onto its op-ed page. It appeared on January 4, 2007, under the muted headline, "A World Free of Nuclear Weapons."

It was a busy news day—Nancy Pelosi was elected Speaker of the House, becoming the first woman to hold that position, and President Bush put General David Petraeus in charge of American forces in Iraq. But the *Journal* article still drew immediate attention. An Associated Press story described the op-ed, emphasizing Kissinger's role. It reported, "Former Secretary of State Henry A. Kissinger and three other prominent American security experts urged the United States on Thursday to lead in the creation of a 'world without nuclear weapons.'"

Agence France-Presse, the French wire service, said in a news dispatch, "The Washington heavyweights say the United States should launch a major effort towards banning all nuclear weapons. Citing nuclear programs in North Korea and Iran, the officials say the world 'is now on the precipice of a new and dangerous nuclear era.'"

As word spread about the article, the critical question for Shultz and his colleagues was whether it would attract support from foreign and defense policy experts. And even more important, could the idea of nuclear disarmament catch fire with any of the leading presidential candidates who were just beginning to launch their 2008 campaigns?

It did not take long to find out.

The article jolted the national security fraternity. It was one thing if Max Kampelman favored the abolition of nuclear weapons, quite another if George Shultz, Henry Kissinger, Bill Perry, and Sam Nunn endorsed the idea. This was the heart of the foreign policy establishment talking, two mainstream Republicans and two benchmark Democrats breaking with their clans to embrace a quixotic cause that had inspired plenty of soaring presidential rhetoric over the years but little serious consideration.

Part of the impact in the defense world was due to timing. The fearsome calculus of Cold War nuclear deterrence no longer seemed to apply, eliminating the reality check that had always made abolition look hopelessly impractical. The new threat was nuclear terrorism, a plausible and immediate danger that America's nuclear arsenal could do little, if anything, to prevent. Maybe abolition wasn't such a wacky idea after all. Maybe the interim steps that the four authors proposed could actually help keep nuclear materials out of the hands of terrorists. And while everyone was thinking about the escalating violence in Iraq, the four men reminded the country that the greatest danger to American security might well be the uncontrolled spread of nuclear weapons and the technology to make them.

Shultz put it this way: "So, here we are twenty or so years later and more countries have nuclear weapons, people are awakening to the problem of proliferation more. I think to a certain extent after the end of the Cold War the subject went to sleep. And there were reductions, the START treaty was implemented. Then the Moscow 2002 treaty pushed things a little further. But there was no verification. It wasn't as vital. And people weren't paying that much attention. And all of a sudden comes this op-ed by four people who are entitled to be listened to."

The article generated a torrent of supportive letters and messages from foreign policy practitioners, far exceeding the expectations of the four authors and Drell. "When we wrote the first article," Kissinger said, "I thought it would be a statement that might attract the attention an occasional op-ed piece receives. But it generated an extraordinary amount of correspondence, many offers of participation by people that one would take very seriously."

Gorbachev chimed in with his own article in the *Journal* at the end of January. Noting that Shultz, Perry, Kissinger, and Nunn were "not known for utopian thinking," Gorbachev declared, "As someone who signed the first treaties on real reductions in nuclear weapons, I feel it is my duty to support their call for urgent action."

At the same time, Sonia Gandhi, head of India's Congress Party, supported the initiative as she welcomed party members to a conference in New Delhi marking the centenary of Mahatma Gandhi's nonviolent resistance movement. Shultz had smartly added a line to the op-ed article quoting Rajiv Gandhi's call for nuclear disarmament during an appearance before the UN General Assembly in 1988.

The four authors and Drell were soon fielding unsolicited offers of financial assistance from two foundations, the Carnegie Corporation of New York and the MacArthur Foundation. Nunn, in a memo to his collaborators, reported that Warren Buffett might be interested in contributing, too. Shultz suggested that the group rally support from former secretaries of state and defense as well as former national security advisers and members of Congress, and that the men see if they could marshal support among leading presidential candidates jockeying to run in 2008. Shultz and Perry recommended that expert papers be prepared about the eight steps toward zero that the *Journal* article outlined, and Nunn proposed a ninth, on verification.

Shultz got to work writing letters to prospective supporters. Some recipients, like Lawrence Eagleburger, a former secretary of state, seemed like promising prospects. Others, like Donald Rumsfeld, who had stepped down as secretary of defense a year earlier, were not.

Within a few months, Shultz and the others could cite an impressive roster of top former government officials who supported the initiative. Republican backers included James A. Baker III, Eagleburger, and Colin Powell, all secretaries of state; Melvin Laird, Frank Carlucci, and William Cohen, defense secretaries; and Richard Allen and Robert McFarlane, national security advisers. Most notably, George H. W. Bush endorsed the plan, but his views were not publicly disclosed, at his request. The Democratic contingent included a former defense secretary, Robert McNamara, three national security advisers, Zbigniew Brzezinski, Anthony Lake, and Samuel Berger, and Warren Christopher and Madeleine Albright, Bill Clinton's secretaries of state.

But for all the support and activity, the future of the initiative seemed uncertain. Having expected a muted response, the four authors and Drell lacked a dynamic game plan to advance their cause. It wasn't even clear who among them would take the lead. One colleague recalled the state of uncertainty: "A number of us see an opportunity for initiative and for developing some leverage on these issues that we've been toiling in the trenches on for a period of decades. But there's not a clear sense of leadership, who should lead the charge. And in particular, we see Sam Nunn wanting to defer to George Shultz, seeing him as the senior person among the group, and this is George's initiative. We see George Shultz, having just finished this conference, which took a lot of energy, deferring to Sam Nunn. . . . A number of us become concerned that, 'Oh my God, we're at this moment in time and it's going to get squandered because they keep saying, "You first! You first!"'"

The solution was to park the initiative at NTI, Nunn's

organization, and devote a good deal of NTI's resources and staff time to the plan, which was dubbed the Nuclear Security Project (NSP). The NTI board approved a $3 million budget for the project, and several foundations, including Carnegie and MacArthur, stepped up to make generous grants. The Hoover Institution retained a role as the convener and host of conferences, publisher of pamphlets and books generated by the project, and the home base for Shultz and Drell.

An ambitious plan to advance the initiative soon took shape at two Stanford meetings attended by Shultz and Drell and a trio of top NTI officials, Joan Rohlfing, Brooke Anderson, and Steve Andreasen. The first meeting was in early March, the second in mid-June. The plan that emerged from the first called for convening a second conference at the Hoover Institution later that year to explore in greater detail the steps that could be taken to move the world toward nuclear disarmament. A new raft of analytical papers would be commissioned for the gathering. The plan also outlined ways to engage members of Congress, recruit other prominent national security experts to support the initiative, reach out to 2008 presidential candidates, conduct a public education campaign, and take the abolition message abroad. The road map included the scheduling of a third conference, in 2008, aimed at broadening support beyond the United States. Shultz commissioned Chester A. Crocker, a former diplomat who had worked with him at the State Department, to prepare a diplomatic action plan on nuclear issues that could serve as a road map for the next administration in Washington.

Shultz and Nunn, effectively, became coleaders of the initiative. The greatest challenge for the men was to both galvanize broad-based enthusiasm for their campaign and win the support of national leaders, starting with the president of the United States. Perry said, "We have taken it upon ourselves to do two things—to try to advance that idea in the United States and bring over the

next generation of political leaders to incorporate it in their thinking of how they should govern. That's one event. The other thrust
is to try to develop in other countries in the world like-minded
leaders. Get people in England and France and Germany, Russia,
China, Japan, India, to be developing programs like this in their
own countries. Because it's quite clear that the United States can
set an example, but we cannot dictate to other countries how they
deal with these problems."

He understood it wouldn't be an easy sell. The prospect of
nuclear terrorism was frightening but seemed remote. The issues
involved were gritty and difficult to influence. In short, it wasn't a
popular subject.

"In a democracy, leaders are also followers," Perry said. "They
try to see what the people are thinking and try to lead them in the
direction they seem to want to go. There are exceptions to that, to
be sure. But it's hard to find cases today of where a leader's taken
an unpopular position and tried to sell it, tried to present it, tried
to get people to accept it."

Paradoxically, Max Kampelman, of all people, was not entirely
pleased by the *Journal* article. He told Jim Goodby it was too tech-
nocratic and too scientific.

"His experience has been that all kinds of detailed proposals
have been advanced over the years, only to end up on the scrap
heap because the political leadership and public interest have been
lacking," Goodby reported to Drell. "Getting that support should
be our first priority. He hopes he will be proved wrong, but
he fears that without presidential backing in a highly visible way,
the follow-on work at Stanford will have no results. He agrees
that the points made in the WSJ article are logically correct but it
misses the real point. He strongly believes that public psychology
has to be altered before anything like a zero option has a serious
chance. He doesn't see that in the work program we have laid out."

Kampelman's lament was consistent with his long-standing

view that the best way forward was to get high-level political support for the initiative, and to bring the initiative before the United Nations for consideration and action. He wanted the president to make the case to the General Assembly.

Wounded pride may have also motivated his dissent. After all, he had resuscitated the idea of eliminating nuclear weapons after the September 11 attacks, he had pressed Shultz and Nunn to support it, and he had generated the emotional high point of the Reykjavik anniversary conference that led directly to the *Wall Street Journal* op-ed piece. Yet he was not invited to sign the article. When asked if that bothered him, he said, "I really am not looking for the credit." He hastened to add, "But I tell you, just so that you know, I've never counted, but I wouldn't be surprised if since that time I haven't made fifty speeches in the United States on this issue."

A milestone was hit in late June, when Margaret Beckett, the British foreign secretary, told a Washington audience that her government supported the call for a world free of nuclear weapons.

With the 2008 presidential election approaching, the five men realized, as Kampelman had advised Goodby, that by far the best way to intensify their campaign was to get the next president to make it a centerpiece of his or her foreign policy. "A president has to make these things happen because they are a priority," Nunn said. "And if he doesn't, they won't."

The Bush administration clearly wasn't going to be helpful. Dick Cheney had given Kampelman a polite hearing but he and other administration officials offered no support. The chilly response was reinforced early in 2008 when Nunn made the case directly to President Bush for redoubling global efforts to control nuclear weapons. The occasion was a visit to the White House by a small group of former American and Russian officials who had started conferring periodically to see if they could spur better relations between the two countries. Henry Kissinger had recruited the American contingent at the suggestion of Vladimir Putin, the Russian president. Kissinger brought aboard Shultz, Perry, and Nunn, along with Robert Rubin, the former Treasury secretary; Martin Feldstein, the Harvard economist; Thomas Graham, a former diplomat; and David O'Reilly, an oil company executive. Yevgeni Primakov, who had served as Russia's foreign minister and prime minister in the 1990s, headed the Russian delegation.

At Kissinger's request, Nunn had prepared some talking points to make a brief presentation to Bush about the need to intensify joint American-Russian efforts to prevent terrorists from obtaining nuclear weapons. Nunn told Bush the world was at a "tipping point" where the United States and Russia recognized the need to better control nuclear weapons and fissile materials, had reached agreement on steps to do so, but had not acted vigorously to implement the accords.

Bush seemed uninterested. "It was really astonishing," one observer at the meeting said. "Here we were, sitting in the Roosevelt Room, yards from the Oval Office, and we're talking about how we could dismantle the threat that hung over our lives for seventy years." The observer said that Bush "couldn't have shown less interest. He jotted a few notes, looked up over his glasses—and then he asked a question about something else." Nunn's recollection was different: "I didn't think he brushed us off. I thought he was interested in it, but it was pretty apparent he hadn't thought very deeply about it."

Even before the Bush meeting, Shultz, Kissinger, Perry, and Nunn had set their sights on senators John McCain, Hillary Clinton, and Barack Obama.

"The breakthrough would be a new president that says, 'I'm going to do this,'" Shultz said in mid-2008. "And then the question is, 'How do you go about it?' That's what Chet Crocker's paper is going to be. . . . If the U.S. government should decide that it wants to work on this, then we're able to say at this point, 'We can help you. Here are these papers on key subjects, which are a starting point. And here are these people, who know something about those subjects and they're willing to come and work. And here are these people, Democrats and Republicans, most of them somebody's heard of, who are willing to stand up behind you and say, "Yes, we agree." ' "

The four men had good lines into the campaigns—Shultz and Kissinger to McCain, Perry and Nunn to the Democratic contenders and their aides. The men did not want their initiative, or nuclear weapons policy in general, to become a partisan campaign issue, so they approached the presidential campaigns gingerly. Over time, Shultz became an unofficial counselor to McCain. After formally endorsing Obama in April 2008, Nunn signed on as an Obama adviser. "That was a big endorsement for us," said Ben Rhodes, an Obama campaign aide and later deputy national security adviser.

Brooke Anderson, a top Nunn aide at NTI who had worked on the National Security Council staff during the Clinton administration, turned out to be a pivotal link to the Obama campaign. Anderson joined the Obama team in 2007, working closely with Susan Rice, one of Obama's senior foreign policy advisers. (The two went on to represent the United States at the United Nations, Rice as permanent representative and Anderson as an ambassador and alternate representative for special political affairs. Anderson later moved to the White House as chief of staff of the National Security Council.) Anderson, familiar with Nunn's thinking about nuclear weapons and the development of the *Journal* op-ed article, was perfectly situated to act as liaison between the abolitionists and Obama.

As Obama stepped onto the national stage in 2007, his marquee foreign policy credential was his opposition to the war in Iraq. From the outset of his campaign, he used the war as a cudgel against Hillary Clinton, who had voted in favor of the 2002 Senate resolution that authorized President Bush to go to war. As an Illinois state senator in 2002, Obama had cautioned against invading Iraq.

Obama was not a nuclear weapons novice when he opened his presidential campaign in 2007, but he initially did not emphasize the issue or call for the elimination of nuclear weapons. His interest in nuclear weapons dated back to the early 1980s when he was a student at Columbia University. During his senior year in 1983, Obama called for the elimination of nuclear weapons in the campus newsmagazine, *Sundial*. His essay, "Breaking the War Mentality," referred caustically to "military-industrial interests" with their "billion-dollar erector sets."

After joining the Senate in 2005, he reengaged nuclear weapons issues, promptly inviting Nunn to Capitol Hill to talk about threat reduction efforts. Obama also started working with—and learning from—Senator Lugar, the Indiana Republican, NTI board member and Sam Nunn's partner in creating the Nunn-Lugar threat reduction program. He traveled to Russia with Lugar in 2005 to get a firsthand look at Russian efforts to secure its weapons and weapons-making materials. Lugar recalled, "When we got there, he was clearly all business—a very careful listener and note taker and a serious student."

In April 2007, in a campaign appearance, Obama told the Chicago Council on Global Affairs that it was essential for the United States to take the lead in "marshalling a global effort to meet a threat that rises above all others in urgency—securing, destroying and stopping the spread of weapons of mass destruction.

"As leaders from Henry Kissinger to George Shultz to Bill Perry to Sam Nunn have all warned," he said, "the actions we are taking today on this issue are simply not adequate to the danger. . . . As President, I will lead a global effort to secure all nuclear weapons and material at vulnerable sites within four years—the most effective way to prevent terrorists from acquiring a bomb."

Obama did not call for the elimination of nuclear weapons that day, nor did he three months later, when he returned to the issue in a wide-ranging foreign policy speech at the Wilson Center in Washington.

The breakthrough came in Chicago on October 2, 2007, the fifth anniversary of his anti–Iraq War speech, a date and place he and his aides had carefully chosen as the right moment to deliver the foreign policy cornerstone address of his young campaign. The plan was to once again focus on Iraq.

Ben Rhodes recalled, "The original conception was, just give a big antiwar speech, Iraq War speech in Chicago, where you say, I was right and everybody else was wrong, and that's why I should be the Democratic nominee, and kind of fire up the base, and we even had satellite events in other states where people would have kind of anti–Iraq War rallies."

Obama preferred a broader approach. He told his aides, "I want to make a bigger argument about the reorientation of our national security policy and I want to put out at least one big idea other than simply ending the war in Iraq," Rhodes said.

Nuclear weapons seemed a natural option, given Obama's interest in the issue. He told Rhodes and his colleagues to make abolition and other nuclear weapons issues a centerpiece of the speech. They had all seen the *Journal* op-ed article; Obama had referred to Shultz, Kissinger, Perry, and Nunn in his April address. This time he would go for broke. "To him it was a no-brainer," Rhodes said. "He said, well, I totally agree with them. . . . He always wanted that to be a cornerstone of his platform."

Rhodes said, "He wanted to use the speech to surface a bigger idea and to again, tie it into his broader argument that we were making, which is that we need to challenge our own assumptions. Part of his point on Iraq was that we got trapped in some pattern of conventional wisdom that kind of cascaded into war. And so in this respect, challenging the conventional wisdom that you can never get to zero, which he saw these guys [Shultz, Kissinger, Perry, and Nunn] do, connected to the notion that we need to challenge ourselves within to think bigger and to be more ambitious in the kinds of worldview that we embrace on national security."

So, Obama told an audience at DePaul University, "Here's what I'll say as president: America seeks a world in which there are no nuclear weapons.

"We will not pursue unilateral disarmament. As long as nuclear weapons exist, we'll retain a strong nuclear deterrent. But we'll keep our commitment under the Nuclear Nonproliferation Treaty on the long road towards eliminating nuclear weapons. We'll work with Russia to take U.S. and Russian ballistic missiles off hair-trigger alert, and to dramatically reduce the stockpiles of our nuclear weapons and material. We'll start by seeking a global ban on the production of fissile material for weapons. And we'll set a goal to expand the U.S.-Russian ban on intermediate-range missiles so that the agreement is global."

Obama did not consult with Nunn before delivering the speech—he did not need to, with Brooke Anderson close at hand. Anderson, Susan Rice, and Ivo Daalder, another Obama adviser who favored rethinking nuclear weapons strategy, helped draft the speech. But campaign aides gave Nunn, Perry, Shultz, and Kissinger advance notification that Obama would embrace their cause in the Chicago address.

A few days after Obama's speech, the quartet gathered again in the Annenberg Room at the Hoover Institution for their second conference, titled "Reykjavik Revisited, Steps Toward a World Free of Nuclear Weapons." The goal this time was to explore in greater detail the steps needed to reduce nuclear threats and move toward zero. Several dozen nuclear weapons experts attended, including many of the people who had participated in the first conference a year earlier.

Nancy Reagan blessed the conference in a letter that Shultz read to the participants. It said, "Dear George, Thank you for letting me know of the new effort to rid the world of nuclear weapons. It was always Ronnie's dream that the world would one day be free of nuclear arms. . . . I'm very encouraged that you are working on this important goal, and I know Ronnie would approve of the careful and serious way it is being approached. Each step is essential to bringing the vision closer to reality. . . . Warmly, Nancy."

The conference soon led to a second op-ed article, and another round of drafting and redrafting that tested Shultz's patience. The paper trail shows multiple versions passed around the group, with Sid Drell, Steve Andreasen, Joan Rohlfing, and Jim Goodby churning out versions in response to suggestions from Shultz, Nunn, and Kissinger.

After reading an initial draft, Nunn sent Shultz, Kissinger, Perry, and Drell a memo outlining his thoughts.

"As we look forward, a major focus of our effort will be to further internationalize the dialogue on the agenda we have put forward. I believe we should try to use this second op-ed to continue this momentum and move us to the international phase.

"As Henry pointed out at our meeting last week, we have the challenge of trying to build consensus in a very disparate international environment. Henry suggested that our task should be to develop common objectives with international leaders, and not fall back on the typical American behavior of creating a 'checklist' of American objectives that we measure others' behavior against. I agree."

By the time the article was ready for publication in late December, approved by the four men, Shultz was worn out. "I said to Sam, 'I'm never going to do that again.' It's just too much work to get everybody signed off on every word."

The *Wall Street Journal* published the article on January 15, 2008. It amplified on the steps laid out in the first op-ed, with an emphasis on international cooperation, as Kissinger and Nunn had urged.

The article ended with a mountaintop analogy that Nunn and

his colleagues at NTI had added to the working draft on December 10, 2007, as the piece was still coming together. Nunn had first used the image in a June speech to the Council on Foreign Relations in New York. He and his colleagues would use it frequently, with minor variations, in the months after the op-ed article was published. The end of the op-ed said: "In some respects, the goal of a world free of nuclear weapons is like the top of a very tall mountain. From the vantage point of our troubled world today, we can't even see the top of the mountain, and it is tempting and easy to say we can't get there from here. But the risks from continuing to go down the mountain or standing pat are too real to ignore. We must chart a course to higher ground where the mountaintop becomes more visible."

Once again, Max Kampelman demurred, calling the article "inadequate." He told Jim Goodby, "As I read the piece and remember the struggles of recent years, I regrettably doubt that the advocacy we champion is any more likely to achieve our goal than it has in the past. . . . The details of the piece are undoubtedly vital and necessary, but inadequate to achieve our goal of 'zero.' "

As mapped out in planning discussions after publication of the first *Wall Street Journal* article, Nunn, Shultz, and Drell took their act abroad in February 2008, appearing in Oslo as the star attractions at a gathering of former international leaders organized by the Norwegian government in collaboration with NTI and the Hoover Institution. The Norwegian foreign minister, Jonas Gahr Støre, endorsed the initiative. Shultz gave an opening address and Nunn delivered a luncheon talk. His speech was titled "The Mountaintop: A World Free of Nuclear Weapons."

"Other than that we both sat and listened," Shultz recalled. "Didn't say anything, just listened. And one of the amazing things was any number of people came up to me during the end of the meeting and said, 'It was so refreshing that you came and listened. Usually Americans don't listen.' "

The next stop was London, where the three men joined Kissinger and Perry to initiate a "Statesmen's Dialogue" with their European peers aimed at broadening support for their initiative. The day began with a breakfast meeting with Foreign Secretary David Miliband, followed by a session with members of Parliament. The discussion went well until a former British defense minister spoke up. "I always got a lot of comfort from knowing if anybody got too fresh with us we could just nuke 'em," the former official said. Shultz recalled the moment with a grin. "That kind of chilled the atmosphere," he said.

While in London, the four men met with Igor Ivanov, a former Russian foreign minister, and Aleksandr Bessmertnykh, the last Soviet foreign minister. Ivanov was close to Vladimir Putin, then the Russian president. Shultz was pleasantly surprised to find that Ivanov's views on nuclear weapons were similar to his own. "I said, 'Igor, let me try a rough translation of what you just said. What you just said was as far as Russia's concerned, the door is open.' He said, 'Absolutely.' At the end of the meeting, he came around to me and Henry and he said, 'I'm going back to Moscow tomorrow and I'm going to tell Putin all about this meeting.'"

Following the Shultz-Kissinger-Perry-Nunn model, clusters of retired foreign and defense ministers from various nations soon produced their own op-ed articles, backing the Americans. Four distinguished Brits—Douglas Hurd, Malcolm Rifkind, David Owen, and George Robertson—delivered one to the *Times* of London in late June. Five Italians weighed in a month later in *Corriere della Sera*. Before too long, a quartet of German luminaries followed suit in the *International Herald Tribune*. By June, NTI had raised $2.25 million to fund the Nuclear Security Project.

The appearance of allied groups was encouraging, with one notable exception. As 2008 progressed, Shultz, Kissinger, Perry, Nunn, and Drell grew alarmed about a comparable effort to put together a "Compact to Eliminate Nuclear Weapons." The group working on the compact would soon call itself Global Zero. On the surface, the two groups seemed complementary. They favored the elimination of nuclear weapons, featured prominent former government officials knowledgeable about nuclear weapons, were generously funded, and were eager to present their case to the public. Bruce Blair, one of the founders of Global Zero, had attended the second Hoover conference, where he made a strong case for taking American and Soviet nuclear missiles off high alert status. Blair knew what he was talking about—he had served as an Air Force launch control officer at a Minuteman missile site.

But Blair and his colleagues thought the best path to nuclear disarmament was negotiation of an international treaty that would set a date for reaching abolition. Shultz and his colleagues were wary of a single-stroke solution, fearing new treaty negotiations would drag on indefinitely. They were also irritated that Blair and his group seemed to suggest to its followers that Shultz, Kissinger, Perry, and Nunn were in agreement with its approach. "We're not in their camp and we don't want anybody to confuse what they're doing with what we're doing," Shultz said in mid-2008. Nunn was especially snappish about the group after learning it had circulated materials that seemed critical of the approach advocated by Shultz, Kissinger, Perry, and Nunn. "He got very agitated," a Nunn friend and NTI board member said. After receiving a revised version of the Compact, Nunn wrote back to Blair: "We hope that our work can be complementary, but we ask that in your future outreach you be careful to point out that our efforts are separate and independent because we do not want to create the impression that we are part of the Compact project."

Nunn, Shultz, Kissinger, and Perry critiqued the Global Zero approach in a progress report they prepared for supporters of the *Wall Street Journal* op-ed articles. Referring to Blair and two of his Global Zero colleagues, Matt Brown and Barry Blechman, it said: "We have been asked but have declined to join the Blair-Brown-Blechman initiative. While the Nuclear Security Project and their effort share the same ultimate goal of a world free of nuclear weapons, the two projects have fundamentally different approaches. The Blair-Brown-Blechman project is centered on global negotiation of a Treaty to eliminate all nuclear weapons by a date certain. We want to strengthen the Nuclear Non-Proliferation Treaty (NPT)—with its core commitment to nuclear disarmament—leading up to an important 2010 NPT Review Conference. If we become engaged in a 'new Treaty' effort, we fear that it would weaken and divert efforts to strengthen the NPT. We also do not want to divert our energy and attention from addressing the urgent and achievable steps that will increase our security today and move us toward the goal of a world free of nuclear weapons."

The tensions between the two groups continued to simmer for months. A later Nunn memo to Kissinger, Shultz, and Perry described a shift in Global Zero strategy that shed the date-certain theme and called for steps like those advocated by Nunn and his colleagues. Nunn was still apprehensive.

The chill eventually made its way into documentary films that each group prepared to heighten public awareness about nuclear threats. The ninety-minute Global Zero film, *Countdown to Zero*, refers not once to the work done by Shultz, Kissinger, Perry, and Nunn. The quartet's film, *Nuclear Tipping Point*, makes no reference to Global Zero. *Nuclear Tipping Point* was distributed free on DVDs; *Countdown to Zero* appeared briefly in movie theaters.

The Shultz quintet opened an important new beachhead in June 2008 when Shultz hosted a dinner for nine evangelical ministers and other Christian leaders at his Stanford home. Although the evangelical community is often identified with politically conservative causes, a number of evangelical ministers have questioned the morality of nuclear weapons and sympathized with the call for eliminating them. It is not a new theological theme. In 1983, the National Conference of Catholic Bishops issued a Pastoral Letter on War and Peace that strongly challenged the nuclear status quo. "Nuclear war threatens the existence of our planet," the letter said. "This is a more menacing threat than any the world has known. It is neither tolerable nor necessary that human beings live under this threat."

At the Shultz dinner, Bill Perry told the ministers of his rising alarm about the threat of nuclear terrorism and described the consequences of such an attack. At one of several elegantly set tables in the Shultzes' large pool house, Shultz and several ministers discussed the moral dimensions of nuclear weapons. Drell spoke of similar issues at another table. The next morning at the Hoover Institution, the three men gave a detailed explanation of their campaign to the evangelical leaders.

The dinner and meeting led to the Two Futures Project, an evangelical program that supports the work of Shultz and his colleagues and spreads the word about nuclear abolition to Christian churches and schools around the country. Tyler Wigg-Stevenson, a Baptist minister and graduate of Swarthmore College and Yale Divinity School, organized the project. He invited Shultz to participate in a news teleconference when the project was launched in April 2009.

The project website describes the movement this way: "The Two Futures Project (2FP) is a movement of American Christians for the abolition of all nuclear weapons. We believe that we face two futures and one choice: a world without nuclear weapons or a world ruined by them. We support concrete and practical steps to reduce nuclear dangers immediately, while pursuing the multilateral, global, irreversible, and verifiable elimination of nuclear weapons, as a biblically-grounded mandate and as a contemporary security imperative."

In October 2010, Bill Perry addressed the board of the National Association of Evangelicals, which gathered in Los Angeles. The board gave him a standing ovation.

As the summer of 2008 sped toward the party nominating conventions, Obama reinforced his abolition message. At a July appearance at Purdue University in Indiana with Sam Nunn and Senator Evan Bayh, the Indiana Democrat, Obama said, "We used to worry about our nuclear stalemate with the Soviet Union. Now, we worry about 50 tons of highly enriched uranium—some of it poorly secured—at civilian nuclear facilities in over forty countries around the world. Now, we worry about the breakdown of a nonproliferation framework that was designed for the bipolar world of the Cold War. . . . We'll make the goal of eliminating all nuclear weapons a central element in our nuclear policy."

Thanks partly to Shultz's advice, McCain also endorsed abolition, as long as it did not undermine American security. In March 2008, he told the Los Angeles World Affairs Council: "Forty years ago, the five declared nuclear powers came together in support of the nuclear Nonproliferation Treaty and pledged to end the arms race and move toward nuclear disarmament. The time has come to renew that commitment. We do not need all the weapons currently in our arsenal. The United States should lead a global effort at nuclear disarmament consistent with our vital interests and the cause of peace."

McCain revisited the issue two months later in Denver. He said, "A quarter of a century ago, President Ronald Reagan declared, 'Our dream is to see the day when nuclear weapons will be banished from the face of the Earth.' That is my dream, too. It is a distant and difficult goal. And we must proceed toward it prudently and pragmatically, and with a focused concern for our security and the security of allies who depend on us. But the Cold War ended almost twenty years ago, and the time has come to take further measures to reduce dramatically the number of nuclear weapons in the world's arsenals."

Shultz took stock of the political landscape in midsummer, noting with satisfaction that both Obama and McCain had endorsed the goal of abolishing nuclear weapons.

Other issues dominated the presidential contest as it roared toward November, including the imploding economy and the war in Iraq. Once Obama and McCain had secured their party nominations, they spent little time discussing nuclear weapons, but Obama spelled out his thinking in September in written responses to questions submitted to his campaign by the Arms Control Association, a private, nonpartisan group based in Washington. The association posted his answers on its website and printed them in *Arms Control Today*, its monthly magazine.

Shultz, Kissinger, Perry, Nunn, and Drell could not have asked for a clearer declaration of support for their agenda. "As president," Obama said, "I will set a new direction in nuclear weapons policy and show the world that America believes in its existing commitment under the nuclear Nonproliferation Treaty to work to ultimately eliminate all nuclear weapons. I fully support reaffirming this goal, as called for by George Shultz, Henry Kissinger, William Perry, and Sam Nunn, as well as the specific steps they propose to move us in that direction."

Nuclear weapons came up briefly again during the first presidential debate, in September at the University of Mississippi. When Jim Lehrer, the moderator, asked the candidates about the likelihood of another terror attack on the continental United States, Obama said, "The biggest threat that we face right now is not a nuclear missile coming over the skies. It's in a suitcase. This is why the issue of nuclear proliferation is so important. It is the—the biggest threat to the United States is a terrorist getting their hands on nuclear weapons. And we—we are spending billions of dollars on missile defense. And I actually believe that we need missile defense, because of Iran and North Korea and the potential for them to obtain or to launch nuclear weapons, but I also believe that, when we are only spending a few hundred million dollars on nuclear proliferation, then we're making a mistake."

Obama's victory in November was a turning point for Shultz

and his colleagues. We will never know how much emphasis McCain might have put on nuclear weapons issues, but it seems unlikely that he would have made nuclear disarmament a signature initiative of his presidency.

Obama did, thanks in no small measure to the groundwork laid by Shultz, Kissinger, Perry, Nunn, and Drell. Obama called Shultz shortly after the election, while still president-elect. "I had never met him," Shultz recalled. "We had a four- or five-minute talk on the telephone. And he asked me about Russia. I gave him my view about that. And then I said, 'You've made a very strong statement about our nuclear-free world initiative during the campaign.' And he said, 'Well, I really meant that. I'm going to follow up on that. It's very important.'"

"There was a direct line of influence from work of these folks to him," Ben Rhodes said. "He looks to them as a source of both substantive input and inspiration, for a couple of reasons. . . . He respects the role that these men have played in American history. Each of them, at important junctures, played key roles in developing our national security policy and our policies in these areas. In addition to the substantive work that they've put into this, so that this is more than just a talking point, they've actually done a lot of hard work to fill in the pieces, to make it something tangible."

It certainly didn't hurt to have two stalwart Republicans providing political cover for a Democratic president who was inclined to call for the elimination of nuclear weapons. Obama might well have championed abolition on his own as a candidate and then as president, but the presence of Shultz and Kissinger at his side, at first figuratively and then literally during several Oval Office visits, was a stout shield against right-wing attacks.

Their example of bipartisanship, as Rhodes noted, is an increasingly rare thing in Washington these days. The notion that politics once stopped at the water's edge when it came to American foreign policy is fuzzy nostalgia. That may have been the case during World War II, and there was a broad consensus during the Cold War that the United States had to make a stand against the Soviet Union and threat of Soviet expansion. But within that consensus vigorous disagreements flared over Vietnam and other American interventions abroad. Yet even those divisions were not as reflexive and scripted as today's clashes, driven by a hyperspeed news cycle, cable television's insatiable appetite for acrimony, and the collapse of the political center in Congress.

As Obama was sworn in as president on January 20, 2009, he seemed hopeful he could overcome Washington's poisonous climate. "On this day," he said in his inaugural address, "we gather because we have chosen hope over fear, unity of purpose over conflict and discord. On this day, we come to proclaim an end to the petty grievances and false promises, the recriminations and worn-out dogmas that for far too long have strangled our politics. We remain a young nation. But in the words of Scripture, the time has come to set aside childish things."

As those hopes quickly faded in 2009 during the rancorous debates over how best to revive the economy and reform the health-care system, Obama's ambitious nuclear agenda could easily have been sidetracked. It was not—thanks to some timely help from Shultz, Kissinger, Perry, Nunn, and Drell.

CHAPTER TWENTY-SIX

Time is not on our side.
—GEORGE SHULTZ

How far President Obama would go on the nuclear front was not entirely clear at first. Sam Nunn fretted that the untested president might be distracted by the onrush of other business. "People many times don't understand that you have to make choices and there have to be priorities," he said a few days after the election. "So he's got to make this a priority, and it's got to be more important than other things."

The four men gave Obama a gentle nudge on January 22, 2009, two days after he was sworn in as president. It came in the form of a brief letter.

"As you know, we have been working together to help build a consensus for reversing reliance on nuclear weapons globally as a contribution to preventing their proliferation into potentially dangerous hands, and ultimately ending them as a threat to the world," the men said. "We are proud of your bold leadership on this issue during your campaign. We join you in believing that we have a window of opportunity to work cooperatively with other nations to reduce risk, increase transparency and build confidence—essential steps required to move a world without nuclear weapons from a vision to a reality.

"We stand ready to assist you and your administration in this endeavor in whatever way we can, and would be privileged to meet with you and members of your national security team to discuss strategies to achieve the vision and the steps. We look forward to your leadership and to working with you on these critical issues."

Hillary Clinton, the freshly minted secretary of state, invited Shultz to meet with her in Washington. A few days after the Obama team took power, Shultz said, "We're in a waiting game now, waiting to see what the administration does. The signs are positive, the White House website has endorsed many of our goals, almost word for word in some cases. I told Hillary you can't let this drift for a year, or it will be gone. You have to make a major effort now. We'll see what happens."

Obama did not disappoint. He decided to make nuclear disarmament the centerpiece of his first overseas trip as president. As the White House prepared for the European visit in April, Obama told his aides, "Let's take this issue that doesn't usually get a lot of attention and let's put it in the biggest platform we can."

They picked Prague as the site. The platform would be Obama's maiden foreign policy speech as president. Gary Samore, a nuclear weapons specialist recruited by Obama to handle weapons of mass destruction issues at the White House, helped draft the speech with Ben Rhodes. "The great thing about writing that speech with Ben is that it was very early in the administration," Samore recalled, "so the other departments were not fully staffed and the bureaucracy was very obedient, because early on in the administration there's a lot of malleability and you can do things very quickly at the stroke of a pen which, once things have been solidified, it takes many interagency meetings before you can reach a judgment. . . . We sent it around to the proper senior people, those few that were actually in office, and got a very quick clearance."

On the fine spring morning of April 6, 2009, Obama faced a

sea of people gathered on the vast cobblestone expanse of Prague's
Hradcany Square and, in effect, made the initiative of Shultz and
his partners the official policy of the United States government.

"So today," he declared, "I state clearly and with conviction
America's commitment to seek the peace and security of a world
without nuclear weapons. I'm not naive. This goal will not be
reached quickly—perhaps not in my lifetime. It will take patience
and persistence. But now we, too, must ignore the voices who tell
us that the world cannot change. We have to insist, 'Yes, we can.'

"Some argue that the spread of these weapons cannot be stopped,
cannot be checked—that we are destined to live in a world where
more nations and more people possess the ultimate tools of destruction. Such fatalism is a deadly adversary, for if we believe
that the spread of nuclear weapons is inevitable, then in some way
we are admitting to ourselves that the use of nuclear weapons is
inevitable. . . . And as a nuclear power, as the only nuclear power
to have used a nuclear weapon, the United States has a moral responsibility to act. We cannot succeed in this endeavor alone, but
we can lead it, we can start it."

Obama went on to delineate a series of practical steps to reduce
nuclear threats in the short and medium term, as the world moved
toward abolition. He promised to negotiate a new arms reduction
treaty with Russia, to reduce the number of warheads in both
nations. He said he would seek Senate ratification of the Comprehensive Nuclear Test-Ban Treaty, an accord it rejected in 1999.
He called for a new global treaty that would end the production
of fissile material used to make warheads. "If we are serious about
stopping the spread of these weapons," he said, "then we should
put an end to the dedicated production of weapons-grade materials
that create them. That's the first step."

Shultz was impressed. "Very powerful speech," he said a few
months later. "Like everything, it needs a lot of following up on,
and action, but the words were eloquent and precise, and hit key

issues. It was an extremely good speech, and I wrote him a note, telling him that."

If much of Obama's speech sounded familiar to Shultz, Kissinger, Nunn, and Perry, it was no coincidence. "A lot of things we took for the Prague speech came right out of their op-ed," recalled Samore. "Of course those are ideas that are also floating around for a long time now. The agenda on the international arms control stage is pretty well established."

When asked to pinpoint the role the men played in the development of the Obama administration's nuclear policies, Samore said: "The most important thing is the marriage between a vision and practical steps, because if you just announce the vision of abolishing nuclear weapons, then that can be seen as naive, and even dangerous. . . . The most important thing that the four horsemen did was to conceive of a strategy that combined a vision, a long-term vision with short-term practical steps that were achievable."

A week after the Prague speech, Shultz, Perry, and Nunn picked up the theme in Rome at a nuclear threat conference jointly hosted by Shultz, Mikhail Gorbachev, and the Italian Foreign Ministry. The meeting was an outgrowth of the planning sessions that had followed publication of the first *Wall Street Journal* op-ed article. Italy was soon to host the annual G-8 meeting and Shultz and his group hoped the Italian government would use its summit role to put nuclear weapons high on the agenda when the world leaders gathered at L'Aquila in July.

The subject of the Rome meeting, held in a grand conference room at the Foreign Ministry, was "Overcoming Nuclear Dangers." It looked like a Cold War reunion. As participants gathered the first morning, Shultz, Gorbachev, and the former Soviet foreign minister Aleksandr Bessmertnykh chatted by the espresso bar outside the conference room, not far from Hans-Dietrich Genscher, the former West German foreign minister. Nunn and Perry circulated around the room, sampling the pastries.

Shultz greeted the seventy or so participants by warning, "Time is not on our side." He talked about the need to take steps that "pull us back from the nuclear precipice" and said "the agenda is reasonably well known and it is daunting."

Gorbachev lamented the glacial pace of change in the nuclear weapons arena. He told the group, "We have to admit that nothing fundamentally new has been achieved in the past decade and a half. The pace of nuclear arms reductions has slowed. The mechanisms of arms control and verification have weakened. The Comprehensive Test Ban Treaty has not entered into force. The quantities of nuclear weapons held by Russia and the United States still far exceed the arsenals of all other nuclear powers taken together, thus making it more difficult to bring them into the process of nuclear disarmament. The regime of nuclear non-proliferation is in jeopardy."

Despite the daunting nine-hour time difference with California, Shultz sat ramrod straight in his chair throughout hours of discussion, never nodding off or even drooping slightly. Perry was no match, dozing off periodically in the conference room. Nunn managed to stay awake, energized by an early-morning workout in the hotel gym, where he appeared around 6 a.m. in gym shorts and the blue dress shirt he had worn the evening before.

For all the hours of sober discussion in the conference hall, the emotional high point of the conference came when Bill Perry addressed the participants after dinner on the first day. The setting was Villa Madama, a sixteenth-century palace on the slopes of Monte Mario, a grand home designed by Raphael for Cardinal Giulio de' Medici, who later became Pope Clement VII. The artistic center of the villa is the *salone*, a grand room with a vaulted ceiling graced with frescoes by Giulio Romano, a Raphael disciple.

As dinner neared an end, and wineglasses were refilled, Perry stood before a simple microphone on a metal stand, dwarfed by the stunning ceiling. Gorbachev and Shultz were seated at a long rectangular table in front of him. "Many of my colleagues have asked me why an old warrior like me would get involved in nuclear dis-armament," Perry said, glancing down at several pages of notes in his hand. His voice was barely audible as he described his role as an intelligence analyst during the Cuban Missile Crisis.

After recalling several other Cold War incidents and his efforts to dismantle nuclear arsenals in Ukraine and other former Soviet republics, he said he thought nuclear threats were diminishing. "At the time, I believed that we were well on our way to dealing with the legacy of the Cold War. But since then, those efforts have stalled and even reversed. . . . It seems as if we are drifting into an unprecedented nuclear catastrophe. And I have come to believe that the only way we have to deal with this nuclear catastrophe is to work to bring an end to nuclear weapons. And that's my answer to people who ask why I am working in this field today.

"No one should believe that it is going to be easy. There are powerful obstacles . . . both in Russia and in the United States. On top of that, most of the other countries in the world are sitting it out. Some of them through an understandable skepticism about whether this is all going to really happen. So there's much difficult work to be done. . . . I believe that this goal is so important that I'm dedicating the remainder of my career in order to achieve it. I do this in the hopes it will create a safer world for my children and my grandchildren."

A month later, Obama made his admiration of the men plain by welcoming them to the Oval Office. After caucusing among themselves at Nunn's Washington office about who should speak for the foursome, Shultz took the lead. "They all said I should be the spokesman for the group," Shultz said. He sat next to Obama in a striped armchair in front of the fireplace, the Oval Office seat reserved for the ranking guest. Kissinger, Perry, and Nunn sat on two facing sofas, along with Rahm Emanuel, then White House chief of staff; James Jones, then national security adviser; and two of Jones's aides, Samore and Michael McFaul.

It was an important symbolic show of mutual support for the president's audacious nuclear agenda. The quartet needed the president's backing to advance their goals; Obama needed the quartet's support to raise nuclear issues above the killing ground of Washington politics.

"The conversation started with him," Shultz said, "and I talked, we went around. Then we had a lot of interaction. I would call it a real conversation, as distinct from people making statements, where you say something, he listens, he responds to it, and so on. And it was clear enough that he is into the subject. He's thought about it, and is aware of the ins and outs of it, or he couldn't have carried on that kind of an easy conversation."

When reporters were escorted into the Oval Office at the end of the meeting, Obama said, "I just had a wonderful discussion with four of the most preeminent national security thinkers that we have—a bipartisan group of George Shultz, Henry Kissinger, Bill Perry, and Sam Nunn—all who've come together and helped inspire policies of this administration in a speech that I gave in Prague, which set forward a long-term vision of a world without nuclear weapons.

"We are going to be pushing this as one of our highest priorities, to take specific steps, measurable steps, verifiable steps, to make progress on this issue, even as we keep a long-term perspective and a long-term vision about what can be achieved. And we can think of no better advisers, counselors, and partners in this process than the four gentlemen who joined us here today.

"We also think this is a reminder of the long tradition of bipartisan foreign policy that has been the hallmark of America at moments of greatest need, and that's the kind of spirit that we hope will be reflected in our administration."

Shultz spoke for the four guests. "All four of us support enthusiastically what the President is doing, as expressed eloquently in his speech in Prague. First of all, we all noticed, on your White House web site, that the first sentence was 'We will work for a world free of nuclear weapons.' That's the vision.

"The second sentence is, 'As long as nuclear weapons are around, we will be sure we have a strong deterrent ourselves.' So we support that notion that we must be conscious of our national security all the way along to zero."

After the meeting, the quartet had a brief encounter with reporters outside the North Lawn entrance to the West Wing, the normal gathering spot for impromptu news conferences by prominent White House visitors. Shultz again spoke for the group. At Kissinger's direction—contrary to his own instincts—Shultz declined to answer any questions.

"Henry was very insistent," Shultz reported. "He said, no questions. And we sort of argued about that, and he said, no questions. If you have questions, the story will be on some contradiction of some kind. That's what the press is trying to do. So you make your statement and leave. No questions. So that's what we did. I was a little surprised, myself, because I've never done anything like that. But anyway, Henry was absolutely insistent that if you didn't do that, you'd get a bum story based on some wrinkle that somebody figured out to have you in disagreement with the president."

That evening Kissinger appeared on Fox News, answering questions about the meeting from Greta Van Susteren, the host of *On the Record*. While reaffirming his support for the elimination of nuclear weapons, he seemed unconvinced the goal could ever be achieved. "We wrote two articles on the subject of how one can reduce the danger of nuclear proliferation and work ultimately, perhaps, toward a world that might have no nuclear weapons," he told Van Susteren. "We support the basic premise of the objective, but also, we strongly support the idea that until that objective is reached, we must maintain adequate forces for deterrence. And so we have to look at the individual steps that can be taken. We need, in a way, sort of a vision and a kind of step-by-step program in order perhaps to get there. Is it possible? At this point, nobody could describe what such a world would look like."

In February 2010, Shultz flew to Paris to address a conference convened by Global Zero. His appearance signaled a modest thaw in relations between Shultz and his partners and Global Zero. He was respectfully received by the large gathering in the elegant Salon Opera at Le Grand Intercontinental Hotel, a few paces from the Paris Opera. Some of the questions asked from the floor after his address were not welcoming, but by and large, the encounter suggested the two groups might find a way to cooperate in the months ahead. Indeed, in February 2011, Bruce Blair, one of the founders of Global Zero, attended a workshop at Stanford on technical disarmament issues organized by Shultz and Drell.

From Paris, Shultz headed to Berlin, where he linked up with Kissinger, Perry, and Nunn for a round of meetings with German officials, continuing the "Statesmen's Dialogues" that they had inaugurated two years earlier in London. They conferred with Chancellor Angela Merkel and consulted with a trio of aging but still sharp fellow Cold Warriors, Helmut Schmidt, the former chancellor; Hans-Dietrich Genscher, a former foreign minister; and Richard von Weizsäcker, who was German president. As the men were whisked around the snowy German capital in a fleet of black Mercedes and called on top government officials, one could almost imagine they were still Washington potentates. A news conference featuring the four Americans and three Germans drew a large pack of reporters and camera crews. The men also dined with German dignitaries at the American Academy in Berlin. Guests at the Hotel Adlon, where the men were staying, stopped to stare at the four Americans, who must have seemed an apparition from the days of the Berlin Wall as they stepped outside onto Pariser Platz, framed by the Brandenburg Gate. Shultz, Kissinger, and Nunn seemed right at home in the spotlight, Perry less so.

For all the attention, it was hard not to notice the advanced age of the Americans and their German counterparts. "Why don't you get some younger people to join your group?" Charlotte Shultz drily asked her husband as they headed to the airport after the news conference with ninety-one-year-old Schmidt, eighty-three-year-old Genscher, and ninety-year-old von Weizsäcker. When he reminded her that Colin Powell and Madeleine Albright had endorsed the initiative, Charlotte said, "I mean someone really young." Shultz laughed heartily. Then he conceded she had a point. Finding a younger generation of prominent and experienced statesmen to carry on the effort is a serious challenge that Shultz, Kissinger, Perry, Nunn, and Drell have not addressed.

The issue was underscored in Munich, the next stop on their German tour. There the men hosted a meeting with former government leaders from around the world. The gathering looked like a geriatric convention, as mostly white-haired men, more than a few leaning on canes, compared notes about their efforts to curtail nuclear arsenals and set a course toward abolition.

Nunn opened the meeting by asking everyone to speak up, since some in the group were hard of hearing. He then recounted a Georgia story about the heavy drinker who was told he would go deaf if he didn't stop drinking. The man stopped for a month, then resumed. When his wife asked why, as Nunn cheerfully told the story, the man replied, "Well, I like what I've been drinking better than what I've been hearing."

The turnout was impressive, including former Italian, French, British, and German leaders, and the commitment to doing away with nuclear weapons was obviously heartfelt. Pointing to Nunn, Kissinger, Perry, and Shultz, von Weizsäcker said, "These men have had enormous impact on our thinking in Europe."

The four men returned to the White House in April 2010 as guests of honor at a screening of *Nuclear Tipping Point*, the documentary about their campaign. Charlotte Shultz, irrepressible as ever, made the trip despite recent hip surgery. She showed up with a walker decked out to look like a San Francisco cable car. As she entered the White House, she tapped a small bell attached to the walker, mimicking the distinctive sound of a cable car. Uniformed Secret Service agents seemed uncertain what to make of the contraption, but they let her by.

Several dozen top national security officials gathered in a ground-floor hallway overlooking the Rose Garden for a reception before the screening. It was like a homecoming for Shultz, Kissinger, Perry, and Nunn, who had spent countless hours at the White House while in office. Some of the younger White House staff members present were clearly pleased to find themselves mingling with Cold War figures they had studied in college and graduate school. One of the twentysomething waiters serving drinks and canapés turned to a guest after Kissinger picked up a drink. "That's a piece of history," she said.

After thirty minutes or so of sipping cocktails, the four men were escorted to the Oval Office for a brief meeting with President Obama. As the group returned, accompanied by Obama, aides opened the doors to the screening room, a plush miniature movie theater that seats roughly sixty people in banked rows. The decor is red and black. Small bags of popcorn awaited at every reclining seat. Secretary of State Hillary Clinton and Robert Gates, then defense secretary, briefly joined the group but said they had to run to other appointments. Obama welcomed the crowd and pointing to the four men, seated in the front row, thanked them for their nuclear initiative. "You can see that I take you seriously," he said. Then he signaled to the projection booth to roll the film.

It was interesting to see many of the civilian and military officials who control the nation's nuclear weapons sit quietly for an hour as the film unspooled. Even though the audience was quite familiar with the issues, the solemn commentary of Shultz, Kissinger, Perry, and Nunn made a stirring impression. (Admiral Mike Mullen, the chairman of the Joint Chiefs of Staff, did polish off his popcorn during the film.) When it ended, Obama again thanked the four men for their efforts and waited patiently by the door to shake hands with everyone as they exited.

That evening, Shultz and his partners and their spouses dined with some of the officials in a private room at the Hay-Adams Hotel. It wasn't a victory dinner, but there was an unmistakable sense of satisfaction and pride that they had come so far in just a few years.

The sense of accomplishment was tempered by the realization that much work remained to be done. Translating their goals, and Obama's, into tangible progress toward nuclear disarmament had barely begun.

CHAPTER TWENTY-SEVEN

*You can repeat until you turn blue in the face that we
want to move towards a world without nuclear weapons, but if you
don't have some real accomplishments, and if you don't get some
things done, you're not going to move very fast, if at all.*
—SAM NUNN

To appreciate the challenges confronting President Obama and George Shultz and his partners as they try to rid the world of nuclear weapons, a visit to the birthplace of the atom bomb can be instructive.

Rusty Gray, a lean, silver-haired metallurgical engineer, spends his days in a warren of small laboratories atop one of the high mesas in Los Alamos, New Mexico, taking apart and testing some of the thousands of components and bits of metal, chemicals, and wiring that go into a nuclear warhead. Unlike his predecessors at the Los Alamos National Laboratory, Gray isn't inventing new nuclear weapons. He's making sure America's old weapons still work.

His labors, and those of hundreds of his colleagues at Los Alamos and other nuclear weapons centers around the nation, will help determine whether the work of Shultz, Kissinger, Perry, Nunn, and Drell ultimately leads to the eradication of nuclear weapons. That may sound paradoxical, since Gray's job is to help keep America's aging weapons in tiptop shape. But in the realm of nuclear disarmament, the difference between maintaining old weapons and building new ones can be the difference between whether a nation is arming or disarming.

With the help of Rusty Gray and his fellow scientists and engineers, the nation is getting by just fine with an arsenal of aging warheads. The last newly manufactured American warhead came off the assembly line outside Amarillo, Texas, in 1989. Thanks to an informal international testing moratorium that the United States honors, no nuclear weapon has been test-fired at the Nevada underground test site since 1992.

The record might look much different if the government had felt compelled to build and test-fire new generations of warheads over the last two decades. That's the way Washington used to ensure the American arsenal was abundantly stocked with reliable weapons. New warheads were periodically produced and test-fired, and older warheads were routinely tested. Once it was clear the weapons were good to go, no one spent much time worrying if they would decay over thirty to forty years and turn into duds. Older weapons could be traded in for new models before aging became an issue. The restocking signaled to the world that Washington was not really serious about its commitment to the Nuclear Non-Proliferation Treaty's language about nuclear disarmament.

Today the labs, manufacturing facilities, test sites, and other secret centers created to make new weapons are largely devoted to ensuring that an aging stockpile remains viable. Or as Rusty Gray said, "It's like when you put the lawn mower away for the winter, you want to be confident it will start at the first pull in the spring."

The work is the centerpiece of what's known as the Stockpile Stewardship Program, a multibillion-dollar government project started in response to congressional legislation in 1992 imposing the moratorium on American nuclear testing and mandating the negotiation of a test ban treaty. The program was initiated by President Clinton in 1993, and later refined after a 1994 Jason study, led by Drell. The Drell group reported warheads could last for years if they were properly maintained and refurbished. The bomb makers, in effect, have been replaced by bomb repairmen equipped with cutting-edge surveillance and diagnostic technologies and some of the world's fastest computers.

The highly sophisticated science has made it possible to run advanced computer simulations of a nuclear explosion that show the unfolding nuclear processes in remarkable detail. Most weapons experts, including Drell, say the work has eliminated the need to test-fire weapons. Some of the scientists and engineers working at Los Alamos said that they had learned more about the workings of a nuclear weapon from the simulations and other diagnostic tools than their predecessors had divined from the 1,051 nuclear weapons tests conducted by the United States from 1945 to 1992.

The shift has not been welcomed by some nuclear weapons advocates, who argue that the United States must design and test new warheads to keep pace with other nations working on new models, including Russia. President George W. Bush thought the case strong enough to order up design work on a new warhead dubbed the Reliable Replacement Warhead, or RRW. Bomb designers at the Los Alamos and Lawrence Livermore laboratories conducted a bakeoff to see who could produce the better weapon. Work was suspended when Congress cut off funding in 2007. Had the United States built the new warhead, a new international warhead development race likely would have started.

Shultz, Kissinger, Perry, and Nunn joined the debate in 2010 with a third op-ed article in the *Wall Street Journal*. Before drafting the article, the four men, plus Drell, visited the Lawrence Livermore National Laboratory in 2009 to take a look at the Stockpile Stewardship Program and related activities. One piece of the maintenance work, the Life Extension Program, focuses directly on maintaining warheads. The directors of the two weapons labs in New Mexico—Los Alamos and Sandia—flew in to California for the discussion, knowing that whatever the former officials said would influence policy and budget debates in Washington.

The op-ed article opened innocuously enough by arguing that the United States must maintain the safety, security, and reliability of its nuclear weapons until disarmament day comes. The punch line—pushed by Drell—came midway through the piece in a reference to a recently completed Jason study of the stewardship program. Jason said that warhead life "could be extended for decades, with no anticipated loss in confidence" under the Life Extension Program and approaches like it. To the nuclear weapons community, the message was clear: Shultz, Kissinger, Perry, and Nunn were satisfied that the programs were keeping the American arsenal in good working order and would do so for years to come, removing the need to develop and test new warheads. To keep Stockpile Stewardship viable, the men called for increased funding for the labs. The article was an important milestone in the new weapon versus old weapon debate, and put the men in line with President Obama, who barred further development of a new warhead when he took office.

The new look of weapons modernization work at Los Alamos is just one example of the kind of fundamental change that will be required to move the world toward nuclear disarmament. As Shultz, Kissinger, Perry, Nunn, and Drell well know, an imposing array of political, diplomatic, and technological forces must be favorably aligned—perhaps perfectly aligned—to reach the goal of abolition. Even if one sets aside some related international problems—such as the need to resolve intractable regional conflicts between India and Pakistan or between Israel and its neighbors in the Middle East—the odds against global nuclear disarmament are formidable. President Obama acknowledged as much during his 2009 appearance in Prague when he said the goal might not be reached in his lifetime.

Considering the forty-one-year age difference between Barack Obama and George Shultz, it is easy to understand why Shultz and his partners have a more compressed time frame in mind. They are impatient to move ahead and are working with a sense of urgency on numerous fronts to advance their campaign. As Sam Nunn said, "You can repeat until you turn blue in the face that we want to move towards a world without nuclear weapons, but if you don't have some real accomplishments, and if you don't get some things done, you're not going to move very fast, if at all."

One of the issues they have studied is reconstitution, the notion that in a nuclear-free world the United States and other countries could maintain the expertise, equipment, and materials needed to build new nuclear weapons if faced with an unforeseen nuclear threat. At first blush, reconstitution seems a nuclear double cross to pure abolitionists. If weapons are to be eliminated, so too should the means to make them. But that outcome is unrealistic. The knowledge of how to make nuclear weapons cannot be eradicated. The next best outcome, many experts believe, is to let nations maintain the ability to produce new weapons so that they will not be left helpless if a rogue country goes nuclear at some point.

It is a provocative idea, but one with obvious appeal to realists like Shultz and his colleagues who want to eliminate nuclear weapons in a responsible way that does not leave the United States vulnerable to unpredictable future enemies.

The idea was championed by Jonathan Schell in *The Abolition*, published in 1984. He wrote: "As reductions continued, the capacity for retaliation would consist less and less of the possession of weapons and more and more of the capacity for rebuilding them, until, at the level of zero, that capacity would be all. Indeed, the more closely we look at the zero point the less of a watershed it seems to be. Examined in detail, it reveals a wide range of alternatives, in which the key issue is no longer the number of weapons in existence but the extent of the capacity and the level of readiness for building more."

The idea is back in vogue today, thanks in part to the work of Shultz, Kissinger, Perry, Nunn, and Drell. Indeed, they have gathered together some of the best minds in the field to study the issue in depth and organized a workshop on related technical issues in 2011.

Reconstitution could come in various forms. Schell initially proposed keeping a bank of bomb-grade materials available so that weapons could be quickly built. Michael O'Hanlon, director of foreign policy research at the Brookings Institution, favors pushing the starting line further back to a world where the production of highly enriched uranium and plutonium has stopped and stocks have been eliminated. Drell and other scientists propose keeping weapons laboratories in operation and a highly skilled workforce in place that can restart the bomb-building process. Some scientists at Los Alamos said continual design work on new warheads is necessary to retain top-flight engineers, but others disagree.

Reconstitution is just one of many issues Shultz and his partners are working on as they try to advance their disarmament initiative. The array of topics provides a good guide to the multiple barriers impeding passage to zero. In the diplomatic arena, Russian resistance to further arms reductions has to be overcome before global negotiations about eliminating nuclear weapons can commence. That will require creative American diplomacy with the Kremlin on a broad array of security issues. In the area of defense policy, the greatest obstacle to abolition is overcoming an entrenched Cold War mind-set in Washington that sees nuclear weapons and nuclear deterrence as indispensable elements of national security. And in the technological realm, there are myriad challenges, such as coming up with ways to verify that nations that say they are going to give up their weapons actually do so and that a clandestine effort to rearm—known in the zero-nukes lexicon as a breakout—can be detected. As the work at Los Alamos suggests, the science of maintaining weapons is demanding and will only become more so during a drawdown of arms that may take decades to complete.

It is a daunting list, and covers only some of the matters that must be resolved if the world is to be free of nuclear arms. No wonder Nunn and his partners talk about creating a base camp partway to the summit they seek to conquer, a place where the world can regroup and prepare for the final ascent. As of early 2012, as this book is published, the summit is visible in the far distance, but barely.

Still, there is reason to be encouraged. When the five men take stock of what has happened since their first *Wall Street Journal* article in 2007, they see significant advances, far beyond their expectations. "I think the progress is astonishing," Shultz said in early 2011.

They have made surprising headway. Their greatest accomplishment is the wave of renewed interest in nuclear disarmament generated by their *Journal* op-ed and subsequent proselytizing. Government rhetoric so far has outdistanced government action, but garnering the support of President Obama and other world leaders, including the unanimous 2009 UN Security Council resolution endorsing the elimination of nuclear weapons, was no small achievement.

President Obama, for his part, has translated verbal support into effective action. In addition to the brisk schedule he set for removing and securing vulnerable stocks of fissile material in places like Poland, he convened a nuclear summit in Washington in April 2010 to enlist the help of other nations in locking down bomb-grade materials. The summit was attended by forty-seven nations, the largest gathering of world leaders organized by an American president since Franklin Roosevelt hosted the 1945 conference in San Francisco that created the United Nations.

In anticipation of the meeting, Chile worked with Andrew Bieniawski and his colleagues in the Global Threat Reduction Initiative to pack up Chile's entire stock of highly enriched uranium and ship it to the United States. At the summit, Ukraine announced it would relinquish the last batch of the highly enriched uranium left over from the Soviet era and Mexico agreed to work with the United States and Canada to convert its research reactor to run on low-enriched uranium. Washington and Moscow also reached agreement after many years of haggling to reduce their copious stockpiles of plutonium over time. The summit communiqué was not binding, but it put the forty-seven nations on record as supporting an ambitious series of twelve steps to reduce nuclear dangers and improve the security of fissile materials.

A month later, the United Nations hosted a conference of 189 nations to review the status of the Nuclear Non-Proliferation Treaty. The mass gathering produced several positive if unenforceable results, including a reaffirmation to eliminate all nuclear weapons and a 2012 deadline for convening a regional conference to eliminate unconventional weapons in the Middle East. The outcome was a considerable improvement over the last review conference, in 2005, which ended in disarray. The positive outcome was partly due to President Obama's commitment to seek the elimination of nuclear weapons.

Later in 2010, Shultz, Kissinger, Perry, and Nunn weighed in on behalf of New START, the latest nuclear arms reduction treaty with Russia. Senate appearances by Kissinger and Perry, and strong endorsements from Nunn and Shultz, helped President Obama win Senate ratification despite stiff Republican resistance. The National Association of Evangelicals and the United States Conference of Catholic Bishops also pressed for ratification. In the end, the treaty was approved by a 71–26 vote, including thirteen Republicans, more than the required two-thirds majority.

The arms cuts called for under the treaty are modest, bringing the number of operational strategic nuclear warheads on each side down to 1,550 from the previous ceiling of 2,200. (There are many thousands more in reserve, not covered by the treaty.) It also limits each nation to seven hundred deployed launchers— land- and sea-based intercontinental missiles and heavy bombers that can deliver warheads to distant targets. That's far more than reasonably needed to deal with current and foreseeable threats, but reaffirming the downward trend in the American and Russian arsenals was important and the renewal of arms talks a necessary precursor to future negotiations about deeper cuts. The treaty also assured the resumption of monitoring and verification measures needed to ensure compliance with arms limits, a critically important step. Verification measures had lapsed at the end of 2009 with the expiration of the previous arms reduction treaty between Washington and Moscow.

In another positive development, Sam Nunn and NTI enlisted the aid of Warren Buffett to help pay for the creation of an international nuclear fuel bank designed to supply low-enriched uranium to countries building nuclear power plants or research reactors. Buffett put up $50 million, on the condition that another $100 million be raised. The additional money was contributed by the United States and thirty other countries. Access to an internationally controlled source of lower-enriched uranium may discourage some countries from building their own enrichment plants, which can easily be used to produce highly enriched uranium suitable for use in nuclear weapons—as Iran seems intent on doing. Nunn and the other men are acutely aware of the global need to manage the production of fissile material in a way that provides fuel for nuclear power reactors without generating bomb-grade uranium.

The fuel bank will be run by the International Atomic Energy Agency, the world body charged with encouraging the peaceful uses of nuclear energy and verifying through inspections that safeguarded nuclear materials are not diverted for military purposes. Kazakhstan has invited the IAEA to locate the fuel bank there.

But these and other recent achievements are merely down payments toward the greater goal that Shultz, Kissinger, Perry, Nunn, and Drell have in mind. As Perry said after Senate ratification of

New START, "If the START treaty was this hard, you can only imagine how difficult the rest will be."

If Obama fails to win a second term, historians may someday say his nuclear weapons agenda hit a high-water mark with Senate ratification of New START. Many of Obama's aides worried that that might be so during the opening months of 2011 as they looked at future prospects for success. Further progress on arms reductions with Moscow is likely to be more difficult than negotiating New START, which proved more arduous than the White House expected. Without deep reductions by the United States and Russia—down to a level of five hundred or so operational warheads on each side—China and other nuclear weapons states are not likely to join talks about trimming their own arsenals and moving toward zero. Reaching an international agreement to end the production of fissile material for weapons programs also won't be easy. As of 2011, Pakistan was the major impediment to international approval of such a ban, which would be codified in a Fissile Material Cut-off Treaty, first proposed by President Clinton in 1993.

Another pivotal step awaited action after New START was approved—gaining Senate ratification of the Comprehensive Nuclear Test-Ban Treaty (CTBT). As the name suggests, the treaty would impose a blanket ban on nuclear weapons testing. After the tense days of the Cuban Missile Crisis, John F. Kennedy and Nikita Khrushchev, the Soviet leader, agreed in 1963 to ban testing in the atmosphere, in outer space, and underwater. In 1974 Washington and Moscow agreed to prohibit underground tests with a yield larger than 150 kilotons, equivalent to 150,000 tons of TNT. Two years later the two nations added an accord regulating underground nuclear explosions for peaceful purposes. Russia has abstained from testing since 1990, the United States since 1992. India, Pakistan, and North Korea have conducted underground tests over the last dozen years.

Drell played a critical role in creating the groundwork for the test-ban treaty when he headed a 1995 Jason study group that said the United States could maintain an effective nuclear stockpile under a full test ban. The report eased concerns in the Clinton administration and helped overcome pressure to settle for a limited accord. Perry used his expertise and clout as defense secretary to beat back Pentagon resistance, and Bill Clinton signed the treaty in 1996. But the Senate rejected it in 1999, following the advice of opponents who said its provisions could not be adequately monitored and enforced because small underground tests might elude detection. They also contended that a test ban would hobble national security by permanently preventing the testing of new warheads.

Though Washington has not test-fired a weapon since 1992, ratification of the treaty is symbolically important beyond its value in providing for on-site inspections and limiting the potential for nuclear modernization. "You can argue that we are in fact following it already, so what difference does it make?" Perry said. "The difference it makes is a profound difference on the attitude of the rest of the world about how serious the U.S. government is about its intentions. And without the rest of the world believing that we're serious, they're not going to be moving down this path. Our leadership, I believe, is essential."

President Obama said in Prague that he would move quickly to resubmit the treaty to the Senate. "To achieve a global ban on nuclear testing, my Administration will immediately and aggressively pursue U.S. ratification of the Comprehensive Test Ban Treaty. After more than five decades of talks, it is time for the testing of nuclear weapons to finally be banned." As of mid-2011, the White House had not acted, fearing it could not muster a two-thirds majority for ratification. Given Republican gains in 2010, and the need to persuade senators who opposed the treaty in 1999 to change their minds, the prospects for approval looked bleak. The question was whether Obama was prepared to expend a great deal of effort on a long-shot ratification campaign.

Drell and other weapons experts are confident that the treaty can be effectively monitored with sensitive seismic sensors and other detection instruments now located at dozens of stations around the world. When the monitoring system is completed, there will be nearly 200 land-based sites as well as undersea and atmospheric monitoring devices, all operated by the CTBT Organization (CTBTO), an organization based in Vienna that was founded in 1996 and will oversee implementation of the treaty if, and when, it goes into force. More than 80 percent of the 337 planned stations are in operation. The system, which was in its infancy when the Senate considered the treaty in 1999, ought to reassure skeptical senators that even a small nuclear test can be detected.

As for the need to test warheads, a new, multibillion-dollar laser instrument at the Lawrence Livermore National Laboratory may add a critical new dimension to scientists' understanding about nuclear fusion, the primary source of explosive energy in a hydrogen bomb. The National Ignition Facility (NIF), as the apparatus is called, looks like one of the elaborate, futuristic weapons complexes once featured in the climactic scenes of James Bond movies. The construction crew that built it told lab officials they didn't believe it was meant for scientific research, but actually was a giant, newfangled antisatellite weapon. In fact, the machine is a real marvel of modern engineering, dedicated to some of the nation's most ambitious scientific goals, including self-sustaining nuclear fusion in a laboratory. If successful, machines like the NIF could, in theory, serve as a clean, virtually inexhaustible source of electric power.

Touring the NIF and talking with Ed Moses, the director, is like stepping into the pages of a science fiction novel. The NIF is made up of 192 lasers, housed in a gigantic ten-story building the size of three football fields. The enormous energy generated by the 192 lasers is funneled into 48 extraordinarily powerful beams that zap a pill-size target capsule containing a tiny amount of hydrogen fuel. The beams can produce 500 trillion watts of power for 20 billionths of a second, generating temperatures of 100 million degrees Celsius and pressures 100 times the earth's atmosphere on the target. Under those extraordinary conditions, in theory, the hydrogen atoms will fuse into helium, releasing thermonuclear energy.

If the system works as Moses predicts, the NIF will give scientists a unique tool for advancing their understanding of the dynamics of a nuclear explosion. They will, in effect, be able to replicate in miniature the forces at work when a warhead is detonated. That, in turn, can further reduce the need to test-fire warheads and would enhance the Stockpile Stewardship Program.

WHATEVER THE FATE of the test-ban treaty, working with the Kremlin on additional arms reductions and attendant matters is the starting point for many items on the checklist to zero. Referring to New START, Perry said, "But even though it was small, it was vital—because everything we need to do in the future, starting with halting the Iranian program, requires working with Russia and showing that we are serious about bringing our own nuclear stockpiles down."

The diplomatic landscape with Russia today bears little resemblance to the world Ronald Reagan and Mikhail Gorbachev faced at Reykjavik. The political conditions for productive arms talks would seem vastly improved, but the balance of military forces that now favors the United States is an obstacle. In a reversal of fortune since the end of the Cold War, Russia's conventional military power has declined as America's has increased, leaving the Kremlin more reliant on its nuclear weapons than it was during the Soviet period. Russian military commanders today are reluctant to give up their nuclear weapons, believing they are the great equalizer if Russia ever faces a military threat from China or the

West. Beyond defense issues, the arsenal sustains Russia's status as a great power even though its economy now ranks tenth in the world, just ahead of India and Spain.

To advance the arms control agenda with Moscow, the United States will need to address a set of intertwined issues, including tactical nuclear arms, ballistic missile defenses, and European security calculations.

Kissinger and his colleagues have tried indirectly to advance the long-term arms control agenda with Moscow through their back-channel, or Track 2, meetings with former high-ranking Russian officials led by former prime minister Yevgeni Primakov. The American and Russian groups have met three times: in Moscow in July 2007, in Washington in January 2008, and in Moscow in March 2009.

Once arms reduction negotiations began in 2009, the former officials left the diplomatic heavy lifting to the two governments. But throughout the talks, Rose Gottemoeller, the chief American negotiator, kept Shultz, Kissinger, Perry, Nunn, and Drell closely informed.

The next order of business with Russia—which the men are already working on—is to reduce, if not eliminate, tactical nuclear weapons, in other words, short-range, battlefield arms. It was this class of weapons, and the prospect that they would be fired in the first hours of an East-West military conflict, that so concerned Sam Nunn during his 1974 visit to NATO as a freshman senator. The United States still has roughly 500 tactical nuclear weapons, including 200–300 gravity bombs that are dropped from airplanes, stationed at bases in Belgium, the Netherlands, Germany, Italy, and Turkey. Russia has kept an estimated 3,800 tactical weapons. The disparity reflects Kremlin concern about the weakened Red Army, the rising military power of China, and potentially restive Muslim nations on Russia's southern border. In 1991 Washington and Moscow pledged to pull back their tactical weapons from border areas (NATO border areas, in the American case) and destroy all warheads built for short-range missiles, artillery shells, and demolition mines. Since the agreement was informal, no verification measures were mandated, and none has been carried out.

One compelling reason to get rid of the tactical weapons is that they are more vulnerable to theft, or at least a politically incendiary breach of security, than are their larger, better-secured strategic cousins. Bill Perry calls them "a terrorist's dream."

There has already been at least one security breach at a NATO base. In February 2010, a small contingent of antinuclear activists easily surmounted a security fence at Kleine Brogel Air Base in eastern Belgium. They made their way unimpeded into an area containing a Weapons Storage Vault, a nuclear weapons bunker that can hold four B61 nuclear bombs. It is unclear if any weapons were present at the time. The group plastered a few antinuke posters on a shelter wall, then nonchalantly strolled out onto a base runway, where they stood around for nearly an hour before security forces arrived. The trespassers were not prosecuted, possibly for fear that a Belgian jury would be sympathetic to the group's antinuclear views.

A more serious assault on the base may have been prevented in 2003 when Belgian authorities arrested Nizar Trabelsi in Brussels after learning he could be connected to terror plots in Europe. The Tunisian immigrant, a professional soccer player in Germany at one time, was convicted in September 2003 on charges of plotting to blow up the canteen at Kleine Brogel frequented by American airmen stationed at the base. He turned out to be associated with al-Qaeda. A Belgian court sentenced him to ten years in prison.

Robertus "Dutch" Remkes, a retired U.S. Air Force general who dealt with American tactical nuclear weapons in Europe from 2006 to 2008, worried that a determined terrorist group could break into one of the shelters and blow off the hardened cap on a bomb vault. He said he doubted a bomb could be removed intact, and even if one were, built-in safeguards would prevent anyone from detonating it. But Remkes warned his fellow officers that terrorists could crack open one of the bombs with an explosive charge, spraying radioactive materials around the site.

He described how an attack would unfold: "If four or five small teams of suicide attackers go at the same time against four different nuclear storage sites, somebody is bound to get through. . . . Jumping over fences and running for a hardened aircraft shelter which is less than 200 meters from the fence, at night or in broad daylight, you're probably going to get to that shelter. And when you get in there, you're probably going to figure out where it is. It's probably where the line is painted on the ground. All this is available on the Internet. . . . And just imagine, even one team is able to make this thing happen."

Remkes predicted that pulling off such an attack would be a spectacular triumph for a terror organization, sending political shock waves across Europe. "Imagine this taking place in a country where we deny that they even exist," he said. His recommendation: withdraw the weapons before they become a liability. "We're never going to use the damn things," he said. Another defense specialist familiar with the B61 bombs agreed. "We don't have anything targeted with them anymore," he said. In 2008, the United States withdrew the last of the 110 B61 bombs that it had based in Britain.

The United States is committed, in principle, to negotiating a deal with Russia to cut tactical nuclear weapons. Russia is wary of a deal because the weapons give added firepower to its weakened conventional forces, especially in the Far East, where Moscow wants to maintain a counterweight to China. America's European allies are divided over the presence of the American weapons on European territory, with some pressing for their removal while others, still nervous about Russia, are reluctant to see them go. NATO leaders essentially dodged the issue at a 2010 summit meeting with bland communiqué language about seeking future reductions.

Tackling tactical nuclear weapons is not possible without addressing broader political and diplomatic dynamics, including European security issues. Sam Nunn put it well: "In Europe, NATO must address a fundamental question. In the years ahead, does NATO want Russia to be inside or outside the Euro-Atlantic security arc? The same question, of course, must be asked by the Russians. If our answer is outside, then it's simple—we both just keep doing what we are now doing and further progress in the nuclear arena will be threatened. If the answer is inside, we and Russia must make major adjustments in strategy."

Perry and Shultz underscored the point after New START was signed but before the Senate ratification vote. Moving beyond New START, they said, would be difficult for Moscow: "Part of the reason for their reluctance to accept further reductions is that Russia considers itself to be encircled by hostile forces in Europe and in Asia. Another part results from the significant asymmetry between United States and Russian conventional military forces. For these reasons, we believe that the next round of negotiations with Russia should not focus solely on nuclear disarmament issues."

Cooperation, rather than competition, in the development of limited missile defenses is essential to future American-Russian relations. President Obama wisely pulled back from the Bush administration's ill-advised decision to base missile defense installations in Poland and the Czech Republic. Moscow overreacted to the plan, which did not threaten Russian security. The scheme was also technically flawed. The best site for radar systems designed to detect the launch and flight path of Iranian missiles so they can be intercepted—the purpose of the system—is actually southern Russia.

Working with Russia on missile defense technologies would remove a long-standing irritant in relations and open the way to future arms reduction agreements. Recognizing the importance of this issue, the Euro-Atlantic Security Initiative (EASI), an international commission cochaired by Nunn, has set up a working group on missile defense issues. Stephen Hadley, George W. Bush's national security adviser during Bush's second term, is one of the study group's leaders. Perry, Drell, and David Holloway, for their part, organized a 2011 meeting at Stanford of Russian and American missile defense experts, hoping to help develop the basis for a future agreement. The Americans reported modest progress at the meeting, including a willingness by the Russians to begin early-warning missile-launch data exchanges that had been put off in recent years.

WHILE THE ROAD to abolition starts in Moscow, it also runs through London, Paris, Beijing, New Delhi, Islamabad, Jerusalem, Pyongyang, and possibly before too long, Tehran. Shultz, Kissinger, Perry, Nunn, and Drell have made a point of traveling to many of these capitals to encourage cooperation on arms reductions. The September 2009 Security Council resolution was a milestone, and the Nuclear Summit in Washington a good step, but turning expressions of support into action has proved difficult. For instance, President Nicolas Sarkozy of France supported the 2009 Security Council resolution calling for abolition, but just a few months later a senior French diplomat sarcastically dismissed the plan at a Global Zero conference in Paris.

Chinese president Hu Jintao also endorsed the Security Council resolution, but China, as it often does on diplomatic matters, has taken a cautious approach to the abolition initiative. China, which first tested a nuclear weapon in 1964, is believed to maintain an arsenal of some four hundred warheads and has always said it would only use the weapons for defensive purposes. As part of a review of nuclear weapons policy, the Obama administration said it would "pursue high-level, bilateral dialogues on strategic stability with both Russia and China which are aimed at fostering more stable, resilient, and transparent strategic relationships."

To give Beijing a nudge, Stanford's John Lewis organized a two-day meeting of American and Chinese nuclear specialists at the university in 2009 that was cohosted by Shultz and Perry. The meeting, attended by several senior Chinese nuclear scientists, was inconclusive, but at least opened informal new lines of communication between the two nations on technical arms issues. Shultz, Kissinger, Perry, and Nunn have also participated in a series of back-channel meetings with their counterparts in China, similar to their Track 2 Russian talks. The working assumption in nuclear weapons circles is that China is unlikely to engage in formal discussions about limiting nuclear weapons or abolishing them until the United States and Russia bring the number of their operational warheads down to around five hundred on each side.

India and Pakistan present their own challenges because tensions between the two nations often spike to crisis levels that could someday uncontrollably accelerate to a nuclear exchange. They have come close to nuclear war at least once over the disputed territory of Kashmir. Both countries keep their nuclear weapons operations opaque to outsiders, including the United States, but Washington has given Pakistan a good deal of advice and equipment to help keep its weapons secure. Given the political turbulence in Pakistan and presence of terror groups, the security of Pakistan's nuclear weapons can't be guaranteed. The diversion of highly enriched uranium from government sites is an even greater danger, as then secretary of defense Robert Gates and the American ambassador in Islamabad warned in 2009. Meanwhile, as officials in Washington worry about the security of Pakistan's nuclear arsenal, Pakistan has quietly been building more and more warheads. American intelligence assessments in 2011 suggested Pakistan would soon have one hundred or more warheads, surpassing Britain as the world's fifth-largest nuclear weapons state after Russia, the United States, France, and China.

As Pakistan was expanding its arsenal, the United States and India were putting into effect an agreement on peaceful nuclear

cooperation. Under the controversial deal, Washington agreed
to allow the transfer of American nuclear fuel and technology
to India, ending a three-decade moratorium prompted by New
Delhi's failure to sign the Nuclear Non-Proliferation Treaty. In
return, India agreed to separate its civilian and military nuclear
programs and place its civilian operations under international
safeguards and inspection. It also agreed to continue its moratorium on weapons tests, improve weapons security, and work
toward an international agreement to ban the production of fissile material for weapons. India is estimated to have sixty to
eighty weapons.

Kissinger and Perry visited India in 2008 to talk about their
nuclear initiative and explore whether India might take part in an
international effort to reduce weapons. Small delegations of nuclear weapons specialists from India and Pakistan visited Stanford
for several days of unpublicized conversation in 2011.

Perry is the group's point man for North Korea, having
dealt with the volatile nation during his stint as defense secretary. He stays in close touch with two Stanford colleagues, Siegfried Hecker and John Lewis, who travel frequently to North
Korea and follow its nuclear activities closely. They were the first
Americans to see a new North Korean uranium enrichment facility in 2010. North Korea's nuclear ambitions, like so much else
about the cloistered nation, are obscure. It has vacillated over the
years from professing no weapons ambitions and giving IAEA
inspectors access to its nuclear facilities to operating a clandestine
weapons program and testing two nuclear devices. Its nuclear
program is believed to have been built, at least in part, with de-
signs and equipment acquired from A. Q. Khan, the Pakistani
nuclear scientist. In turn, North Korea has exported its nuclear
technology to other nations, including Libya and Syria. With
China, North Korea's only international friend, unwilling to
lean hard on its neighbor, the prospects for enlisting North Korea

in a disarmament compact looked unpromising as this book went
to press.

Perry, Shultz, and the others have no easy answers for Iran. They
agree that an Iranian bomb would be a severe, if not fatal, setback
for their initiative. If Iran develops nuclear weapons, other nations
in the neighborhood may be tempted to do the same, including
Syria, Saudi Arabia, and Turkey, which as a NATO member has
served for years as a base for American nuclear weapons. The 2011
overthrow of Hosni Mubarak in Egypt and popular unrest in other
Middle East nations may dampen the nuclear ambitions of some
countries, but an Iranian nuclear arsenal is likely to be a volatile
factor in the region. Fortunately, the Iranian weapons program was
slowed in 2010 by an American-Israeli covert operation that contaminated Iran's uranium enrichment plant with a disabling computer worm called Stuxnet. In January 2011, the *New York Times*
reported that the program "appears to have wiped out roughly a
fifth of Iran's nuclear centrifuges and helped delay, though not destroy, Tehran's ability to make its first nuclear arms." By mid-2011,
the Iranians seemed to have overcome the cyberattack and production of enriched uranium at Natanz was recovering.

Perry fears that the intersection of terrorism and the weapons
programs in North Korea and Iran will push nuclear threats out of
control. "If Iran and North Korea cannot be stopped from building nuclear arsenals," he said, "I believe that we will cross that tipping point, with consequences that will be dangerous beyond most
people's imagination."

THE DEFENSE DOCTRINES and military forces born of the nuclear age are powerful barriers to nuclear disarmament. The massive investment in nuclear arms that the nation made during the
Cold War will take many decades to unwind. Like most defense
experts, Robert Gates just doesn't see how nuclear weapons can be

undone. He is not opposed to the idea, in principle. "I don't have a problem with it from a philosophical stance," he said while still at the Pentagon. Nor does he object to the efforts of Shultz, Kissinger, Perry, Nunn, and Drell. "I think by setting the vision, they sort of provided an umbrella for more aggressive nonproliferation and arms reductions endeavors."

But he can't imagine how it would work. "Practically, I for one don't see how you put the genie back in the bottle. And I don't know how you could ever have the confidence you would require that some other nation-state couldn't covertly develop the capability, even if others gave it up."

He added with a grin, "The good news is, I don't have to worry about implementing it."

General Kevin Chilton, who commanded American strategic nuclear forces from 2007 to 2011, echoed the views of many fellow officers when he argued that the world would not necessarily be a safer place absent nuclear weapons. "There's been century after century of devastating warfare, with untold numbers of human lives lost and interrupted in tragedies and probably culminating in World War II. Millions, tens of millions of people around the world killed and affected by that conflict. We haven't seen that since the advent of nuclear weapons. In fact, we've seen great restraint. It doesn't mean warfare has gone away, but we've seen great restraint from the great powers."

So, two decades after the disintegration of the Soviet Union, American defense policy still pivots around the notion that a large nuclear arsenal is the best guarantor against attack. Though the number of missiles and warheads has fallen well below Cold War levels, the Pentagon continues to believe that the United States cannot do without 1,550 operational warheads at high alert, ready to fire at a moment's notice, with another 3,500 in reserve. That's enough nuclear firepower, as Senator Lamar Alexander said during the Senate debate on New START, "to blow any attacker to Kingdom Come."

The United States still relies on a triad of weapons systems—land-based missiles, submarine-based missiles, and long-range bombers—to deliver warheads to distant targets. Retaining that force, in theory, deters other nuclear weapons states from initiating a nuclear attack against the United States and might give pause to enemies armed with biological or chemical weapons.

General Chilton outlined the rationale. "The arsenal that is maintained by Russia today still poses an existential threat to the United States," he said. "What has changed dramatically is the geopolitical Cold War clash of ideals between those two, between the U.S. and the Soviet Union, communism versus democratic form of government. But that's a political change that could change overnight. So you don't want to bet the farm on a consistent political structure that could change quickly by doing anything rash on the way as you reduce."

But that sort of logic seems obsolete. In an op-ed article in late 2010, three men who literally labored at the heart of America's nuclear weapons complex—launch-duty officers at underground missile bunkers—aptly described the doctrine of nuclear deterrence today as "an outmoded strategy dealing with an obsolete threat."

We are no longer locked in a volatile standoff with another superpower. Russia and the United States may not be the best of friends, but they are not going to wage nuclear war against one another. China is a rising power with a nuclear arsenal, but for now its rapidly growing economy is more relevant to American power than its military forces. An attack by a nuclear-armed North Korea or Iran might justify a retaliatory strike with a handful of nuclear weapons, not hundreds. The failure of thousands of nuclear weapons to deter a terrorist attack was painfully evident on September 11, 2001.

One of the nation's top military officers, a man intimately familiar with American nuclear weapons strategy, told a group of defense analysts and scholars in 2010 that he could imagine very few circumstances under which the United States would use even a handful of nuclear weapons. He said he saw no existential threat to the United States equivalent to the Soviet Union and offered no scenario for launching hundreds of warheads. Even the use of a few seemed a remote option. That led several high-powered conference participants to ask afterward, as one put it, "If you never plan to use them, why do you have them?"

Colin Powell, who served as chairman of the Joint Chiefs, national security adviser, and secretary of state, frequently makes the same point. "The thing I convinced myself of after all these years of exposure to the use of nuclear weapons is that they were useless," he said. "They could not be used."

Yet many defense planners and politicians remain enthralled by the concept of nuclear deterrence. As Shultz, Kissinger, Perry, and Nunn said, "Today the Cold War is almost 20 years behind us, but many leaders and publics cannot conceive of deterrence without a strategy of mutual assured destruction."

Perry and Drell ran into a stone wall of resistance at a 2009 Washington meeting of defense experts convened by the directors of the Los Alamos and Lawrence Livermore national laboratories. As Perry put it, "In this group, and in other groups I've been with, I find ourselves talking past each other." Most speakers at the gathering defended the need to maintain a gargantuan nuclear deterrent and several indirectly attacked the abolition initiative. One participant suggested that the number of American warheads should be determined by Pentagon target planners, implying that American defense policy and arms negotiating guidance should be set by military officers rather than the president and secretaries of state and defense.

When the time came for Perry to address the group, he was uncharacteristically agitated. In a rare display of anger, he said, "I've heard some discussion here today about numbers, and thousands of numbers have been thrown out as the goal for the next reduction.

Secretary Gates has said he would consider 1,500. It's been pointed out that numbers should not be the realm of the politician, but the realm of the target planner. I disagree. The target planners come up with the numbers on the basis of political guidance, for God's sake!"

The enduring devotion to nuclear deterrence theory was evident at a two-day conference on the subject cohosted by the Hoover Institution and NTI and organized by Shultz, Drell, and Jim Goodby in late 2010, and attended by Perry, Kissinger, and Nunn. The participants were, by and large, reform-minded deterrence experts, but even this group struggled to escape the grip of Cold War theory. Patrick Morgan, a defense specialist at the University of California, Irvine, only half jokingly referred to the doctrine as "The Thing." Jonathan Schell compared the challenge of coming up with a new defense paradigm to finding a way out of the labyrinth. Richard Perle, one of the fiercest defenders of the nuclear faith during the Cold War, told the group he was surprised at the persistence of Cold War thinking in the room. He argued that still talking about launch-on-warning, a Cold War issue, was lunacy. He said that the days are gone when the United States should be worrying about how many weapons survive a Russian first strike, and that focusing on nuclear arms reductions is a distraction from the urgent threat of nuclear-armed terrorists.

Harald Müller, director of the Peace Research Institute Frankfurt, put it provocatively at the conference: "Deterrence is not just a strategy, it is a social relationship built on institutionalized distrust and worst-case thinking under the assumption of actual or potential enmity. It is maintained by an extensive institutional and physical infrastructure which reproduces itself into eternity by the production of enemy analyses at home and the production of distrust abroad."

President Obama waded into the nuclear deterrence thicket when his administration conducted a reassessment of United States nuclear policy and forces. The Pentagon, not exactly a hotbed of new thinking about nuclear forces, led the review. Realizing the study could set a new policy framework for American nuclear forces, Bill Perry and Sam Nunn, working with fellow Democrats in the White House and Pentagon, did the best they could to persuade the administration to rethink nuclear policy. Their efforts were not entirely successful. The Nuclear Posture Review, as the report was called, vividly reflected the compromises required to hold the support of the nuclear old guard.

It made some significant course corrections. The review started by emphasizing the threat of nuclear terrorism and the spread of nuclear weapons and technology, issues not treated so prominently in similar reviews by earlier administrations. The report said:

"As President Obama has made clear, today's most immediate and extreme danger is nuclear terrorism. Al Qaeda and their extremist allies are seeking nuclear weapons. We must assume they would use such weapons if they managed to obtain them. The vulnerability to theft or seizure of vast stocks of such nuclear materials around the world, and the availability of sensitive equipment and technologies in the nuclear black market, create a serious risk that terrorists may acquire what they need to build a nuclear weapon.

"Today's other pressing threat is nuclear proliferation. Additional countries—especially those at odds with the United States, its allies and partners, and the broader international community—may acquire nuclear weapons."

It also acknowledged, "The massive nuclear arsenal we inherited from the Cold War era of bipolar military confrontation is poorly suited to address the challenges posed by suicidal terrorists and unfriendly regimes seeking nuclear weapons. Therefore, it is essential that we better align our nuclear policies and posture to our most urgent priorities—preventing nuclear terrorism and nuclear proliferation."

The review wisely pulled back from the Bush administration's excessively aggressive reliance on nuclear weapons as the ultimate retaliation against an enemy that attacked the United States with chemical or biological weapons. And more broadly, it stepped gingerly toward diminishing America's reliance on nuclear weapons to deter attacks. But it stopped short of declaring that the use of nuclear weapons would be reserved solely to counter a nuclear attack. This was a source of contention in the administration, and proponents of a more progressive policy, including Bill Perry, had to settle for the statement that Washington would only consider the use of nuclear weapons in "extreme circumstances" to defend its vital interests and those of its allies.

In a corollary assertion, the review said Washington would not use or threaten to use nuclear weapons against nonnuclear states that adhere to the Nuclear Non-Proliferation Treaty—an assurance to most nations but a pointed warning to North Korea and prospectively to Iran.

But the review was still suffused with Cold War thinking and failed, in some instances, to advance the enlightened policy goals that Obama outlined in Prague in 2009.

Thanks to the review, nearly all of America's 450 land-based Minuteman III long-range, nuclear-tipped missiles will remain on alert, meaning they can be launched within minutes if the president gives the order. (The missiles are being stripped of their multiple-warhead clusters, a process known as deMIRVing.) The alert status may have been desirable when nuclear war with the Soviet Union seemed possible, but it's hard to imagine a contingency today when the United States would need to launch hundreds of missiles in an instant. The bristling posture of so many missiles needlessly keeps the nuclear balance between the United States and Russia on a razor's edge and risks an accidental or unauthorized launch.

If the idea, in part, is to have the missiles ready to use against a target other than Russia, the alert status makes even less sense. One defense planner said, "There is no target we can address without overflying Russia, just because of the physical location. So that basically takes them out of the game for anything, other than calling up Russia and saying, 'Hey, we're going to launch a couple hundred of these over the top of you. Don't worry about it; just duck.'"

In another Cold War anachronism, Washington will retain a three-pronged nuclear offense, relying on land- and submarine-based missiles and bombers to deliver nuclear weapons during a conflict. It's hard to believe, but fifty years after a nuclear-armed B-52 bomber cruised menacingly across movie screens in *Dr. Strangelove*, seventy-six of the hulking airplanes, refurbished over the years, remain in service to carry nuclear weapons. The Navy will maintain fourteen Ohio-class submarines, behemoths of the sea that are each outfitted with twenty-four nuclear-tipped Trident missiles.

The justification for maintaining the triad seems unhinged from the realities of today's threats, or any likely to develop in coming decades. General Chilton, the strategic forces commander, defended the system. "The triad's existence was developed to really make sure that the Soviets, and today any potential adversary, would never mistakenly assume that they could, with a preemptive attack, disarm the United States and not suffer a devastating retaliation blow." He said, "That was the purpose of the triad, that you had a survivable leg, you had a responsive leg."

But other than Russia, which no longer is an enemy, what country today has the offensive firepower to wipe out America's land-based missiles? The answer: none.

Chilton argued that the redundancies in the triad remain an important element of American defense planning. He said, "You could imagine if you had a problem with your submarine leg of your triad, whether it be with the warheads or the boats themselves, you could re-alert B-52s and you would still sustain a survivable leg of the triad that would deter an adversary from thinking they could decapitate you or neutralize your retaliatory capability."

It all sounds as if the Cold War never ended and the United States still faces the possibility of a decapitating nuclear attack. Moreover, the idea that all the Ohio-class submarines or their Trident missiles could be simultaneously immobilized seems outlandish.

Pitching the triad forward, the 2010 nuclear review reaffirmed plans to develop a new generation of missile-equipped submarines and new solid-fuel rocket motors to propel future missiles. Keeping the defense industrial base up to speed with technological advances makes sense, but the Pentagon has a knack for throwing money at ill-conceived, mismanaged projects that does not bode well for costly new investments in nuclear forces.

For Shultz, Kissinger, Perry, Nunn, and Drell, the Nuclear Posture Review was a positive step, but it was far from a road map to abolition.

IF THE UNITED States ever sweeps away its Cold War cobwebs, how could it and other countries manage a nuclear countdown to zero? And once there, how could they sustain a nonnuclear equilibrium?

Realizing that answers to these questions are a precondition for nuclear disarmament, Shultz and his partners have spent a good deal of time trying to come up with sensible suggestions for what nuclear specialists call end-state issues. The ideas they are exploring are far from perfect or comprehensive, but they do suggest there is a way forward.

The five men start with a phased drawdown of American and Russian weapons that eventually expands to include other nuclear-armed nations. They imagine a reconsideration of defense strategy to make it less dependent on nuclear weapons and favor new technical measures that can verify the elimination of nuclear weapons and the maintenance of a nonnuclear state.

A core problem is adapting deterrence theory to a nonnuclear world. Bernard Brodie, one of the first and most influential nuclear weapons theorists, accurately predicted the shape of nuclear deterrence not long after the 1945 surrender of Japan. He said, "Thus far the chief purpose of our military establishment has been to win wars. From now on its chief purpose must be to avert them. It can have almost no other useful purpose."

Yet, while it is true, as General Chilton suggested, that the presence of nuclear weapons has inhibited global war, and the blockbuster American and Soviet arsenals sustained an uneasy Cold War peace, a great deal of blood has been shed in local and regional military conflicts since the bomb was invented. Nuclear weapons did not prevent the Korean War or the Vietnam War, nor the Soviet invasion of Afghanistan or Saddam Hussein's occupation of Kuwait. Moreover, a nuclear deterrent is also only as credible as the prospect that nuclear weapons would actually be used, and there is only the barest chance today that the United States would fire its weapons in self-defense. That seems especially so given the nature of current threats—trying to retaliate against al-Qaeda with a nuclear volley makes little sense.

That means the United States is left with an overwhelmingly powerful arsenal of weapons for which there is no obvious target, and a deterrence strategy that lacks credibility. We are like a muscle-bound giant. As Shultz, Drell, and Jim Goodby have noted, "Much has changed in the past twenty years, yet the basic concepts about how deterrence works have changed hardly at all in the popular imagination and even in a number of official statements about national policy. Conventional concepts about deterrence need to be reconsidered in the context of the specific contemporary threats our nation faces. Otherwise, national security policies will become detached from the reality that they are devised to influence, and our national security will become endangered."

What to do? Shultz, Kissinger, Perry, and Nunn gave their answer in another *Wall Street Journal* op-ed article in March 2011. As with the three earlier *Journal* articles, it took weeks of discussion and numerous drafts to come to agreement. They haggled for two weeks over the use of one word in the essay before settling on a final version that could be submitted to the *Journal*. The nub of their assessment: "Nations should move forward together with a series of conceptual and practical steps toward deterrence that do not rely primarily on nuclear weapons or nuclear threats to maintain international peace and security."

Shultz and his colleagues did not go into detail, but it would seem logical that the United States and Russia should scale back to a modest number of weapons more relevant to today's threat, and no longer pivot defense strategy around the threat of massive nuclear retaliation. America's conventional military forces, even if they are reduced over time, can provide ample firepower to defend the country and look after its interests abroad. And new technologies, such as hypersonic weapons that can deliver powerful conventional warheads to distant targets, are on the drawing board. Using a conventional intercontinental missile for that purpose sounds appealing on paper. Such a missile strike, for instance, might have reached the Afghan redoubt where Osama bin Laden was sighted in 1998 in time to kill him. The subsonic cruise missiles fired at President Clinton's order arrived too late. But launching long-range missiles runs the risk that Russia would think it was coming under attack as ballistic missiles headed in its direction.

If the nuclear deterrence spell can be broken, the path to nuclear disarmament will look more navigable. Reconstitution is likely to be a central element of any approach. A host of difficult issues are associated with reconstitution. One involves the terms of an international treaty that would govern a zero world, including permissible reconstitution enterprises. Another issue is how to monitor nuclear arsenals as they come down toward zero, and at zero, and how to ensure that reconstitution facilities operate within treaty limits. These can be arcane matters that scientists like Drell are exploring and are grist for niche publications like *Nuclear Weapons Journal*, which is published by the Los Alamos National Laboratory.

The science of arms monitoring has come a long way since the 1940s and early '50s, when the United States dispatched manned aircraft along the periphery of the Soviet Union hoping to get a glimpse of military installations inside its borders. The U-2 spy plane gave Washington a deeper look inside the Soviet Union from 1956 to 1960. Since then, spy satellites have provided a torrent of data by photographing and using other surveillance technologies while orbiting overhead. In recent years, more intrusive practices have been employed, including on-site inspections of military bases and missile factories. Ronald Reagan never tired of using the phrase "Trust but verify" when discussing arms control issues.

Edward M. Ifft, a former State Department on-site arms inspector and an expert on these matters, imagines four stages of monitoring and verifying a zero world. At stage one, the starting point for final reductions would have to be confirmed—if the number of warheads or delivery vehicles that a nation starts with were unknown, counting down to zero would be impossible. Then the retirement and dismantlement of warheads, or at least their separation from delivery systems like missiles, would have to be meticulously tracked. Next, the removal and storage or disposal of fissile material must be monitored. Last, surveillance would be required to ensure that reconstitution activities—at defense labs, bomb-making facilities, missile bases, and so on—did not exceed international limits.

The United States and other nations have some experience monitoring these sorts of things, but the degree of difficulty would be much higher in dealing with a countdown to zero and reconstitution facilities and materials. Drell and Goodby described a few techniques involved: "National technical means [satellites], data exchanges, on-site inspections (both routine ones and those prompted by a challenge), perimeter and portal continuous monitoring, tags and seals, sensors and detection devices to monitor nuclear activity and the resulting effluents, remote viewing as conducted already by the International Atomic

Energy Agency, and—no less important—human intelligence, or good old-fashioned spying."

In 2011, Drell and Christopher Stubbs, a Harvard physicist, came up with an ingenious proposal to expand aerial surveillance already conducted under the 2002 Open Skies Treaty. Dwight Eisenhower suggested in 1955 that countries open their skies to aerial surveillance of military installations by other nations but the Kremlin quickly rejected the idea. It was reborn after the Cold War. There have been more than 750 such flights involving dozens of countries since 2002. In 2010, the United States conducted fourteen Open Skies flights over Russia, and Russia conducted six in American airspace. Airmen and technical crews from both nations participated in both sets of flights.

Drell and Stubbs suggested that the practice could be used to monitor various aspects of a zero treaty and reconstitution activities. Flights, for instance, could be used to sample atmospheric gases and particulates that can signal the production of fissile materials. Aerial surveillance could also provide higher resolution images of ground facilities than spy satellites do. Exotic new monitoring technologies may appear in coming years, including laser-based techniques to detect uranium and its compounds from afar.

Their work fits nicely into the approach that Shultz, Kissinger, Perry, Nunn, and Drell have taken since the first *Wall Street Journal* article. "We have always insisted on saying, 'Let us test each proposition and see how it actually works and see whether it can be made to work,'" Kissinger said. "And we have not come to a point yet where one could say, 'It's unworkable.' And that I consider great progress."

ON A MILD early-spring evening in 2011, George Shultz, Bill Perry, and Sam Nunn made their way to Capitol Hill for a screening of *Nuclear Tipping Point* at the Library of Congress. James Billington, an esteemed historian who has directed the library for more than twenty years, invited members of Congress to the gathering in the ornate Members' Room at the Thomas Jefferson Building, just down the block from the Supreme Court. Following the screening, Shultz, Perry, and Nunn would field questions from lawmakers.

A grand total of two House members showed up, and one left right after the screening. Shultz and Perry had traveled from California just to attend the event. The failure of lawmakers to show up—a dozen or so congressional staff members did appear—reflected a general braking of the momentum that Shultz and his partners had generated so effectively over the past few years. Prospects for Senate ratification of the test-ban treaty seemed uncertain, at best. The White House was considering how to advance Obama's nuclear agenda in the months before the 2012 presidential election. Absent Senate action on the test-ban treaty, or tangible progress with Russia on the next set of nuclear arms reduction issues, the most promising arena was the continuing effort to lock down vulnerable fissile materials overseas. South Korea will host a second nuclear summit in March 2012 designed to reinforce efforts to reach the goals set at the forty-seven-nation gathering Obama hosted in Washington in 2010.

After the Library of Congress event, Shultz and his partners regrouped over dinner at the Hay-Adams Hotel, across Lafayette Square from the White House. They seemed undeterred. The next milestone for them was a May conference in London organized by Des Browne, a former British defense secretary who has taken the lead in mobilizing European support for the abolition initiative. Rather than being deflated, Shultz, Nunn, and Perry brainstormed with NTI executives about other steps they could take to spur new action. Back in California the next afternoon, Shultz and Perry headed directly from the airport to Stanford to resume work on their initiative.

The London meeting gave a new jolt of energy to the disarmament campaign. A large contingent of former and current

defense and diplomatic officials from more than a dozen nations, including Australia, Britain, China, Denmark, Germany, India, Italy, Japan, Pakistan, Russia, and the United
States, converged on Lancaster House for the two-day gathering. NTI and the Hoover Institution cohosted the meeting
with Browne's organization, the European Leadership Network
for Multilateral Nuclear Disarmament and Non-proliferation
(ELN). The theme was "Deterrence: Its Past and Future."

The conference setting, the Great Gallery in Lancaster House,
imparted a sense of grandeur to the discussion as the two dozen or so
participants conferred under a vaulted ceiling and gilded columns.
The former officials discussed an array of nuclear policy issues and
practical steps to reduce nuclear threats, including removing more
American and Russian intercontinental missiles from high-alert
status, downsizing nuclear arsenals, and securing fissile materials.

Barriers to disarmament were evident as General Jehangir
Karamat, the former chairman of Pakistan's Joint Chiefs of Staff,
and General V. R. Raghavan, a former top Indian officer, verbally
sparred over their national interests and mutual enmity. Giving
up nuclear weapons was not a goal either man seemed seriously
willing to entertain, but as Nunn observed during a break in the
discussion, simply getting the two men in the same room to talk
about nuclear arms was an encouraging step.

Malcolm Rifkind, former British foreign secretary and defense minister, delivered a rousing dinner address, paying tribute
to Shultz, Kissinger, Perry, and Nunn for reviving interest in the
cause of nuclear disarmament. As the meeting broke up, Nunn
headed to Moscow for further discussions with Russian officials.

In his autumn course on technology and national security,
Bill Perry can turn emotional as he talks about his career and the
United States, which he calls "the country I love so much and to
which I owe so much."

He likes to leave students with a parting thought. He calls it "a benediction." He begins with a quotation from John F. Kennedy: "Too many of us think that it is impossible to contain proliferation. But that is a dangerous and defeatist belief. It leads to the conclusion that nuclear terrorism or nuclear war is inevitable; that we are gripped by forces that we cannot control.

"We need not accept that view. Our problems are man-made; and therefore they can be solved by man."

Perry goes on, "I would amend Kennedy's statement only to say that the solutions must come from men and women."

Then, as he packs up his papers, he says: "My generation was responsible for building up this fearsome nuclear arsenal. And my generation has now started the task of dismantling it. But we will not be able to finish this task. So we will have to pass the baton on to your generation."

Perry might have added a parting thought from Kissinger, who has said, "Once nuclear weapons are used, we will be driven to take global measures to prevent it. So some of us have said, let's ask ourselves, 'If we have to do it afterwards, why don't we do it now?'"

ACKNOWLEDGMENTS

Book writing is at once the most singular and social of disciplines. Singular because there is no intermediary between writer and pen or keyboard. Social because the gathering of information for a nonfiction book like this one requires interaction with hundreds of people from the principal characters to the anonymous staff member who disappears into the recesses of a repository of historical papers to locate an invaluable document. I relied on the good advice and indispensable assistance of dozens of people during the three years I worked on this book.

Gabriela Aoun, my research assistant from start to finish, was my irreplaceable partner in this enterprise. She jumped to the head of a long line of qualified applicants by politely but firmly pressing her case, and that same quiet determination proved to be one of many attributes as we dug into the careers of George Shultz, Henry Kissinger, Bill Perry, Sam Nunn, and Sid Drell. Gabriela, a Princeton graduate, provided critical assistance in every phase of the project. Her fine research skills produced dozens of carefully organized binders packed with historical materials, many drawn from long hours burrowing into archival collections. Her research reports on various aspects of Cold War history and nuclear weapons policy were acute and well written. Her thoughtful advice about the shape and scope of the book helped to bring a sprawling project into focus. Once I began writing, Gabriela critiqued draft chapters with an insightful eye for both thematic points and fine-grain detail. Along the way she was invariably collegial and effervescent. Gabriela's great character and values defined everything she did.

I am grateful to George Shultz, Henry Kissinger, Bill Perry, Sam Nunn, and Sid Drell for cooperating with Gabriela's and my research work. They cleared time on their busy calendars for numerous interviews, invited me to countless public and private appearances, and welcomed me on several overseas expeditions. They understood from the outset that I would exercise sole control over the content of the book and never challenged that principle, even when it was clear that reporting for the book involved historical and policy matters they would have preferred not to exhume. Shultz, Nunn, and Drell provided access to previously closed personal archives and other historical materials, including, in Nunn's case, an oral history he prepared as his service in the Senate neared an end. These proved to be rich resources that helped to fill out the chronicles of their careers.

Aides to each of the men were most helpful: Susan Schendel, who works with Shultz; Deborah Gordon, Perry's executive aide; Bonnie Rose, in Drell's office; and Jessee Leporin, on Kissinger's staff. Paige Mathes, who handled much of the administrative and record-keeping work involved with the nuclear disarmament initiative at the Hoover Institution, helped Gabriela and me in countless ways.

Sam Nunn's colleagues at the Nuclear Threat Initiative (NTI) provided assistance on many fronts, including a reconstruction of meetings, conversations, and correspondence that led to the 2007 *Wall Street Journal* op-ed article that launched the nuclear initiative. Charles Curtis, Joan Rohlfing, Deborah Rosenblum, Steve Andreasen, and Isabelle Williams at NTI were unfailingly helpful. Cathy Gwin, who has worked with Nunn for years, was figuratively at my side every step of the way, opening doors in Washington and Atlanta, excavating Senate history, keeping me apprised of new developments, and clearing the way for me to attend closed events in the United States and abroad. Cathy is one of the most capable and fair-minded public affairs executives I have dealt with over four decades of reporting in Washington.

I am indebted to Vartan Gregorian, the president of the Carnegie Corporation of New York, who contributed pivotal financial support. Vartan and Stephen Del Rosso, director of Carnegie's International Peace and Security Program, approved a grant at a critical moment when my funding resources were near depletion. Carnegie also supported my previous book on spy satellites.

My colleagues at Stanford University supported the project in tangible and intangible ways. Chip Blacker, director of the Freeman Spogli Institute for International Studies (FSI), encouraged me to do the book and provided the financial assistance that made it possible to have a full-time research assistant. John Raisian, director of the Hoover Institution, welcomed me to Stanford and worked with Chip to help get me settled at FSI.

My academic home at Stanford for the past three years has been the Center for International Security and Cooperation (CISAC), which is part of FSI. Scott Sagan and Sig Hecker, CISAC codirectors, welcomed me to the center as a consulting professor and provided workspace for Gabriela and me. What a home it has been! CISAC is populated with nuclear weapons experts, starting with Scott, one of the nation's leading scholars on nuclear weapons policy, and Sig, who ran the Los Alamos National Laboratory for years before coming to Stanford. Both men generously shared their knowledge with me and made me feel at home. Tino Cuellar, who succeeded Scott as codirector in 2011, reaffirmed the warm welcome. Lynn Eden, CISAC's research director and a nuclear weapons expert in her own right, offered expertise and wise counsel. David Holloway, historian and nuclear policy expert, graciously pointed me to research materials and guided me through the arcane world of nuclear weapons. Liz Gardner, who keeps CISAC humming as administrative chief, helped smooth my transition from journalism to the academy. Tracy Hill made the logistics of CISAC look easy. I am also grateful to the many other CISAC colleagues who offered a helping hand.

My return to Stanford after forty years in journalism was made all the more pleasant and productive by the welcome I received from John Hennessy, Stanford's president, and John Etchemendy, the provost. Gerhard Casper, who served as Stanford president from 1992 to 2000, played a key role in helping me get the book project launched and anchored at Stanford.

I had the good fortune to find three excellent part-time research assistants who worked with Gabriela intermittently, in each case for a few months. Kolby Hanson, now on assignment for Teach For America, tackled George Shultz's early years and wartime service; Niko Milonopoulos delved into Henry Kissinger's handling of nuclear weapons policy; and Jason Saltoun-Ebin scoured the Reagan Library for materials related to George Shultz's service as secretary of state. The dozens of interviews conducted for this project were transcribed by Christine Sinnott.

A number of former colleagues in the Washington bureau of the *New York Times* shared information and insights with me, including Peter Baker, Elisabeth Bumiller, Helene Cooper, Mark Mazzetti, David Sanger, Eric Schmitt, Scott Shane, and Thom Shanker.

This book is built in part on the research and analytical work of the many men and women who examined Cold War history and the nuclear age long before I began this project. Their books and essays appear in the bibliography. My book would not have been possible without their work. Those to whom I am especially indebted include Richard Rhodes, whose four-volume history of the nuclear age is the starting point for any historical exploration of the period, and Richard Reeves, whose books about the Kennedy, Nixon, and Reagan presidencies are filled with illuminating information. My thanks, too, to Barton Bernstein, the Stanford historian who set me on my own journey through nuclear history during my senior year at the university, when I wrote a paper for him about Robert Oppenheimer, the scientific director of the Manhattan Project.

A host of former and current government officials spent time with me reviewing Cold War history and more contemporary affairs, and telling me about their dealings with the five principal characters in the book. So, too, did many men and women who worked with Shultz, Kissinger, Perry, Nunn, and Drell in other roles. Those who spoke for the record are listed. Those who could not speak for attribution because they discussed sensitive or classified information, or felt they could not speak candidly about the five men for the record, are not named. The information gleaned from all the interviews was essential to assembling the book.

The National Security Archive at George Washington University maintains a trove of declassified government papers, including voluminous files involving national security decision making during the Cold War. Tom Blanton, the director, and his colleagues guided Gabriela and me through the archive's collections, many of which are assembled and analyzed in thoughtful electronic briefing books. William Burr, a senior analyst, has edited several invaluable collections about nuclear weapons policy during the Cold War.

Half a dozen intrepid experts in the field agreed to read draft chapters of my book or the entire manuscript. I am grateful for their suggestions, and the opportunity they gave me to correct mistakes and misperceptions. The group included Scott Sagan and David Holloway at Stanford, and Bud Wheelon, the founding director of the CIA's science and technology directorate. I first encountered Bud when researching my book about spy satellites. Joseph Martz, a senior scientist at Los Alamos National Laboratory, checked several chapters for technical accuracy. I met Joe when he turned up one day in the office next to mine at CISAC, where he spent a year as a visiting fellow. Needless to say, any errors that remain are solely my responsibility.

Ever since we worked together for Clay Felker at *Esquire* in the late 1970s, Binky Urban has been my indispensable guide to the publishing world and an astute evaluator of my book ideas. When I first broached the idea for this book to Binky in 2008, she smartly tossed back my draft proposal with instructions to start over again. She was quite right. But even in that ill-defined draft, Binky recognized the potential for a book and encouraged me to pursue it. No one knows the book business better than Binky and I have repeatedly benefited from her sound advice and loyal friendship.

Tim Duggan at HarperCollins embraced the improved book proposal from the outset. His enthusiasm for the project was contagious. Once he got a look at the manuscript, he made many fine suggestions and his deft editing improved the book in innumerable ways from the narrative architecture and biographical portraits of the five men to the analysis of nuclear weapons policy. I first heard from Tim when I was still at the *Times*. His encouraging notes always raised my spirits and opened the way to a productive and enjoyable collaboration. Tim's colleague, Emily Cunningham, was most helpful as we moved through the editing and production process.

No group was more important to the project than my family. My brother, William Taubman, a Cold War scholar and Pulitzer Prize–winning biographer, generously informed my work with his insights and information. Michael and Greg Taubman, my sons, provided unflagging encouragement. Felicity Barringer, my wife of four decades, was my constant supporter, sounding board, and discerning adviser. Her editing suggestions helped me sharpen and refine the book. Felicity patiently endured the many weekends

I absented myself from outdoor recreation in the California sunshine to concentrate on the book. I like to think my weekend vanishing act abetted her training for a hundred-mile bike ride along the California coast from Carmel to the Hearst Castle at San Simeon in September 2010. I followed behind by car that day, awed by her strength and stamina.

Stanford, California
October 2011

NOTES

PREFACE

x **The article proposed:** George P. Shultz, William J. Perry, Henry A. Kissinger, and Sam Nunn, "A World Free of Nuclear Weapons," *Wall Street Journal*, Jan. 4, 2007.

xiv **A high-powered international commission:** Gareth Evans and Yoriko Kawaguchi, cochairs, "Eliminating Nuclear Threats: A Practical Agenda for Global Policymakers," International Commission on Nuclear Non-Proliferation and Disarmament, November 2009. Bill Perry served as a commission member.

xvi **Despite American and Russian efforts:** Roughly speaking, there are 2,100 tons of bomb-grade fissile material stored in various places around the world, enough to make thousands of nuclear weapons. Most of it is securely stored in the United States and Russia, but enough remains at inadequately protected sites in other countries to make dozens of weapons.

xvi **"If you were to ask":** Robert Gates interview, Aug. 7, 2009.

xviii **"Our age has stolen":** Henry Kissinger, "Our Nuclear Nightmare," *Newsweek*, Feb. 7, 2009.

CHAPTER ONE

5 **"candyass":** Walter Isaacson, David Beckwith, and Dick Thompson, "Shultz: Thinker and Doer," *Time*, July 5, 1982.

5 **In 1996, Osama bin Laden addressed:** The poem said:

Oh William, tomorrow you will be informed
As to which young man will face your swaggering brother
A youngster enters the midst of battle smiling, and
Retreats with his spearhead stained with blood.

Quoted in Steve Coll, *Ghost Wars: The Secret History of the CIA, Afghanistan, and Bin Laden, from the Soviet Invasion to September 10, 2011* (New York: Penguin, 2005), p. 10.

8   **Federation of Atomic Scientists:** The Federation of Atomic Scientists is now called the Federation of American Scientists.

8   **pithy films:** *On the Beach* was directed by Stanley Kramer and released in 1959. *Dr. Strangelove or: How I Learned to Stop Worrying and Love the Bomb* was directed by Stanley Kubrick and released in 1964.

8   **"to provide hope for":** "The Challenge of Peace: God's Promise and Our Response," Pastoral Letter on War and Peace by the National Conference of Catholic Bishops, May 3, 1983.

8   **"Today, every inhabitant":** President John F. Kennedy before the United Nations General Assembly, Sept. 25, 1961, UCSB American Presidency Project.

9   **"pursue negotiations":** Treaty on the Non-Proliferation of Nuclear Weapons, Article VI, www.state.gov/t/isn/trty/16281.htm.

9   **"This is a very reassuring":** Lyndon Johnson, press conference, White House, July 1, 1968, UCSB American Presidency Project.

9   **"elimination of all nuclear":** Jimmy Carter, Inaugural Address, Jan. 20, 1977, UCSB American Presidency Project.

9   **In 1963, John Kennedy predicted:** President John F. Kennedy, News Conference, Washington, DC, Mar. 21, 1963, John F. Kennedy Library and Museum, www.jfklibrary.org/Research/Ready-Reference/Press-Conferences/News-Conference-52.aspx. Robert S. McNamara, President Kennedy's defense secretary, had prepared a memo for the president a few weeks earlier outlining his expectations for the spread of nuclear nations. It included a table listing the nations that McNamara and his aides thought might become nuclear weapons states in the years ahead. The nations considered most likely to do so were China, Egypt, Israel, and West Germany. Nations regarded as less likely included Australia, Belgium, Brazil, Canada, India, Italy, Japan, Netherlands, Norway, Sweden, and Switzerland. U.S. secretary of defense Robert McNamara to President John F. Kennedy, "The Diffusion of Nuclear Weapons with and without a Test Ban Agreement," memorandum, Feb. 12, 1963, Digital National Security Archive (DNSA), document no. NP00941.

10   **"More powerful than the tread":** Victor Hugo. The actual quote: "All the forces in the world are not so powerful as an idea whose time has come."

10   **"I don't think anybody":** Barack Obama, Remarks by the President in the Oval Office, May 19, 2009, White House transcript.

11   **"This very institution":** Barack Obama, Remarks to the UN Security Council on Non-Proliferation and Nuclear Disarmament, Sept. 24, 2009, White House transcript.

11   **"We were just sitting in the corner":** Sam Nunn comment to author, Dec. 20, 2010.

12   **"Thank you so much":** George H. W. Bush letter to George Shultz, Mar.

7, 2007, Nuclear Security Project archives, Office of George Shultz, Stanford University.

12   **"I know all four of us"**: George Shultz remarks at Millennium Hotel dinner, New York, Sept. 24, 2009.

13   **"It was in some ways"**: William J. Perry remarks at Millennium Hotel dinner, New York, Sept. 24, 2009.

14   **"The dividing line"**: James Schlesinger remarks at the 2010 Strategic Deterrence Symposium, Strategic Command (STRATCOM), Omaha, NE, Aug. 11, 2010.

14   **"We agree that the strongest"**: John Deutch and Harold Brown, "The Nuclear Disarmament Fantasy," *Wall Street Journal*, Nov. 19, 2007.

14   **"All four of us"**: George Shultz interview, Aug. 25, 2008.

15   **"He's the best man"**: As told by McGeorge Bundy to Father Bryan J. Hehir and subsequently quoted by Hehir in his remarks at the Center for International Security and Cooperation's Annual Drell Lecture, "The Politics and Ethics of Nonproliferation," Stanford University, Dec. 6, 2005.

17   **"Some people take"**: Sam Nunn in *Nuclear Tipping Point*, written and directed by Ben Goddard, Nuclear Security Project, 2010.

18   **"My generation was responsible"**: William J. Perry remarks before Management Science and Engineering 193 class, Stanford University, Oct. 27, 2009.

18   **"I think Samuel Johnson"**: Albert "Bud" Wheelon interview, Mar. 21, 2009. The actual quote from Johnson reads, "Depend upon it, Sir, when a man knows he is to be hanged in a fortnight, it concentrates his mind wonderfully." James Boswell, *The Life of Samuel Johnson* (New York: Penguin Classics, 1986).

CHAPTER TWO

20   **Prime Minister David Cameron:** The Prime Minister's office confirmed that the meeting with Prime Minister Cameron and Chancellor Osborne took place.

20   **"He's blown hot"**: James Goodby interview, July 1, 2009.

20   **"I had never learned"**: George P. Shultz, *Turmoil and Triumph: My Years as Secretary of State* (New York: Charles Scribner's Sons, 1993), p. 780.

21   **"were insane, just insane"**: George Shultz remarks at ninetieth birthday gala, San Francisco, Dec. 13, 2010.

21   **"spiritual father of this enterprise"**: Henry Kissinger remarks at the American Academy in Berlin, Feb. 3, 2010.

21   **"I think it probably did"**: Goodby interview, July 1, 2009.

21   **"I'm very optimistic"**: George Shultz remarks at the Global Zero Summit, Paris, Feb. 2, 2010.

21   **"Bill sees his great success"**: Harold Brown interview, July 8, 2009.

22   **"That's the way it read to me"**: George Shultz interview, July 1, 2009.

22 **"I saw my duty"**: William J. Perry interview, Feb. 22, 2011.

23 **"I think he very quickly"**: Goodby interview, July 1, 2009.

24 **"I confess when it started"**: Henry Kissinger interview, conducted by *Nuclear Tipping Point* filmmakers, Mar. 14, 2010, Nuclear Threat Initiative.

24 **"Henry's always hard"**: Brown interview, July 8, 2009.

24 **"He's told me that, too"**: Perry interview, Feb. 22, 2011.

25 **"Well, he signed it"**: George Shultz interview, Aug. 27, 2010.

25 **"First, let's remember"**: Nunn statement to author, Dec. 20, 2010.

26 **"Both Sam and I"**: Kissinger interview, Jan. 27, 2009.

26 **"Henry Kissinger did more"**: Goodby interview, July 1, 2009.

27 **"You've got to seek"**: Sidney Drell interview, Feb. 14, 2011.

27 **In 1983 he cofounded the Center:** The center was later renamed the Center for International Security and Cooperation. Drell quit the center in 1989 after the university refused to give it the authority to appoint faculty members.

28 **"I appreciate the kind remarks"**: Henry Kissinger dinner remarks at Hoover Institution conference, "Deterrence: Its Past and Future," Stanford University, Nov. 11, 2010.

28 **"Is Sam Nunn too smart"**: Phil Gailey, "Sam Nunn's Rising Star," *New York Times Magazine*, Jan. 4, 1987.

29 **"I read every word"**: Sam Nunn interview, Nov. 18, 2008.

29 **"How about this"**: Stephen Colbert and Sam Nunn, *The Colbert Report*, Comedy Central, June 9, 2010.

30 **"Soviet strategy"**: Richard M. Nixon and Henry A. Kissinger, "An Arms Agreement—On Two Conditions," *Washington Post*, Apr. 26, 1987.

30 **"He stressed that the Reagan"**: Anatoly Dobrynin, *In Confidence: Moscow's Ambassador to America's Six Cold War Presidents 1962–1986* (New York: Times Books, 1995), p. 548.

31 **"if I could choose one"**: Henry Kissinger, *Years of Upheaval* (Boston: Little, Brown, 1982), p. 81.

31 **"They're entitled to their opinions"**: Shultz interview, July 1, 2009.

31 **"Henry loves to manipulate things"**: George Shultz dinner remarks at Hoover Institution conference, "Deterrence: Its Past and Future," Stanford University, Nov. 11, 2010.

31 **"I have to say that"**: Henry Kissinger dinner remarks at Hoover Institution conference, "Deterrence: Its Past and Future," Stanford University, Nov. 11, 2010.

32 **"constitutional crisis"**: Michael R. Gordon, "Reagan Is Warned by Senator Nunn Over ABM Treaty," *New York Times*, Feb. 7, 1987.

32 **"He's a much better golfer"**: Shultz interview, Aug. 27, 2010.

32 **"pretty good golfer"**: Nunn interview, Sept. 1, 2010.

32   **"It was a complex game":** Elisabeth Bumiller, "Gentle George and The Quiet Roar," *Washington Post*, Dec. 14, 1982.

32   **"You get away with":** George Shultz comment to author, Dec. 11, 2010.

33   **Perry's 1994 confirmation hearing:** Bill Clinton nominated William J. Perry to succeed Les Aspin as defense secretary after his first choice, Admiral Bobby Ray Inman, a former director of the National Security Agency and deputy director of the CIA, withdrew from consideration.

33   **"I don't seek publicity":** Perry interview, Feb. 22, 2011.

34   **"cc" line:** E-mail from Sam Nunn, Oct. 24, 2008. The author received a copy.

35   **"Sid, we've come a long way":** Drell comment to author, Apr. 2008.

36   **"We are in a race":** Sam Nunn, "The Race Between Cooperation and Catastrophe," remarks before the National Press Club, Mar. 9, 2005.

CHAPTER THREE

37   **dubbed "Little Boy" by its American makers:** The account of the Hiroshima project was taken in 2009 from the Department of Energy's history of the Manhattan Project, www.cfo.doe.gov/me70/manhattan/hiroshima.htm. The page is no longer available on the DOE website.

39   **"Today, the Cold War":** Barack Obama remarks in Hradcany Square, Prague, Apr. 5, 2009, White House transcript.

39   **The danger is likely:** William J. Broad, "Laser Advances in Nuclear Fuel Stir Terror Fear," *New York Times*, Aug. 20, 2011.

40   **"When this first bomb":** William Perry interview, Aug. 14, 2008.

40   **"The downtown area":** Ashton B. Carter, Michael M. May, and William J. Perry, "The Day After: Action Following a Nuclear Blast in a U.S. City," *Washington Quarterly*, Autumn 2007, pp. 5–6.

41   **"low-probability, high-impact":** Perry interview, Aug. 14, 2008.

41   **"It's the remote":** Perry interview, Aug. 14, 2008.

41   **"We have to get past":** William J. Broad, "New Advice on the Unthinkable: How to Survive a Nuclear Bomb," *New York Times*, Dec. 16, 2010.

42   *Securing the Bomb:* Matthew Bunn, *Securing the Bomb 2010: Securing All Nuclear Materials in Four Years*, Project on Managing the Atom, Belfer Center for Science and International Affairs, John F. Kennedy School of Government, Harvard University; commissioned by the Nuclear Threat Initiative, Apr. 2010, p. v.

44   **The Baader-Meinhof Gang:** Michael Krepon, "When Terrorists Were West Germans," *Arms Control Wonk*, Feb. 11, 2010, http://krepon.armscontrolwonk.com/archive/2623/when-terrorists-were-west-germans.

44   **Tokyo subway system:** Sara A. Daly, John V. Parachini, and William Rosenau, "Aum Shinrikyo, Al Qaeda, and the Kinshasa Reactor: Implications of Three

Case Studies for Combating Nuclear Terrorism," RAND Corporation, Santa Monica, CA, 2005, www.rand.org/pubs/documented_briefings/DB458.

44   **And al-Qaeda has made no secret:** David Albright, "Al Qaeda's Nuclear Program: Through the Window of Seized Documents," *Special Forum* 47, Nautilus Institute, Berkeley, CA, Nov. 6, 2002; Bunn, *Securing the Bomb 2010*, p. 13.

44   **"Al Qaeda's patient":** Rolf Mowatt-Larssen, "Al-Qaeda Weapons of Mass Destruction Threat: Hype or Reality?" Belfer Center for Science and International Affairs, John F. Kennedy School of Government, Harvard University, Jan. 2010, pp. 5–6.

45   **"Our number one concern":** Interview by author with American intelligence official in Washington, DC, Nov. 11, 2008.

45   **"If they are allowed":** Robert Gates interview, Aug. 7, 2009. Gates stepped down from the post in July 2011 and was succeeded by Leon Panetta.

47   **A. Q. Khan:** Douglas Frantz and Catherine Collins, *The Man from Pakistan: The True Story of the World's Most Dangerous Nuclear Smuggler* (New York: Twelve, 2007), pp. xv–xvi.

47   **"Our view is as long":** Gates interview, Aug. 7, 2009.

48   **"I doubt that they would":** Perry interview, Feb. 22, 2011.

48   **"We had no details":** CIA background briefing; under ground rules officials could not be identified, Apr. 24, 2008.

49   **uranium rather than plutonium:** The relatively pure form of plutonium, Pu-239, preferred for use in nuclear weapons, is produced by nuclear reactors as the highly enriched uranium that fuels the reactors decays during reactor operation.

49   **"barriers to analysis":** Author interview with government intelligence analysts, Nov. 20, 2008.

50   **potentially serious smuggling scheme:** A full account of this case can be found in Lawrence Scott Sheet's April 2008 story for *The Atlantic*, "A Smuggler's Story," and in a 2008 report by Michael Bronner, "100 Grams (and Counting . . .): Notes from the Nuclear Underworld," published by the Managing the Atom Project, Harvard University.

51   **"In 2003, 2004, and 2005":** Archil Pavlenishvili interview, Nov. 17, 2010.

51   **"Even in the United States":** Author interview with government intelligence analysts, Nov. 20, 2008.

51   **"We assess that undetected":** "Annual Report to Congress on the Safety and Security of Russian Nuclear Facilities and Military Forces," Central Intelligence Agency, Dec. 2004, p. 5.

52   **"There is sufficient material":** Porter J. Goss, "Global Intelligence Challenges 2005: Meeting Long-Term Challenges with a Long-Term Strategy," Testimony Before the Senate Select Committee on Intelligence, Feb. 16, 2005.

53   **"Well, we think that right now":** Pavlenishvili interview, Nov. 17, 2010.

53   **"A single bomb of this type":** Letter from Albert Einstein to Franklin D. Roosevelt, Aug. 2, 1939, Franklin D. Roosevelt Presidential Library Online Archives, Box 5, Alexander Sachs Folder.

55   **"The driver is setting":** Pascal Fias interview, Nov. 15, 2010.

56   **"I believe these actions":** Robert Gates statement from the Pentagon, June 5, 2008, Department of Defense website.

56   **"This had all happened so gradually":** Gates interview, Aug. 7, 2009.

CHAPTER FOUR

58   **For years, Poland's:** The account of the National Nuclear Security Administration's activities in Poland comes from a trip the author took there in September 2010 with a number of NNSA officials.

60   **The hardest part of nuclear bomb making:** The phenomenal explosive force of fission weapons comes from the splitting of atoms in the fission process. A very few select isotopes of certain heavy elements, such as naturally occurring uranium-235 (U-235) or man-made plutonium-239 (Pu-239), are capable of this process. In each case, as the core of the atom, or nucleus, splits, subatomic particles known as neutrons dart out of the nucleus. They, in turn, strike and split other nuclei in a cascading chain reaction. Each time an atom splits, a tiny amount of its mass is converted into energy. As the chain reaction accelerates swiftly in an instant, a tremendous burst of energy is produced. The progression was captured by Einstein's formula, $E=mc^2$. It says that a tiny piece of matter multiplied by the speed of light squared equals a huge amount of energy.

Highly enriched uranium, a refined form of naturally occurring uranium, happens to be fissile material ideally suited to sustaining fission chain reactions. It is produced by concentrating the U-235 isotope in natural uranium, nature's heaviest element. Uranium in its natural form is benign and unsuitable for use in a nuclear weapon. Through a process known as enrichment, U-235 can be concentrated in the uranium. At higher levels of enrichment, it becomes weapons-grade matter.

A hydrogen bomb, which no one imagines a terror group could possibly manufacture, is actually two nuclear weapon stages operating in tandem in one package. The detonation of the first stage, called the primary, generates the nuclear forces that activate the second stage, known as the secondary. Much of the energy in the second stage arises from fusion, the reverse of fission. In a fusion weapon, light nuclei such as isotopes of hydrogen fuse together to create a heavier atom, a process that also releases a jolt of energy, since this heavier atom has slightly less mass than the original hydrogen isotopes.

60   **A 1977 U.S. government study:** Matthew Bunn, *Securing the Bomb: Securing All Nuclear Materials in Four Years,* Project on Managing the Atom, Belfer Center

for Science and International Affairs, John F. Kennedy School of Government, Harvard University, commissioned by the Nuclear Threat Initiative, Nov. 2008, p. 6. Original source: U.S. Congress, Office of Technology Assessment, *Nuclear Proliferation and Safeguards* (Washington, DC: OTA, 1977).

60 **research reactors around the world:** Nearly all research reactors are either government operated or managed by universities. Twenty or so American universities run research reactors, and until recently, many of those machines were also poorly secured. With help from the Energy Department, seventeen American university reactors that ran on highly enriched uranium have been converted to operate on lower enriched uranium. Reactors at the Massachusetts Institute of Technology and the University of Missouri are slated for conversion.

61 **The Maria reactor in Poland:** The other Polish reactor, the EWA reactor, was decommissioned in 1995.

62 **The programs are not perfect:** Most of the work has involved massive military stockpiles rather than the relatively small amounts of weapons-grade material found at research reactors like the ones in Poland. When the Soviet Union broke apart, tons of bomb-grade fissile material were left exposed to possible theft or diversion. Nuclear security was shaky in Russia, which inherited the bulk of the Soviet arsenal. Some 3,200 nuclear weapons and large amounts of bomb-grade uranium were inadequately secured in the newly independent states of Ukraine, Belarus, and Kazakhstan. Galvanized by Sam Nunn, and later sustained by Bill Perry, among others, Washington provided financial aid and technical assistance to help the four nations upgrade security, dismantle weapons, and keep nuclear scientists employed. In one remarkable program, highly enriched uranium from Soviet-era warheads is sold to the United States, where it is turned into fuel for nuclear power plants. Roughly 10 percent of America's electric power today comes from uranium once contained in Soviet warheads aimed at the United States.

62 **In a 2010 report:** "Nuclear Proliferation; Comprehensive U.S. Planning and Better Foreign Cooperation Needed to Secure Vulnerable Nuclear Materials Worldwide," report of the Government Accountability Office, Dec. 15, 2010.

62 **has cost American taxpayers:** Figures provided by the National Nuclear Security Administration.

64 **"This is the largest":** Andrew Bieniawski interview with Geoff Blumfiel of National Public Radio, Sep. 24, 2010.

68 **"our major concern":** Jane Perlez, David E. Sanger, and Eric Schmitt, "Wary Dance With Pakistan in Nuclear World," *New York Times*, Dec. 1, 2010.

CHAPTER FIVE

73 **the birthplace of the nuclear weapons age:** The description of Trinity Site is based on the author's visit on April 4, 2009.

73   **"Now, I am become":** *The Day After Trinity,* directed by Jon Else (Santa
      Monica, CA: Pyramid Films, 1980).

74   **"Suddenly, there was an enormous flash":** Richard Rhodes, *The Making
      of the Atomic Bomb* (New York: Simon & Schuster, 1986), p. 672. Original source:
      I. I. Rabi, *Science: The Center of Culture* (New York: World, 1970), p. 138.

76   **"We're hardly out of port":** George Shultz interview, Sept. 2, 2002.

76   **"The main feeling":** William Perry interview, Nov. 10, 2008.

76   **"I was taking an engineering course":** Perry interview, Nov. 10, 2008.

77   **"I heard they just dropped":** Sidney Drell interview, Aug. 7, 2008.

77   **"I knew it was a big event":** Henry Kissinger interview, Jan. 27, 2009.

78   **"From Stettin in the Baltic":** Winston Churchill, remarks upon receiving an
      honorary degree, Westminster College, Fulton, MO, Mar. 5, 1946.

79   **"There has always been":** Later that day, the White House said: "The President
      wants to make it certain that there is no misinterpretation of his answers to ques-
      tions at his press conference today about the use of the atom bomb. Naturally, there
      has been consideration of this subject since the outbreak of the hostilities in Korea,
      just as there is consideration of the use of all military weapons whenever our forces
      are in combat. Consideration of the use of any weapon is always implicit in the very
      possession of that weapon. However, it should be emphasized, that, by law, only the
      President can authorize the use of the atom bomb, and no such authorization has
      been given. If and when such authorization should be given, the military commander
      in the field would have charge of the tactical delivery of the weapon. In brief, the
      replies to the questions at today's press conference do not represent any change in this
      situation." Harry Truman, press conference, Executive Office Building, Nov. 30,
      1950, UCSB American Presidency Project.

79   **The nuclear arms race:** Fact sheet provided to author by the Department of
      Energy, "Increasing Transparency in the U.S. Nuclear Weapons Stockpile," May
      3, 2010.

80   **"There is a kind":** James E. Goodby, *At the Borderline of Armageddon: How Amer-
      ican Presidents Managed the Atom Bomb* (Lanham, MD: Rowman & Littlefield,
      2006), p. 80. Original source: Robert S. McNamara, *The Essence of Security: Re-
      flections in Office* (New York: Harper & Row, 1968), p. 166.

81   **massive retaliation:** Secretary of State John Foster Dulles enunciated the doc-
      trine in a 1954 speech.

81   **"Gentlemen, you don't have":** Fred Kaplan, *The Wizards of Armageddon* (Stan-
      ford, CA: Stanford University Press, 1983), p. 223.

81   **"Kahn proposed":** Kaplan, *The Wizards of Armageddon,* p. 223.

82   **Dead Hand:** For a full account, see David E. Hoffman, *The Dead Hand: The
      Untold Story of the Cold War Arms Race and Its Dangerous Legacy* (New York: Dou-
      bleday, 2009).

82   **"We simply cannot"**: Albert D. Wheelon, "Corona: The First Reconnaissance
      Satellites," *Physics Today*, Feb. 1997, p. 24.

CHAPTER SIX

83   **"I still remember the names"**: William Perry interview, Nov. 10, 2008. In one
      of the most prominent early naval confrontations of the war, shelling and torpedoes
      from the British ships damaged the German vessel, which had successfully attacked
      merchant ships in the South Atlantic earlier in 1939. After ordering the *Graf Spee*
      to safer waters in the port of Montevideo and mistakenly determining that she
      faced a formidable British flotilla, the ship's captain, Hans Langsdorf, scuttled the
      Graf Spee in the River Plate. Hitler was infuriated by the decision and a few days
      later, Captain Langsdorf committed suicide. U.S. Department of the Navy, Naval
      Historical Center, Battle of the River Plate, Dec. 1939.

83   **"I was deeply interested"**: William Perry interview, Nov. 10, 2008.

83   **"That wouldn't be my first"**: Edward Perry interview, May 21, 2009.

84   **"hard to get close to"**: Ed Perry interview, May 21, 2009.

84   **"Mother was not only"**: Edward Perry, unpublished memoir, p. 7.

84   **"Bill was very fond"**: Lee Perry interview, Mar. 4, 2009.

85   **"Bill and Lee could"**: Ed Perry interview, May, 21, 2009.

85   **"Bill used to love"**: Lee Perry interview, Mar. 4, 2009.

85   **"I wanted to be part"**: William Perry interview, Nov. 10, 2008.

86   **"You just couldn't believe"**: William Perry interview, Nov. 10, 2008.

87   **"I found it very interesting"**: William Perry interview, Nov. 10, 2008.

87   **"I always thought I was"**: Sidney Drell interview, Aug. 12, 2009. The other bi-
      ographical comments from Drell in this chapter were made in the same interview.

89   **"this guy Einstein"**: According to Drell, he saw Einstein walking around
      Princeton's campus, but never met him.

91   **"He was a brilliant"**: Sidney Dancoff died of cancer in 1950, a year after Drell
      received his Ph.D.

92   **"My parents would have"**: Harriet Drell comment to author, 2009.

92   **"I just imagine"**: Persis Drell interview, Oct. 3, 2008.

92   **Julian Schwinger**: Julian Schwinger shared the 1965 Nobel Prize in Physics
      with Richard Feynman.

CHAPTER SEVEN

95   **the U-2 spy plane**: The CIA conducted twenty-four U-2 flights over Soviet
      territory from July 4, 1956, to May 1, 1960, when one of the planes and its pilot,
      Francis Gary Powers, were shot down by an improved Soviet antiaircraft missile.

96   **"Bill is a very pragmatic"**: Paul Kaminski interview, Jan. 28, 2009.

96   **research work at Stanford:** Stanford's connection to defense research, and the university's own classified research projects, became a focal point for campus antiwar protesters during the Vietnam War.

96   **"a rare thing":** Lew Franklin interview, Nov. 10, 2008.

96   **"cerebral approach":** William Perry interview, Nov. 10, 2008.

99   **"one of the great breakthroughs":** Albert Wheelon interview, Mar. 19, 2009.

100   **"The only people they had cleared":** William Perry interview, Nov. 10, 2008.

101   **"We were the two kids":** Wheelon interview, Mar. 19, 2009.

101   **"Unlike most panels":** William Perry, Stanford University, Jan. 18, 1999.

102   **"I received a phone call":** William Perry remarks at the "Overcoming Nuclear Dangers" Conference, Rome, Apr. 16, 2009.

103   **"Right from the beginning":** James Bjorken, foreword to published remarks by Sidney Drell in *Beam Line* 28, no. 2 (Summer 1998): 2–3. *Beam Line* is an in-house periodical produced by the SLAC National Accelerator Laboratory.

104   **"I was upstairs":** Sidney Drell interview, Aug. 12, 2009.

104   **"Screwdriver Report":** Wolfgang K. H. Panofsky, *Panofsky on Physics, Politics and Peace: Pief Remembers* (New York: Springer, 2007), pp. 60–63.

105   **The Jasons:** For a more detailed history of the Jasons, see Ann Finkbeiner, *The Jasons: The Secret History of Science's Postwar Elite* (New York: Viking Penguin, 2006).

106   **"We showed that it would":** Sidney Drell interview, Sept. 9, 2009.

106   **"Sid and I were both":** William Perry interview, Feb. 22, 2011.

106   **"Bud and Sid":** William Perry interview, Aug. 14, 2008.

107   **"Call it entrapment":** Sidney Drell, *Nuclear Weapons, Scientists and the Post–Cold War Challenge* (Hackensack, NJ: World Scientific, 2007), p. 41.

CHAPTER EIGHT

108   **"He said he wanted":** Sidney Drell, "Reminiscences of Work on National Reconnaissance," in *Nuclear Weapons, Scientists and the Post–Cold War Challenge* (Hackensack, NJ: World Scientific, 2007), pp. 39–44.

109   **"The streaks were":** Albert Wheelon interview, Mar. 19, 2009.

110   **"I learned, to my amazement":** Drell, *Nuclear Weapons, Scientists and the Post–Cold War Challenge*, pp. 39–44.

110   **Luis Alvarez:** Alvarez was awarded the Nobel Prize in Physics in 1968 for his work in particle physics.

110   **"There was a list of hypotheses":** Wheelon interview, Mar. 19, 2009.

113   **"Over time":** Sidney Drell remarks at Rumford Prize award ceremony, American Academy of Arts and Sciences, Boston, Oct. 12, 2008.

113 **"It is my personal conviction":** Sidney Drell, retirement remarks, published in *Beam Line* 28, no. 2 (Summer 1998): 8–9.

113 **"For millennia":** Father Bryan J. Hehir, "Ethical Considerations of Living in the Nuclear Age," Conference on Building a Safer 21st Century, Stanford University, Dec. 6, 1987.

113 **"In the words of a religious person":** Sidney Drell interview, Apr. 26, 2011.

114 **"Deterrence is acceptable":** Sidney Drell interview, Aug. 7, 2008. The pastoral letter said, "Deterrence is not an adequate strategy as a long-term basis for peace; it is a transitional strategy justifiable only in conjunction with resolute determination to pursue arms control and disarmament." "The Challenge of Peace: God's Promise and Our Response," Pastoral Letter on War and Peace by the National Conference of Catholic Bishops, May 3, 1983.

114 **"I struggled like many people":** Sidney Drell interview, Aug. 7, 2008.

115 **No First Use:** Sidney Drell interview, May 20, 2011.

116 **"You know how staff meetings go":** Gilbert Decker interview, Dec. 19, 2008.

117 **"I said, wait a minute":** William Perry interview, Nov. 10, 2008.

118 **Rhyolite:** The satellite project's secrecy was compromised by two TRW employees, who sold technical information about the project to the Soviets. The story of this damaging episode is told by Robert Lindsey in *The Falcon and the Snowman: A True Story of Friendship and Espionage* (New York: Simon & Schuster, 1979).

118 **Soviet radar installation:** Frank Eliot, "Moon Bounce Elint," *Studies in Intelligence* (Spring 1967): 59–65.

119 **"Bill was always a big proponent":** Decker interview, Dec. 19, 2008.

119 **"Dave had a motto":** William Perry remarks at the Leadership Symposium, Stanford University, Apr. 7, 2009.

CHAPTER NINE

121 **Louis and Paula Kissinger:** Details on Kissinger's early years from Walter Isaacson, *Kissinger: A Biography* (New York: Simon & Schuster, 1992), and Robert Dallek, *Nixon and Kissinger: Partners in Power* (New York: HarperCollins, 2007).

121 **"That part of my childhood":** Isaacson, *Kissinger*, p. 26. Original source: Bernard Law Collier, "The Road to Peking," *New York Times Magazine*, Nov. 14, 1971.

121 **"Kissinger is a strong man":** Isaacson, *Kissinger*, p. 29. Original source: Interview with Isaacson, May 14, 1988.

122 **Kissinger's military service:** Isaacson, *Kissinger*, pp. 47–55.

124 **"Whenever peace":** Isaacson, *Kissinger*, pp. 74–75.

124 **"At that time the conventional wisdom":** Henry Kissinger interview, Jan. 27, 2009.

125 **One day, in a chance:** Isaacson, *Kissinger*, p. 82. Kissinger himself provided a

somewhat different account of his encounter with Arthur Schlesinger Jr. Speaking at a Stanford dinner on November 11, 2010, he said: "I was writing about nineteenth-century diplomacy when I was walking across Harvard Yard in the rain with Arthur Schlesinger and he had just received a letter from Tom Finletter, who had been Secretary of the Air Force, advocating the doctrine of massive retaliation. He handed me that letter and asked, 'What do you think of this?' So I wrote him a memo of what I thought of it. I hadn't thought of it much before, but he made me think of it. He then sent this letter to *Foreign Affairs*. It was the first article I ever published."

126 **"Given the power of modern weapons":** Henry Kissinger, *Nuclear Weapons and Foreign Policy* (New York: Norton, 1969), p. 14.

126 **"For the first time":** Isaacson, *Kissinger*, pp. 88–89. Original source: Russell Baker, "U.S. Reconsidering 'Small-War' Theory," *New York Times*, Aug. 11, 1957.

126 **"That was sort of an attractive":** Henry Kissinger dinner remarks, Hoover Institution conference, "Deterrence: Its Past and Future," Stanford University, Nov. 11, 2010.

CHAPTER TEN

128 **"He said, 'You're taking part'":** George Shultz interview, Nov. 2, 2009.

129 **George Pratt Shultz was born:** Details on George Shultz's early years from George Shultz interview, Sept. 2, 2009, and George Shultz, *Turmoil and Triumph: My Years as Secretary of State* (New York: Charles Scribner's Sons, 1993).

130 **sometime around 1918:** George Shultz is not certain about the date of his parents' marriage, nor does he have any record of the wedding date.

131 **"Maybe he's brilliant":** Elisabeth Bumiller, "Gentle George and The Quiet Roar," *Washington Post*, Dec. 14, 1982.

131 **"In this game":** George Shultz interview, Sept. 2, 2009.

132 **field research for his senior thesis:** Shultz later established fellowships that provide funding for fieldwork for undergraduate and graduate students at Princeton and for graduate students at MIT and Stanford.

132 **"They had zero education":** Shultz interview, Sept. 2, 2009.

133 **"By April 1943":** George Shultz, *Turmoil and Triumph*, p. 26.

134 **"I went in about":** Shultz interview, Sept. 2, 2009.

135 **"I can remember times":** Shultz interview, Sept. 2, 2009.

135 **"Physics, of course":** Shultz interview, Sept. 2, 2009.

136 **"No, she'll come":** "Secretary of State's Wife a Frequent Traveling Companion," Associated Press, Aug. 8, 1988.

136 **"I would read these things":** George Shultz remarks at Hoover Institution conference, "Deterrence: Its Past and Future," Stanford University, Nov. 11, 2010.

136 **"In the Nation's Service"**: Shultz, *Turmoil and Triumph*, pp. 27–28.

137 **"I asked Al"**: Johan Van Overtveldt, *The Chicago School: How the University of Chicago Assembled the Thinkers Who Revolutionized Economics and Business* (Chicago: Agate, 2007), p. 324.

137 **"I had to create an environment conducive"**: Shultz, *Turmoil and Triumph*, p. 28.

CHAPTER ELEVEN

139 **"a most attractive"**: "Miss Elizabeth Cannon weds Mr. Sam A. Nunn," Sam Nunn archives, Emory University, Series 2, Box 1, unidentified newspaper.

139 **"My father had a great influence"**: Warren Brown, "Senator Sam Nunn," *Sky Magazine*, Nov. 1983. Sam Nunn Sr. was actually fifty when Nunn was born.

139 **Nunn, who fought:** The 82nd Division became the 82nd Airborne Division in 1942.

139 **"In the early thirties"**: "Tribute to Samuel Augustus Nunn," Aug. 16, 1965, Sam Nunn archives, Emory University, Series 3, Box 3.

140 **"Red-hot Sam Nunn"**: Charlie Roberts, "Senator Nunn, the Athlete," *Atlanta Constitution*, Nov. 10, 1972.

140 **"He was a tremendous rebounder"**: Roberts, "Senator Nunn, the Athlete."

140 **"He really knew"**: Skip Korson, "Georgia's Sam Nunn," *Macon Magazine*, Summer 1988.

140 **"He said he'd be afraid"**: Korson, "Georgia's Sam Nunn."

140 **"If I had been six-foot-four"**: Brown, "Senator Sam Nunn."

141 **"I followed his career"**: Sam Nunn interview, Nov. 18, 2008.

141 **"I have a great opportunity"**: Sam Nunn letter to his parents, undated, Sam Nunn archives, Emory University, Series 2, Box 5.

142 **"That made a huge impression"**: Nunn interview, Nov. 18, 2008.

142 **"Uncle Carl was going over"**: Nunn interview, Nov. 18, 2008.

143 **"He was sort of a hawk"**: Nunn interview, Nov. 18, 2008.

143 **"It had a big effect on me"**: Nunn interview, Nov. 18, 2008.

143 **"I didn't tell him"**: *Atlanta Journal-Constitution*, June 11, 1978, Sam Nunn archives, Emory University, Series 2, Box 4, unidentified article.

143 **"I really wanted"**: Sam Nunn interview, Sept. 1, 2010.

143 **racial tensions:** Nunn interview, Sept. 1, 2010; Thomas A. Johnson, "300 Start a 5-Day Protest March in Georgia, Despite Plea by Maddox," *New York Times*, May 20, 1970.

145 **"The only person"**: Richard B. Ray letter to Irvin Goodroe, Jan. 13, 1971, Sam Nunn archives, Emory University, Series 4, Box 3.

145 **"They basically weren't demanding"**: Nunn interview, Sept. 1, 2010.

146 **"damn fool":** James F. Cook, *Carl Vinson: Patriarch of the Armed Forces* (Macon, GA: Mercer University Press, 2004), p. 350.

146 **"Good gracious, what in the world?":** Korson, "Georgia's Sam Nunn."

146 **"I decided I either":** Nunn interview, Sept. 1, 2010.

147 **"I'm really worried about David's":** "Senate Foes Square Off," United Press International, Sam Nunn archives, Emory University, Series 2, Box 2, n.d.

147 **second youngest:** Joe Biden Jr. of Delaware was the youngest candidate at age thirty. He and Nunn both entered the Senate in 1973.

147 **"end the dictatorship":** *Warner-Robins Journal*, July 12, 1972.

147 **endorsement of George Wallace:** Nunn interview, Sept. 1, 2010.

149 **Nunn easily won:** George McGovern won 25 percent of the Georgia vote.

CHAPTER TWELVE

154 **"I wanted to be sure":** George Shultz, *Turmoil and Triumph: My Years as Secretary of State* (New York: Charles Scribner's Sons, 1993), pp. 8–9.

154 **"What does that candyass":** Walter Isaacson, David Beckwith, and Dick Thompson, "Shultz: Thinker and Doer," *Time*, July 5, 1982.

155 **"He didn't get secretary":** Richard Nixon, John Dean, and Bob Haldeman. Location: Oval Office. "You can't screw about with the IRS," Sept. 15, 1972, 5:24–6:17 p.m., Oval Office. White House Tapes, Presidential Recordings Program, Miller Center of Public Affairs, University of Virginia, http://whitehouse tapes.net.

155 **Oval Office conversation:** Aug. 3, 1972: The President, Haldeman, and Ehrlichman, 9:44–10:40 a.m., Oval Office, and August 3, 1972: The President and Ehrlichman, 5–5:30 p.m., Executive Office Building. Stanley I. Kutler, ed., *Abuse of Power: The New Nixon Tapes* (New York: The Free Press, 1997), pp. 112–19.

156 **"At first when I showed up":** George Shultz remarks at Hoover Institution conference, "Deterrence: Its Past and Future," Stanford University, Nov. 11, 2010.

156 **"We had a little tripartite":** George Shultz remarks at Hoover Institution conference: "Deterrence: Its Past and Future," Stanford University, Nov. 11, 2010.

157 **"When it came to":** George Shultz with Timothy J. Naftali, May 10, 2007, Stanford, California. Richard Nixon Presidential Library and Museum, Richard Nixon Oral History Project, Yorba Linda, California.

157 **"We had fun talking about golf":** George Shultz interview, Sept. 2, 2009.

CHAPTER THIRTEEN

160 **"the fundamental concept":** William Burr, "The Nixon Administration, the 'Horror Strategy,' and the Search for Limited Nuclear Options, 1969–1972," *Journal of Cold War Studies* 7, no. 3 (Summer 2005): 41.

160 **At the time, the United States:** Fact sheet provided to author by the

Department of Energy, "Increasing Transparency in the U.S. Nuclear Weapons Stockpile," May 3, 2010.

160 **Favorable terms by some calculations meant:** National Security Council Staff, "Strategic Policy Issues," circa February 1, 1969, National Security Archive Electronic Briefing Book No. 173, Doc. 2. Original source: National Archives, Nixon Presidential Materials Project, Henry A. Kissinger Office Files, Box 3, Folder: Strategic Policy Issues.

160 **"No matter what":** Burr, "The Nixon Administration, the 'Horror Strategy,' and the Search for Limited Nuclear Options, 1969–1972," p. 34. For original citation, see "NSC Meeting—February 19, 1969," in National Archives, Nixon Presidential Materials Project, National Security Council Institutional Files, H-109, National Security Council Minutes Originals 1969, p. 1.

160 **"Is this the best they can do?":** Burr, "The Nixon Administration, the 'Horror Strategy,' and the Search for Limited Nuclear Options, 1969–1972," p. 48.

160 **"argued that massive":** Burr, "The Nixon Administration, the 'Horror Strategy,' and the Search for Limited Nuclear Options, 1969–1972," p. 49. For original citation, see "Notes on NSC Meeting 14 February 1969," in National Archives, Nixon Presidential Materials Project.

161 **"I thought it was sort of agreed":** Kissinger interview, Jan. 27, 2009.

163 **"We were in a number of situations":** Kissinger interview, Jan. 27, 2009.

163 **Duck Hook:** Seymour M. Hersh disclosed the Duck Hook scheme in his book *The Price of Power: Kissinger in the Nixon White House* (New York: Summit Books, 1983), and William Burr, a senior analyst at the National Security Archive, and Jeffrey Kimball, a professor of history at Miami University, provided a full account, based on declassified records of the Nixon administration, in "Nixon's Secret Nuclear Alert: Vietnam War Diplomacy and the Joint Chiefs of Staff Readiness Test, October 1969," *Cold War History* 3, no. 2 (Jan. 2003): 113–56.

163 **"I would regretfully find":** Scott D. Sagan and Jeremi Suri, "The Madman Nuclear Alert," *International Security* 27, no. 4 (Spring 2003): 159.

163 **"I refuse to believe":** "Nixon White House Considered Nuclear Options Against North Vietnam, Declassified Documents Reveal," edited by William Burr and Jeffrey Kimball, National Security Archive Electronic Briefing Book No. 195, July 31, 2006. Original source: Jeffrey Kimball, *Nixon's Vietnam War* (Lawrence, KS: University of Kansas Press, 1998.), 163.

164 **"He cannot, for example":** Memorandum from Tony Lake and Roger Morris, NSC Staff, to Captain [Rembrandt] Robinson, Subject: Draft Memorandum to the President on Contingency Study, 29 September 1969, NSA Electronic Briefing Book No. 195, Doc. 1. Original source: folder 4: VIETNAM: (General Files), Sep 69–Nov 69, Box 74, National Security Council Files: Subject Files, Nixon Presidential Materials Project, National Archives.

164 **"Important Questions"**: "Memorandum for the President from Henry A. Kissinger, Subject: Contingency Military Operations Against North Vietnam, 2 October 1969, Attachment: 'Important Questions,'" NSA Electronic Briefing Book No. 195, Document 2I. Original source: Top Secret/Sensitive Vietnam Contingency Planning, HAK, Oct. 2, 1969 [2 of 2], Box 89, NSC Files: Subject Files, Nixon Presidential Materials, National Archives.

165 **"If the adversary feels"**: Sagan and Suri, "The Madman Nuclear Alert," p. 162. Original Nixon citation can be found in Richard Nixon, *The Real War* (New York: Warner Books, 1980), pp. 254–56. Subsequent information on Nixon's "madman strategy" and its 1969 implementation is derived from Sagan and Suri, whose article was based largely on declassified documents obtained by the National Security Archive.

166 **"Kissinger has all sorts"**: Diary Entry, Friday, October 17, H. R. Haldeman Diary, NSA Electronic Briefing Book No. 81, Doc. 8. Original Source: Nixon Presidential Materials Project, Special Files, Hand-written Journals and Diaries of Harry Robbins Haldeman.

168 **"We were determined"**: Henry Kissinger, *Years of Upheaval* (Boston: Little, Brown, 1982), p. 580.

168 **"Should I wake up"**: Robert Dallek, *Nixon and Kissinger: Partners in Power* (New York: HarperCollins, 2007), p. 530. Original source: National Archives. Richard Nixon Presidential Library and Museum. Henry A. Kissinger Telephone Conversation Transcripts (Telcons). Chronological File. Box 23. Oct. 24, 1973.

169 **"suggestion of unilateral"**: Dallek, *Nixon and Kissinger*, p. 531. For a copy of the message, see the National Security Archive's "The October War and U.S. Policy," "Nixon to Brezhnev, 25 October 1973, delivered to Soviet Embassy, 5:40 a.m.," Doc. 73.

169 **"opposed to the unilateral"**: Kissinger, *Years of Upheaval*, pp. 594–5.

169 **"I may say that"**: Henry Kissinger news conference, Oct. 25, 1973.

170 **"You and I were the only"**: Dallek, *Nixon and Kissinger*, p. 530. For transcripts of the Oct. 24, 1973, conversations between Kissinger and Haig, see the Digital National Security Archive, "The Kissinger Telephone Conversations: A Record of U.S. Diplomacy, 1969–1977," Documents KA11413 and KA11416.

171 **"That's irrelevant to the problem"**: Henry Kissinger interview, Jan. 27, 2009.

171 **"I cannot think"**: Henry Kissinger remarks at Hoover Institution conference, "Deterrence: Its Past and Future," Stanford University, Nov. 11, 2010.

171 **"I can't honestly say"**: Brent Scowcroft interview, Mar. 3, 2010.

171 **"We were much more interested"**: Kissinger interview, Jan. 27, 2009.

174 **"I tried to introduce"**: Kissinger interview, Jan. 27, 2009.

174 **"In some respects"**: Henry Kissinger interview, Jan. 27, 2009.

175 **"The first strategic arms limitation agreement"**: James E. Goodby, *At the Borderline of Armageddon: How American Presidents Managed the Atom Bomb* (Lanham, MD: Rowman & Littlefield, 2006), p. 93.

CHAPTER FOURTEEN

177 **"From the beginning"**: Richard Garwin memo, Dec. 2, 1969, Sidney Drell's personal files.

178 **"I am always amazed"**: Sidney Drell letter to Donald Hornig, Dec. 30, 1967, Sidney Drell's personal files.

178 **"Sid's an insider type"**: James Bjorken interview, Sept. 21, 2009.

179 **1966 Jason study:** Ann Finkbeiner, *The Jasons: The Secret History of Science's Postwar Elite* (New York: Viking, 2006), pp. 90–117.

179 **Jason also studied:** Finkbeiner, *The Jasons*, pp. 90–117.

179 **"Many people"**: Finkbeiner, *The Jasons*, p. 93.

179 **in Corsica:** Gloria B. Lubkin, "Protestors Harass Jason Physicists," *Physics Today* 25, no. 10 (Oct. 1972): 62–63.

180 **passionate critique:** Charlie Schwartz et al., "Science Against the People: The Story of Jason—The Elite Group of Academic Scientists Who, As Technical Consultants to the Pentagon, Have Developed the Latest Weapon Against Peoples' Liberation Struggles: 'Automated Warfare,'" Scientists and Engineers for Social and Political Action, Dec. 1972, http://socrates.berkeley.edu/~schwrtz/SftP/Jason.html.

182 **"I was obviously troubled"**: Sidney Drell interview, Oct. 6, 2009.

183 *Science and Government:* C. P. Snow, *Science and Government (The Godkin Lectures at Harvard University, 1961)* (Cambridge, MA: Harvard University Press, 1961).

183 **"I convinced myself"**: Sidney Drell interview, Oct. 6, 2009.

183 **"We should have told Mr. McNamara"**: Murph Goldberger interview, June 8, 2009.

CHAPTER FIFTEEN

185 **"Radar is an"**: Sidney Drell paper, Aug. 5, 1971, Sidney Drell's personal files.

185 **"George dropped out"**: Richard Garwin interview, Nov. 25, 2008.

185 **"We must get"**: Sidney Drell memo, Sidney Drell's personal files.

185 **"Henry was national security adviser"**: Garwin interview, Nov. 25, 2008.

186 **"I felt he wanted something"**: Paul Doty interview, May 20, 2009.

186 **"Inform David"**: "Topics for Conversation with Dr. David," Sidney Drell memo, Sept. 23, 1970, Sidney Drell's personal files.

186 **"Garwin was the smartest"**: Doty interview, May 20, 2009.

187 **"We just knew that our"**: Doty interview, May 20, 2009.

187 **"I was dead set"**: Garwin interview, Nov. 25, 2009.

187 **"So Henry himself":** Garwin interview, Oct. 25, 2009. The interview and subsequent profile of Kissinger produced by Fallaci included footage showing classified documents at the White House, which caused Kissinger considerable grief when the broadcast was aired. Kissinger describes the interview and regrets his comments in his book *The White House Years* (Boston: Little, Brown, 2009), pp. 1409–10.

188 **"The name of the enclosed":** Jack Ruina letter to Doty group, Dec. 28, 1969, Paul Doty's personal files.

188 **"I would say":** Walter Isaacson, *Kissinger: A Biography* (New York: Simon & Schuster, 1992), p. 322.

188 **"There was no weapon":** Henry Kissinger interview, Jan. 27, 2009.

189 **"That's a Henryism":** Sidney Drell interview, Oct. 6, 2009.

189 **It exploited a breakthrough:** The Bell Labs scientists, Willard S. Boyle and George E. Smith, won the 2009 Nobel Prize in Physics for their development of the semiconductor devices.

189 **FROG:** President's Foreign Intelligence Advisory Board, Memorandum for President's File, Subject: President's Foreign Intelligence Advisory Board Meeting with the President, June 4, 1971, National Security Archive Electronic Briefing Book: Science Technology and the CIA, Doc. 32. Original source: National Archives, Nixon Presidential Materials, President's Office Files.

190 **"What really broke":** Doty interview, May 20, 2009.

CHAPTER SIXTEEN

192 **"What is necessary":** "Sakharov letter to Drell, Feb. 3, 1983," in Kenneth W. Thompson, ed., *Sidney Drell on Arms Control* (Lanham, MD: University Press of America, 1988), p. 97.

192 **"He's saying exactly":** Sidney Drell interview, Feb. 14, 2011.

193 **"The unchecked growth":** Sidney Drell and Sergei P. Kapitza, eds., *Sakharov Remembered: A Tribute by Friends and Colleagues* (New York: American Institute of Physics, 1991), p. 118.

193 **a family dinner:** Sidney Drell remarks at Stanford University, Feb. 21, 1980, and at the National Academy of Sciences, Nov. 13, 1988, Hoover Institution archives, Sidney Drell files.

194 **"think Faulkner is":** Sidney Drell travelogue, Aug. 6, 1976, Hoover Institution archives, Sidney Drell files.

194 **"It took me close to an hour":** Sidney Drell travelogue, Aug. 6, 1976, Hoover Institution archives, Sidney Drell files.

194 **"a great scientist":** Sidney Drell remarks at Rockefeller University, May 1–2, 1981, Hoover Institution archives, Sidney Drell files.

195 **In 1983, he produced an essay:** Andrei Sakharov, "The Danger of Thermo-

Nuclear War: An Open Letter to Dr. Sidney Drell," *Foreign Affairs* 61, no. 5 (Summer 1983).

195 **Drell disagreed:** Letter from Sidney Drell to Andrei Sakharov, Sept. 20, 1983, Hoover Institution archives, Sidney Drell files.

196 **"In Tbilisi":** Letter from Andrei Sakharov to Sidney Drell, Dec. 8, 1980, Hoover Institution archives, Sidney Drell files.

196 **"It was marvelous news":** Letter from Sidney Drell to Andrei Sakharov, Dec. 23, 1986, Hoover Institution archives, Sidney Drell files.

197 **"Andrei Sakharov is one":** Drell and Kapitza, eds., *Sakharov Remembered*, p. x.

CHAPTER SEVENTEEN

198 **"to be his legs and eyes":** Sam Nunn oral history, Nuclear Threat Initiative, vol. 1, p. 63.

198 **"Use them or lose them":** Nunn oral history, vol. 1, p. 71.

199 **"I felt it was imperative":** Sam Nunn interview, Nov. 18, 2008.

200 **"Groucho held the pistol up":** Nunn oral history, vol. 1, p. 85.

200 **"We were not going to":** Nunn interview, Nov. 18, 2008.

200 **"One of the last stops":** Nunn oral history, vol. 1, p. 72.

201 **"That had a huge effect":** Nunn interview, Nov. 18, 2008.

201 **"The nuclear threshold in Europe":** Sam Nunn, "Policy, Troops and the NATO Alliance," Report of Senator Sam Nunn to the Committee of Armed Services, Apr. 2, 1974, p. 3, Lexis-Nexis Congressional Record.

202 **many military issues:** Once Nunn became chairman of the manpower subcommittee in 1974, he became active on many military service issues, including the switch from conscription to all-volunteer military forces that began in 1973. When Jimmy Carter presented the Senate with a treaty giving up American control of the Panama Canal come 1999, Nunn had to choose between Carter's plan and the prevailing view in Georgia that Washington should retain control. "It was a campaign year, and this, without any doubt, was the most volatile, dangerous political vote that I ever had to cast, certainly one that I would have to cast in a campaign year," he recalled. With several other Democrats ready to follow Nunn's lead, his vote to ratify was critical to approval of the treaty, which was narrowly ratified on March 17, 1978, by a vote of 68–32 [Nunn oral history, vol. 1, p. 6].

202 **He reported that:** "Vietnam and Cambodia," Washington Special Actions Group Meeting, Jan. 7, 1975, Digital National Security Archive.

203 **"a series of misjudgments":** Sam Nunn, "Vietnam Aid—The Painful Options," Report of Senator Sam Nunn to the Committee on Armed Services, United States Senate, Feb. 12, 1975, p. 15, Lexis-Nexis Congressional Record.

203 **"our nation would have":** Nunn, "Vietnam Aid—The Painful Options," p. 9.

204 **"It is the central thesis":** Sam Nunn and Senator Dewey F. Bartlett, "NATO and the New Soviet Threat," Report of Senator Sam Nunn and Senator Dewey F. Bartlett to the Committee on Armed Services, United States Senate, Jan. 24, 1977, p. 1.

CHAPTER EIGHTEEN

205 **"He got the call":** Lee Perry interview, Mar. 4, 2009.

206 **"Weigh that against the job":** David Fubini, *Let Me Explain: Eugene G. Fubini's Life in Defense of America* (Santa Fe: Sunstone Press, 2009), p. 248.

206 **"I said, now I'm down to number five":** Harold Brown interview, July 8, 2009.

206 **"This was probably":** William Perry interview, Aug. 14, 2008.

207 **"I believe that this":** Nominations of William James Perry and David Emerson Mann, Hearing before the Committee on Armed Services, U.S. Senate, Mar. 25, 1977.

208 **"I can still remember":** Perry interview, Aug. 14, 2008.

208 **"We must make the most":** "Nominations of William J. Perry, Harold W. Chase and George A. Peapples," Committee on Armed Services, United States Senate, Nov. 1, 1977.

208 **"offset strategy":** Ashton B. Carter and William J. Perry, *Preventive Defense: A New Security Strategy for America* (Washington, DC: Brookings Institution Press, 1999), pp. 179–80.

208 **"There was a long history":** Brown interview, July 8, 2009.

209 **"careful, analytical, low-key":** Brown interview, July 8, 2009.

209 **"He got some early pieces":** Paul Kaminski interview, Jan. 28, 2009.

210 **SR-71:** The SR-71 was never used in Soviet airspace.

210 **Russian scientist:** David C. Aronstein, *Have Blue and the F-117: Evolution of the "Stealth" Fighter* (Reston, VA: American Institute of Aeronautics and Astronautics, 1997), p. 20.

211 **"a diamond beveled":** Ben R. Rich and Leo Janos, *Skunk Works: A Personal Memoir of My Years of Lockheed* (Boston: Little, Brown, 1996), p. 26.

211 **"Have Blue":** Rick Atkinson, "Stealth: From 18-inch Model to $70 Billion Muddle," *Washington Post*, Oct. 8, 1989.

211 **"Here's the stealth bomber":** Atkinson, "Stealth."

212 **airborne radar system:** The system, built by Boeing, was known as AWACS: Airborne Warning and Control System. The plane had a Boeing 707 airframe with a radar unit attached to the top.

212 **"That was a tough development":** Perry interview, Aug. 14, 2008.

213 **"I think that we essentially":** Brown interview, July 8, 2009.

CHAPTER NINETEEN

215 **North American Air Defense Command (NORAD):** The name was officially changed to North American Aerospace Defense Command in March 1981.

215 **"I still remember":** William Perry interview with *Nuclear Tipping Point* filmmakers, Sept. 1, 2010, Nuclear Threat Initiative papers.

215 **"That call is engraved":** Perry initially recalled that the cause of the malfunction was that someone at NORAD had mistakenly placed a training tape in the computer system. That had happened during a similar false alarm in 1979, that did not occur in the middle of the night. See Scott Sagan, *The Limits of Safety: Organizations, Accidents and Nuclear Weapons* (Princeton, NJ: Princeton University Press, 1993), p. 228.

216 **"It's the most sane":** Robert D. McFadden, "Samuel T. Cohen, Neutron Bomb Inventor, Dies at 89," *New York Times*, Dec. 1, 2010.

217 **"I had come to the conclusion":** Sam Nunn oral history, Sept. 3, 1996, vol. 1, p. 138.

217 **"inconsistent pronouncements":** Don Oberdorfer, "Carter, Kissinger Agree on Global Ills, Divide on Reasons," *Washington Post*, Apr. 11, 1980. In 1981, Reagan approved production of seven hundred neutron warheads and three types of warheads were stockpiled by the United States. The last of the weapons were retired in 1992 and all were dismantled by 2003.

217 **hearings in the spring of 1978:** Department of Defense Authorization for Appropriations for Fiscal Year 1979, Hearings before the Committee on Armed Services U.S. Senate on S. 2571, Part 9- Research and Development, Apr. 5, 10, 11, 13, 14, 20; May 8, 1978.

218 **That gave rise to:** Robert A. Hoover, *The MX Controversy: A Guide to Issues and References* (Claremont, CA: Regina Books, 1982), pp. 12–27.

219 **Other proposals:** The coastal submarines, much smaller than their ocean-going cousins, would each have carried two MX missiles attached outside the pressure hull and aligned parallel to the hull. The missiles would rotate to vertical after they were launched.

219 **"no further changes":** Tom Wicker, "Saving Nevada and Utah," *New York Times*, June 20, 1980.

219 **Salt Lake City:** "Headline: Bill Moyers' Journal: The MX Debate," May 13, 1980, Public Broadcasting Service, Vanderbilt Television Archive.

221 **"We had a very convoluted":** William Perry interview, Aug. 14, 2008. In 1982, President Reagan decided to base one hundred MX missiles in one hundred closely spaced, superhardened silos in Wyoming.

221 *New Yorker* **cartoon:** Dana Fradon, *New Yorker*, June 1, 1981.

222 **"At the time":** William Perry remarks before Management Science and Engineering 193 class, Stanford University, Oct. 27, 2009.

222 **"All of these things I've described":** Perry interview, Aug. 14, 2008.

CHAPTER TWENTY

225 **"It's a fair statement":** George Shultz interview, Feb. 3, 2011.

226 **"The worst day":** George Shultz interview, Sept. 2, 2009.

227 **antinuclear rally:** Paul Lettow, *Ronald Reagan and His Quest to Abolish Nuclear Weapons* (New York: Random House, 2006), pp. 3–5.

227 **Reagan often expressed doubts:** Lettow, *Ronald Reagan and His Quest to Abolish Nuclear Weapons*, pp. 21–23. The two aides were Ed Meese and Caspar Weinberger.

227 **"we kept our world":** Ronald Reagan, "Address at the Republican National Convention in Kansas City," Aug. 19, 1976, UCSB American Presidency Project.

228 **"The decision to launch":** Ronald Reagan, *An American Life: The Autobiography* (New York: Simon & Schuster, 1990), p. 257.

228 **"they reserve unto themselves":** Ronald Reagan remarks at a White House news conference in the Old Executive Office Building, Washington, DC, Jan. 29, 1981, UCSB Presidency Project.

228 **"the march of freedom":** Ronald Reagan address to the members of the British Parliament, London, June 8, 1982, UCSB American Presidency Project.

229 **"an evil empire":** Ronald Reagan, Remarks at Annual Convention of the National Association of Evangelicals, Orlando, FL, Mar. 8, 1983, UCSB American Presidency Project.

229 **National Security Decision Directive 75:** National Security Decision Directive 75, Jan. 17, 1983, Ronald Reagan Presidential Library, White House Staff and Office, Paul Thompson Files, Box 52, National Security Decision Directives—Book II [NSDDs 75–83].

229 **"I found myself astonished":** Lou Cannon, *Ronald Reagan: The Role of a Lifetime* (New York: Touchstone/Simon & Schuster, 1991), p. 259.

230 **"I could not believe":** Martin Anderson and Annelise Anderson, *Reagan's Secret War: The Untold Story of His Fight to Save the World from Nuclear Disaster* (New York: Crown, 2009), p. 50. Original source: Richard Pipes's journal, quoted in a letter from Pipes to Annelise Anderson, Nov. 2, 2002.

230 ***The Fate of the Earth:*** Jonathan Schell's *The Fate of the Earth* originated as a three-part series of articles in the *New Yorker*. The book won the *Los Angeles Times* book prize and was nominated for a Pulitzer Prize.

231 **"zero-zero" proposal:** Reagan, *An American Life*, pp. 550–51.

231 **"George Shultz has done":** James Mann, *The Rebellion of Ronald Reagan: A History of the End of the Cold War* (New York: Viking, 2009), p. 14. Original source: Memo to President-elect Ronald Reagan from Richard Nixon, Nov. 17, 1980, Richard Nixon Library.

232 **"I also learned that the Soviets were tough":** George Shultz, *Turmoil and Triumph: My Years as Secretary of State* (New York: Charles Scribner's Sons, 1993), p. 119.

232 **Helmut Schmidt:** George Shultz interview, Aug. 25, 2008.

233 **"From a half century":** Shultz, *Turmoil and Triumph,* p. 501.

233 **"He encouraged people":** James Goodby interview, July 1, 2009.

233 **1967 visit:** Lettow, *Ronald Reagan and His Quest to Abolish Nuclear Weapons,* p. 19.

234 **"There must be something":** Shultz, *Turmoil and Triumph,* pp. 261–62.

234 **"The JCS [Joint Chiefs of Staff] estimates":** NCS/NSPG Meeting: 1981–1989 Minutes, Dec. 3, 1981, Cabinet Room, Ronald Reagan Library.

234 **He said it reinforced Reagan's view:** Shultz interview, Feb. 3, 2011.

235 **"During the course of the discussion":** Shultz interview, Feb. 3, 2011.

235 **"We don't have the technology":** Shultz, *Turmoil and Triumph,* p. 250.

236 **"a unilateral executive":** Michael R. Gordon, "Reagan Is Warned by Senator Nunn over ABM Treaty," *New York Times,* Feb. 7, 1987.

236 **"I found great":** Shultz, *Turmoil and Triumph,* p. 250.

236 **Speaking from the Oval Office:** Ronald Reagan, "Address to the Nation on Defense and National Security," Oval Office, Mar. 23, 1983, UCSB American Presidency Project.

237 **"a tendency to rely":** Shultz, *Turmoil and Triumph,* p. 263.

237 **"quack medicine":** Sidney D. Drell, *In the Shadow of the Bomb: Physics and Arms Control* (New York: American Institute of Physics, 1993), p. 217.

238 **"Our analysis raises":** Sidney Drell, Philip J. Farley, and David Holloway, "Preserving the ABM Treaty: A Critique of the Reagan Strategic Defense Initiative," *International Security* 9, no. 2 (Autumn 1984): 89.

238 **"The problem with Star Wars":** Warren Froelich, "'Star Wars' Proposal Faulted; Ex-Defense Aide Sees Soviet Buildup, Arms Treaty Peril," *San Diego Union-Tribune,* Nov. 2, 1984.

238 **"We see virtually":** Charles Corddry, "Star Wars: It's Headed for Earth," *San Diego Union-Tribune,* Dec. 2, 1986.

238 **"President Reagan's":** Henry Kissinger, "Cutting Defense: The Wrong Idea," *Washington Post,* Mar. 5, 1985.

239 **"pipe-dream":** George Shultz, *Turmoil and Triumph,* p. 250. Richard Burt is now the United States chair of Global Zero, another organization advocating the complete elimination of nuclear weapons.

239 **"The president has noticed":** Shultz, *Turmoil and Triumph,* p. 376.

239 **"I told the president":** Shultz, *Turmoil and Triumph,* p. 466.

239 **"He was annoyed":** Shultz, *Turmoil and Triumph,* p. 505.

240 **"We should go easy":** NCS/NSPG Meeting: 1981–1989 Minutes, "Strategic

Defense Initiative," Nov. 30, 1983, 11:00–12:04 a.m., Cabinet Room, NSPG folder 0071, box 91306, Ronald Reagan Library.

240 **"They all thought Reagan":** George Shultz interview, Aug. 27, 2010.

240 **"If you win 48":** James Mann, *The Rebellion of Ronald Reagan*, p. 43. In an interview on May 19, 2009, Tom Simons recounted the same comment to the author with a slight variation in Shultz's wording. The actual number of states that Reagan won was forty-nine, not forty-eight.

240 **showcase article:** George P. Shultz, "Shaping American Foreign Policy: New Realities and New Ways of Thinking," *Foreign Affairs* 63, no. 4 (Spring 1985): 705–22.

241 **"I like Mr. Gorbachev":** Margaret Thatcher, TV interview for the BBC, Dec. 17, 1984, retrieved from the Margaret Thatcher Foundation, www.margaret thatcher.org/document/105592.

242 **"In Gorbachev":** Shultz, *Turmoil and Triumph*, p. 532.

242 **questioned Shultz's judgment:** The gap left Shultz wary of intelligence reports, and he often speaks with disdain about American intelligence agencies. Robert Gates, who headed the CIA analytical division during the Reagan presidency and was a Soviet specialist, returned the favor in his memoirs. He said, "Shultz was not a team player unless he could be coach, captain and quarterback. Unlike Haig, though, he always remembered who owned the team." Robert Gates, *From the Shadows: The Ultimate Insider's Story of Five Presidents and How They Won the Cold War* (New York: Simon & Schuster, 1996), p. 279.

243 **Shultz got an assist:** Suzanne Massie's best-known book is *Land of the Firebird: The Beauty of Old Russia* (New York: Simon & Schuster, 1980).

245 **"agreed a nuclear war":** "Union of Soviet Socialist Republics–United States: Documents from the Geneva Summit, November 21, 1985," U.S. Department of State Bulletin 86, no. 2106 (Jan. 1986): 7–11.

245 **"Personally, I thought":** Shultz, *Turmoil and Triumph*, p. 602.

245 **"This is our first indication":** Shultz, *Turmoil and Triumph*, p. 700.

246 **"It's a good idea":** Jack F. Matlock, *Reagan and Gorbachev: How the Cold War Ended* (New York: Random House, 2005), p. 207.

247 **"would not be":** "Dear Mr. President," Mikhail Gorbachev letter to Ronald Reagan, Sept. 15, 1986, Reykjavik File, National Security Archive, George Washington University, Washington, DC, NSA Electronic Briefing Book No. 203, edited by Svetlana Savranskaya and Thomas Blanton, Document 1.

247 **"We go into Reykjavik":** "Gorbachev's Goals and Tactics at Reykjavik," National Security Council (Stephen Sestanovich), Oct. 4, 1986, Reykjavik File, National Security Archive, George Washington University, Washington, DC, NSA Electronic Briefing Book No. 203, edited by Svetlana Savranskaya and Thomas Blanton, Document 6.

CHAPTER TWENTY-ONE

248 **"That's what alarmed people":** George Shultz interview, Aug. 27, 2010.

250 **"to sweep Reagan":** Jack F. Matlock, *Reagan and Gorbachev: How the Cold War Ended* (New York: Random House, 2005), p. 211. Original source: Anatoly Chernyaev, *My Six Years with Gorbachev* (University Park: Pennsylvania State University Press, 2000), p. 81.

250 **"Our goal is to prevent":** Gorbachev's instructions for the group preparing for Reykjavik, Oct. 4, 1986, Reykjavik File, National Security Archive, George Washington University, Washington, DC, NSA Electronic Briefing Book No. 203, edited by Svetlana Savranskaya and Thomas Blanton, Document 5.

250 **"The right[-wing politicians]":** USSR CC CPSU Politburo session on preparations for Reykjavik, Oct. 8, 1986, Reykjavik File, National Security Archive, George Washington University, Washington, DC, NSA Electronic Briefing Book No. 203, edited by Svetlana Savranskaya and Thomas Blanton, Document 8.

251 **"The accident at the Chernobyl":** Mikhail Gorbachev, *Memoirs* (New York: Doubleday, 1996), p. 189.

251 **"Chernobyl has altered":** NCS/NSPG Meeting: 1981–1989 Minutes, "U.S.-Soviet Relations," 2:00–2:45 p.m., Situation Room, June 12, 1986, Ronald Reagan Library.

252 **"Gorbachev must go":** Memorandum to the President, Secretary of State George Shultz, "Subject: Reykjavik," Oct. 2, 1986, Reykjavik File, National Security Archive, George Washington University, Washington, DC, NSA Electronic Briefing Book No. 203, edited by Svetlana Savranskaya and Thomas Blanton, Document 4.

252 **Soviet ship:** Hotel space in Reykjavik was limited and the cruise ship, called *Georgi Ots*, also provided more secure and private quarters for the Soviet delegation.

252 **On Saturday morning:** This account of the summit talks is based on notes taken during the Reagan-Gorbachev meetings by American and Soviet note takers. The Soviet notes were made public by the Gorbachev Foundation in 1993 and published that year by Mirovaya Ekonomika i Mezhdunarodnye Otnosheniya. The notes were subsequently translated into English by the Foreign Broadcast Information Service and published on August 30, 1993. The State Department notes were declassified on January 14, 2000. Both sets of notes are available at the National Security Archive: Reykjavik File, National Security Archive, George Washington University, Washington, DC, NSA Electronic Briefing Book No. 203, edited by Svetlana Savranskaya and Thomas Blanton.

254 **leaders were talking seriously:** George Shultz, *Turmoil and Triumph: My Years as Secretary of State* (New York: Charles Scribner's Sons, 1993), p. 762.

254   **"This is the best Soviet":** Shultz, *Turmoil and Triumph*, pp. 760–62.

254   **"He and I had at it":** Ronald Reagan, *An American Life: The Autobiography* (New York: Simon & Schuster, 1990), p. 676.

255   **"George and I":** Reagan, *An American Life*, p. 677.

258   **"There is still time":** Reagan, *An American Life*, p. 679.

258   **"The President's performance":** George Shultz Press Conference from Iceland, NBC, Oct. 12, 1986, and George Shultz Press Conference from Iceland, CBS, Oct. 12, 1986, Ronald Reagan Presidential Library.

259   **"My first, overwhelming, intention":** Gorbachev, *Memoirs*, p. 419.

259   **"This exchange":** Tom Simons interview, May 19, 2009.

260   **"She handbagged me":** In various public appearances over the years, including to the author, Shultz has described this encounter with Prime Minister Thatcher.

261   **"The reality of the actual":** Shultz, *Turmoil and Triumph*, p. 774.

261   **"Sometimes people asked me why":** George Shultz interview, Feb. 3, 2011.

261   **"he only landed":** Shultz, *Turmoil and Triumph*, p. 775.

262   **"The nuclear age":** George Shultz, "Nuclear Weapons, Arms Control, and the Future of Deterrence," remarks before the International House of Chicago and *Chicago Sun-Times* Forum, University of Chicago, U.S. State Department Bulletin, Jan. 1987.

262   **"I struggled with that speech":** Shultz interview, Feb. 3, 2011.

262   **"I want to ensure":** Memorandum for the President, John M. Poindexter, "Subject: Guidance for Post-Reykjavik Follow-up Activities," Nov. 1, 1986, Reykjavik File, National Security Archive, George Washington University, Washington, DC, NSA Electronic Briefing Book No. 203, edited by Svetlana Savranskaya and Thomas Blanton, Document 24.

263   **"They will probably":** "Meeting with the Joint Chiefs of Staff, Alton G. Keel [Executive Secretary of the National Security Council], 18 December 1986," Reykjavik File, National Security Archive, George Washington University, Washington, DC, NSA Electronic Briefing Book No. 203, edited by Svetlana Savranskaya and Thomas Blanton, Document 29.

264   **"As for SDI":** Henry Kissinger, "Reagan Was Right to Shun 'Accords' That Were Traps," *Los Angeles Times*, Oct. 19, 1986.

265   **"If we strike":** Richard M. Nixon and Henry A. Kissinger, "An Arms Agreement— On Two Conditions," *Washington Post*, Apr. 26, 1987.

265   **"I got in one":** James Mann, *The Rebellion of Ronald Reagan: A History of the End of the Cold War* (New York: Viking, 2009), p. 53. Original source: Richard Nixon, "Memorandum to the File, Meeting with President Reagan at the White House, 5 p.m., April 28, 1987."

265   **"undoes forty years":** Mann, *The Rebellion of Ronald Reagan*, p. 254. Original

source: Memo to President-elect Ronald Reagan from Richard Nixon, Nov. 17, 1980, Richard Nixon Library.

266 **"The most conservative"**: Henry A. Kissinger, "A New Era for NATO," *Newsweek*, Oct. 12, 1987.

266 **"euphoria"**: Henry A. Kissinger, "The Dangers Ahead," *Newsweek*, Dec. 21, 1987.

266 **"Arms–Control Fever"**: Henry A. Kissinger, "Arms-Control Fever," *Washington Post*, Jan. 19, 1987.

267 **"It is one thing"**: Letter from George Shultz to Henry Kissinger, Jan. 19, 1988, Hoover Institution archives, George Shultz papers, Box 535.

267 **"I notice that we will be at Mandalay"**: Letter from Henry Kissinger to George Shultz, June 22, 1988, Hoover Institution archives, George Shultz papers, Box 535.

268 **"His basic principle"**: James Goodby interview, July 1, 2009.

268 **intermediate-range missile treaty:** The United States and Soviet Union eventually destroyed a total of 2,692 short- and intermediate-range missiles. The Soviet Union destroyed 889 of its intermediate-range missiles and 957 shorter-range missiles, and the U.S. destroyed 677 and 169, respectively. "The INF Treaty and the Washington Summit: 20 Years Later," Electronic Briefing Book No. 238, Digital National Security Archive, www.gwu.edu/~nsarchiv/NSAEBB/NSAEBB238/index.htm.

269 **"I was very upset"**: Shultz interview, Aug. 27, 2010.

270 **"The world was not ready"**: Shultz interview, Feb. 3, 2010.

270 **"If we could just talk"**: NSC/NSPG Meeting: 1981–1989 Minutes, "United States Arms Control Positions," Sept. 8, 1987, 1:15 p.m.–2:15 p.m., Situation Room, NSPG folder 0165, box 91309, Ronald Reagan Library.

270 **"What exactly do you mean"**: Shultz interview, Feb. 3, 2010.

CHAPTER TWENTY-TWO

271 **"I've seen him answer questions"**: Sam Nunn oral history, vol. 2, p. 158.

272 **"proliferation of weapons"**: Sam Nunn oral history, vol. 2, p. 159.

272 **Richard Lugar:** Senator Lugar serves today as an NTI board member and remains very engaged with nuclear weapons issues as the ranking Republican on the Foreign Relations Committee. But he does not agree with Nunn's call to abolish nuclear weapons. He told the *National Journal* in 2010: "I've talked to Sam Nunn and all the others that you mention about this subject of a world without nuclear weapons. They express the concept as being at the base of a mountain shrouded in clouds and trying to formulate a strategy for getting to the top even though they can't see it. So I don't fault them or President Obama for talking about a world without nuclear weapons, but neither do I think it is a particularly good idea to

express the process in that way. Quite frankly, it's been plenty difficult enough just trying to get down to the 1,500-warhead limit in New START.

"Talk of 'no nukes' also invites opposition from those who see it as a sign of weakness in those who lack the backbone to face the world as it is. I don't think that criticism is fair, but it's out there. So it seems to me that the more practical path is to move incrementally ahead, taking warheads off of missiles one at a time, steadily building trust and transparency into a process that makes misunderstandings less likely." James Kitfield, "Lugar: Pass New START Now," *National Journal*, July 17, 2010, p. 9.

272 **In an influential report:** Sidney Drell and Charles Townes, "The Report of the Nuclear Weapons Safety Panel," Committee on Armed Services, Hearing before the House of Representatives, Dec. 18, 1990.

273 **"All hell broke loose":** Sam Nunn oral history, vol. 2, p. 147.

274 **Ashton Carter:** Ashton B. Carter, Kurt Campbell, Steven Miller, and Charles Zraket, "Soviet Nuclear Fission: Control of the Nuclear Arsenal in a Disintegrating Soviet Union," Center for Science and International Affairs, Harvard University, Nov. 1991.

274 **"The study predicted":** Ashton B. Carter and William J. Perry, *Preventive Defense: A New Security Strategy for America* (Washington, DC: Brookings Institution Press, 1999), p. 71.

275 **Nunn and Lugar invited:** Richard Rhodes, *Twilight of the Bombs: Recent Challenges, New Dangers, and the Prospects for a World Without Nuclear Weapons* (New York: Knopf, 2010), pp. 104–5.

275 **White House strategy to reduce overall:** George H. W. Bush, "Address to the Nation on Reducing United States and Soviet Nuclear Weapons," Sept. 27, 1991, White House, UCSB American Presidency Project.

276 **"It just shows you":** Sam Nunn oral history, vol. 2, p. 167.

277 **"I told Sam and David":** William Perry interview, Aug. 14, 2008.

277 **"Perry took this":** Gloria Duffy interview, Feb. 2, 2011.

277 **"When we took office":** Carter and Perry, *Preventive Defense*, p. 77.

278 **"They assumed":** William Perry remarks at the Leadership Symposium, Stanford University, Apr. 7, 2009.

279 **"There was a lot of mentality":** Duffy interview, Feb. 2, 2011.

279 **"Across one wall":** Carter and Perry, *Preventive Defense*, pp. 1–2.

280 **"In place of nuclear missile silos":** Carter and Perry, *Preventive Defense*, p. 7.

281 **"what kind of madmen":** Bradley Graham, "U.S., Russia Reach Accord on Europe Treaty; Perry, Grachev Achieve 'Meeting of the Minds' on Border-Area Conventional Forces," *Washington Post*, Oct. 29, 1995.

281 **"Project Sapphire":** For a more thorough account of the operation, see Rhodes, *The Twilight of the Bombs*, pp. 148–54.

281 **The results:** For updated numbers, see the Nunn–Lugar Scorecard on Senator Richard Lugar's official website, http://lugar.senate.gov/nunnlugar/index.html.

282 **"The Cold War was over":** Sam Nunn interview, Sept. 1, 2010.

283 **Hambrecht & Quist:** Hambrecht & Quist was later acquired by Chase Manhattan Bank and is now part of JPMorgan Chase.

283 **"At Pervomaysk":** Carter and Perry, *Preventive Defense*, p. 8.

CHAPTER TWENTY-THREE

288 **"I would not absolutely":** Brent Scowcroft interview, Mar. 3, 2010.

289 **"I didn't know how to get to zero":** William Perry interview, Aug. 14, 2008.

289 **"The national security":** Henry A. Kissinger, "Sense, Sensibility, and Nuclear Weapons," *New York Post*, June 7, 1998.

290 **"You were the inspiration":** E-mail from Sam Nunn to Max Kampelman, Mar. 15, 2007, Nuclear Threat Initiative papers.

290 **"Max was on George's State Department":** Sam Nunn interview, Sept. 1, 2010.

290 **"I don't even know":** Max Kampelman interview, Mar. 25, 2010.

291 **"The rabbi who advised":** "Legends in the Law: A Conversation with Max Kampelman," *Washington Lawyer,* Feb. 2006, retrieved from www.dcbar.org/for_lawyers/resources/legends_in_the_law/kampelman.cfm.

292 **"I said, 'Mr. President'":** Kampelman interview, Mar. 3, 2010.

292 **"I said, 'Ted'":** Nunn interview, Sept. 1, 2010.

293 **"catalyze a global":** Memo to President George W. Bush, from Richard Lugar, Sam Nunn, Pete V. Domenici, et al., "A Bush–Putin Initiative Against Catastrophic Terrorism," Dec. 18, 2001, Nuclear Threat Initiative papers.

294 **"It wasn't 'let's engage'":** Nunn interview, Sept. 1, 2010.

294 **"For the foreseeable future":** John Deutch, Henry Kissinger, and Brent Scowcroft, "Test-Ban Treaty: Let's Wait Awhile," *Washington Post*, Oct. 10, 1999.

295 **"I knew about Sid":** George Shultz interview, Aug. 25, 2010.

295 **"I clearly didn't call":** Sidney Drell interview, Aug. 7, 2008.

296 **"George has enormous confidence":** Sam Nunn interview, Nov. 18, 2008.

296 **"Sid is very":** Shultz interview, Aug. 25, 2008.

296 **"I've always admired":** Nunn interview, Nov. 18, 2008.

297 **"Would also like":** Memo from Sam Nunn to George Shultz, "Key Points on Nuclear Weapons/RAND," July 28, 2003, Nuclear Security Project papers, Office of George Shultz, Stanford University.

297 **"That's where it started":** Nunn interview, Nov. 18, 2008.

297 **recommendations to Condoleezza Rice:** Memorandum from George Shultz to Condoleezza Rice, "Memorandum on Reducing the Danger from Nuclear Weapons and Improving the Security of Nuclear Materials," Aug. 14, 2003,

Nuclear Security Project papers, Office of George Shultz, Stanford University.

298 **In a cover letter to Bush:** Letter from George Shultz to President George W. Bush, Aug. 14, 2003, Nuclear Security Project archives, Office of George Shultz, Stanford University.

298 **"I was disappointed":** Nunn interview, Sept. 1, 2010.

299 **"I remember being disappointed":** George Shultz interview, Aug. 27, 2010.

299 **"We first engaged Secretary Shultz":** "Next Steps on Strategic Forces Project," NTI staff memo to Charles Curtis, Nov. 8, 2004, Nuclear Threat Initiative papers.

300 **fortuitous connection:** Andreasen wasn't the only NTI staff member who knew Drell. Joan Rohlfing, the senior vice president for programs at the time, had spent a year at Stanford in the late 1980s as a graduate student, at Drell's invitation. The two first met in 1983 when Rohlfing was an undergraduate at the University of Illinois at Urbana-Champaign. When Drell visited the campus, where he had done his Ph.D. work, she interviewed him for the student radio station. Rohlfing is now president of NTI.

300 **in *Foreign Affairs*:** The Drell-Andreasen letter took exception to a *Foreign Affairs* article by John Deutch, a former CIA director and deputy secretary of defense. The Deutch article, as summarized by *Foreign Affairs,* argued: "The nuclear threat has been transformed since the end of the Cold War, but Washington's nuclear posture has not changed to meet it. The United States should scale back its arsenal while allowing limited nuclear tests, shaping its nuclear force to bolster non-proliferation without undermining deterrence." *Foreign Affairs*, January–February 2005. Andreasen and Drell objected to Deutch's assertion that underground nuclear weapons testing might need to be resumed and his call to revise the Comprehensive Test Ban Treaty. Their letter to *Foreign Affairs* (March–April 2005) said:

John Deutch correctly concludes in "A Nuclear Posture for Today" (Jan./Feb. 2005) that the United States lacks a convincing rationale for the structure of its current nuclear force and for the policies guiding the management of its nuclear weapons. He rightly asserts that countering the proliferation of nuclear weapons should become as high a priority as deterring nuclear attacks. Yet although Deutch is right to propose substantially reducing the United States' deployed nuclear arsenal, he is wrong to advocate possible new nuclear tests or changing the terms of the Comprehensive Test Ban Treaty (CTBT).

During the recent presidential campaign, George W. Bush identified the spread of nuclear weapons and their possible use by terrorists as the most serious threat to the nation. To strengthen the NPT and stem nuclear proliferation, Bush should continue the U.S. moratorium on nuclear testing, initiate a bipartisan process with the Senate to achieve CTBT ratification, and work to secure ratification by other key states.

300 **"It was a good":** Letter from Max Kampelman to Steve Andreasen. Mar. 22, 2005, Nuclear Threat Initiative papers.

300 **"Reagan Was Right":** Steve Andreasen, "Reagan Was Right: Let's Ban Ballistic Missiles," *Survival* 46, no. 1 (Spring 2006): 117–30.

300 **"When I went to see him":** Steve Andreasen, NTI staff interview, Mar. 23, 2010.

301 **"He's much more":** Andreasen, NTI staff interview, Mar. 23, 2010.

301 **"I thought it was very":** Joan Rohlfing, NTI staff interview, Mar. 23, 2010.

301 **"Increasingly, we are":** Sam Nunn, "The Race Between Cooperation and Catastrophe," Remarks before the National Press Club, Mar. 9, 2005.

301 **"The only way to":** Concept paper prepared by Steve Andreasen for Max Kampelman, "K-1," July 4, 2005, Nuclear Threat Initiative papers.

302 **"My own hesitation":** E-mail from Max Kampelman to Steve Andreasen, July 13, 2005, "Re: Nuclear Concept Paper: K-3 Draft," Nuclear Threat Initiative papers.

302 **"The United States should":** Draft op-ed piece prepared by Steve Andreasen for Max Kampelman, "'Zero' Weapons of Mass Destruction," Nov. 20, 2005, Nuclear Threat Initiative papers.

302 **"I couldn't buy":** Nunn interview, Sept. 1, 2010.

302 **"But I have to say":** Kampelman interview, Mar. 3, 2010.

303 **"I found his reaction":** "Summary of Kampelman's November 16 meeting with Vice President Cheney," Nuclear Threat Initiative papers.

304 **"We said, we're not getting":** Drell interview, Aug. 7, 2008.

304 **"Our idea was not":** Shultz interview, Aug. 25, 2008.

304 **"As I look back over":** Goodby interview, July 1, 2009.

305 **"My conclusion":** Perry interview, Aug. 14, 2008.

CHAPTER TWENTY-FOUR

306 **"This message is not designed":** Message from Max Kampelman to Sidney Drell and George Shultz, Feb. 15, 2006, Nuclear Threat Initiative papers.

306 **"He called me and said":** Max Kampelman interview, Mar. 3, 2010.

307 **"I welcome any suggestions":** Letter from George Shultz to Max Kampelman, March 31, 2006, Nuclear Threat Initiative papers. The Andersons' book was published in 2009. Martin Anderson and Annelise Anderson, *Reagan's Secret War: The Untold Story of His Fight to Save the World from Nuclear Disaster* (New York: Crown, 2009).

307 **"I thought, just out of the blue":** George Shultz interview, Aug. 27, 2010.

307 **Kampelman's article:** Max Kampelman, "Bombs Away," *New York Times*, Apr. 24, 2006.

307 **The article ended:** Martin Luther King used the "ought" and "is" comparison in his book *Strength to Love*. "This strange dichotomy, this agonizing gulf between the *ought* and the *is*, represents the tragic theme of man's earthly pilgrimage." Martin Luther King Jr., *Strength to Love* (Cleveland: First Fortress, 1981), p. 40.

307 **"Max's column":** E-mail from Sidney Drell to Steve Andreasen, Apr. 25, 2006, Nuclear Threat Initiative papers.

308 **"He'd say, 'How many people'":** Sam Nunn interview, Sept. 1, 2010.

308 **"I think it became":** Charles Curtis interview, Mar. 23, 2010.

309 **"parallelism":** Memo from Steve Andreasen to Sam Nunn, "June 27 Meeting with Secretary Shultz, Dr. Perry and Sid Drell," June 16, 2006, Nuclear Threat Initiative papers.

309 **"We sat around":** George Shultz interview, Aug. 25, 2008.

309 **"Shultz, I think it":** Curtis interview, Mar. 23, 2010.

310 **"It was just brilliant":** Sam Nunn interview, Nov. 18, 2008.

310 **The Nuclear Outlook:** "The Nuclear Outlook and What Can Be Done About It," Nuclear Security Project papers, Office of George Shultz, Stanford University.

313 **"I would say":** Nunn interview, Sept. 1, 2010.

313 **action on the:** Memo from Sam Nunn to George Shultz, "Comments on Your Nuclear Outlook Memo," July 13, 2006, Nuclear Security Project papers, Office of George Shultz, Stanford University.

314 **"Henry, who has":** George Shultz interview, Aug. 25, 2008.

315 **"When I was in":** Henry Kissinger remarks at the American Academy of Diplomacy, State Department, Washington, DC, Dec. 14, 2005.

315 **"I quickly let":** Kampelman interview, Mar. 3, 2010.

315 **"In the Cold War":** Henry Kissinger interview with *Nuclear Tipping Point* filmmakers, Mar. 14, 2010, Nuclear Threat Initiative papers.

316 **"George Shultz and I":** Kissinger interview, Jan. 27, 2009.

317 **"the most eloquent":** Steve Andreasen, Nuclear Security Project Chronology, Nuclear Threat Initiative papers.

317 **Kampelman called:** Max Kampelman, "The Power of the Ought," Remarks at Hoover Institution Conference, "Implications of the Reykjavik Summit on Its Twentieth Anniversary," Stanford University, Oct. 11, 2006.

318 **"That was a masterful":** Steve Andreasen, NTI staff interview, Mar. 23, 2010.

318 **"Ordinarily, you can't":** William Perry interview, Aug. 14, 2008.

318 **Andreasen started drafting:** Steve Andreasen draft, "The Problem, The Vision, The Steps," Oct. 13, 2006, Nuclear Security Project papers, Office of George Shultz, Stanford University.

319 **"We thought that would":** Shultz interview, Aug. 25, 2008.

319 **"He thinks the only":** Joan Rohlfing, NTI staff interview, Mar. 23, 2010.

320 **"I have come to the"**: Nunn interview, Nov. 18, 2008.

320 **Nunn sent Shultz a letter:** Letter from Sam Nunn to George Shultz, Nov. 15, 2006, Nuclear Security Project papers, Office of George Shultz, Stanford University.

320 **"Our good efforts"**: Message from Sid Drell to Steve Andreasen, Nov. 29, 2006, Nuclear Threat Initiative papers.

320 **"I've added"**: Sam Nunn letter to George Shultz, Dec. 8, 2006, Nuclear Security Project papers, Office of George Shultz, Stanford University.

321 **"free from the *threat*"**: Curtis interview, Mar. 23, 2010.

321 **origins of which remain murky:** None of the people involved in the preparation of the article could recall the genesis of the idea that Nunn, and later Kissinger, endorse the aspirations outlined in the article but not sign it as coauthors. George Shultz said it might have been suggested after the October conference at the Hoover Institution to overcome the fact that Nunn and Kissinger had been unable to attend the meeting.

321 **"This was a suggestion"**: Rohlfing, NTI staff interview, Mar. 23, 2010.

321 **"I didn't like that"**: Nunn interview, Sept. 1, 2010.

322 **"I don't think anyone"**: Kissinger interview, Jan. 27, 2009.

323 **"I send you"**: Facsimile from Henry Kissinger to George Shultz, Dec. 26, 2006, Nuclear Security Project papers, Office of George Shultz, Stanford University.

323 **"Henry was always"**: Shultz interview, Aug. 27, 2010.

323 **"I'd say Shultz"**: Nunn interview, Nov. 18, 2008.

323 **Drell demurred:** Shultz interview, Aug. 29, 2010.

CHAPTER TWENTY-FIVE

324 **"A World Free"**: George P. Shultz, William J. Perry, Henry A. Kissinger, and Sam Nunn, "A World Free of Nuclear Weapons," *Wall Street Journal*, Jan. 4, 2007. The op-ed article noted in an addendum that the following people, who attended the October 2006 Reykjavik Twentieth Anniversary Conference at the Hoover Institution, also endorsed the op-ed piece: Martin Anderson, Steve Andreasen, Michael Armacost, William Crowe, James Goodby, Thomas Graham Jr., Thomas Henriksen, David Holloway, Max Kampelman, Jack Matlock, John McLaughlin, Don Oberdorfer, Rozanne Ridgway, Henry Rowen, Roald Sagdeev, and Abraham Sofaer.

324 **drew immediate attention:** Oddly, the *Wall Street Journal* newsroom failed to take note of the scoop that had appeared on the paper's editorial pages. The editorial pages, for their part, followed up the next day with a dyspeptic letter to the editor from John L. Sorg, a reader in McCordsville, Indiana. The headline was "Four Pollyannas of the Apocalypse." Sorg wrote, "I am not a statesman like

the four authors, yet I am compelled to express my shock at their pollyanish-ness and downright naivete. Actually, the only surprise to me is George P. Shultz. He worked for and with Ronald Reagan as secretary of state and he should understand the necessity of 'Peace through Strength' at least as much as he understands the word 'Kumbaya.'" John L. Sorg, "Four Pollyannas of the Apocalypse," letter, *Wall Street Journal*, Jan. 5, 2007.

324 **"Former Secretary":** George Gedda, "Kissinger, Other Eminent Security Experts Urge 'World Without Nuclear Weapons,'" Associated Press, Jan. 4, 2007.

324 **"The Washington heavyweights":** "Former US Policy Honchos Call for World Free of Nuclear Arms," Agence France-Presse, Jan. 4, 2007.

325 **"So, here we are":** George Shultz interview, Aug. 25, 2008.

326 **"When we wrote":** Henry Kissinger in *Nuclear Tipping Point*, written and directed by Ben Goddard (Nuclear Security Project, 2010).

326 **"not known for":** Mikhail S. Gorbachev, "The Nuclear Threat," *Wall Street Journal*, Jan. 31, 2007.

327 **Shultz got to work:** The postpublication activities cited here are based on the Nuclear Security Project papers, Office of George Shultz, Stanford University.

328 **An ambitious plan:** "The Vision of Reykjavik: Toward a Nuclear Weapon Free World Strategy", Mar. 1, 2007. Nuclear Threat Initiative. A refined version of the March 1 memo was completed on March 15.

328 **"We have taken it upon":** William Perry interview, Aug. 14, 2008.

329 **"His experience":** E-mail from James Goodby to Sid Drell, "Max Kampelman's Ideas," May 16, 2007, Nuclear Security Project papers, Office of George Shultz, Stanford University.

330 **"I really am not":** Max Kampelman interview, Mar. 25, 2010.

330 **"A president has to":** Sam Nunn interview, Nov. 18, 2008.

331 **"It was really":** David E. Sanger, *The Inheritance: The World Obama Confronts and the Challenges to American Power* (New York: Crown, 2009), pp. 412–13.

331 **"I didn't think he":** Sam Nunn interview, Sept. 1, 2010.

331 **"The breakthrough would be":** Shultz interview, Aug. 25, 2008.

332 **"That was a big endorsement":** Ben Rhodes, in Ben Rhodes and Gary Samore interview, Aug. 4, 2010.

333 **His interest in nuclear weapons:** Barack Obama, "Breaking the War Mentality," *Sundial* 7, no. 12 (Mar. 10, 1983). David E. Sanger and William J. Broad mentioned the article in "The Long Arc of a Nuclear-Free Vision," *New York Times*, July 5, 2009.

333 **"As leaders from":** Barack Obama, Remarks to the Chicago Council on Global Affairs, Apr. 23, 2007, UCSB American Presidency Project.

334 **speech at the Wilson Center:** Barack Obama, Remarks in Washington, DC: "The War We Need to Win," Aug. 1, 2007, UCSB American Presidency Project.

334 **The breakthrough:** Barack Obama, Remarks in Chicago: "A New Beginning," DePaul University, Oct. 2, 2007.

334 **"The original conception":** Ben Rhodes, in Rhodes and Samore interview, Aug. 4, 2010.

335 **"Here's what I'll say":** Barack Obama, Remarks in Chicago: "A New Beginning," Oct. 2, 2007.

335 **"Dear George":** Letter from Nancy Reagan to George Shultz, Oct. 4, 2007, Nuclear Security Project archives, Office of George Shultz, Stanford University.

336 **"As we look forward":** Memo from Sam Nunn to Shultz, Kissinger, Perry, and Drell, Oct. 31, 2007, Nuclear Security Project papers, Office of George Shultz, Stanford University.

336 **"I said to Sam":** Shultz interview, Aug. 25, 2008.

336 **The *Wall Street Journal* published the article:** George P. Shultz, William J. Perry, Henry A. Kissinger, and Sam Nunn, "Toward a Nuclear-Free World," *Wall Street Journal*, Jan. 15, 2008.

The steps outlined in the article were, in the authors' words:

Extend key provisions of the Strategic Arms Reduction Treaty of 1991.

Take steps to increase the warning and decision times for the launch of all nuclear armed ballistic missiles, thereby reducing risks of accidental or unauthorized attacks.

Discard any existing operational plans for massive attacks that still remain from the Cold War days.

Undertake negotiations toward developing cooperative multilateral ballistic-missile defense and early warning systems, as proposed by Presidents Bush and Putin at their 2002 Moscow summit meeting.

Accelerate work to provide the highest possible standards of security for nuclear weapons, as well as for nuclear materials everywhere in the world, to prevent terrorists from acquiring a nuclear bomb.

Start a dialogue, including within NATO and with Russia, on consolidating the nuclear weapons designed for forward deployment to enhance their security, and as a first step toward careful accounting for them and their eventual elimination.

Strengthen the means of monitoring compliance with the nuclear Non-Proliferation Treaty (NPT) as a counter to the global spread of advanced technologies.

Adopt a process for bringing the Comprehensive Test Ban Treaty (CTBT) into effect, which would strengthen the NPT and aid international monitoring of nuclear activities.

337 **June speech:** Sam Nunn, "The Mountaintop: A World Free of Nuclear Weapons," remarks before the Council on Foreign Relations, June 14, 2007.

337 **"inadequate":** E-mail from Max Kampelman to Jim Goodby, Dec. 18, 2007, Nuclear Security Project papers, Office of George Shultz, Stanford University.

337 **"The Mountaintop":** Sam Nunn, "The Mountaintop: A World Free of Nuclear Weapons," remarks in Oslo, Norway, Feb. 27, 2008.

337 **"Other than that":** Shultz interview, Aug. 25, 2008.

338 **clusters of retired foreign and defense:** Over time, NTI developed partnerships with thirteen foreign organizations to help advance the disarmament initiative and interim steps to reduce nuclear threats. The organizations were based in Argentina, Australia, Britain, Germany, Japan, Russia, and Sweden, among other nations.

339 **Global Zero:** Other Global Zero leaders include Barry Blechman, cofounder of the Henry L. Stimson Center, a nonpartisan Washington think tank, and Matt Brown, former Rhode Island secretary of state. Richard Burt, former ambassador to Germany and assistant secretary of state, has also played a leading role.

339 **"We're not in their":** Shultz interview, Aug. 25, 2008.

339 **"We hope that our work":** Letter from Sam Nunn to Bruce Blair, Apr. 22, 2008, Nuclear Security Project papers, Office of George Shultz, Stanford University.

339 **"We have been asked":** Draft letter to NSP supporters by Shultz et al., July 10, 2008, Nuclear Security Project papers, Office of George Shultz, Stanford University.

340 **documentary films:** *Nuclear Tipping Point* was written and directed by Ben Goddard and produced by the Nuclear Threat Initiative. Free DVDs of the film are distributed through www.nucleartippingpoint.org. *Countdown to Zero* was written and directed by Lucy Walker and produced by Lawrence Bender. It showed in theaters nationwide briefly as well as at the 2010 Sundance and Cannes film festivals.

341 **"Nuclear war threatens":** "The Challenge of Peace: God's Promise and Our Response," Pastoral Letter on War and Peace by the National Conference of Catholic Bishops, May 3, 1983.

341 **Two Futures Project:** http://twofuturesproject.org. The roster of evangelical ministers who support the effort includes Leith Anderson, president of the National Association of Evangelicals, and Ronald J. Sider, president of Evangelicals for Social Action. For the full list of endorsers, see http://twofuturesproject.org/endorsers.

342 **"We used to":** Barack Obama, Remarks in West Lafayette, Indiana, July 16, 2008, UCSB American Presidency Project.

342 **"Forty years":** John McCain, "Foreign Policy: Where We Go From Here," Los Angeles World Affairs Council, Mar. 26, 2008.

342 **"A quarter of a century"**: John McCain, remarks at the University of Denver, May 27, 2008, John McCain campaign website (no longer exists).

343 **"As president"**: "Arms Control Today 2008 Presidential Q&A: Democratic Nominee Barack Obama," *Arms Control Today*, Sept. 24, 2008. Senator McCain did not respond to the ACA questions. www.armscontrol.org/system/files/Obama_Q-A_FINAL_Dec10_2008.pdf.

343 **"The biggest threat"**: First Presidential Debate, Sept. 26, 2008, University of Mississippi, transcript at http://elections.nytimes.com/2008/president/debates/first-presidential-debate.html.

344 **"I had never"**: George Shultz interview, July 1, 2009.

344 **"There was a direct line"**: Ben Rhodes, in Ben Rhodes and Gary Samore interview, Aug. 4, 2010.

345 **"On this day"**: Barack Obama, Inaugural Address, Washington, DC, Jan. 20, 2009, UCSB American Presidency Project.

CHAPTER TWENTY-SIX

346 **"People many times"**: Sam Nunn interview, Nov. 18, 2008.

346 **"As you know"**: Letter from Shultz, Kissinger, Perry, and Nunn to President Obama, Jan. 22, 2009, Nuclear Security Project papers, Office of George Shultz, Stanford University.

347 **"We're in a waiting game"**: George Shultz interview, Feb. 9, 2009.

347 **"Let's take this issue"**: Ben Rhodes and Gary Samore interview, Aug. 3, 2010.

348 **"So today"**: Barack Obama remarks in Hradcany Square, Prague, Apr. 5, 2009, White House transcript.

348 **"Very powerful"**: George Shultz interview, July 1, 2009.

349 **"The most important"**: Gary Samore, in Rhodes and Samore interview, Aug. 3, 2010.

350 **"Time is not"**: George Shultz remarks at the "Overcoming Nuclear Dangers" Conference, Rome, Apr. 16, 2009.

350 **"We have to admit"**: Mikhail Gorbachev remarks at the "Overcoming Nuclear Dangers" Conference, Rome, Apr. 16, 2009.

350 **"Many of my"**: William J. Perry dinner remarks at the "Overcoming Nuclear Dangers" Conference, Rome, Apr. 16, 2009.

351 **"They all said I"**: Shultz interview, July 1, 2009.

352 **"All four of us"**: George Shultz remarks in the Oval Office, May 19, 2009, White House transcript.

353 **"Henry was very"**: Shultz interview, July 1, 2009.

353 **"We wrote two"**: "Henry Kissinger on the Pakistan Meeting with Obama," *On the Record with Greta Van Susteren*, Fox News, May 19, 2009.

355 **"Why don't you get"**: The author rode with them to the airport.

355 **in Munich:** The author attended the Munich Security Conference in 2010, along with Shultz, Kissinger, Perry, and Nunn.

355 **guests of honor at a screening:** The author attended the screening.

CHAPTER TWENTY-SEVEN

358 **Los Alamos:** The author visited the Los Alamos National Laboratory in New Mexico, Oct. 8 and 9, 2009.

359 **"It's like when you":** Rusty Gray, comment to author at Los Alamos.

359 **Jason study, led by Drell:** Sidney Drell et al., *Science-Based Stockpile Stewardship* (McLean, VA: MITRE Corporation, Nov. 1994).

360 **The bomb makers:** Scientists and engineers at Los Alamos and other national laboratories also design and develop new technologies to detect and help prevent the spread of nuclear weapons and materials.

360 **nuclear weapons tests:** Between 1945 and 1992, the United States conducted 1,051 nuclear tests; 215 of those were atmospheric (underwater tests included) and 836 were underground tests. The Soviet Union/Russia conducted 715 nuclear tests over the same period, 219 of which were atmospheric (underwater included) and 496 were underground. See Robert Standish Norris and Thomas B. Cochran, "United States Nuclear Tests, July 1945 to 31 December 1992," Natural Resources Defense Council, Feb. 1, 1994, pp. 1–2; and Pavel Podvig, ed., *Russian Strategic Nuclear Forces* (Cambridge: MIT Press, 2001), pp. 439–40.

360 **third op-ed:** George P. Shultz, William J. Perry, Henry A. Kissinger, and Sam Nunn, "How to Protect Our Nuclear Deterrent," *Wall Street Journal*, Jan. 20, 2009.

360 **visited the Lawrence Livermore National Laboratory:** At the time of the visit, Drell and Perry served on the governing boards that oversee the management of the Livermore and Los Alamos labs. Perry left the boards in October 2010 when he became a member of the Energy Department advisory board.

360 **Life Extension Program:** The program is designed to include the rebuilding of pits for some older warheads when that is deemed necessary. A pit is the spherical chamber containing plutonium that is the core of a modern warhead.

362 **"You can repeat":** Sam Nunn interview, Sept. 1, 2010.

362 **"As reductions continued":** Jonathan Schell, *The Fate of the Earth and The Abolition* (Stanford: Stanford University Press, 2000), p. 153.

363 **Michael O'Hanlon:** Michael E. O'Hanlon, *A Skeptic's Case for Nuclear Disarmament* (Washington, DC: Brookings Institution Press, 2010).

364 **"I think the progress":** George Shultz interview, Feb. 3, 2011.

364 **nuclear summit:** The name of the summit was the Nuclear Security Summit. It took place on April 12 and 13, 2010.

365 **A month later:** The 2010 Review Conference of the Parties to the Treaty on the Non-Proliferation of Nuclear Weapons took place May 3–28, 2010.

366 **International Atomic Energy Agency:** Though an independent agency, the
IAEA, which was established in 1957 as an outgrowth of President Eisenhower's Atoms for Peace program, reports annually to the United Nations General
Assembly, and at times, to the Security Council. IAEA inspectors are responsible for monitoring compliance with safeguard agreements under which nations
like Iraq and Iran agree to limit their nuclear activities, such as uranium enrichment, to peaceful purposes. IAEA inspectors correctly determined before
the 2003 American invasion of Iraq that Saddam Hussein's nuclear weapons
program was moribund. The IAEA's enforcement powers, however, are limited and nations like North Korea that are intent on developing weapons can
simply bar agency inspectors from monitoring their nuclear facilities. The UN
can impose sanctions in such cases and try to prevent the shipment of nuclear-
related equipment to outlier countries, but there is no guarantee that weapons
programs can be blocked.

367 **"If the START":** David E. Sanger, "Obama Nuclear Agenda Only Gets Harder
After Treaty," *New York Times*, Dec. 22, 2010.

367 **a blanket ban:** The Treaty Banning Nuclear Weapons Tests in the Atmosphere,
in Outer Space and Under Water, also known as the Partial Test Ban Treaty, was
signed on August 5, 1963. The Threshold Test Ban Treaty was signed on July 3,
1974, but did not enter into force until March 31, 1976. On May 28, 1976, the
United States and Soviet Union signed the Underground Nuclear Explosions for
Peaceful Purposes Treaty.

367 **Drell played a critical role:** Sidney Drell et al., *JASON Nuclear Testing Study:
Summary and Conclusions* (McLean, VA: MITRE Corporation, Aug. 3, 1995).

368 **"You can argue":** William Perry interview, Feb. 22, 2011.

368 **"To achieve a global ban":** Barack Obama remarks in Hradcany Square,
Prague, Apr. 5, 2009, White House transcript.

369 **monitoring system:** "New Impetus for Test Ban Treaty," *Strategic Comments*
(International Institute for Strategic Studies) 15, no. 6 (Aug. 2009).

369 **CTBTO:** The CTBTO currently goes by a different name that will remain
until the treaty goes into force: Preparatory Commission for the Comprehensive
Nuclear-Test-Ban Organization.

369 **National Ignition Facility:** The author visited the NIF on April 9, 2009.

370 **"But even though":** William Perry interview, Feb. 22, 2011.

371 **its economy now ranks tenth:** Economy rankings come from the CIA World
Fact Book.

371 **The American and Russian groups:** A fourth meeting planned in Washington in December 2009 was canceled at the request of the Bush administration
after the military conflict between Russia and Georgia earlier that year.

371 **Rose Gottemoeller:** Gottemoeller also participated in a conference the men

organized at the Hoover Institution in 2010 about rethinking the role of nuclear deterrence in American defense strategy. As the director for Russia, Ukraine, and Eurasia affairs at the Clinton White House, Gottemoeller worked closely with Perry on the denuclearization of Ukraine, Kazakhstan, and Belarus.

371 **The United States still has roughly:** Walter Pincus, "Russian Tactical Nuclear Weapons Still an Issue after START Treaty Ratification," *Washington Post*, Dec. 27, 2010.

372 **"a terrorist's dream":** William Perry remarks at *Nuclear Tipping Point* screening, Library of Congress, Washington, DC, Mar. 8, 2011.

372 **Nizar Trabelsi:** "18 Guilty in Terror Trial in Belgium; 3 Linked to Plot on NATO," *New York Times*, Oct. 1, 2003.

373 **"If four or five":** General Robertus Remkes interview, Nov. 4, 2007.

374 **"In Europe":** Sam Nunn remarks to the InterAction Council 28th Annual Plenary Meeting, Hiroshima, Apr. 18, 2010, Nuclear Threat Initiative.

374 **"Part of the reason":** William J. Perry and George P. Shultz, "How to Build on the Start Treaty," *New York Times*, Apr. 10, 2010.

374 **limited missile defenses:** Limited missile defenses, unlike Reagan's dream of a missile shield, would be designed to intercept a handful of missiles, not dozens or hundreds. As a result, a limited system would not neutralize American or Russian nuclear forces as the two countries move to reduce their arsenals.

374 **Euro-Atlantic Security Initiative:** The Initiative was established and is supported by the Carnegie Endowment for International Peace. In addition to Nunn, the other cochairs are Wolfgang Ischinger, former German deputy foreign minister and ambassador to the United States, and Igor Ivanov, former Russian foreign minister. The cochair of the missile defense working group, with Stephen Hadley, is Vyacheslav Trubnikov, a retired Soviet diplomat and former director of the Russian Foreign Intelligence Service.

375 **"pursue high-level":** "Nuclear Posture Review Report," Department of Defense, Apr. 2010, Executive Summary.

376 **Pakistan's nuclear weapons:** David E. Sanger and Eric Schmitt, "Pakistani Nuclear Arms Pose Challenge to U.S. Policy," *New York Times*, Jan. 31, 2011.

377 **Stanford colleagues:** Siegfried Hecker was director of the Los Alamos National Laboratory, 1986–97, and is codirector of Stanford's Center for International Security and Cooperation. John Lewis is an expert on Chinese politics and U.S.-China relations and a professor of Chinese politics, emeritus, at Stanford University.

378 **"appears to have":** William Broad, John Markoff, and David E. Sanger, "Israeli Test on Worm Called Crucial in Iran Nuclear Delay," *New York Times*, Jan. 15, 2011.

378 **"If Iran and North Korea":** William Perry remarks at the 2011 Robert McNamara Lecture on War and Peace, Harvard University, Feb. 24, 2011.

379   **"I don't have a problem":** Robert Gates interview, Aug. 7, 2009.

379   **"There's been century":** General Kevin Chilton interview, Aug. 9, 2010.

380   **"The arsenal":** Chilton interview, Aug. 9, 2010.

380   **"an outmoded strategy":** Bruce Blair, Damon Bosetti, and Brian Weeden, "Bombs Away," *New York Times*, Dec. 6, 2010.

381   **"If you never plan":** The author attended the conference.

381   **"The thing I convinced myself":** Colin Powell in *Nuclear Tipping Point*, directed by Ben Goddard (Nuclear Security Project, 2010).

381   **"Today the Cold War":** Henry Kissinger, William J. Perry, Sam Nunn, and George P. Shultz, "A World Free of Nuclear Weapons," *Wall Street Journal*, Jan. 4, 2007, p. A15.

381   **"I've heard some discussion":** William J. Perry remarks at the Conference on Strategic Weapons in the 21st Century, cosponsored by Lawrence Livermore and Los Alamos national laboratories, Washington, DC, Jan. 29, 2009.

382   **two-day conference:** The conference was called "Deterrence: Its Past and Future," and took place at the Hoover Institution, Stanford University, on November 11 and 12, 2010.

384   **"extreme circumstances":** Nuclear Posture Review Report, Department of Defense, Apr. 2010, p. viii.

385   **"The triad's existence":** Chilton interview, Aug. 9, 2010.

386   **end-state issues:** Sid Drell and Jim Goodby described some of them in *A World Without Nuclear Weapons: End-State Issues* (Stanford: Hoover Institution Press, 2009). A number of other essays and papers have looked at the same set of issues. These include *The Abolition* by Jonathan Schell (Stanford: Stanford University Press, 2000); "Abolishing Nuclear Weapons," by George Perkovich and James M. Acton (London: Routledge for The International Institute for Strategic Studies, 2008); "Shared Responsibilities for Nuclear Disarmament: A Global Debate," by Scott D. Sagan (Cambridge: American Academy of Arts and Sciences, 2010); and "A Skeptic's Case for Nuclear Disarmament," by Michael E. O'Hanlon (Washington, DC: Brookings Institution Press, 2010).

387   **"Thus far":** Bernard Brodie, Frederick Sherwood Dunn, and Arnold Wolfers, *The Absolute Weapon: Atomic Power and World Order* (New York: Harcourt Brace, 1946).

387   **"Much has changed":** Invitation from the Hoover Institution for Conference on Nuclear Deterrence, delivered Sept. 13, 2010.

388   **"Nations should move":** Kissinger et al., "A World Free of Nuclear Weapons." Shultz, Perry, and Nunn preferred to say "steps toward deterrence that do not rely ultimately on nuclear weapons . . ." Kissinger, unwilling to lean that far toward marginalizing nuclear weapons, insisted on "steps toward deterrence that do not rely primarily on nuclear weapons . . ."

389 **"National technical means":** Drell and Goodby, *A World Without Nuclear Weapons*, p. 15.

390 **Open Skies Treaty:** U.S. Department of State Bureau of Arms Control, Verification and Compliance Euro-Atlantic Security Affairs.

390 **"We have always":** Henry Kissinger in *Nuclear Tipping Point*.

390 **at the Library of Congress:** The author attended the screening.

393 **"My generation was":** William Perry remarks before Management Science and Engineering 193 class, Stanford University, Oct. 27, 2009.

393 **"Once nuclear weapons":** Kissinger in *Nuclear Tipping Point*.

BIBLIOGRAPHY

INTERVIEWS AND ORAL HISTORIES
Interview List
with Gabriela Aoun
Lew Franklin, December 18, 2008, Stanford University
with Philip Taubman
Michael R. Anastasio, October 9, 2009, Los Alamos, NM
Steve Andreasen, Cathy Gwin, and Joan Rohlfing, March 23, 2010, Washington, DC
John R. Bass, November 18, 2010, Tbilisi, Georgia
Andrew Bieniawski, September 25, 2010, Warsaw, Poland
James Bjorken, September 21, 2009, Palo Alto, CA
Shlomo Brom, April 21, 2009, Tel Aviv
Harold Brown, July 8, 2009, San Diego
General James Cartwright, March 11, 2010, Washington, DC
General Kevin Chilton, August 9, 2010, Omaha, NE
Richard Combs, July 12, 2009, Three Rivers, CA
Charles Curtis, March 23, 2010, Washington, DC
Gilbert Decker, December 19, 2008, Los Gatos, CA
Paul Doty, May 20, 2009, Cambridge, MA
Persis Drell, October 3, 2008, Palo Alto, CA
Sidney Drell, August 7, 2008, August 12, 2009, September 2, 2009, October 6, 2009, February 14, 2011, Stanford, CA
Gloria Duffy, February 2, 2011, San Francisco
Pascal Fias, November 15, 2010, Antwerp, Belgium
Gideon Frank, April 22, 2009, Tel Aviv
Lew Franklin, December 10, 2008, Stanford, CA
Richard Garwin, November 25, 2008, Scarsdale, NY
Robert Gates, August 7, 2009, Washington, DC
Marvin Goldberger, April 8, 2009, La Jolla, CA
James Goodby, July 1, 2009, Stanford, CA

Mikhail Gorbachev, April 17, 2009, Rome

Olli Heinonen, April 24, 2009, Vienna

David Huizenga, July 12, 2010, Washington, DC

Israeli Defense Force Intelligence analyst, April 19, 2009, Tel Aviv

Paul Kaminski, January 28, 2009, Fairfax Station, VA

Max Kampelman, March 25, 2010, Washington, DC

Henry Kissinger, January 27, 2009, New York

Meir Litvak, April 21, 2009, Tel Aviv

David Makhardze, November 18, 2010, Tbilisi, Georgia

Edward Moses, April 9, 2009, Livermore, CA

Sam Nunn, November 18, 2008, Atlanta, GA; September 1, 2010, El Paso, TX

Alexander Okitashvili, November 17, 2010, Tbilisi, Georgia

Archil Pavlenishvili, November 17, 2010, Tbilisi, Georgia

Tanja Peeters, November 15, 2010, Antwerp, Belgium

Ed Perry, May 21, 2009, Brunswick, ME

Lee Perry, March 4, 2009, Palo Alto, CA

William Perry, August 14, 2008, November 10, 2008, February 22, 2011,
   Stanford, CA

Tariq Rauf, April 24, 2009, Vienna

General Robertus Remkes, Ret., November 4, 2010, Edenton, NC

Ben Rhodes and Gary Samore, August 5, 2010, Washington, DC

Condoleezza Rice, April 21, 2010, Stanford, CA

Brent Scowcroft, March 23, 2010, Washington, DC

George Shultz, August 25, 2008, July 1, 2009, September 2, 2009, August 27, 2010,
   February 3, 2011, Stanford, CA

Thomas Simons, May 19, 2009, Cambridge, MA

Ephraim Sneh, April 20, 2009, Tel Aviv

Albert "Bud" Wheelon, March 21, 2009, Montecito, CA

with Nuclear Tipping Point *filmmakers*

Henry Kissinger, March 14, 2010

William Perry, September 1, 2010

Richard Nixon Presidential Library and Museum, Richard Nixon Oral History Project,
Yorba Linda, CA

George Shultz, with Timothy J. Naftali, May 10, 2007, Stanford, CA

University of Virginia, Miller Center of Public Affairs, Presidential Oral History Pro-
gram, Ronald Reagan Oral History Project, Charlottesville, VA

George Shultz, with Stephen Knott, Marc Selverstone, and James Sterling Young, December 18, 2002

Nuclear Threat Initiative offices, Washington, DC

Sam Nunn Oral History, vols. 1 and 2, September 3 and 5, 1996, Washington, DC

ARCHIVES AND LIBRARIES

Emory University, Manuscript, Archives and Rare Book Library, Atlanta, GA

Hoover Institution, Archival Collections, Stanford, CA

Hoover Institution, Nuclear Security Project papers, Stanford, CA

National Security Archive, George Washington University, Washington, DC

Princeton University, Seeley G. Mudd Manuscript Library, Princeton, NJ

Richard Nixon Presidential Library, Yorba Linda, CA

Ronald Reagan Presidential Library, Simi Valley, CA

BOOKS

Alter, Jonathan. *The Promise: President Obama, Year One.* New York: Simon & Schuster, 2010.

Anderson, Martin, and Annelise Anderson. *Reagan's Secret War: The Untold Story of His Fight to Save the World from Nuclear Disaster.* New York: Crown, 2009.

Aronstein, David C., and Albert C. Piccirillo. *Have Blue and the F-117A: Evolution of the "Stealth Fighter."* Reston, VA: American Institute of Aeronautics and Astronautics, 1997.

Bernstein, Jeremy. *Plutonium: A History of the World's Most Dangerous Element.* Ithaca, NY: Cornell University Press, 2007.

Beschloss, Michael R., and Strobe Talbott. *At the Highest Levels: The Inside Story of the End of the Cold War.* Boston: Little, Brown, 1993.

Boswell, James. *The Life of Samuel Johnson.* New York: Penguin Classics, 1986.

Burr, William, ed. *The Kissinger Transcripts: The Top-Secret Talks with Beijing and Moscow.* New York: New Press, 1998.

Cannon, Lou. *President Reagan: The Role of a Lifetime.* New York: Touchstone/Simon & Schuster, 1991.

Carter, Ashton B., and William J. Perry. *Preventive Defense: A New Security Strategy for America.* Washington, DC: Brookings Institution Press, 1999.

Chernyaev, Anatoly. *My Six Years with Gorbachev.* University Park: Pennsylvania State University Press, 2000.

Christopher, Warren. *Chances of a Lifetime.* New York: Scribner, 2001.

Cirincione, Joseph. *Bomb Scare: The History and Future of Nuclear Weapons.* New York: Columbia University Press, 2007.

Cohen, Samuel. *The Neutron Bomb: Political, Technological and Military Issues.* Cambridge, MA: Institute for Foreign Policy Analysis, 1978.

——. *The Truth About the Neutron Bomb: The Inventor of the Bomb Speaks Out.* New York: William Morrow, 1983.

Coll, Steve. *Ghost Wars: The Secret History of the CIA, Afghanistan, and Bin Laden, from the Soviet Invasion to September 10, 2001.* New York: Penguin, 2005.

Collins, Catherine, and Douglas Frantz. *Fallout: The True Story of the CIA's Secret War on Nuclear Trafficking.* New York: Free Press, 2011.

Combs, Dick. *Inside the Soviet Alternative Universe: The Cold War's End and the Soviet Union's Fall Appraised.* University Park: Pennsylvania State University Press, 2008.

Cook, James F. *Carl Vinson: Patriarch of the Armed Forces.* Macon, GA: Mercer University Press, 2004.

Cooke, Stephanie. *In Mortal Hands: A Cautionary History of the Nuclear Age.* New York: Bloomsbury, 2009.

Dallek, Robert. *Nixon and Kissinger: Partners in Power.* New York: HarperCollins, 2007.

Dobbs, Michael. *One Minute to Midnight: Kennedy, Khrushchev, and Castro on the Brink of Nuclear War.* New York: Knopf, 2008.

Dobrynin, Anatoly. *In Confidence: Moscow's Ambassador to America's Six Cold War Presidents 1962–1986.* New York: Times Books, 1995.

Drell, Sidney D. *In the Shadow of the Bomb: Physics and Arms Control.* New York: American Institute of Physics, 1993.

————. *Nuclear Weapons, Scientists, and the Post–Cold War Challenge.* Hackensack, NJ: World Scientific, 2007.

Drell, Sidney D., and James E. Goodby. *A World Without Nuclear Weapons: End-State Issues.* Stanford, CA: Hoover Institution Press, 2009.

Drell, Sidney D., and Sergei P. Kapitza, eds. *Sakharov Remembered: A Tribute by Friends and Colleagues.* New York: American Institute of Physics, 1991.

Enthoven, Alain C., and K. Wayne Smith. *How Much Is Enough? Shaping the Defense Program, 1961–1969.* Santa Monica, CA: RAND Corporation, 2005.

Finkbeiner, Ann. *The Jasons: The Secret History of Science's Postwar Elite.* New York: Viking, 2006.

FitzGerald, Frances. *Way Out There in the Blue: Reagan, Star Wars and the End of the Cold War.* New York: Simon & Schuster, 2000.

Frantz, Douglas, and Catherine Collins. *The Man from Pakistan: The True Story of the World's Most Dangerous Nuclear Smuggler.* New York: Twelve, 2007.

Fubini, David G. *Let Me Explain: Eugene G. Fubini's Life in Defense of America.* Santa Fe: Sunstone Books, 2009.

Gates, Robert M. *From the Shadows: The Ultimate Insider's Story of Five Presidents and How They Won the Cold War.* New York: Simon & Schuster, 1996.

Ghamari-Tabrizi, Sharon. *The Worlds of Herman Kahn: The Intuitive Science of Thermonuclear War.* Cambridge, MA: Harvard University Press, 2005.

Goldstein, Gordon M. *Lessons in Disaster: McGeorge Bundy and the Path to War in Vietnam.* New York: Times Books, 2008.

Goodby, James E. *At the Borderline of Armageddon: How American Presidents Managed the Atom Bomb.* Lanham, MD: Rowman & Littlefield, 2006.

Gorbachev, Mikhail. *Memoirs.* New York: Bantam, 1997.

Hersh, Seymour M. *The Price of Power: Kissinger in the Nixon White House.* New York: Summit Books, 1983.

Hinderstein, Corey, ed. *Cultivating Confidence: Verification, Monitoring and Enforcement for a World Free of Nuclear Weapons*. Stanford, CA: Hoover Institution Press, 2010.

Hoffman, David E. *The Dead Hand: The Untold Story of the Cold War Arms Race and Its Dangerous Legacy*. New York: Doubleday, 2009.

Holloway, David. *Stalin and the Bomb*. New Haven, CT: Yale University Press, 1994.

Hoover, Robert A. *The MX Controversy: A Guide to Issues and References*. Claremont, CA: Regina Books, 1982.

Horne, Alistair. *Kissinger: 1973, The Crucial Year*. New York: Simon & Schuster, 2009.

Isaacson, Walter. *Kissinger: A Biography*. New York: Simon & Schuster, 1992.

Kahn, Herman. *On Thermonuclear War*. New Brunswick, NJ: Transaction, 2007.

Kaplan, Fred. *The Wizards of Armageddon*. Stanford, CA: Stanford University Press, 1983.

Kennedy, Robert F. *Thirteen Days: A Memoir of the Cuban Missile Crisis*. New York: Norton, 1971.

Kenney, Martin. *Understanding Silicon Valley: The Anatomy of an Entrepreneurial Region*. Stanford, CA: Stanford University Press, 2000.

Kimball, Jeffrey. *Nixon's Vietnam War*. Lawrence, KS: University of Kansas Press, 1998.

Kissinger, Henry. *Nuclear Weapons and Foreign Policy*. New York: Norton, 1969.

————. *The White House Years*. Boston: Little, Brown, 2009.

————. *Years of Upheaval*. Boston: Little, Brown, 1982.

Kutler, Stanley I., ed. *Abuse of Power: The New Nixon Tapes*. New York: The Free Press, 1997.

Lamont, Lansing. *Day of Trinity*. New York: Atheneum, 1965.

Leebaert, Derek. *Magic and Mayhem: The Delusions of American Foreign Policy from Korea to Afghanistan*. New York: Simon & Schuster, 2010.

Leslie, Stuart W. *The Cold War and American Science: The Military-Industrial-Academic Complex at MIT and Stanford*. New York: Columbia University Press, 1993.

Lettow, Paul. *Ronald Reagan and His Quest to Abolish Nuclear Weapons*. New York: Random House, 2006.

Lindsey, Robert. *The Falcon and the Snowman: A True Story of Friendship and Espionage*. Guilford, CT: Lyons Press, 2002.

Lowen, Rebecca S. *Creating the Cold War University: The Transformation of Stanford*. Berkeley: University of California Press, 1997.

Mann, James. *The Rebellion of Ronald Reagan: A History of the End of the Cold War*. New York: Viking, 2009.

Mann, Robert. *The Walls of Jericho: Lyndon Johnson, Hubert Humphrey, Richard Russell, and the Struggle for Civil Rights*. New York: Harcourt Brace, 1996.

Matlock, Jack F., Jr. *Reagan and Gorbachev: How the Cold War Ended*. New York: Random House, 2005.

McNamara, Robert S. *The Essence of Security: Reflections in Office*. New York: Harper & Row, 1968.

————. *In Retrospect: The Tragedy and Lessons of Vietnam.* With Brian VanDeMark. New York: Times Books, 1995.

Muller, Richard A. *Physics for Future Presidents: The Science Behind the Headlines.* New York: Norton, 2008.

O'Hanlon, Michael E. *A Skeptic's Case for Nuclear Disarmament.* Washington, DC: Brookings Institution Press, 2010.

Panofsky, William K. H. *Panofsky on Physics, Politics and Peace: Pief Remembers.* New York: Springer, 2007.

Rabi, I. I. *Science: The Center of Culture.* New York: World, 1970.

Reagan, Ronald. *An American Life: The Autobiography.* New York: Simon & Schuster, 1990.

————. *The Reagan Diaries.* Edited by Douglas Brinkley. New York: HarperCollins, 2007.

Reed, Thomas C., and Danny B. Stillman. *The Nuclear Express: A Political History of the Bomb and Its Proliferation.* Minneapolis: Zenith Press, 2009.

Reeves, Richard. *President Kennedy: Profile of Power.* New York: Touchstone, 1993.

————. *President Nixon: Alone in the White House.* New York: Simon & Schuster, 2002.

————. *President Reagan: The Triumph of Imagination.* New York: Simon & Schuster, 2005.

Rhodes, Richard. *Arsenals of Folly.* New York: Knopf, 2007.

————. *Dark Sun: The Making of the Hydrogen Bomb.* New York: Simon & Schuster, 1995.

————. *The Making of the Atomic Bomb.* New York: Simon & Schuster, 1986.

————. *The Twilight of the Bombs: Recent Challenges, New Dangers, and the Prospects for a World Without Nuclear Weapons.* New York: Knopf, 2010.

Rich, Ben R., and Leo Janos. *Skunk Works: A Personal Memoir of My Years at Lockheed.* Boston: Little, Brown, 1996.

Richelson, Jeffrey T. *Defusing Armageddon: Inside NEST, America's Secret Nuclear Bomb Squad.* New York: Norton, 2009.

Sagan, Scott D., ed. *Inside Nuclear South Asia.* Stanford, CA: Stanford University Press, 2009.

————. *The Limits of Safety: Organizations, Accidents and Nuclear Weapons.* Princeton, NJ: Princeton University Press, 1993.

Sanger, David E. *The Inheritance: The World Obama Confronts and the Challenges to American Power.* New York: Crown, 2009.

Schell, Jonathan. *The Fate of the Earth and The Abolition.* Stanford, CA: Stanford University Press, 2000.

Schulzinger, Robert D. *U.S. Diplomacy Since 1900.* New York: Oxford University Press, 2002.

Sheehan, Neil. *A Fiery Peace in a Cold War: Bernard Schriever and the Ultimate Weapon.* New York: Random House, 2009.

Shields, John M., and William C. Potter, eds. *Dismantling the Cold War: U.S. and NIS Perspectives on the Nunn-Lugar Cooperative Threat Reduction Program.* Cambridge, MA: MIT Press, 1997.

Shultz, George P. *Ideas and Action.* Erie, PA: Free to Choose Press, 2010.

————. *Turmoil and Triumph: My Years as Secretary of State*. New York: Charles Scribner's Sons, 1993.

Shultz, George P., Sidney D. Drell, and James E. Goodby, eds. *Deterrence: Its Past and Future*. Stanford, CA: Hoover Institution Press, 2011.

Snow, C. P. *Science and Government*. Cambridge, MA: Harvard University Press, 1961.

Suri, Jeremi. *Henry Kissinger and the American Century*. Cambridge, MA: Belknap Press, 2007.

Suskind, Ron. *The One Percent Doctrine: Deep Inside America's Pursuit of Its Enemies Since 9/11*. New York: Simon & Schuster, 2006.

————. *The Way of the World: A Story of Truth and Hope in an Age of Extremism*. New York: Harper, 2008.

Talbott, Strobe. *Deadly Gambits: The Vivid Inside Story of Arms Control Negotiations*. New York: Vintage Books, 1985.

Tenet, George. *At the Center of the Storm: My Years at the CIA*. With Bill Harlow. New York: HarperCollins, 2007.

Thompson, Kenneth W., ed. *Sam Nunn on Arms Control*. Lanham, MD: University Press of America, 1987.

————, ed. *Sidney Drell on Arms Control*. Lanham, MD: University Press of America, 1988.

Thompson, Nicholas. *The Hawk and the Dove: Paul Nitze, George Kennan and the History of the Cold War*. New York: Henry Holt, 2009.

Van Overtveldt, Johan. *The Chicago School: How the University of Chicago Assembled the Thinkers Who Revolutionized Economics and Business*. Chicago: Agate, 2007.

Wasserman, Sherri L. *The Neutron Bomb Controversy: A Study in Alliance Politics*. New York: Praeger, 1983.

Woods, Jeff. *Richard B. Russell: Southern Nationalism and American Foreign Policy*. Lanham, MD: Rowman & Littlefield, 2007.

Woodward, Bob. *Obama's Wars*. New York: Simon & Schuster, 2010.

Wrong, Michela. *In the Footsteps of Mr. Kurtz: Living on the Brink of Disaster in Mobutu's Congo*. New York: Perennial, 2002.

Younger, Stephen M. *The Bomb: A New History*. New York: HarperCollins, 2009.

Zoellner, Tom. *Uranium: War, Energy, and the Rock That Shaped the World*. New York: Viking, 2009.

REPORTS

Annual Report to Congress on the Safety and Security of Russian Nuclear Facilities and Military Forces. National Intelligence Council, December 2004.

Bunn, Matthew. *Securing the Bomb: Securing All Nuclear Materials in Four Years*. Project on Managing the Atom, Belfer Center for Science and International Affairs, John F. Kennedy School of Government, Harvard University, November 2008.

Bunn, Matthew. *Securing the Bomb 2010: Securing All Nuclear Materials in Four Years*.

Project on Managing the Atom, Belfer Center for Science and International Affairs, John F. Kennedy School of Government, Harvard University, Commissioned by the Nuclear Threat Initiative, April 2010.

Carter, Ashton B., Kurt M. Campbell, Steven E. Miller, and Charles A. Zraket. *Soviet Nuclear Fission: Control of the Nuclear Arsenal in a Disintegrating Soviet Union.* Cambridge, MA: Center for Science and International Affairs, Harvard University, November 1991.

Carter, Ashton B., Michael M. May, and William J. Perry. *The Day After: Action in the 24 Hours Following a Nuclear Blast in an American City.* Cambridge, MA: Preventive Defense Project, May 31, 2007.

Daly, Sara A., John V. Parachini, and William Rosenau. *"Aum Shinrikyo, Al Qaeda, and the Kinshasa Reactor: Implications of Three Case Studies for Combating Nuclear Terrorism."* RAND Corporation, Santa Monica, CA, 2005.

Drell, Sidney, et al. *JASON Nuclear Testing Study: Summary and Conclusions.* McLean, VA, MITRE Corporation, August 3, 1995.

Drell, Sidney, et al. *Science-Based Stockpile Stewardship.* McLean, VA: MITRE Corporation, November 1994.

Drell, Sidney, John S. Foster, and Charles Townes. *The Report of the Panel on Nuclear Weapons Safety of the House Armed Services Committee,* December 1990.

Evans, Gareth, and Yoriko Kawaguchi, cochairs. *Eliminating Nuclear Threats: A Practical Agenda for Global Policymakers.* Canberra/Tokyo: International Commission on Nuclear Non-Proliferation and Disarmament, November 2009.

Global Fissile Material Report 2009: A Path to Nuclear Disarmament. Fourth annual report of the International Panel on Fissile Materials, September 2009.

Mowatt-Larssen, Rolf. *Al-Qaeda Weapons of Mass Destruction Threat: Hype or Reality?* Belfer Center for Science and International Affairs, John F. Kennedy School of Government, Harvard University, January 2010.

Murphy, Paul, Rt. Hon. *Report into the London Terrorist Attacks on 7 July 2005.* Intelligence and Security Committee, London, May 2006.

Nuclear Posture Review Report, Department of Defense, April 2010.

Nuclear Proliferation: Comprehensive U.S. Planning and Better Foreign Cooperation Needed to Secure Vulnerable Nuclear Materials Worldwide. Report of the Government Accountability Office, December 15, 2010.

Nunn, Sam. *Policy, Troops and the NATO Alliance.* Report of Senator Sam Nunn to the Committee on Armed Services, United States Senate, April 2, 1974.

———. *Vietnam Aid—The Painful Options.* Report of Senator Sam Nunn to the Committee on Armed Services, United States Senate, February 12, 1975.

Nunn, Sam, and Dewey F. Bartlett. *NATO and the New Soviet Threat.* Report of Senator Sam Nunn and Senator Dewey F. Bartlett to the Committee on Armed Services, United States Senate, January 24, 1977.

Perry, William J., and James R. Schlesinger. *America's Strategic Posture: The Final Report of the Congressional Commission on the Strategic Posture of the United States.* Washington, DC: United States Institute of Peace Press, 2009.

Perry, William J., and Brent Scowcroft. "U.S. Nuclear Weapons Policy: Independent Task Force Report No. 62." Council on Foreign Relations, 2009.

Schwartz, Charlie, et al. *Science Against the People: The Story of Jason—The Elite Group of Academic Scientists Who, As Technical Consultants to the Pentagon, Have Developed the Latest Weapon Against Peoples' Liberation Struggles: "Automated Warfare."* Scientists and Engineers for Social and Political Action, December 1972.

ARTICLES

Andreasen, Steve. "Reagan Was Right: Let's Ban Ballistic Missiles." *Survival* 46, no. 1 (Spring 2006).

Apple, R. W., Jr. "Washington Talk; Remaking of Sam Nunn With '92 in the Distance." *New York Times*, Dec. 20, 1990.

"Arms Control Today 2008 Presidential Exclusive: Democratic Nominee Barack Obama." *Arms Control Today*, Sept. 24, 2008, www.armscontrol.org/2008election.

Atkinson, Rick. "How Stealth's Consensus Crumbled; As Costs Became Clearer, Political Climate and Priorities Changed." *Washington Post*, Oct. 10, 1989.

———. "Stealth: From 18-inch Model to $70 Billion Muddle." *Washington Post*, Oct. 8, 1989.

———. "Unraveling Stealth's 'Black World'; Questions of Cost and Mission Arise Amid Debate Over Secrecy." *Washington Post*, Oct. 9, 1989.

Baker, Russell. "U.S. Reconsidering 'Small-War' Theory." *New York Times*, Aug. 11, 1957.

Bjorken, James. Foreword to published remarks by Sidney Drell. *Beam Line* 28, no. 2 (Summer 1998).

Broad, William J. "Laser Advances in Nuclear Fuel Stir Terror Fear." *New York Times*, Aug. 20, 2011.

———. "New Advice on the Unthinkable: How to Survive a Nuclear Bomb." *New York Times*, Dec. 16, 2010.

Broad, William J., John Markoff, and David E. Sanger. "Israeli Test on Worm Called Crucial in Iran Nuclear Delay." *New York Times*, Jan. 15, 2011.

Brown, Warren. "Senator Sam Nunn." *Sky Magazine*, Nov. 1983.

Bumiller, Elisabeth. "Gentle George and The Quiet Roar." *Washington Post*, Dec. 14, 1982.

Burr, William. "The Nixon Administration, the 'Horror Strategy,' and the Search for Limited Nuclear Options, 1969–1972." National Security Archive.

Corddry, Charles. "Star Wars: It's Headed for Earth." *San Diego Union-Tribune*, Dec. 2, 1986.

Crowley, Michael. "The Stuff Sam Nunn's Nightmares Are Made Of." *New York Times Magazine*, Feb. 25, 2007.

Deutch, John, and Harold Brown. "The Nuclear Disarmament Fantasy." *Wall Street Journal*, Nov. 19, 2007.

Deutch, John, Henry A. Kissinger, and Brent Scowcroft. "Test-Ban Treaty: Let's Wait Awhile." *Washington Post*, Oct. 10, 1999.

Drell, Sidney D. Retirement remarks. *Beam Line* 28, no. 2 (Summer 1998).

Drell, Sidney D., Philip J. Farley, and David Holloway. "Preserving the ABM Treaty: A Critique of the Reagan Strategic Defense Initiative." *International Security* 9, no. 2 (Autumn 1984): 59–91.

"18 Guilty in Terror Trial in Belgium; 3 Linked to Plot on NATO." *New York Times*, Oct. 1, 2003.

Eliot, Frank. "Moon Bounce Elint." *Studies in Intelligence*, Spring 1967.

"Former US Policy Honchos Call for World Free of Nuclear Arms." *Agence France-Presse*, Jan. 4, 2007.

Froelich, Warren. "'Star Wars' Proposal Faulted; Ex-Defense Aide Sees Soviet Buildup, Arms Treaty Peril." *San Diego Union-Tribune*, Nov. 2, 1984.

Gailey, Phil. "Sam Nunn's Rising Star." *New York Times Magazine*, Jan. 4, 1987.

Gedda, George. "Kissinger, Other Eminent Security Experts Urge 'World Without Nuclear Weapons.'" Associated Press, Jan. 4, 2007.

Gorbachev, Mikhail S. "The Nuclear Threat." *Wall Street Journal*, Jan. 31, 2007.

Gordon Jackson, Michael. "Beyond Brinkmanship: Eisenhower, Nuclear War Fighting, and Korea, 1953–1968." *Presidential Studies Quarterly* 35, no. 1 (Mar. 2005).

Gordon, Michael R. "Reagan Is Warned by Senator Nunn Over ABM Treaty." *New York Times*, Feb. 7, 1987.

Graham, Bradley. "U.S., Russia Reach Accord on Europe Treaty; Perry, Grachev Achieve 'Meeting of the Minds' on Border-Area Conventional Forces." *Washington Post*, Oct. 29, 1995.

Isaacson, Walter, David Beckwith, and Dick Thompson. "Shultz: Thinker and Doer." *Time*, July 5, 1982.

Johnson, Thomas A. "300 Start a 5-Day Protest March in Georgia, Despite Plea by Maddox." *New York Times*, May 20, 1970.

Kampelman, Max M. "Bombs Away." *New York Times*, Apr. 24, 2006.

Kissinger, Henry A. "Arms-Control Fever." *Washington Post*, Jan. 19, 1988.

———. "Cutting Defense: The Wrong Idea." *Washington Post*, Mar. 5, 1985.

———. "The Dangers Ahead." *Newsweek*, Dec. 21, 1987.

———. "A New Era for NATO." *Newsweek*, Oct. 12, 1987.

———. "Our Nuclear Nightmare." *Newsweek*, Feb. 7, 2009.

———. "Reagan Was Right to Shun 'Accords' That Were Traps." *Los Angeles Times*, Oct. 19, 1986.

———. "Sense, Sensibility, and Nuclear Weapons." *New York Post*, June 7, 1998.

Kitfield, James. "Lugar: Pass New START Now." *National Journal*, July 17, 2010.

Korson, Skip. "Georgia's Sam Nunn." *Macon Magazine*, Summer 1988.

"Legends in the Law: A Conversation with Max Kampelman." *Washington Lawyer*, Feb. 2006.

Krepon, Michael. "When Terrorists Were West Germans." *Arms Control Wonk*, Feb. 11, 2010, http://krepon.armscontrolwonk.com/archive/2623when-terrorists-were-west-germans.

Lubkin, Gloria B. "Protestors Harass Jason Physicists." *Physics Today* 25, no. 10 (Oct. 1972).

McFadden, Robert D. "Samuel T. Cohen, Neutron Bomb Inventor, Dies at 89." *New York Times*, Dec. 1, 2010.

"New Impetus for Test Ban Treaty." *Strategic Comments* (International Institute for Strategic Studies) 15, no. 6 (Aug. 2009).

Nixon, Richard M., and Henry A. Kissinger. "An Arms Agreement—On Two Conditions." *Washington Post*, Apr. 26, 1987.

Obama, Barack. "Breaking the War Mentality." *Sundial* 7, no. 12 (Mar. 10, 1983).

Oberdorfer, Don. "Carter, Kissinger Agree on Global Ills, Divide on Reasons." *Washington Post*, Apr. 11, 1980.

Perlez, Jane, David E. Sanger, and Eric Schmitt. "Wary Dance With Pakistan in Nuclear World." *New York Times*, Dec. 1, 2010.

Pincus, Walter. "Russian Tactical Nuclear Weapons Still an Issue after START Treaty Ratification." *Washington Post*, Dec. 27, 2010.

Roberts, Charlie. "Senator Nunn, the Athlete." *Atlanta Constitution*, Nov. 10, 1972.

Sagan, Scott D., and Jeremi Suri. "The Madman Nuclear Alert." *International Security* 27, no. 4 (Spring 2003).

Sakharov, Andrei. "The Danger of Thermo-Nuclear War: An Open Letter to Dr. Sidney Drell." *Foreign Affairs* 61, no. 5 (Summer 1983).

Sanger, David E. "Obama Nuclear Agenda Only Gets Harder After Treaty." *New York Times*, Dec. 22, 2010.

Sanger, David E., and Eric Schmitt. "Pakistani Nuclear Arms Pose Challenge to U.S. Policy." *New York Times*, Jan. 31, 2011.

"Secretary of State's Wife a Frequent Traveling Companion." Associated Press, Aug. 8, 1988.

Shultz, George P. "Shaping American Foreign Policy: New Realities and New Ways of Thinking." *Foreign Affairs* 63, no. 4 (Spring 1985): 705–22.

Shultz, George P., William J. Perry, Henry A. Kissinger, and Sam Nunn. "How to Protect Our Nuclear Deterrent." *Wall Street Journal*, Jan. 20, 2009.

———. "Toward a Nuclear-Free World." *Wall Street Journal*, Jan. 15, 2008.

———. "A World Free of Nuclear Weapons." *Wall Street Journal*, Jan. 4, 2007.

"3 Groups Begin Public Relations Assault on 'Star Wars' project." *San Diego Union-Tribune*, Oct. 23, 1986.

Wheelon, Albert D. "Corona: The First Reconnaissance Satellites." *Physics Today*, Feb. 1997.

Wicker, Tom. "Saving Nevada and Utah." *New York Times*, June 20, 1980.

SPEECHES, CORRESPONDENCE, PAMPHLETS, VIDEOS

Beckett, Margaret. "A World Free of Nuclear Weapons?" Carnegie International Nonproliferation Conference, Washington, DC, June 25, 2007.

Bill Moyers' Journal: The MX Debate. May 13, 1980, Public Broadcasting Service. Vanderbilt Television Archive.

Bush, George H. W. "Address to the Nation on Reducing United States and Soviet Nuclear Weapons." White House, Sept. 27, 1991. UCSB American Presidency Project.

———. Letter to George Shultz, Mar. 7, 2007. Nuclear Security Project archives, Office of George Shultz, Stanford University.

Carter, Jimmy. Inaugural Address, Jan. 20, 1977. UCSB American Presidency Project.

"The Challenge of Peace: God's Promise and Our Response." Pastoral Letter on War and Peace, National Conference of Catholic Bishops, May 3, 1983.

Churchill, Winston. Remarks upon receiving an honorary degree, Westminster College, Fulton, MO, Mar. 5, 1946.

The Colbert Report. Comedy Central, June 9, 2010.

Drell, Sidney. Remarks at Rumford Prize award ceremony, American Academy of Arts and Sciences, Boston, Oct. 12, 2008.

Einstein, Albert. Letter to Franklin D. Roosevelt, Aug. 2, 1939, Franklin D. Roosevelt Presidential Library Online Archives, Box 5, Alexander Sachs Folder.

Eisenhower, Dwight D. President's News Conference on Mar. 16, 1955. UCSB American Presidency Project.

———. President's News Conference on Mar. 23, 1955. UCSB American Presidency Project.

Gates, Robert. Statement from the Pentagon, June 5, 2008. Department of Defense website.

Goddard, Ben. *Nuclear Tipping Point*. Directed by Ben Goddard. Nuclear Security Project, 2010.

Gorbachev, Mikhail. Remarks at Overcoming Nuclear Dangers Conference, Rome, Apr. 16, 2009.

Hehir, Bryan J. "Ethical Considerations of Living in the Nuclear Age." Conference on Building a Safer 21st Century, Stanford University, Dec. 6, 1987.

———. "The Politics and Ethics of Nonproliferation," Center for International Security and Cooperation's Annual Drell Lecture. Stanford University, Dec. 6, 2005.

"Henry Kissinger on the Pakistan Meeting with Obama." *On the Record with Greta Van Susteren*. Fox News, May 19, 2009.

"Increasing Transparency in the U.S. Nuclear Weapons Stockpile." Department of Energy Fact Sheet, May 3, 2010.

Kampelman, Max. "The Power of the Ought." Remarks at Hoover Institution Conference: "Implications of the Reykjavik Summit on Its Twentieth Anniversary," Stanford University, Oct. 11, 2006.

Kennedy, John F. Speech before the United Nations General Assembly, Sept. 25, 1961. UCSB American Presidency Project.

Kissinger, Henry. Remarks at American Academy in Berlin, Feb. 3, 2010.

———. Remarks at American Academy of Diplomacy, United States State Department, Washington, DC, Dec. 14, 2005.

———. Remarks at Hoover Institution Conference, "Deterrence: Its Past and Future," Stanford University, Nov. 11, 2010.

McCain, John. Remarks at University of Denver, May 27, 2008. John McCain campaign website [no longer exists].

———. "U.S. Foreign Policy: Where We Go From Here." Remarks before the Los Angeles World Affairs Council, Mar. 26, 2008.

Nunn, Sam. "The Mountaintop: A World Free of Nuclear Weapons." Remarks before the Council on Foreign Relations, June 14, 2007.

———. "The Mountaintop: A World Free of Nuclear Weapons." Remarks in Oslo, Feb. 27, 2008.

———. "The Race Between Cooperation and Catastrophe." Remarks before the National Press Club, Mar. 9, 2005.

Obama, Barack. First Presidential Debate, University of Mississippi, Sept. 26, 2008.

———. Inaugural Address, Washington, DC, Jan. 20, 2009. UCSB American Presidency Project.

———. Remarks by the President in the Oval Office, May 19, 2009. White House transcript.

———. Remarks in Chicago: "A New Beginning," Oct. 2, 2007. UCSB American Presidency Project.

———. Remarks in Hradcany Square, Prague, Apr. 5, 2009. White House transcript.

———. Remarks in Washington, DC: "The War We Need to Win," Aug. 1, 2007. UCSB American Presidency Project.

———. Remarks in West Lafayette, Indiana, July 16, 2008. UCSB American Presidency Project.

———. Remarks to Chicago Council on Global Affairs, Apr. 23, 2007. UCSB American Presidency Project.

Perry, William. Remarks at Millennium Hotel dinner, New York, Sept. 24, 2009.

———. Remarks at Leadership Symposium, Stanford University, Apr. 7, 2009.

———. Remarks at "Overcoming Nuclear Dangers" Conference, Rome, Apr. 16, 2009.

————. Remarks at 2011 Robert McNamara Lecture on War and Peace, Harvard University, Feb. 24, 2011.

————. Remarks before Management Science and Engineering 193 class, Stanford University, Oct. 27, 2009.

Reagan, Ronald. "Address at the Republican National Convention in Kansas City." Aug. 19, 1976. UCSB American Presidency Project.

————. "Address to the Nation on Defense and National Security." Oval Office, Mar. 23, 1983. UCSB American Presidency Project.

————. Remarks at Annual Convention of the National Association of Evangelicals. Orlando, FL, Mar. 8, 1983. UCSB American Presidency Project.

————. Remarks at White House news conference in the Old Executive Office Building, Washington, DC, Jan. 29, 1981. UCSB American Presidency Project.

Schlesinger, James. Remarks at 2010 Strategic Deterrence Symposium, Strategic Command (STRATCOM), Omaha, NE, Aug. 11, 2010.

Shultz, George. "Nuclear Weapons, Arms Control, and the Future of Deterrence." Remarks before the International House of Chicago and *Chicago Sun-Times* Forum, University of Chicago. U.S. State Department Bulletin, Jan. 1987.

————. Press Conference from Iceland, CBS, Oct. 12, 1986. Ronald Reagan Presidential Library.

————. Press Conference from Iceland, NBC, Oct. 12, 1986. Ronald Reagan Presidential Library.

————. Remarks at Global Zero Summit, Paris, Feb. 2, 2010.

————. Remarks at Hoover Institution conference, "Deterrence: Its Past and Future," Stanford University, Nov. 11, 2010.

————. Remarks at Millennium Hotel dinner, New York, Sept. 24, 2009.

————. Remarks at ninetieth birthday gala, San Francisco, Dec. 13, 2010.

————. Remarks at "Overcoming Nuclear Dangers" Conference, Rome, Apr. 16, 2009.

————. Remarks in Oval Office. May 19, 2009. White House transcript.

Thatcher, Margaret. TV Interview for BBC, Dec. 17, 1984. Retrieved from the Margaret Thatcher Foundation, www.margaretthatcher.org/document/105592.

HEARINGS AND TESTIMONIES

D'Agostino, Thomas P. "Statement of Thomas P. D'Agostino, Undersecretary for Nuclear Security and Administrator for National Nuclear Security Administration, U.S. Department of Energy, On Reducing the Cost of the U.S. Nuclear Weapons Complex Before the House Appropriations Committee Subcommittee on Energy and Water Development," Mar. 17, 2009.

Goss, Porter J. "Global Intelligence Challenges 2005: Meeting Long-Term Challenges with a Long-Term Strategy." Testimony Before the Senate Select Committee on Intelligence, Feb. 16, 2005.

Kissinger, Henry. "Statement of Dr. Henry A. Kissinger Before the Senate Foreign Relations Committee," May 25, 2010.

"Nominations of William James Perry and David Emerson Mann." Committee on Armed Services, United States Senate, Mar. 25, 1977.

"Nominations of William J. Perry, Harold W. Chase and George A. Peapples." Committee on Armed Services, United States Senate, Nov. 1, 1977.

Nunn, Sam. "Statement by Former Senator Sam Nunn, Co-Chairman, Nuclear Threat Initiative. The New START Treaty. United States Senate Committee on Armed Services," July 27, 2010.

Perry, William J. "Statement of William J. Perry Regarding Submission of the New START for Consent and Ratification." Senate Foreign Relations Committee, Apr. 29, 2010.

VISITS

Lawrence Livermore National Laboratory, April 2009.

Los Alamos National Laboratory, October 2009.

Poland, September 2010.

Republic of Georgia, November 2010.

Trinity Site, New Mexico, April 2009.

INDEX